A Conductor's Guide to Choral-Orchestral Works

Jonathan D. Green

The Scarecrow Press, Inc.
Lanham, Maryland, and Oxford

SCARECROW PRESS, INC.

Published in the United States of America
by Scarecrow Press, Inc.
A Member of the Rowman & Littlefield Publishing Group
4501 Forbes Blvd., Suite 200, Lanham, MD 20706
www.scarecrowpress.com

PO Box 317
Oxford
OX2 9RU, UK

Copyright © 1994 by Jonathan D. Green
First paperback edition 2003

British Library Cataloguing in Publication Information Available

The hardback edition of this book was previously cataloged by the Library of
Congress as follows:

Green, Jonathan D., 1964-
    A conductor's guide to choral-orchestral works / by
Jonathan D. Green.
        p. cm.
    "Works to be included must be for full chorus and
orchestra, containing some English text, composed
between 1900 and 1972"--Introd.
    Revision of the author's thesis (D.M.A.) --University of
North Carolina at Greensboro.
    Includes bibliographical references and discography p.
    ISBN 0-8108-2712-3(acid-free paper)
    1. Choruses with orchestra--20th century--Bibliography.
I. Title.
ML128.C48G7 1994
016.7825--dc20   93-6388

⊖™ The paper used in this publication meets the minimum requirements of
American National Standard for Information Sciences—Permanence of
Paper for Printed Library Materials, ANSI/NISO Z39.48-1992.
Manufactured in the United States of America.

ISBN: 0-8108-4720-5   (paper)

This book is dedicated to my dear friend

John Charles Swan

who showed me that words and music may
have a common ground

TABLE OF CONTENTS

Introduction

The purpose of this book is to catalogue large-scale works in English for mixed choir and orchestra, which will be defined as an instrumental ensemble containing a string section. Some of the works may use multiple languages, one of which must be English. This catalogue is to be a reference tool for conductors in their programing and pre-rehearsal preparation. Information for each work will include (if available): a biographical sketch of the composer, selected bibliography, performance times, discography, publishers, editions, availability of performance materials, location of autographs, instrumentation, text sources, performance issues, a brief history of the piece, and information regarding any solo roles.

Works to be included must be for full chorus and orchestra, containing some English text, and composed between 1900 and 1972. These works were originally chosen for having at least one citation indicating a length of twenty or more minutes. During the course of this study, certain works were found to be slightly shorter; however these pieces were retained if they proved no less than fifteen minutes long. The last qualification for inclusion is that performance materials are commercially available.

Related Research

Numerous studies have been made of various performance issues regarding a selected repertoire. A number of catalogues of works for men's choirs have been made, the most thorough of which is that edited by J. Merrill Knapp[1] Charles C. Burnsworth[2] has compiled a

xi

---

[1] J. Merrill Knapp, editor: *Selected List of Music for Men's Voices.* Princeton, NJ: Princeton University Press, 1952.

[2] Charles C. Burnsworth: *Choral Music for Women's Voices.* Metuchen, NJ: Scarecrow Press, 1968.

descriptive guide to music for women's choirs which provides more detailed information about each work.

Sergius Kagen[3] addressed the quality, range and tessitura of vocal solos. The present study incorporates Kagen's methods in the evaluation of solo roles within each work. Instrumentation and performance times of orchestral works have been listed by David Daniel[4], Eslinger and Daugherty[5], Daugherty and Simons[6], and Margaret K. Farish[7]. These lists, while extensive, are often incomplete or inconsistent with the actual scores. In this study, such information has been confirmed in the scores, publishers' listings, and performance records.

The most complete listing of works contained in this study can be found in Thurston Dox's study of large American choral works[8]. Dox includes score locations, publishers, some bibliographic materials, and occasional listings of instrumentation and performance times.

There are currently no reference sources for this specific repertoire, nor is there any source which addresses the range of performance considerations included in this present study. Such a source would be invaluable to conductors in selecting works for concerts, as well a

xii

[3] Sergius Kagen: *Music for the Voice*, revised. Bloomington, IN: University of Indiana Press, 1968.

[4] David Daniel: *Orchestra Music: A Source Book*. Metuchen, NJ: Scarecrow Press, 1972.

[5] Gary S. Eslinger and F. Mark Daugherty, editors: *Sacred Choral Music in Print*, second edition. 2 volumes. Philadelphia: Musicdata: 1985.

[6] F. Mark Daugherty and Susan H. Simons, editors: *Secular Choral Music in Print*, second edition. 2 volumes. Philadelphia: Musicdata, 1987.

[7] Margaret K. Farish: *Orchestra Music in Print*. Philadelphia: Musicdata, 1979.

[8] Thurston Dox: *American Oratorios and Cantatas: a Catalogue of Works Written in the United States from Colonial Times to 1985*. 2 volumes. Metuchen, NJ: Scarecrow Press, 1986.

providing a starting point for rehearsal preparation and score study.

Procedures

Each entry includes a listing of the performance time which has been determined by averaging all cited times found including those in scores, catalogues, reviews, and recordings. For most of the works these timings were in virtual consensus. Marked discrepancies between timings are cited independently.

All known text sources are listed with a cross-referenced listing of text sources in the first appendix. Complete vocal and instrumental performing forces are listed for each work. All inconsistencies are addressed in the "performance issues" entry for the given work.

When available, information regarding the first performance of each work is listed, as is the location of the composer's autograph of the score or a facsimile of it. All available editions are listed, as are the sources and conditions for acquiring them (rental/purchase).

The core of this study is the "performance issues" section of each entry. It describes the compositional language and notable characteristics of each work. Important limitations to successful performance and important rehearsal considerations are addressed.

Each work has been labeled with regard to the difficulty of the orchestra and chorus roles. Five gradations of difficulty have been used: easy, medium easy, medium, medium difficult, and difficult. These are subjective labels determined by detailed score study. Easy works are those which are accessible to inexperienced ensembles. Those labeled difficult are within the abilities of only the most skilled performing organizations, and even for them demanding of extensive rehearsal time. Most entries also include a brief prose explanation of their difficulty.

In addition to the selected bibliography presented for each composer, a specific bibliography is provided for each work when such material has been available. An exhaustive discography has been compiled for each work from the date of its composition through January of 1993.

Preceding the body of the catalogue is a chapter which presents musical and textual trends observed throughout the studied repertoire. Following the catalogue is a cross-referenced table of text sources and a complete list of music publishers for the works evaluated.

This book is an adaptation of my dissertation toward the Doctorate of Musical Arts at the University of North Carolina at Greensboro. Much of the research was based upon access to full scores many of which were loaned to me by the publishers as part of my regular perusal of music in preparation for the programming of each concert season. I hope that this text will bring these works and publishing companies a deserved increase in circulation.

It is my pleasure to thank the members of my advisory committee: Dr. Eddie Bass, Dr. William Carroll, Dr. Kelley Griffith, and Mr. Robert Gutter for their assistance in determining the format and style of this study. I am indebted to my wife, Ms. Lynn Buck for her patience and proofreading skills. My father, Mr. Gary Green aided me with church music and hymn-tune information, and my mother, Mrs. Justine Green provided much useful discographic information. Dr. Richard Wursten and Mr. Ted Hunyter, music librarians of the University of North Carolina at Greensboro; and Dr. P. Alston Jones and Mr. Eric Childress, librarians of Elon College, provided much support in locating bibliographic information and allowing generous access to restricted materials. I am grateful to Dr. James Sherbon and Mrs. Martha Rierson for the generous assistance in the navigation of the academic process. I am glad to thank Elon College, and particularly Dean Clair Myers for their continued support. And I am most grateful to my doctoral advisor, Dr. Richard Cox, for his dedication to this project, his tireless support, and sage advice.

CHAPTER I

DEVELOPMENTS AND TRENDS

The primary purpose of this study is to provide a reference source of large choral-orchestral works containing some English texts, which were composed between 1900 and 1972. The sole criteria for inclusion were length, language of text, dates of composition, and commercial availability of performance materials.

It is relevant to state here that seven organizations stood out in the numbers of commissions and performances from the total body of works studied. They are the Koussevitsky Foundation of the Library of Congress, the Birmingham Choral Festival conducted by Hans Richter, the Ann Arbor May Festival, the Cincinnati May Festival, the Robert Shaw Chorale conducted by Robert Shaw, the Interracial Choir of New York conducted by Harold Aks, and the Collegiate Chorale conducted by Abraham Kaplan.

This preliminary chapter will serve as a summation of the trends and commonalities exhibited in the examined repertoire. Among these developments are examples of most of the significant musical techniques explored by composers during this period. The most distinctive development, however, is the text themes and sources. These truly distinguish these works from the rest of the twentieth-century repertoire. The developments in musical practices and text selections, respectively, will be examined below.

Musical Developments

Within most musical genres of this century, composers have explored virtually every known compositional technique. This is reflected in the choral-orchestral repertoire. It is important to note that in the works surveyed, the choral writing is consistently more conservative than its orchestral complement. There is also very little

imitative counterpoint in any of these works. Most of the choral parts
are harmonically conceived and primarily homophonic in construction.
The only prominent exception to this observation regarding
contrapuntal practices is Michael Tippett's *Shires Suite*. The choral
contingent of this work is a collection of canons. Within the
remaining works, even the more contrapuntally complex works remain
vertical in conception with the interplay of parts being merely the result
of rhythmic juxtaposition rather than the product of calculated part-
writing. Each compositional device observed in this study will be cited
and described.

Serial Procedures

Of the eighty-nine works studied, five used the twelve-tone
technique, although none used it exclusively. The most consistent use
of the serial process occurs in Ross Lee Finney's *Still Are New Worlds*
and *Martyr's Elegy*. In both of these works, the composer constructs
tetrads of similar voicing for the choir, treating them in a manner
resembling traditional chords. By maintaining consistent voicing and
using conspicuous harmonic support from the orchestra, Finney greatly
enhances the learnability of these works. Similarly, Peter Mennin, in
his *Cantata de Virtute: The Pied Piper*, uses traditional part-writing
methods within passages of serial content. Once again, the composer
imitates traditional tonal procedures within an atonal context. It
appears that such an approach is an attempt to ensure accessibility to
the choir, as is suggested by the fact that the melodic contours and
harmonic voicings of the instrumental parts of the above works do not
similarly emulate tonal practices. Mennin's composition begins with a
strict use of serial methods, but gradually works its way toward tonal
material at the end. The metamorphosis from atonal to tonal is gradual
and the pitch treatment in the middle sections uses inner-voice
statements of the tone-row against an otherwise freely-tonal
surrounding. The conflict of pitch materials is finally won by E^b
major. Unlike Finney, Mennin often gives the voices no support from
the accompaniment, but the linearity of the vocal writing helps to
maintain accessibility.

In *When Lilacs Last in the Dooryard Bloom'd*, Roger Sessions
often states all twelve discrete pitches without repetition; however, he
does not do this systematically. There is no single sequence of these
pitches which appears to be distinguished as a motivic device.
Sessions's work remains strictly atonal without adopting any rigorous
serial practice.

The opening of Vincent Persichetti's *Creation* divides the choir
into twelve parts which utter a tone-cluster containing all twelve

discrete pitches. This, while prolonged, is an effect rather than a systematic compositional practice. Persichetti uses this cluster to musically represent the primordial ooze whence order is to come. As the process of creation is outlined in the text, the ensemble enters a diatonic and ordered tonal environment.

Complex Rhythmic Structures

There are brief occurrences of multiple simultaneous divisions of the beat, as well as frequent changes of meter in many of the works examined. In general, the majority of challenging temporal elements are assigned to the orchestra. Most of the choral parts thus remain rhythmically "square."

The most common polymetric event is the simultaneous use of 6/8 and 2/4 meters, a device which dates back to the music of Hector Berlioz. More distinctive are runs of unusual and differing divisions of the beat being stated concurrently. These instrumental figures are reminiscent of similar figures in the piano music of Chopin. The latter cross-relations were not assigned to the singers.

Five works are distinguished by particularly complex rhythmic content. They are Sessions's *When Lilacs Last in the Dooryard Bloom'd*, Schuller's *The Power Within Us*, Dett's *The Ordering of Moses*, Tippett's *The Vision of St. Augustine*, and Britten's *War Requiem*. All of these works have frequent metric changes, frequently displaced downbeats, and unusual borrowed divisions. The Tippett, Schuller, and Sessions pieces are challenging because of their constant variety and general avoidance of a consistent metric pulse. Dett's work has frequent scalar flourishes which impose divisions of 6, 7, 8, 9, 10, 11, and 13 to the beat with no apparent reason for the variety. The Britten is unique for its use of metric modulations. In this work, separate portions of the ensemble are assigned different note values for a common pulse. These disparate values are exchanged in opposition to each other. This creates the visual impression of concurrent accelerandi and ritardandi to the performers while the actual pulse remains constant.

Electronic Tape

Three works included the presence of pre-recorded material on magnetic tape which is to be played at designated points in the score. Finney's *Still Are New Worlds* and *Martyr's Elegy* both contain electronically synthesized sounds which are preserved as taped music. In this way, the composer is able to introduce non-acoustic sounds into his ensemble. In both works the presence of the taped sounds is indicated by a line running through the score. There are no indications within the score of any events on the tape and thus no clear integration is possible between the live and recorded sounds. Only the concurrence of sound can be maintained.

Leonard Bernstein uses pre-recorded material in his *Mass*. An unusual feature of the taped portion of the work is that it is entirely traditionally-acoustic musical sounds. The taped music is fully notated in the score, and should be recorded by the musicians (especially solo singers) who are to participate in the live sections of the performance. These recorded passages represent the most difficult music in the piece. The opportunity to preserve a "best" version of these often challenging sections is an asset for performers of limited experience. The purpose of the tape, which is indicated as quadraphonic, is in part to create multidirectional sound sources from a single ensemble. It also is linked to the indicated theatrical treatment of the work. The score appears to allow a freedom of interpretation as to the quantity of the music to be pre-recorded.

Bernstein's work also includes electronic organs and electric guitars. Likewise, David Del Tredici's *Pop-pourri* features a concertato rock band which is assigned wholly-notated and non-idiomatic passages. It also uses electronic amplification of the soprano soloist which also includes the use of a bull-horn for dramatic effect.

Jazz Influences

Characteristics of African-American music have been incorporated into concert works since the second decade of this century. Four of the works in this survey have conspicuously included idiomatic uses of jazz material.

The oldest of these is Dett's *The Ordering of Moses* which incorporates actual African-American folk music. The composer uses the spiritual "Go Down Moses" as the principal thematic material of the entire oratorio. As he develops the theme, it takes on jazz rhythms of the 1920s and early 1930s. Dett also uses frequent non-functional seventh and ninth chords which were a prominent feature of the dance music of that era.

Constant Lambert's *The Rio Grande* and Dave Brubeck's *The Light in the Wilderness* both feature jazz-based solos for piano. Lambert's composition is thoroughly composed in the manner of George Gershwin's concert works. Brubeck's piece is more fundamentally jazz-related. It reflects the performing proclivities of the composer in its feature of a jazz combo. There are optional opportunities for extensive improvised piano solos.

Leonard Bernstein uses a remarkable variety of musical styles in his *Mass*. This work is a multi-media event which exploits the musical practices of the concert hall and of the "pop" culture of the late

1960s. In addition to the extensive use of jazz harmonies (particularly ninth and eleventh chords), Bernstein imitates the musical styles of rock-and-roll and the music of the "beat" generation.

A final composition must be discussed within this category. It too uses African-American musical sources, but not idiomatically. In *A Child of Our Time*, Michael Tippett uses black spirituals in a role similar to that of the chorales in Bach's Passions. Tippett's work is a Passion of sorts for the world's downtrodden. He uses the music of enslaved blacks as an eloquent expression of the futility felt by the oppressed of mankind. He does not, however, attempt to maintain the musical style of his sources. He preserves the melody and text of the spirituals, but sets them in the style of early twentieth-century English choral music.

Intrumental Soloists

In the manner of Beethoven's Choral Fantasy, three of the works feature an instrumental soloist with the choir and orchestra. Arthur Bliss includes a solo flute part in his Pastoral: *Lie Strewn the White Flocks.* Here the flutist's role is to portray a shepherd and Pan, both of whom have close associations with the flute. The fourth movement is for flute solo, timpani, and strings. It is entitled "Pan's Sarabande."

The other two pieces which feature solo instruments are Brubeck's *Light in the Wilderness* and Lambert's *Rio Grande.* Both of these compositions serve as vehicles for jazz-related piano solos as described above.

Free Repetition

Well before the rise of interest in the ostinato music popularized by Steve Reich and Philip Glass which has come to be inaccurately known as minimalism, Alan Hovhaness incorporated such techniques into many of his works. In his *Magnificat* and *Cantata: Praise the Lord with Psaltery,* he notates ostinato figures which repeat freely with concurrent metric independence. Hovhaness uses this device to create the effect of an instrumental "murmur." He applies a similar technique to some of the vocal passages as well. Bernstein uses the same technique in his *Kaddish Symphony.*

Chant

Some of the choral uses of aforementioned free repetition in Hovhaness's music are in the style of Mozarabic chant. Gustav Holst uses actual Gregorian chant in his *Hymn to Jesus.* In this composition, the composer quotes "Vexilla regis" and "Pange lingua."

Each of these chants is written in traditional metric notation with the stated intention of free performance. Holst suggests that the trombonist who begins the work should familiarize himself with the style and nuances of these chants disregarding the literalism of the notation. Anglican chant notation is used in one passage of Elgar's *The Apostles*.

Narrator

The role of a narrator has existed in choral-orchestral works for centuries, as in the Evangelists of baroque Passions. In this century, composers have introduced spoken narrations into many of these works. The spoken texts serve as literal narrations, introductions, or as a way to present text unhampered by a musical setting. This sometimes appears to be a way of introducing a considerable amount of text within a restricted time span. It is also a method of avoiding the musical challenges of unmetered texts. In some works, particularly Bernstein's *Kaddish Symphony* and Bliss's *Morning Heroes*, the use of spoken texts is clearly for dramatic intensity.

Speaking Choir

The success of spoken narration, combined with Schoenberg's development of *Sprechstimme*, has led to the introduction of spoken passages for the choirs. These are sometimes unmeasured, producing a glossolalial effect as in the freely spoken passages of Holst's *Hymn of Jesus* and Samuel Adler's *The Binding*. More often, the spoken passages are rhythmically notated using the unified speech as a dramatic sonority which is clearly integrated in the surrounding musical fabric. Examples of this include David Amram's *A Year in Our Land* and Elie Siegmeister's *I Have a Dream*. In the latter of these works, the use of choral speaking helps to emphasize key portions of the text.

There is evidence of a third use of speaking choirs. In certain works, it appears to be a way for composers to use a pitch vocabulary which is not easily absorbed by most choirs. By introducing extended spoken sections, the quantity of challenging note learning for the vocal ensemble is diminished. In Finney's *Still Are New Worlds* and *Martyr's Elegy* and Mennin's *Cantata de Virtute: The Pied Piper*, there are extended sections for rhythmic speaking in the choir. These passages are well chosen and very convincing, but under close examination it is clear that this is an attempt to assure that the entire choral portion of the pieces can be learned. The location of these spoken parts in the middle of each of the works creates a well-conceived textural architecture and an ideal resting place for a choir which has been singing material through calculated intervals.

Gebrauchsmusik

During this century numerous composers have recognized the need for good musical literature for amateur soloists and ensembles. Seven of the works were composed for amateur ensembles. Of them, Tippett's *Shires Suite*, Gunther Schuller's *The Power Within Us*, and Adler's *A Whole Bunch of Fun* are written for unusually strong student groups. Tippett's choral writing is fairly representative of the abilities of younger musicians, but the orchestral complement is technically demanding.

Robert Ward's *Earth Shall Be Fair* is a model of technical consideration. The work is for the combined choral forces of a large church music program (adult SATB, youth SATB, and children in unison). The difficulty of each choir's part is a reflection of their expected abilities. The level of the adult choir, while the most difficult, is within the ability of a typical large church choir. The orchestra is also written conservatively, allowing for the probable resources of such a music program.

Britten's *St. Nicolas* was written for the use of combined amateur and professional forces. As he states in the score, the tenor soloist, string quintet, piano I, and percussion I all require experienced performers. The remaining instrumental roles and other singers may and probably should be amateur musicians. Britten extends an invitation for all to participate to his audience by including two congregationally-sung hymns.

Finney's *Pilgrim Psalms* is an arrangement for chorus and orchestra of the tunes and texts of the *Ainsworth Psalter*. It and Mennin's *Christmas Story* are the works accessible to the least experienced ensembles. Finney's orchestral writing is also very conservative whereas Mennin's accompaniment requires seasoned players. It is ironic that the easiest and most difficult works in this study are by the same two composers.

Textual Developments

The most significant trends to be observed in the choral-orchestral repertoire in this century are the content and selection process for the texts. The textual themes of such works from previous centuries are religious, mythological, or literary; however, in the twentieth century, the social consciousness of the artist as composer is reflected in a diversity of texts which address prominent inequities of the human condition. Likewise, composers of this century have frequently elected to select their texts from a number of authors rather than from a single literary source.

Multiple Text Sources

More than a quarter of the works reviewed contained texts from more than a single author. Two of these pieces were settings of a group of texts selected by a literary figure. Finney's *Still Are New Worlds* is about the dissolution of the belief of a finite universe as a response to the discovery of new stars. The composer chose a set of texts which were compiled by Marjorie Hope Nicholson in *The Breaking of the Circle*, which serves as an anthology of remarks by poets and scientists of the time. Ned Rorem chose Paul Goodman's *Dead of Spring* as the source of verses for his *The Poet's Requiem*. It too, serves as an anthology, in this case one concerned with our relationship to death.

The more common approach exhibited in these works is that of the composer as compiler. The breadth of source materials evidenced in these compositions betrays the intimate involvement in literature among this century's composers. In many of the works, the composer becomes a critic of sorts, drawing upon the "finest" available expressions of each concept to be addressed within the piece. To some extent the composer becomes a collaborator in the poetic process by his juxtaposition of varied text sources. The following are a few of the more prominent works which form a collage of numerous poetic sources.

Adler's *A Whole Bunch of Fun* is a setting of collected texts which reveal the humorous side of students' views of school. The poets whose works are included are Lewis Carroll, Marianne Moore, Theodore Roethke, Eleanor Farjeon, P. D. Eastman, George Whicher, and Ogden Nash.

In his *A Year in Our Land*, David Amram uses the writings of James Baldwin, John Dos Passos, Jack Kerouac, John Steinbeck, Thomas Wolfe, and Walt Whitman. Each of the selections addresses a particular aspect of the failure of the "American dream," including transience as a failed pursuit of happiness, religious injustice, social inequities of homosexuals, and urban blight.

Ward's *Sweet Freedom's Song* is written as a commemoration of the Battles of Lexington and Concord. The composer and his wife, Mary, collected quotations from broadsides of the time, with which they combined biblical texts and verses from hymns associated with the colonial era. In addition to editing the aforementioned texts, the Wards wholly authored the verses for one of the movements.

The role of the composer as author is also present in Bernstein's *Mass* and *Kaddish Symphony*. In both of these works, Bernstein penned verses to link other pre-existing texts. Mennin wrote the words for his *Christmas Story*, paraphrasing traditional carols and biblical models. In a similar fashion, Hovhaness adapted scripture for his *Easter Cantata*, and Persichetti authored a poetic translation of the Latin text of the *Stabat Mater*. Edward Elgar adapted scripture into a dramatic form for his *The Apostles* and *The Kingdom*.

In *Cantata de Virtute: The Pied Piper*, Mennin combines Robert Browning's *The Pied Piper of Hamelin* with two thirteenth-century sacred poems and portions of the Requiem Mass. By thoughtful arrangement of these sources, he develops a thought-provoking allegory between the Pied Piper myth and the very real transience of life. Parallel to this, Persichetti compiled approximately one hundred sources from mythology, poetry, and science all pertaining to the genesis of our universe for his *Creation*. The composer's arrangement of the verses, and the unity imposed upon them by the music, fosters the sense of a realization of a unified creation myth rather than a survey of disparate possibilities.

Certain compositions are apparently intended to represent thematic anthologies as in Britten's *Spring Symphony*, which combines thirteen varied poetic views of spring. Likewise, Ralph Vaughan Williams's *Hodie* serves as a narrative of the Christmas myth from the alternate perspectives of scripture, liturgy, and the poetry of five centuries. In his *Dona Nobis Pacem*, Vaughan Williams expresses his pacifism through his setting of the *Agnus Dei*, scriptural quotations calling for peace, John Bright's "Angel of Death" speech, and portions of Walt Whitman's "Drum Taps." Beyond the apparent attempt to combine the best expressions of various aspects surrounding a single theme, the anthologizing composer seems to be reinforcing the validity of his cause through a multiplicity of corroborating sources.

Following the model of Brahms's *Ein deutsches Requiem*, a number of twentieth-century composers have elected to consolidate relevant texts of bereavement into a work of memorial tribute. Herbert Howells, in reaction to his son's untimely death, compiled a series of memorial texts which focussed upon themes of light for his *Hymnus Paradisi*. These were taken from the Requiem Mass, Psalms 23 and 121, the Burial Service from the Book of Common Prayer, and the Salisbury Diurnal.

Three other works which combine the Latin Requiem Mass with other English texts are Britten's *War Requiem*, John Foulds's *World Requiem*, and Nicholas Flagello's *The Passion of Martin Luther King*. The last of these uses extracts from Dr. King's speeches which are given to a baritone soloist. The choir sings only passages from the *Missa pro defunctis*. Foulds's composition combines portions of the Requiem Mass with biblical passages, the "Benedicite," and verses by

Kabir and the composer's paramour, Maude MacCarthy. In the *War Requiem*, Britten integrates passages of the Requiem Mass with poems by Wilfred Owen, a pacifist who was slain in the trenches during the First World War.

Polylingual Texts

Seven of the compositions here studied combine texts of two languages and two contain lines from three. Britten's *War Requiem*, Flagello's *The Passion of Martin Luther King*, Foulds's *World Requiem*, Howells's *Hymnus Paradisi*, and Vaughan Williams's *Hodie* and *Sancta Civitas* all combine English and Latin texts. Bernstein's *Kaddish Symphony* is divided into English and Hebrew sections, and his *Mass* unites English, Latin and Hebrew texts. Tippett's *The Vision of St. Augustine*, despite its English title, contains only a single line of English, which occurs at the composition's conclusion. The remainder of the work is in Latin with brief interjections of nonsensical Greek. The latter passages mentioned are unconnected Greek utterances set in a manner meant to portray glossolalia and religious fervor.

Text Themes

As indicated by the works discussed above, numerous compositions in this century have been written in response to significant political and social events. Edward Elgar's *The Spirit of England*, Foulds's *World Requiem*, Frederick Delius's *Requiem* (on a text of Nietzsche), and Bliss's *Morning Heroes* were all composed as memorials to the slain of World War I. Other works which were written as general anti-war statements include Britten's *War Requiem* and Vaughan Williams's *Dona Nobis Pacem* and *Sancta Civitas*.

Other works are written in commemoration of great figures lost in our time, while the texts of these pieces remain metaphoric. Walt Whitman wrote his poem, "When Lilacs Last in the Dooryard Bloom'd," in reaction to the death of Abraham Lincoln. This text is used in two of the works reviewed. Paul Hindemith's setting was commissioned by Robert Shaw as a memorial tribute to Franklin D. Roosevelt. Two decades later, Roger Sessions set the same poem to honor the memory of Robert Kennedy and Martin Luther King, Jr. King is also commemorated in the Flagello's *The Passion of Martin Luther King* and Elie Siegmeister's *I Have a Dream*.

Text Sources

The texts of these works are drawn from a wide variety of sources. Most authors are represented by a single work; however, a few are distinguished by appearing in a number of different works.

Selections from the Bible are found in twenty of the compositions. Five of these feature Isaiah: Vaughan Williams's *Hodie*, Creston's *Isaiah's Prophecy*, Mennin's *Christmas Story*, and Rogers's *The Prophet Isaiah* are pieces celebrating the Christmas season. As can be seen in the Bernstein pieces already mentioned, Jewish themes have entered the concert hall in this century. Among them is Robert Starer's *Ariel* which also draws upon Isaiah; in this case, however, it is treated from the perspective of an as yet to be fulfilled messianic prophecy. Adler's *The Binding* is also drawn from traditional Jewish theological writings as compiled by the composer's father.

The Book of Common Prayer is quoted in Howells's *Hymnus Paradisi* and Vaughan Williams's *Hodie*. Lewis Carroll is represented in Adler's *A Whole Bunch of Fun* and David Del Tredici's *Pop-Pourri*. The collaborative efforts of John Fletcher and Francis Beaumont are in Bliss's *Pastoral: Lie Strewn the White Flocks*, Britten's *Spring Symphony*, and Holst's *First Choral Symphony*. Roman Catholic Liturgy is used in nine works, some in Latin as discussed above and the remainder in translation. William Drummond's poetry is in Ulysses Kay's *Phoebus Arise* and Vaughan Williams's *Hodie*. Edmund Spenser is also represented in the *Hodie* and Britten's *Spring Symphony*. John Milton's poetry is found in Britten's *Spring Symphony*, Vaughan Williams's *Hodie*, and Healey Willan's *Coronation Suite*. The latter two works both feature Milton's "Ring Out Ye Crystal Spheres."

Three other single texts are represented in works by two composers. Carl Sandburg's *The Corn Huskers* has been set as *The Prairie* by Normand Lockwood and Lukas Foss. Whitman's "When Lilacs Last in the Dooryard Bloom'd" has been set, as mentioned above, by Hindemith and Sessions. The same poet's "Drum Taps" has been set by Howard Hanson in *Three Songs from "Drum Taps"* and William Schuman in *A Free Song*.

It is Whitman who has become the poet of choice for composers of large works in this century. Including the already mentioned pieces, Whitman poems can be found in fourteen works, more than four times the number of any other individual author. Wannamaker has catalogued settings of Whitman's text by over 200 composers.[1] Nearly all of these are choral. The relationship between the poet's words and composers' choice of group singing is a reflection of the universality of Whitman's poetic voice.

---

[1] J.R. Wannamaker: *The Musical Settings of the Poetry of Walt Whitman: A Study of Theme, Structure, and Prosody.* University of Minnesota: Dissertation, 1972.

"Whitman himself likened his treatment of phrase, cadence, and thematic development to music, possibly one of the reasons for the attraction of his work to composers."[2] "Whitman's nationalistic views of equal opportunity, concern for the individual, hope for the destiny of the American people, and the musical attributes of his poetry provide a varied basis of attraction for composers."[3] It is also Whitman's dedication to the prospect of peace and the sincerity of his commemorations to the deceased which have so profoundly drawn composers to his work. And it is these themes which have come to be the foundation of the finest works of this repertoire.

Conclusion

The choral-orchestral repertoire is representative of the principal technical devices which have been explored throughout this century's musical genres. The increased performing difficulties associated with these procedures have been relegated to the orchestra or soloists. The choral writing, while more challenging in terms of pitch material, has become virtually non-contrapuntal with an apparent consensus of composers that such an approach enhances performing accessibility. This conclusion is reinforced by the consistent presence of contrapuntal material in the orchestral writing of these same works.

While the text themes of previous centuries remain a viable pursuit for modern composers, the social conscience of the musical creator has become particularly evident in the selection of texts in the works of this century. The role of composer as propagandist and giver of tribute has come to prominence. Unlike the choral-orchestral works of the past, the contributions to the repertoire from this century frequently address and reflect the moral and historical concerns of composers and listeners alike. This trend is affirmed by the predilection of composers for Whitman's poetry. The universality of his texts is the typification of populism. Composers have thus expressed these ideas through the most populist ensemble, the choir. As concert halls became the domain of the middle class in the nineteenth century making the music to be for the people, in the twentieth century the content of

---

[2] Donald Jenni: "Whitman, Walt," in *The New Grove Dictionary of American Music*, edited by H. Wiley Hitchcock, iv: 521. 4 volumes. London: Macmillan, 1986.

[3] Lou Stem Mize: *A Study of Selected Choral Settings of Walt Whitman Poems*. Florida State University: Dissertation, 1967.

these works has now made it of the people.

CHAPTER II

SURVEY OF WORKS

Adler, Samuel (b. Mannheim, Germany, 4 March 1928)

Life: Adler is the son of trained musicians; his father was a cantor and composer of Jewish liturgical music. His family emigrated to the United States in 1939, where he attended Boston University (BMus 1948) and Harvard (MA 1950). His composition teachers include Aaron Copland, Paul Fromm, Paul Hindemith, Hugo Norden, Walter Piston, and Randall Thompson. He also studied conducting with Serge Koussevitsky at Tanglewood. Joining the Army in 1950, he organized the Seventh Army Symphony Orchestra. From 1957-66, Adler taught composition at North Texas State University, and since then has served on the faculty of the Eastman School. He is recipient of the Army Medal of Honor for musical service; Ford Foundation, Rockefeller, and NEA Awards; a Koussevitsky Foundation commission; and a Guggenheim Fellowship. Adler's works utilize varied techniques including dance rhythms, diatonicism, free atonality, serialism, ostinati, folk themes, improvisation, and aleatoric devices.[4]

---

[4] Marie Wolf: "Adler, Samuel," in *The New Grove Dictionary of American Music*, edited by H. Wiley Hitchcock, i: 8-9. 4 volumes. London: Macmillan, 1986.

Writings: *Anthology for the Teaching of Choral Conducting* (New York: Holt, Rhinehart, and Winston, 1971), *Sightsinging, Pitch, Interval, Rhythm* (New York: W.W. Norton,1979), and *A Study of Orchestration* (New York: W.W. Norton, 1982, revised 1991).

Principal Works: *opera - The Outcast of Poker Flat* (1959), *The Wrestler* (1971), *The Disappointment* (1974); *ballet - The Waking* (1978); *orchestral* - 6 Symphonies (1953, 1957, 1960, 1967, 1975, and 1985); many chamber works, songs, and liturgical works.

Selected Composer Bibliography

Rothmüller, Aron Marko: *The Music of Jews: An Historical Appreciation*, second edition. South Brunswick, NJ: Yoseloff, 1967.

Wolf, Marie: "Adler, Samuel," in *The New Grove Dictionary of American Music*, edited by H. Wiley Hitchcock, i: 8-9. 4 volumes. London: Macmillan, 1986.

The Binding (1967)

Duration: ca. 50 minutes

Text: The Book of Genesis, chapter 22; teachings of Midrash and Aggadah, as compiled by Hugo Chaim Adler (the composer's father) and adapted to English by Albert Friedlander.

Performing Forces: *voices*: 2 sopranos, mezzo-soprano, tenor, and baritone soloists; SATB choir; *orchestra*: piccolo, 2 flutes, 2 oboes (oboe II double English horn), 2 clarinets, bass clarinet, 2 bassoons, 4 horns, 3 trumpets in C, 3 trombones, tuba, timpani (5 drums), percussion (3 players - snare drum, tenor drum, bass drum, crash cymbals, suspended cymbal, tam-tam, triangle, temple blocks, wood block, xylophone, glockenspiel), harp, and strings.

First Performance: 4 May 1967; Temple Emanu-El, Dallas, TX; Temple Emanu-El Choir, Dallas Chamber Music Society; conducted by the composer.

Edition: *The Binding* is published and distributed by Oxford University Press. The piano-vocal score is available for purchase; orchestral materials may be rented.

Autograph: The full score is a facsimile of the composer's manuscript.

Notes: This work was commissioned by Temple Emanu-El, North Texas State University, and the Dallas Chamber Music Society. "This work is dedicated to the 'thousands of sons' who have fallen, and will continue to fall as long as man misunderstands the cry of the 'Living God' as taught and clarified by this legend, and by the sayings of the Prophets of Israel." The score begins with a brief Hebrew phrase which has been phonetically transcribed. It is a dramatically conceived work which is through-composed.

Performance Issues: The choral writing is mostly homophonic, and there are divisi passages in all parts. Adler's work has some tonal orientation, but is generally freely chromatic. The choral parts are the most harmonically stable, while the soloists and orchestra have much polymodal/polytonal material. There is an unmeasured section beginning in the fourth bar after [52]. In this same section of the score, the soloists are asked to approximate pitches within a specific rhythm. At [57], the choir is to divide into even groups which speak five metrically independent lines. The score calls for 2 percussionists, but 3 are needed. There is rapid unison passagework in the strings and winds. *Soloists*: soprano, range: c'-b", tessitura: g'-e", lyric and sustained; Isaac (a boy or young girl) - soprano, range: e'-a^{b}", tessitura: a'-f', clear and lyric; narrator - alto, range: g-g", tessitura: d'-d", strong and speech-like; tenor (also Satan), range: c-a', tessitura: g-f', bright with broad leaps; baritone (also Abraham), range: A^{b}-f', tessitura: B-b, declamatory and powerful. This is an imaginative and well crafted work, which is also a moving and sincere presentation of the biblical legend of Isaac and Abraham. *Choir*: medium difficult; *Orchestra*: medium difficult.

Discography: As of January 1993, no commercial recording has been made available.

Selected Bibliography

Douglass, Robert: [review], *American Choral Review*, x/4 (1968), 194-196.

A Whole Bunch of Fun (1969)

Duration: ca. 20 minutes

Text: Lewis Carroll, Marianne Moore, Theodore Roethke, Eleanor Farjeon, P. D. Eastman, Ogden Nash, and G. F. Whicher

Performing Forces: *voices*: mezzo-soprano or baritone soloists; SATB, SSA, and SA Choirs; *orchestra*: 3 flutes, 2 oboes, 3 clarinets, 2 bassoons, 2 horns, 2 trumpets, 3 trombones, tuba, timpani, percussion (3 players - snare drum, tenor drum, bass drum, tambourine, crash cymbals, suspended cymbal, triangle, wood block, temple blocks, ratchet, xylophone), and strings.

First Performance: November 1971; Rochester, NY; Penfield Central School District Choirs, Rochester Philharmonic, conducted by the composer.[5]

Edition: *A Whole Bunch of Fun* is published and distributed by Oxford University Press. The piano-vocal score is available for purchase; orchestral materials are available on rental.

Autograph: The full score is a facsimile of the composer's manuscript.

Notes: *A Whole Bunch of Fun* was commissioned by the Music Department of Penfield (a suburb of Rochester, NY) Central School District, James E. Dumm, supervisor of music. The texts are tongue-in-cheek comments relating to students' feelings about school. The piece is organized into nine movements as follows:

1. Rules and Regulations   Lewis Carroll
2. To His Royal Highness the Dauphin   Marianne Moore

---

[5] telephone interview with Samuel Adler, August 1992.

3.	Limericks	Theodore Roethke
	a. The Yak	
	b. Myrtle	
4.	The Ballad of the Cat	Eleanor Farjeon
5.	The Ballad of the Dog	P. D. Eastman
6.	More About Myrtle	Theodore Roethke
	a. Myrtle's Cousin	
	b. Goo-Girl	
7.	Three Fables	Marianne Moore
	a. O to be a Dragon	
	b. To a Chameleon	
	c. A Jellyfish	
8.	I will Arise and Go Now	Ogden Nash
9.	Time for Sadness	George F. Whicher

Performance Issues: This work was written for performance by a good public-school music program. Adler has very intelligently crafted a work of attractive and sophisticated music which is within the means of such students. The humor of the texts carries over into the music with some isolated vocal hisses and choral stuttering, but such devices are used with wit. The texts of this piece make it appropriate only for student ensembles. It is not simplistic, and while the choral parts could be mastered by school choirs of medium skill, the orchestra parts require a first-rate school orchestra. The choral writing incorporates unisons and paired doublings within each choir, but there are intricate exchanges between these groups. The fourth and fifth movements have extended passages for speaking choirs. The choirs are combined in only the first, fifth, and last movements leaving each ensemble responsible for only three or four movements. The mixed choir has divisi in all parts and contains the most challenging vocal music with many elements of extended tonality. *Soloist*: mezzo-soprano (or baritone an octave lower), range: b'-e", tessitura: e^{b}'-c". This role sings only the second movement, and is well within the ability of a good high school singer. The singer must have a clear voice which is articulate and flexible. *Choir*: medium easy; *Orchestra*: medium.

Discography: As of January 1993, no commercial recording has been made available.

Amram, David Werner (b. Philadelphia, PA, 17 November 1930).

Life: Amram was educated at Oberlin Conservatory (1 year, 1948) and then George Washington University where he graduated with a BA in history in 1952. He played horn in the National Symphony Orchestra and then the Seventh Army Orchestra with which he toured Europe for three years, returning to the U.S. in 1955. He then enrolled in the Manhattan School of Music, studying with Dmitri Mitropoulos, Vittorio Giannini, and Gunther Schuller. In association with Joseph Papp, he composed incidental music for 25 Shakespeare plays for use in the New York Shakespeare Festival. In 1959, he received the Pulitzer prize for his incidental music to MacLeish's *J. B.* He was the first composer-in-residence with the New York Philharmonic (1966-67). He has made many tours as an emissary for the State Department and the World Council of Churches.

Principal Works: *orchestral*: *Autobiography* (1959), *Shakespearean Concerto* (1959), Horn Concerto (1965), *Brazilian Memories* (1973), *Travels* (1984); *vocal*: *Friday Evening Service* (1960), *Let Us Remember* (1965), and *The Trail of Beauty* (1976).

Selected Composer Bibliography

Amram, David: *Vibrations: The Adventures and Musical Times of David Amram.* New York: Knopf, 1968.
"Amram, David (Werner)," *Current Biography Yearbook,* xxx (November 1969); New York: H. W. Wilson Company.
Petersen, Barbara: "Amram, David," in *The New Grove Dictionary of American Music,* edited by H. Wiley Hitchcock, i: 44-45. 4 volumes. London: Macmillan, 1986.

A Year in Our Land (1964)

Duration: ca. 25 minutes

Text: The texts of this work reflect both the idealism and frustration of the American experience. Amram has selected his texts from the following sources: James Baldwin's *Another Country* is about the troubles of love within a biracial and bisexual context; John Dos Passos's *Manhattan Transfer* is a portrayal of the dissatisfaction with the American dream as experienced by city dwellers; In *Lonesome Traveler,* Jack Kerouac presents an analysis of the transience of human experience and of America as paradise lost; John Steinbeck's *Travels with Charley* is an autobiographical tale of a cross-country trip with his dog, Charley; *The Web and the Rock* of Thomas Wolfe is an autobiographical novel of a young author recently moved to New York, its central theme is the conflicts between Christian and Jew, and rural and city folk; and lastly, Walt Whitman's *Leaves of Grass* is lifetime collection of particularly American poems reflecting the author's views and experiences.[6]

Performing Forces: *voices*: soprano, alto, tenor, and bass soloists; SATB choir; *orchestra*: 2 flutes, 2 oboes (oboe II doubling English horn), 2 clarinets (clarinet II doubling bass clarinet), 2 bassoons (bassoon II doubling contrabassoon), 2 horns, 2 trumpets, 2 trombones, timpani, percussion (3 players - snare drum, bass drum, bongos, tom toms, crash cymbals, suspended cymbal, Chinese gong, triangle, xylophone, Parsifal chime), piano, and strings.

First Performance: 13 May 1964; New York; Interracial Choir; conducted by Harold Aks.

Edition: *A Year in Our Land* is published and distributed by C. F. Peters. Piano-vocal score is available for purchase; orchestral materials are available for rental.

Autograph: The full score is a facsimile of the composer's manuscript.

Notes: Amram's choice of diverse texts describes the four seasons in America. He has organized it into six sections as follows:

	Prologue (Baldwin)	choir
1.	Spring in the East (Dos Passos)	soprano solo and choir
2.	Summer in the West (Kerouac)	tenor solo and choir
3.	Autumn in the North (Steinbeck)	alto solo and choir
4.	Winter in the South (Wolfe)	bass solo and choir
	Epilogue (Whitman)	SATB solos and choir

---

[6] George and Barbara Perkins and Phillip Leininger: *Benét's Reader's Encyclopedia of American Literature.* New York: Harper Collins, 1991.

Performance Issues: The choral writing is diatonic with logogenic rhythms. The choir has some rhythmic speaking including some prolonged and exaggerated vocal sounds. There is a high sustained prelude for solo trumpet. There are a number of dramatically subtle solos for the concertmaster. The Parsifal chime can be achieved by striking the low strings of the piano with a large bass-drum or tam-tam beater. There is no tempo indicated for the third movement. *Soloists*: soprano, range: d'-a", tessitura: f'-f', lyric and flexible with long phrases; alto, range: f#-g", tessitura: e'-d", rhythmic and lyrical; tenor, range: d-b♭', tessitura: f-e♭' (there is one falsetto f"), it is a declamatory and rapidly articulated role; bass, range: F#-d', tessitura: B-b, forceful and articulate. The orchestration is transparent and varied and well within the ability of a moderate college orchestra. The rhythmic intricacy of the vocal writing and orchestrational style suggest a medium-sized choir. The choral parts are sophisticated and very sensitive to the text, demanding a reasonably experienced ensemble. This is an excellent piece for teaching textual nuances. The text is also unusual in its currency of social issues. *Choir*: medium; *Orchestra*: medium easy.

Discography: Interracial Chorale and Orchestra; conducted by Harold Aks. Recorded in 1965. AY-200 [LP mono].

Selected Bibliography

Cranna, Clifford: [review], *Notes*, xxxviii/2 (March 1980).

Barber, Samuel (b. West Chester, PA, 9 March 1910; d. New York, 23 January 1981).

Life: Barber began to study piano at the age of six, and composed his first piece, *Sadness*, the following year. He entered the Curtis Institute in 1924 (BMus 1933), where he studied piano with George Boyle and Isabelle Vengerova, voice with Emilio de Gorgoza, conducting with Fritz Reiner, and composition with Rosario Scalero. At Curtis Barber met his longtime companion Gian Carlo Menotti. The two young composers toured Italy in the summers of 1931 and 1932. A series of awards allowed them to spend much of the next four years studying and performing throughout Europe. Barber returned to the Curtis Institute (1939-42) to teach orchestration and direct a chamber choir. Beginning in 1942, he devoted his career entirely to composition. Barber's music is lyrical and generally tonal in concept although often charged with strong dissonances. He uses classical formal structures throughout his works. Barber's music is consistently refined with frequent juxtapositions of angular and rhythmically aggressive passages with exceptionally elegant and languid melodies. His musical language is highly personal combining a tonal fabric reminiscent of the nineteenth century with a twentieth-century cosmopolitan sensibility.[7]

Awards: American Prix de Rome (1935), Pulitzer Traveling Scholarship (1935), Guggenheim Fellowship (1945), New York Music Critics' Circle Award (1947 for Concerto for Violoncello), 2 Pulitzer Prizes (1958 for *Vanessa*, 1963 for Concerto for Piano), Henry Hadley Medal (1958). In 1964 he was commissioned to compose an opera for the opening of the Metropolitan Opera House in Lincoln Center (1966, *Antony and Cleopatra*). He was elected to the Institute (1941) and Academy (1958) of the American Academy and Institute of Arts and Letters, and was vice president of the Executive Board of the International Music Council of UNESCO (1952).

Principal Works: *operas - Vanessa* (1956-7), *A Hand of Bridge* (1953), *Antony and Cleopatra* (1966); *ballets - Medea* (1946), *Souvenirs* (1952); *orchestral - The School for Scandal* (1931-3), *Music for a Scene from Shelley* (1933), *Symphony in One Movement* (1936), *Adagio for Strings* [adapted from movement 2 of his String Quartet] (1936), *Essay for Orchestra* (1937), Violin Concerto (1939), *Second Essay* (1942), Symphony no. 2 (1944), *Capricorn Concerto* (1944), Cello Concerto (1945), Piano Concerto (1962), *Third Essay* (1978); *choral - A Stopwatch and an Ordinance Map* (1940), *Reincarnations* (1937), *Prayers of Kierkegaard* (1954), *Twelfth Night* (1968); and many songs and chamber pieces.

Selected Composer Bibliography

"Barber, Samuel," *Current Biography Yearbook*, v (September 1944); obituary, lxii (March 1981); New York: H. W. Wilson Company.
Broder, Nathan: *Samuel Barber*. New York: G. Schirmer, 1954.
Heinsheimer, Hans: "Samuel Barber: Maverick Composer," *Keynote*, iv/1 (1980), 7.

---

[7] Harold Gleason and Walter Becker: "Samuel Barber," in *20th-Century American Composers*. Music Literature Outlines, series iv. Bloomington, IN: Indiana University Press, revised 1981.

Gleason, Harold, and Walter Becker: "Samuel Barber," in *20th-century American Composers*. Music Literature Outlines, series iv. Bloomington: Indiana University Press, revised 1981.

Hennessee, Don A.: *Samuel Barber: A Bio-bibliography*. Westport, CT: Greenwood Press, 1985.

Jackson, Richard, and Barbara Heyman: "Samuel Barber," *The New Grove Twentieth-Century American Masters*, 243-262. New York: W.W. Norton, 1986.

Heyman, Barbara: *Samuel Barber: A Documentary Study of His Works*. Dissertation, CUNY, [no date of registration as of January 1993].

_____: *Samuel Barber: The Composer and His Music*. New York: Oxford University Press, 1992.

The Lovers, op. 43 (1971)

Duration: ca. 31 minutes

Text: Pablo Neruda's *Veinte poemas de amor y una canción desperada* (1924), the last of which is the source for *The Lovers*. Translations are by Christopher Logue and W. S. Merwin.

Performing Forces: *voices*: soprano and baritone soloists; choir; *orchestra*: piccolo, 2 flutes, alto flute, 2 oboes, English horn, 2 clarinets, bass clarinet, bassoon, 4 horns, 3 trumpets, 3 trombones, tuba, timpani, percussion (3 players - bass drum, bongo drums, cymbals, antique cymbal (1), tam tam, triangle, wood blocks (high, low), 3 bell trees, xylophone), celeste, harp, piano, and strings.

First Performance: 22 September 1971; Philadelphia; Tom Krause; Temple University Choirs, Philadelphia Orchestra; conducted by Eugene Ormandy.

Edition: *The Lovers* is published and distributed by G. Schirmer. The piano-vocal and study scores are for sale; orchestral materials may be rented.

Autograph: The composer's manuscripts are in the Library of Congress.

Notes: This work was commissioned by the Girard Bank of Philadelphia and dedicated to Valentin Herranz. It is in ten sections as follows:

	Prelude	orchestra
	Prelude	orchestra
I.	Body of a woman	baritone solo
II.	Lithe girl, brown girl	men's choir, a few women
III.	In the hot depth of this summer	women's choir
IV.	Close your eyes	choir
V.	The Fortunate Isles	choir, small soprano solo
VI.	Sometimes	baritone solo
VII.	We have lost even this twilight	choir
VIII.	Tonight I can write	baritone solo
IX.	Cemetery of kisses	choir

About the work, the composer states:

> It was one of my most challenging but stimulating undertakings...I was fascinated by the *Twenty Poems of Love and a Song of Sadness* by Pablo Neruda...I was inspired by them and wanted to set a number of them to music. The poems themselves are extremely erotic, and some of the Girard board members raised their eyebrows. Finally, I asked them whether they didn't have love affairs in Philadelphia and learned that they did...At any rate, the bank thought about it all and gave me complete freedom.[8]

Performance Issues: The full score is in C and sounding at pitch with the exception of the mallet percussion and double basses which are notated traditionally. The choral writing is contrapuntally complex, exploiting imitation at the fourth with great rhythmic variety. The rhythms are generated by the prosody of the text. There are divisi in all of the choral ranks including a three-part division for the basses. The vocal writing is chromatic, but tonally grounded. Most of the choral material is independently lyrical and clearly supported by the accompaniment. The double

---

[8] as quoted in Phillip Huscher: notes for recording of Samuel Barber's *The Lovers*. Performed by Dale Duesing, Sarah Reese; Chicago Symphony Orchestra and Chorus; conducted by Andrew Schenck. Koch International Classics: 3-7125-2H1, 1992.

basses are required to play numerous low c#'s and d's, for which an extension would be more adequate than merely tuning down. This score is less rhapsodic than many of Barber's other vocal works. The orchestration is imaginative and colorful and presents few challenges to ensemble coordination. The instrumental parts are not notably difficult with the exception of clarinet I and the lower strings, who should be strong players. The scoring suggests a fairly large string section and a large choir. With substantial rehearsal time this work could be performed by a choir of limited experience. The text is about a love affair; it is filled with eloquent, erotic allusions. *Soloists*: soprano, range: d'-f#", tessitura: d'-d", lyrical, and only eight measures long, it should be assigned to a member of the choir; baritone, range: G#-f' with an optional f#', tessitura: e-d', declamatory with rapid text articulation. *Choir*: medium difficult; *Orchestra*: medium difficult.

Discography: Sarah Reese, soprano, Dale Duesing, baritone; Chicago Symphony Orchestra and Chorus; conducted by Andrew Schenck. Recorded: October 1991. Koch International Classics: 37125-2H1 [DDD].

Selected Bibliography

[review of premiere], *New York Times* (24 September 1971), 36:6.
Turock: "Philharmonic Hall," *Music Journal*, xxx (January 1972), 75.
Mussulman, John A.: *Dear People...Robert Shaw: A Biography.* Bloomington, IN: Indiana University Press, 1979; 243-4.

Bernstein, Leonard (b. Lawrence, MA, 25 August 1918; d. New York, 14 October 1990).

Life: Bernstein was educated at the Boston Latin School and Harvard (BA 1939). He entered the Curtis Institute in 1941, where he studied conducting with Fritz Reiner and orchestration with Randall Thompson. He also studied conducting with Serge Koussevitsky and composition with Aaron Copland and Paul Hindemith at Tanglewood (1940-2). He was catapulted to fame as a conductor when he substituted for the ailing Bruno Walter in a national radio broadcast. After a year as joint principal conductor, with Dmitri Mitropoulos, he was named sole conductor of the New York Philharmonic (1958-69), retiring as conductor laureate. He was one of the most influential and renowned conductors of this century. His compositions are marked by an inventive integration of jazz music with elements of concert music.

His melodies are very technically crafted in terms of intervallic organization, while retaining qualities of popular music.[9] Throughout his works there is a common theme of man's struggle with unstable beliefs and the pursuit to find faith.[10] His skills as a communicator were displayed in the many educational programs given on national television with the New York Philharmonic, and through his popular books on musical topics.

Writings: *The Joy of Music* (1959), *Young People's Concerts for Reading and Listening* (1962, revised and enlarged 1970), *The Infinite Variety of Music* (1966), *The Unanswered Question* (1976), and *Findings* (1982).

Principal Works: *musicals/operas - On the Town* (1944), *Trouble in Tahiti* (1951), *Wonderful Town* (1953), *Candide* (1956, revised 1973), *West Side Story* (1957), *1600 Pennsylvania Avenue* (1976), *A Quiet Place* (1983); *ballets - Fancy Free* (1944), *Facsimile* (1946), Symphony no. 1, "Jeremiah" (1942), Symphony no. 2, "The Age of Anxiety" (1949), Symphony no. 3, "Kaddish" (1961-63); *choral - Chichester Psalms* (1965); *film music - On the Waterfront* (1954).

Selected Composer Bibliography

"Bernstein, Leonard," *Current Biography Yearbook*, v (February 1944); xxi (February 1960); New York: H. W. Wilson Company.

Bernstein, Leonard: *The Joy of Music*. New York: Simon and Schuster, 1959.

_____: *The Infinite Variety of Music*. New York: Simon and Schuster, 1966.

_____: *The Unanswered Question*. Cambridge, MA: Harvard University Press, 1976.

_____: *Findings*. New York: Simon and Schuster, 1982.

Hughes, Allen: "Leonard Bernstein: Musical Personality of 1960," *Musical America* (January 1961), 15.

---

[9] Joseph Machlis: *Introduction to Contemporary Music*, 575-76. New York: W.W. Norton, 1961.

[10] Joan Peyser: *Bernstein: A Biography*. New York: Beechtree Books, 1987.

Leonard Bernstein: A Catalogue of His Works. New York: Boosey and Hawkes, 1978.

Robinson, Paul: *Bernstein (Art of the Conductor).* New York: Vanguard Press of Simon and Schuster, 1982.

Peyser, Joan: "Leonard Bernstein," *The New Grove Twentieth-Century American Masters,* 291-306. New York: W.W. Norton, 1986.

_____: *Bernstein: A Biography.* New York: Beechtree Books, 1987.

Fluegel, Jane, editor: *Bernstein Remembered.* New York: Carroll and Graf, 1991.

Kaddish, Symphony No. 3 (1961-63)

Duration: ca. 40 minutes

Text: traditional Hebrew text, narrator's text is by the composer

Performing Forces: *voices*: speaker, soprano soloist; SATB choir, boy choir; *orchestra*: 4 flutes (flutes III and IV doubling piccolo), 2 oboes, English horn, clarinet in E^b, 2 clarinets in B^b and A, bass clarinet, alto saxophone, 2 bassoons, contrabassoon, 4 horns, trumpet in D, 3 trumpets in C, 3 trombones, tuba, timpani (5), percussion (7 players - snare drum, field drum, tenor drum, bass drum, Israeli hand drum, 3 bongos, tambourine, crash cymbals, 2 suspended cymbals, finger cymbals, crotales (E, G, B, C), tam-tam, triangle, 3 temple blocks, wood block, sandpaper blocks, rasp, whip, ratchet, maracas, claves, xylophone, glockenspiel, vibraphone, chimes), celeste, harp, piano, and strings.

First Performance: 10 December 1963; Tel Aviv; Hannah Rovina, speaker; Jennie Tourel, soprano; Israel Philharmonic Orchestra, choirs prepared by Abraham Kaplan and Isaac Graziani; conducted by the composer.

Boston Premiere: 31 January 1964; Boston, MA; Felicia Montealegre, speaker; Jennie Tourel, soprano; New England Conservatory Chorus, prepared by Lorna Cooke DeVaron, Columbus Boychoir prepared by Donald Bryant; Boston Symphony; conducted by Charles Munch.

Premiere of Revised Version: 25 August 1977; Mainz; Michael Wager, speaker; Montserrat Caballé, soprano; Wiener

Jeunesse Chor prepared by Günther Theuring, Wiener Sängerknaben prepared by Uwe Harrer; Israel Philharmonic; conducted by the composer.

Edition: *The Kaddish Symphony* is published by Jalni Publications and distributed by Boosey and Hawkes. Piano-vocal and study scores are available for purchase; orchestral materials available for rental.

Autograph: A copy of the composer's manuscript is in the possession of Boosey and Hawkes.

Notes: The work is dedicated "To the Beloved Memory of John F. Kennedy." "Kaddish," is a prayer from the Jewish service for the dead; it is however, also about life. The symphony is a quest for faith; it is an attempt to fit an ancient God into a contemporary belief. Bernstein attempts to achieve this by broadening the scope of the believer to comprehend the role of a deity within a changing world. The "Kaddish" serves as a requiem for the God of the past and prayer for the God of today. The English text is reserved for the narrator. These issues are revisited from an ecumenical perspective in *Mass*. Bernstein has arranged this symphony into three parts which are further divided into seven movements as follows:

    I.   Invocation. Adagio
         Kaddish 1. L'istesso tempo - Allegro molto

    II. Din-Torah. Di nuovo adagio
         Kaddish 2. Andante con tenerezza

    III. Scherzo. Presto Scherzando, sempre pianissimo
         Kaddish 3. Sostenuto
         Finale. Adagio come nel "Din-Torah"

In the score are the following notes:

> *Kaddish* (Symphony No. 3) is the belated result of a joint commission by the Koussevitsky Music Foundation and the Boston Symphony Orchestra, on the occasion of the Orchestra's seventy-fifth anniversary in 1955. Intensive work on the Symphony was begun in the summer of 1961, at Martha's Vineyard, continued at the

MacDowell Colony, in New Hampshire, in the summer of 1962, and completed on August 19, 1963, at Fairfield, Connecticut. The orchestration was achieved in three weeks of November, 1963. . . On November 22, 1963, Bernstein had come to the orchestration of the final *amen* section of the Symphony when, abruptly, fate commanded the dedication: "To the beloved memory of John F. Kennedy."

Because he was not satisfied with the original version, the composer, in 1977, made some revisions. This included a few cuts, some musical re-writing [sic] and even more re-writing of the spoken text. Furthermore, he made it possible for the speaker to be either a woman or a man.

Performance Issues: This is a chromatic and rhythmically charged work. The chromaticisms reflect Bernstein's unique combination of classical traditions with Jewish folk songs and jazz. It is filled with displaced downbeats, constantly changing meters, cross-rhythms, unusual and varied beat divisions, and erratically-placed accents. The beginning of the score has the text of the Kaddish prayer in Aramaic with a translation, a phonetic transliteration and a guide to the symbols used. The transliteration is in the Sephardic dialect and is used in place of the text in the score. The choral writing is very chromatic, but supported by the accompaniment. Bernstein frequently utilizes paired doublings and choral unisons. The vocal counterpoint rarely exceeds two levels of simultaneous melodic motion. The choir is asked to clap, stomp, and to hum on low-register pitches which are up to the discretion of the singers. Beginning two bars after [M], the choir has an 8-part cadenza; for this the composer states, "Each of the 8 groups has its own inner conductor, who beats that group's separate pulse. The beat may be passed along through the section, but there should be as little visual disturbance as possible." This cadenza creates 8 ostinati in diverse tempos which ultimately fade to nothing. The choral parts are not only musically difficult, but also physically challenging. All of the orchestral parts contain very difficult passages and constant rhythmic challenges. The score is thoroughly bowed. The timpanist is asked to play improvised pitches within a given rhythm at [F]. The narration is never notated in definite rhythm, but it is made to correspond to measures, or the score indicates specific beats upon which phrases are to begin. *Soloist*: soprano, range: c'-b$^{b'''}$, tessitura: a'-g'', requires a clear and lyric voice capable of sustained phrases. This is a remarkably challenging piece for all involved in its performance. It is an equally magnificent musical expression of faith and the human condition, well worth the effort of those few ensembles capable of executing it. *Choir*: difficult; *Orchestra*: difficult.

Discography: Jennie Tourel, mezzo-soprano; Felicia Montealegre, speaker; Camerata Singers, Columbus Boychoir, New York Philharmonic; conducted by Bernstein. Recorded 15 and 17 April 1964. Columbia: KL-6005 [LP]; re-released as Sony: SM3K 47162 [ADD].

Montserrat Caballé, soprano; Michael Wager, speaker; Vienna Academy Chamber Choir, Wiener Sängerknaben, Israel Philharmonic Orchestra; conducted by Bernstein. Recorded 1978. Deutsche Grammophon: 2530.968(10)-2530.970(10) [LP]; re-released as 423582-2 GH [ADD].

Selected Bibliography

Davis, Peter: "Bernstein as Symphonist," *New York Times* (26 November 1978), section II, 17.

Gottlieb, Jack: "Symbols of Faith in the Music of Leonard Bernstein," *The Musical Quarterly*, lxvi (1980), 14.

Bernard, Andrew: *Two Musical Perspectives of Twentieth-Century Pacifism: An Analytical and Historical View of Britten's "War Requiem" and Bernstein's "Kaddish Symphony."* University of Washington: Dissertation, 1990.

Mass (1970-71)

Duration: ca. 95 minutes

Text: Latin Liturgy, Bernstein, and Stephen Schwartz

Performing Forces: *voices*: Celebrant (baritone), boy soprano; SATB choir, boy choir; *orchestra*: 2 flutes, 2 oboes (oboe II doubling English horn), 3 clarinets (clarinet III doubling E^{b} clarinet, bass clarinet, and saxophones), 2 bassoons (bassoon II doubling contrabassoon), 4 horns, 4 trumpets, 3 trombones, tuba, 4 electric guitars, 2 electronic keyboards, percussion (38 pieces), 2 Allen organs, harp, and strings.

First Performance: 8 September 1971; Kennedy Center, Washington, DC; Alan Titus - Celebrant; Norman Scribner Choir; conducted by Maurice Peress.

Revision: arranged for chamber orchestra by Maurice Peress (1972)

Performing Forces: *voices*: Celebrant (baritone), boy soprano, choir of 12, boy choir of 10, Street Ensemble of 16, 3 dancers; *orchestra*: flute (doubling clarinet and saxophone), horn, trumpet, trombone, tuba, bass guitar, electric piano, harp, organ, percussion (2 players), 1 violin.

First Performance: 26 December 1972; Los Angeles; conducted by Maurice Peress.

Edition: *Mass* is published by Amberson and distributed by Boosey and Hawkes. The piano-vocal score (47108c) is for sale. The full score and orchestral materials are available by rental.

Autograph: A copy of the composer's manuscript is in the possession of Boosey and Hawkes.

Notes: The original orchestrations are by Bernstein, Hershy Kay, and Jonathan Tunick. The work was composed for the opening of the John F. Kennedy Center in Washington, DC, at the request of Jacqueline Kennedy Onassis. *Mass* combines the words of the Roman Catholic Mass with additional Hebrew prayers and original English text. The work uses the liturgy of the Mass as the basis for a work of musical theater in the manner of a semi-staged oratorio. The liturgy serves as an exploration of faith, its demise and ultimate reaffirmation. *Mass* is organized as follows:

I. DEVOTIONS BEFORE MASS
    1. Antiphon: *Kyrie Eleison*
    2. Hymn and Psalm: "A Simple Song"
    3. Responsory: *Alleluia*
II. FIRST INTROIT (Rondo)
    1. Prefatory Prayers
    2. Thrice-Triple Canon: *Dominus Vobiscum*
III. SECOND INTROIT
    1. *In nomine Patris*
    2. Prayer for the Congregation (Chorale: "Almighty Father")

Performance Issues: This work is a remarkable amalgamation of styles ranging from marches to jazz to classical to rock. In this writer's opinion, it is an effective and sincere composition, which although it contains many pop-music elements of the period is capable of sustaining its musical worth in the future. Bernstein's craft transcends the possible snares of questionable taste which often plague works of this nature. This is a very rhythmic composition with frequent use of odd-legged meters and ostinati. The choral writing is generally diatonic and variable in texture and treatment including choral unisons, chorales, and strict canons. There are divisi for as many as twelve parts for the choir, but many of these involve substantial overlaps. At some sections, some of the men must sing in falsetto. There are also some spoken passages for the Celebrant and members of the choir. The score indicates that the *Kyrie Eleison* is to be on a quadraphonic tape which successively is played from four speakers placed at the corners of the audience. This could certainly be modified and even adapted to live presentation. The most difficult portions of the score are those which are on the tape. Viola d'amore and shawm are included on this tape, which might require rescoring if an entirely live performance were executed. There are some minor staging indications and suggestions for some offstage playing and singing. *Soloists*: Celebrant - baritone/tenor, range: E-a', tessitura: f-e', this role requires a lyric voice, endurance, and strong acting skills; boy soprano, range: d'-g", tessitura: f'-f", this solo is tuneful, sustained, and carefully supported by the accompaniment. There are a number of smaller solo roles which should be assigned to members of the ensemble: 1st Rock Singer - tenor, range: e-f#', tessitura: b-e'; 2nd Rock Singer - baritone, range: e^b-e^b', tessitura: g-d'; 3rd Rock Singer - baritone, range: f#-f#', tessitura: f#-f#'; 1st Blues Singer - baritone, range: c-g'; tessitura: g-d'; 2nd Blues Singer - alto, range: d^b'-g", tessitura: g'-d"; 3rd Blues Singer - baritone, range: d^b-g', tessitura: g-d'; Descant - tenor/countertenor, range: b-a", tessitura: e'-a"; soprano 1, range: d'-f", tessitura: g'-e^b"; soprano 2, range: d'-f", tessitura: f'-e^b"; soprano 3, range: d'-a", tessitura: a'-g"; tenor 1, range: d-f', tessitura: g-e^b'; tenor 2, range: d-f', tessitura: f-e^b'; tenor 3, range: d-a', tessitura: a-g'. *Choir*: medium difficult; *Orchestra*: medium difficult.

Discography: Alan Titus; Norman Scribner Choir, Berkshire Boys' Choir; conducted by the composer. Recorded in 1971. CBS: M2K-44593 [ADD]; re-released as SONY: SM3K 47154.

Selected Bibliography

Berlinski, Herman: "Bernstein's *Mass*," *Sacred Music*, ic/1 (1972), 3.

Goemanne, Noel: "Open Forum: The Controversial Bernstein Mass: Another Point of View," *Sacred Music*, ic (1973), 33.

Pearlmutter, Alan: "Bernstein's Mass Revisited: A Guide to Using a Contemporary Work to Teach Music Concepts," *Music Educators Journal*, 1 lxi (1974), 34.

Cottle, William Andrew, Sr.: *Social Commentary in Vocal Music in the Twentieth Century as Evidenced by Leonard Bernstein's "Mass."* University of Northern Colorado: Dissertation, 1978.

Andre, Don Alan: *Leonard Bernstein's "Mass" as Social and Political Commentary on the Sixties.* University of Washington: Dissertation, 1979.

DeSesa, Gary: *A Comparison between Descriptive Analysis of Leonard Bernstein's Mass and the Musical Implications of the Critical Evaluations Thereof.* New York University: Dissertation, 1985.

Bliss, Sir Arthur (b. London, 2 August 1891; d. London, 27 March 1975).

Life: Bliss was the son of a native of Springfield, MA, Francis E. Bliss, who had moved to England as chairman of the Anglo-American Oil Company in 1888. Arthur Bliss was a student of Gustav Holst, Ralph Vaughan Williams, and Charles Villiers Stanford at the Royal College of Music. His studies were interrupted by military service (1916-18). Bliss was discharged after having been gassed. He became a professor at the RCM in 1921, resigning after a year to dedicate all of his time to composition. He did however teach again for two years in California 1923-25. There he established contacts with Leopold Stokowski and the Coolidge Foundation. Bliss was music director of the BBC (1942-44), and was made Master of the Queen's Musick in 1953, succeeding Arnold Bax. He was knighted in 1950, made Knight Commander of the Royal Victorian Order in 1969, and a Companion of Honour in 1971. Bliss's music maintains a tonal center, expanding upon it via chromaticisms and modal melodic material. His harmonies are tertian, although often nonfunctional and containing many parallel ninth and eleventh chords. His orchestration is lush, continuing in the style of English mysticism established by his teachers and Delius.[11]

Principal Works: *film scores - Of Things to Come* (1935), *Men of Two Worlds*; *operas - The Olympians* (1949), *Tobias and the Angel* (1960); *ballets - Checkmate* (1937), *Miracle in the Gorbals* (1944), *Adam Zero* (1946); *orchestral - Color Symphony* (1922); *vocal - Serenade* (1929), *The Beatitudes* (1962), *A Knot of Riddles* (1963), *The World is Charged with the Grandeur of God* (1969).

---

[11] Stewart R. Craggs: *Arthur Bliss: A Bio-Bibliography.* New York: Greenwood Press, 1988.

Selected Composer Bibliography

Bliss, Arthur: *As I Remember* [autobiography]. London: Faber and Faber, 1970.

Palmer, Christopher: *Bliss.* Sevenoaks, England: Novello, 1972.

Craggs, Stewart R.: *Sir Arthur Bliss: A Preliminary Survey and Synthesis of Materials for the Study of his Music.* 4 volumes. University of Strathclyde, Glasgow, Scotland: Dissertation, 1982.

_____: *Arthur Bliss: A Bio-Bibliography.* New York: Greenwood Press, 1988.

Bliss, Arthur: *Bliss on Music: Selected Writings of Arthur Bliss,* edited by Gregory Roscow. New York: Oxford University Press, 1991.

Pastoral: Lie Strewn the White Flocks
(1928-29)

Duration: ca. 30-33 minutes

Text: adapted from Ben Jonson, John Fletcher, Poliziano, Robert Nichols, and Theocritus

Performing Forces: *voices*: mezzo-soprano soloist; choir; *orchestra*: flute, timpani, and strings.

First Performance: 8 May 1929; Bishopsgate Institute, London; Odette de Foras, mezzo-soprano; Gilbert Barton, flute; Harold Brooke Choir and Orchestra; conducted by Harold Brooke.

Edition: *Pastoral* is published by Novello and distributed by Theodore Presser Company. The piano-vocal score for sale; orchestral materials are available through rental.

Autograph: It is in the possession of Lady Bliss in London.

Notes: This work was commissioned by the Harold Brooke Choir, and is dedicated to Edward Elgar. The composer notes that if "The Pigeon Song" is omitted, the piece can be performed by choir and orchestra only.

I.	Prelude - strings	
II.	The Shepherd's Holiday	Jonson
III.	A Hymn to Pan	Fletcher
IV.	Pan's Sarabande - flute and orchestra	

V.	Pan and Echo	Poliziano
VI.	The Naiad's Music	Nichols
VII.	The Pigeon Song - mezzo soprano	Nichols
VIII.	Song of the Reapers	Theocritus
IX.	Finale	
	The Shepherd's Night Song	Nichols

Performance Issues: The choral and string parts are divided. The finale includes some *a cappella* passages which are quite simple. The vocal writing is strictly homophonic, using functional harmonies within a fabric of constantly shifting tonal centers. The string writing is conservative and practical. This score is playable by any college-level orchestra and is certainly worth the consideration of many youth orchestras. The flute part is treated as a featured solo. It demands an expert player capable of dramatic nuance and technical flexibility. *Soloist*: mezzo-soprano, range: d'-f#'', tessitura: f'-d'', requiring a lyric voice capable of rapid articulation. This is a fairly simple work with graceful tunes and varied dance rhythms. It is a practical selection for an ensemble of limited means and experience, and is certainly deserving of the consideration of advanced groups as well. *Choir*: medium easy; *Orchestra*: medium easy.

Discography: Sybil Michelow, mezzo-soprano; Norman Knight, flute; Bruckner-Mahler Choir of London, London Chamber Orchestra; conducted by Wyn Morris. Recorded in 1970. Pye Virtuoso: TPLS 13036 [LP].
Shirley Minty, mezzo-soprano; Judith Pearce, flute; Holst Singers and Orchestra; conducted by Hilary Davan Wetton. Recorded in 1985. Hyperion: CDA-66175 [ADD].
Della Jones, mezzo-soprano; The Sinfonia Chorus, Northern Sinfonia; conducted by Richard Hickox. Chandos: CHAN 8886 [DDD].

Selected Bibliography

Thompson, Oscar: "Forecast and Review," *Modern Music*, vii/2 (February/March 1930), 30.

Morning Heroes (1929-30)

Duration: ca. 60-65 minutes

Text: adapted from: Homer, Li Tai Po, Walt Whitman, Wilfred Owen, and Robert Nichols

Performing Forces: *voices*: narrator; choir; *orchestra*: 3 flutes (flute III doubling piccolo), 3 oboes, English horn, 2 clarinets, bass clarinet, 3 bassoons, contrabassoon, 4 horns, 3 trumpets, 3 trombones, tuba, 2 timpanists, percussion (2 players - bass drum, snare drum, tenor drum, cymbals, gong), harp, and strings.

The composer states that if necessary the following parts may be omitted: flute III, oboe II, bass clarinet, contrabassoon, timpani II, and percussion II.

First Performance: 22 October 1930; St. Andrew's Hall, Norwich, England; Basil Maine, narrator; Festival Chorus, Queen's Hall Orchestra; conducted by Bliss.

Edition: *Morning Heroes* is published by Novello and distributed by Theodore Presser Company. The piano-vocal score (15551) is for sale; orchestral materials are available through rental.

Autograph: The composer's manuscript is in the University Library, Cambridge.

Notes: This work was commissioned by the Norfolk and Norwich 33rd Triennial Music Festival, and "Dedicated to the memory of my brother Francis Kennard Bliss and all other comrades killed in battle." The work is in five movements as follows:

I.	Hector's Farewell to Andromache	Homer, from the *Iliad*
II.	The City Arming	Whitman, from *Drum Taps*
III.	Vigil	Li-Tai-Po
	The Bivouac's Flame	from *Drum Taps*
IV.	Achilles Goes Forth to Battle	from the *Iliad*
	The Heroes	from the *Iliad*
V.	Spring Offensive	Wilfred Owen
	Dawn on the Somme	Robert Nichols

Morning Heroes is subtitled a Symphony. The fifteen-minute third movement may be performed separately.

Performance Issues: The narrator speaks throughout the first movement and at the beginning of the fifth movement only. The composer states in the score of the first movement

> [It] is to be declaimed dramatically. Correct timing between the Orator and Conductor is necessary only at the bars marked *, but each speech should end approximately where indicated. Bar by bar synchronization throughout, which will restrict the orator, should naturally not be attempted, nor on any account must the flow of the music be interrupted.

The choral writing is triadic and mostly homophonic. At times, Bliss divides the choir into pairs which he treats antiphonally or casts into contrasting homophonic groups. The independent vocal lines move by step or triadic leap. All of the choral parts are supported harmonically by the accompaniment. The orchestra parts are well written and fairly demanding, remaining within the abilities of an above average college of community ensemble. The orchestration requires a large choir, which must be moderately experienced, with a strong men's section. This is a beautiful work in the style of Vaughan Williams and Howells which very elegantly sets a collection of poignant texts. *Choir*: medium easy; *Orchestra*: medium.

Discography: John Westbrook, speaker; Liverpool Philharmonic Choir, Royal Liverpool Philharmonic Orchestra; conducted by Charles Groves. Recorded in 1975. His Master's Voice: SAN 365 [LP].

Selected Bibliography

Bliss, Arthur: "Arthur Bliss's Morning Heroes," *Monthly Musical Record*, lx (1 October 1930), 289-91.

Grace, Harvey: "Morning Heroes," *The Musical Times*, lxx (October 1930), 881-6.

Blom, Eric: "Morning Heroes," *The Music Teacher* (March 1931), 149-50.

Burn, Andrew: "Now, Trumpeter for Thy Close," *The Musical Times*, cxxvi (November 1985), 666-8.

Foreman, Lewis: *From Parry to Britten: British Music in Letters 1900-1945*, 104, 140, 141, 167, 292. Portland, OR: Amadeus Press, 1987.

Golden   Cantata ("Music   in   the   Golden Form") (1963)

Duration: ca. 28 minutes

Text: Kathleen Raine

Performing Forces: *voices*: tenor soloist; choir; *orchestra*: 3 flutes (all doubling piccolo), 2 oboes, 2 clarinets, 2 bassoons, 4 horns, 3 trumpets, 3 trombones, tuba, timpani, percussion (at least 3 players - snare drum, tenor drum, bass drum, crash cymbals, suspended cymbal, triangle, wood block, glockenspiel, xylophone, chimes), celeste, harp, organ (pedals only), and strings.

First Performance: 18 February 1964; The Guildhall, Cambridge; Wilfred Brown; Cambridge University Musical Society Chorus and Orchestra; conducted by Bliss.

Edition: *Golden Cantata* is published by Novello and distributed by Theodore Presser Company. The piano-vocal score is for sale; orchestral materials are available through rental.

Autograph: It is in the possession of Lady Bliss in London. The full score is a facsimile of the composer's manuscript.

Notes: *The Golden Cantata* was commissioned by and is dedicated to the Cambridge University Musical Society to mark the Quincentenary of the first recorded degree in music being awarded by Cambridge University in 1464. It is in eight movements which are played without pause.

Performance Issues: The full score of this work is extremely difficult to read and much of the performance indications and text is completely illegible. This is a tonal composition with primarily homophonic and unison choral writing. The soprano part is, at times, divided. In the final movement, successive phrases are sung by the full choir or a semi-choir. The scoring is very skillful and quite varied, presenting some challenges for good ensemble playing, as there are constant shifts of primary instruments and regular melodic exchanges between diverse instruments. *Soloist*: tenor, range: d-a$^{b'}$; tessitura: f-f': this is a sustained and brilliant role with an optional c" at the end. The tenor soloist sings only in the seventh movement. The choral part is accessible to a choir of moderate experience and size. The complexity of orchestral integration requires a professional level ensemble. *Choir*: medium easy; *Orchestra*: difficult.

Discography: As of January 1993, no commercial recording has been made available.

Selected Bibliography

Sadie, Stanley: "The Golden Cantata," *The Musical Times*, cv (April 1960), 283.

Britten, (Edward) Benjamin (b. Lowestoft, 22 November 1913; d. Aldeburgh, 4 December 1976).

Life: Britten has been this century's most successful composer of opera in English.[12] As a youth, he studied piano with Harold Samuel and composition with Frank Bridge. He attended the Royal College of Music (1930-3), but was unhappy with an official refusal to allow him to study in Vienna with Alban Berg. He began having music published at the age of 17 and in 1936 started writing music for the G.P.O. Film Unit. In 1939, he and lifelong companion Peter Pears followed W. H. Auden to the U.S., staying until 1942. Upon his return to England, he and Pears settled in Aldeburgh where he began the Aldeburgh Festival in 1948. He was a made a Companion of Honour (1953), received the Order of Merit (1965), and became the first composer to be made a Life Peer: Lord Britten of Aldeburgh (1976). His music is characterized by an exceptional lyric gift, innovative rhythms, and a unique extension of tonality through modal exploration. He enjoyed writing music for amateurs which is consistently of complete artistic integrity. Most of all, he had a distinctive sensibility for setting texts. His texts are generally concerned with themes of lost innocence and the relationship between an outsider and society. Both of these themes border upon autobiography.[13]

---

[12] Robert P. Morgan: *Twentieth-Century Music*, 272-78. New York: W.W. Norton, 1991.

[13] Peter Evans: "Benjamin Britten," *The New Grove Twentieth-Century English Masters*, 239-296. New York: W.W. Norton, 1986.

Principal Works: *opera* - *Paul Bunyan* (1940-1), *Peter Grimes* (1945), *The Rape of Lucretia* (1946), *Albert Herring* (1947), *Billy Budd* (1951, revised 1960), *Gloriana* (1953), *The Turn of the Screw* (1954), *A Midsummer Night's Dream* (1960), *Owen Wingrave* (1971), *Death in Venice* (1973); *orchestra* - Sinfonietta (1932), Simple Symphony (1934), Variations on a Theme of Frank Bridge (1937), Piano Concerto (1938, revised 1945), Violin Concerto (1939, revised 1958), *Sinfonia da Requiem* (1940), *Young Person's Guide to the Orchestra* (1946), Cello Symphony (1963); *choral* - *Hymn to the Virgin* (1930, revised 1934), *A Boy was Born* (1933, revised 1955), *Ceremony of Carols* (1942), *Hymn to St. Cecilia* (1942), *Rejoice in the Lamb* (1943), *Five Flower Songs* (1950), *Cantata Academica* (1959), *Cantata Misericordium* (1963), *Children's Crusade* (1968); *solo vocal* - *Les Illuminations* (1939), *Serenade* (1943), *Nocturne* (1958), *Phaedra* (1975); and many folk song arrangements and chamber works.

Selected Composer Bibliography

"Britten, Benjamin (Edward)," *Current Biography Yearbook,* iii (October 1942); xxii (April 1961); obituary, xxxviii (February 1977); New York: H. W. Wilson Company.

Mitchell, Donald, and Hans Keller: *Benjamin Britten.* London: Rockcliff, 1952 (reprinted, Westport, CT: Greenwood Press, 1972).

Hansler, George E.: *Stylistic Characteristics and Trends in the Choral Music of Five Twentieth-Century Composers: A Study of the Choral Works of Benjamin Britten, Gerald Finzi, Constant Lambert, Michael Tippett, and William Walton.* New York University: Dissertation, 1957.

Benjamin Britten: A Catalogue of His Works. New York: Boosey and Hawkes, 1973.

Kennedy, Michael: *Britten.* London: Dent, 1981.

Palmer, Christopher, editor: *The Britten Companion.* London: Faber and Faber, 1984.

Evans, Peter: "Benjamin Britten," *The New Grove Twentieth-Century English Masters,* 239-296. New York: W.W. Norton, 1986.

Mitchell, Donald: *Britten (Edward) Benjamin, Baron Britten (1913-76) The Dictionary of National Biography 1971-80.* Oxford: Oxford University Press, 1986.

Evans, John, Philip Reed, and Paul Wilson: *A Britten Sourcebook.* Aldeburgh, Suffolk: Britten-Pears Library, 1987.

Whittall, Arnold: *The Music of Britten and Tippett: Studies in Themes and Techniques,* second edition. Cambridge: Cambridge University Press, 1990.

Saint Nicolas, op. 42 (1948)

Duration: ca. 50-55 minutes

Text: Eric Crozier

Performing Forces: *voices*: Saint Nicolas - tenor, soprano, alto soloists, and 4 treble soloists; SA gallery choir, SATB choir; *orchestra*: organ, piano 4-hands, percussion (at least 2 players - timpani, snare drum, tenor drum, tambourine, cymbal, gong, triangle, whip), and strings.

First Performance: 5 June 1948, Aldeburgh, England; Peter Pears, Aldeburgh Festival Chorus, conducted by Leslie Woodgate.

commissioner's first performance: 24 July 1948; Peter Pears, Lancing College Ensembles; gallery choir led by Jasper Rooper, performance conducted by Britten.

Edition: *Saint Nicolas* is published and distributed by Boosey and Hawkes. The piano-vocal score (#16469, arranged by Arthur Oldham) and miniature score (#16528) are for sale; orchestral materials are available for rental.

Autograph: A copy of the composer's manuscript is in the possession of the Britten-Pears Library in Aldeburgh, Suffolk.

Notes: *Saint Nicolas* was composed for performance at the centenary celebrations of Lancing College. St. Nicolas was the Bishop of Myra and is the patron saint of children, seamen, and travelers. The libretto presents vignettes from the Saint's life, and is organized as follows:

1.	Introduction	-	Tenor and Choir
2.	Birth of Nicolas	-	Treble and SA-Choir
3.	Nicolas devotes himself to God	-	Tenor
4.	He journeys to Palestine	-	Tenor,TB-Choir, Gallery Choir
5.	He comes to Myra and is chosen Bishop	-	Tenor, Choir, Gallery Choir,and congregation
6.	Nicolas from Prison	-	Tenor
7.	Nicolas and the Pickled Boys	-	Tenor, 3 Trebles, Choir, and Gallery Choir

8. His Piety and Marvellous Works - 7-part Semi-Choir
9. The Death of Nicolas - Tenor, Choir, and
congregation

Performance Issues: Britten has included the following note in the full score:

As stated in the dedication, *Saint Nicolas* was written to be performed at the centenary of a school, when it was sung by the combined choirs of three boys' schools (the main chorus) and one girls' school (the gallery-choir). It is therefore suitable for performance by any numerically big chorus, even if the singers are not very experienced. The choir in the gallery should have a separate conductor.

The string parts are not very sophisticated and can be played by amateur players, preferably led by a professional quintet. The piano duet part is also of moderate difficulty. The first percussion is obbligato and should be played by a professional drummer, who may play as many of the instruments included in the second part as is feasible; the second part is ad libitum and may be played by as many gifted and/or enthusiastic amateurs as there are instruments. On the other hand, the solo tenor part, as can easily be seen, is no amateur matter. The conductor must be cool-headed and should turn to the congregation/audience to conduct them in the two hymns.

The two sections which include congregational singing utilizing traditional hymn tunes: #5 - "Old 100th," and #9 -"God moves in a mysterious way his wonders to perform." The words of these should be made available to the audience. The choral writing is rhythmically conservative, homophonic, and triadically conceived. There are four two-measure solos for a treble voice portraying the young boy Nicolas (movement #2), and one for tenor as the young man Nicolas (movement #3). There are some string solos, which argues for the importance of secure principal players. There are some unmeasured passages for the gallery-choir and soloist which are underscored by *ad libitum* ostinati. This is an excellent work for ensembles of limited experience, but should not be neglected by established groups as it is a most effective piece. The element of congregational participation also makes this an ideal item for a concertized church service. *Soloist*: tenor, range: d-g#'; tessitura:

g-f'; lyric, sustained, and very demanding. *Choir*: medium easy; *Orchestra*: medium easy.

Discography: Peter Pears, tenor; David Hemmings, treble; Aldeburgh Festival Chorus and Orchestra; conducted by Britten. Recorded in 1955. London: LXT 5060 [LP]. Re-released as London: 425714-2 LM [ADD].
Robert Tear, tenor; King's College Choir, Academy of St. Martin in the Fields; conducted by Sir David Willcocks. Seraphim: 60296 [LP].

Selected Bibliography

Holst, Imogen: "Britten's *Saint Nicolas*," *Tempo*, x (1948-49), 23.
Mitchell, Donald: "A Note on *Saint Nicolas*: some points on Britten's style," *Music Survey*, ii (Spring 1950).
Crozier, Eric: "Saint Nicolas," *Aldeburgh Festival Programme Book* (1949).

Spring Symphony, op. 44 (1949)

Duration: ca. 43-45 minutes

Text: various, see "notes" below

Performing Forces: *voices*: soprano, alto, and tenor soloists; SATB choir, children's choir; *orchestra*: 3 flutes (flute III doubling alto-flute and piccolo), 2 oboes, English horn, 2 clarinets, bass clarinet, 2 bassoons, contrabassoon, 4 horns, 3 trumpets, 3 trombones, tuba, cow horn, timpani, percussion (5 players - snare drum, tenor drum, bass drum, tambourine, cymbals, gong, wood block, castanets, xylophone, vibraphone, chimes), 2 harps, and strings.

First Performance: 9 July 1949; Holland Festival, Amsterdam; Jo Vincent, Kathleen Ferrier, Peter Pears; Boy's Choir of the St. Willibrorduskerk in Rotterdam, Mixed Choir of the Dutch Radio, Concertgebouw Orchestra; conducted by Eduard van Beinum.

American premiere: 13 August 1949; Berkshire Festival in Tanglewood; Boston Symphony Orchestra; conducted by Serge Koussevitsky.

Edition: *Spring Symphony* is published and distributed by Boosey and Hawkes. Piano-vocal (prepared by Arthur Oldham, B. & H. 16868) and study (B. & H. 16904) scores are available for purchase; orchestral materials are available for rental.

Autograph: A copy of the composer's manuscript is in the possession of the Britten-Pears Library in Aldeburgh, Suffolk.

Notes: Commissioned by Serge Koussevitsky and the Boston Symphony, *Spring Symphony* is in four movements which are subdivided as follows:

Part I	1.	Introduction (Shine out, fair sun)	Anon. 16th-century
	2.	The Merry Cuckoo	Edmund Spenser
	3.	Spring, the Sweet Spring	Thomas Nashe
	4.	The Driving Boy	George Peele and John Clare
	5.	The Morning Star	John Milton
Part II	1.	Welcome Maids of Honor	Robert Herrick
	2.	Waters above	Henry Vaughan
	3.	Out on the Lawn I lie in Bed	W. H. Auden
Part III	1.	When will my May come	Richard Barnefield
	2.	Fair and Fair	George Peele
	3.	Sound the Flute	William Blake
Part IV	1.	Finale (London, to thee I do present)	Beaumont and Fletcher
	2.	Soomer is icumen in	Anon. 13th-century

Performance Issues: The score indicates four percussionists, but five players are well advised. The wind parts are all technically challenging, containing frequent polyrhythms, and rapid unison passage-work between diverse instruments. The winds are more prominent than the strings throughout the piece. Both harp parts are difficult, but challenging passages are exchanged between the players. There are prominent brass fanfares in "Out on the Lawn I lie in Bed" and "Sound the Flute!" There are some melodic lines passed between string parts in the "Finale" at rehearsal # 10, and in the violins in "Waters above." The choral parts are well written for the voices and are accompanied by thin textures guaranteeing a successful balance. The choir is often asked to sing unaccompanied. The choral parts are often dissonant and contrapuntally intricate, but the harmonic tensions are approached in a logical linear fashion. There are frequent paired doublings at the octave between S and T, and A and B; however, these passages contain many deceptive sevenths and ninths. There are constant overlappings of texts creating a challenge to textual clarity and rhythmic cohesion. The Boys' Choir is written in unison with occasional optional divisi for sections which may be too high for some of the boys, except for "Sound the Flute!" which has two opposing treble parts. The boys are also asked to whistle a written part on pages 32-42. On pages 23, 25, and 28 there are cadenzas for the soloists, ad lib. The "Finale" is very dense with a complex overlapping of contrasting parts. *Soloists*: soprano, range: d#'- b", tessitura: g'- f", lyrical with long sustained lines, and some light and rapid sections, particularly in "Fair and fair;" alto, range: a- f#", tessitura: e'-c", generally sustained and lyric except for ensemble writing; tenor, range: d#- b', tessitura: g-g', declamatory with high sustained singing and soft, crisp articulations in the top of the voice. This is typical of the parts which Britten wrote for Peter Pears. *Choir*: medium difficult; *Orchestra*: medium difficult.

Discography: Jennifer Vyvyan, Norma Procter, Peter Pears; Royal Opera House Choir and Orchestra; conducted by Britten. Recorded in 1961. London: SXL 2264 [LP]. Re-released as London: 425153-2 LM [ADD].
Elizabeth Gale, Alfreda Hodgson, Martyn Hill; Southend Boy's Choir; London Symphony Chorus and Orchestra; conducted by Richard Hickox. Recorded in 1990. Chandos: CHAN 8855 [DDD].

Selected Bibliography

Britten, Benjamin: "A Note on the *Spring Symphony*," *Music Survey*, ii (Spring 1950).
Ottaway, Hugh: "Spring Symphony," *Monthly Musical Record*, lxxx (September 1950).
Blom, Eric: "Vernal Anthology," *Observer* (2 December 1951).
Stein, Erwin: *Orpheus in New Guises*. London: Rockcliff Press, 1953.

War Requiem, op. 66 (1961)

Duration: ca. 85 minutes

Text: The Requiem Mass and Wilfred Owen

Performing Forces: *voices*: soprano, tenor, and baritone soloists, SATB choir, boy choir; *orchestra*: 3 flutes (flute III doubling piccolo), 2 oboes, English horn, 3 clarinets (clarinet III doubling clarinet in E^b and bass-clarinet), 2 bassoon, contrabassoon, 6 horns, 4 trumpets in C, 3 trombones, tuba, piano, organ*, timpani, percussion (4 players - 2 side drums, tenor drum, bass drum, tambourine, cymbals, gong, triangle, castanets, whip, temple blocks, glockenspiel, vibraphone, crotales [C and F#], bells [C and F#]), and strings; *chamber orchestra*: flute (doubling piccolo), oboe (doubling English horn), clarinet (B^b and A), bassoon, horn, percussion (1 player - timpani, side drum, bass drum, cymbal, gong), harp, 2 violins, viola, cello, double bass.

* "The Boy Choir is accompanied throughout by an organ, and it may be advisable to use an harmonium or portable organ for this purpose since the sound should be distant. A grand organ (ad lib,) plays with the orchestra in the last movement only (Britten's note in the score)."

First Performance: 30 May 1962; St. Michael's Cathedral, Coventry; Heather Harper, Peter Pears, Dietrich Fischer-Dieskau; Coventry Festival Chorus, City of Birmingham Symphony, Melos Ensemble, Boys of Holy Trinity, Leamington and Stratford; conducted by Meredith Davies and the composer.

Edition: *War Requiem* is published and distributed by Boosey and Hawkes. The study score (HPS 742), and piano-vocal score are all available for purchase; orchestral materials are available for rental.

Autograph: A copy of the composer's manuscript is in the possession of the Britten-Pears Library in Aldeburgh, Suffolk.

Notes: *War Requiem* was commissioned for the festival celebrating the consecration of St. Michael's Cathedral, Coventry. Wilfred Owen was a pacifist poet who was killed while serving in the trenches during the First World War. The poetry used was written in the field of battle. It should be noted that the "In Paradisum" section of the *Missa pro defunctis* is not included in this work.

Performance Issues: This is a very sophisticated work in which Britten exercises all of his extended twentieth-century compositional techniques. He uses regularly shifting tonal references within a fairly diatonic harmonic language, often exploring polytonality. This pitch language is especially evident in his polarization of pitch centers a tritone apart. Elements of indeterminacy are used in sections of chant, primarily in the *Sanctus*. In the setting of the text, "*Aspera me*," the notation for the choir is quadruply augmented from that of the orchestra. These relationships are later reversed; thus, as separate portions of the ensemble are assigned different notes values for a common pulse, the beat values are exchanged in opposition to each other. This creates the visual impression of concurrent accellerandi and ritardandi to the performers while the actual pulse remains constant. The choral writing exploits inner tonal relationships and logogenic rhythms. In the vocal parts, Britten exploits many contrapuntal devices including imitation, inversion, and retrogression of diatonic material. Most of the choral material is clearly supported by the accompaniment, and there are divisi in all of the choral parts. There are incidents of polymeters and differing concurrent tempos between sections of the ensembles. The recitatives are exceptionally complex, especially in the *Libera me*. The chamber orchestra and soloists should be separated from the full orchestra and chorus. The Boy Choir should be far removed from the rest of the ensemble. Two conductors may be needed because of these distances and the independence of the two orchestras which includes sections that overlap in different tempos. The *Offertorium* contains a section at rehearsal #69 in which Britten quotes his own *Canticle III, Abraham and Isaac.* Such a reference is surely Britten's attempt to underline the metaphor of men sacrificing their sons. The orchestration is greatly varied with difficult passages in many of the individual parts, but it presents greater challenges in the integration of the ensemble. There are numerous cross-rhythms, including: 7 against 6, 5 against 4, 4 against 3, and 3 against 2. The orchestration suggests a large string section and a large choir. The coordination of the diverse ensembles and their disposition requires a substantial amount of planning. *Soloists*: soprano, range: c'-b", tessitura: a'-f#", lyric with sustained and florid phrases; tenor, range: d-g#', tessitura: g-f', declamatory and powerful with great flexibility; baritone, range: A-f', tessitura: d-d'; powerful, lyric, and clear. *Choir*: difficult; *Orchestra*: difficult.

Discography: Galina Vishnevskaya, Peter Pears, Dietrich Fischer-Dieskau; Bach Choir, Highgate School Boys' Choir, London Symphony Orchestra, Melos Ensemble; conducted by the composer. Recorded in 1963. London: OSA 1255 [LP]; re-released as London: 414383-2 LH2 [ADD].

Elisabeth Söderstrom, Robert Tear, Thomas Allen; Trebles of Christ Church Cathedral Choir, City of Birmingham Symphony Orchestra and Choir; conducted by Simon Rattle. Angel: CDC-47033 [DDD].

Lorna Haywood, Anthony Rolfe Johnson, Benjamin Luxon; Atlanta Symphony Orchestra and Chorus; conducted by Robert Shaw. Telarc: CD-80157 [DDD].

Heather Harper, Philip Langridge, John Shirley-Quirk; London Symphony Orchestra and Chorus, Choristers of St. Paul's Cathedral; conducted by Richard Hickox. Chandos: CHAN 8983/4 [DDD].

Selected Bibliography

Evans, Peter: "Britten's *War Requiem*" *Tempo*, lxi-lxii (1962), 20.

Robertson, Alec: "Britten's *War Requiem*," *The Musical Times*, ciii (1962), 308.

Whittall, Arnold: "Tonal Instability in Britten's *War Requiem*," *The Music Review*, xxiv (1963), 201.

Boyd, Malcolm: "Britten, Verdi and the Requiem," *Tempo*, lxxxvi (1968), 2.

Cox, Richard: "Student Concern Fires *War Requiem* Venture," *Choral Journal*, xi/1 (1970).

Hall, William Dawson: *The Requiem Mass: A Study of Performance Practices from the Baroque Era to the Present Day as Related to Four Requiem Settings by Gilles, Mozart, Verdi, and Britten.* University of Southern Califoria: Dissertation, 1970.

Juul-Hansen, A.: "Benjamin Britten's *War Requiem* and Wilfred Owen's text," *Musikforskning*, iii (1977).

Bernard, Andrew: *Two Musical Perspectives of Twentieth-Century Pacifism: An Analytical and Historical View of Britten's "War Requiem" and Bernstein's "Kaddish Symphony."* University of Washington: Dissertation, 1990.

Page, Gordon Keith: *Melodic Unification in Benjamin Brittem's "War Requiem."* Southwestern Baptist Theological Seminary: Dissertation, 1991.

Brubeck, David (b. Concord, CA, 6 December 1920).

Life: Brubeck attended the College of the Pacific as a music major, studying composition with Darius Milhaud at Mills College. With other students, he founded the Jazz Workshop Ensemble which ultimately led to the establishment of the Dave Brubeck Quartet. This group had a variety of members, the most famous combination being: Brubeck (piano), Paul Desmond (saxophone), Joe Morello (drums), and Eugene Wright (double bass). The ensemble helped to popularize the use of unusual meters in jazz. The best known of these pieces is *Take Five*, which was the first instrumental jazz recording to sell a million copies.[14] He has written a number of concert works which combine jazz and European traditions.

Principal Concert Works: *ballets - A Maiden in the Tower* (1956), *Points on Jazz* (1961); *cantatas - The Gates of Justice* (1969), *Truth is Fallen* (1971), *La fiesta de la poseda* (1975); *oratorios - Beloved Son* (1975), *Festival Mass to Hope* (1980); and a number of works for jazz combo and orchestra.

Selected Composer Bibliography

"Brubeck, Dave," *Current Biography Yearbook*, xvii (March 1956); New York: H. W. Wilson Company.

Brubeck, Dave: *Autobiography of Dave Brubeck.* New York: 1972.[15]

Stuessy, Clarence Joseph, Jr.: *The Confluence of Jazz and Classical Forms from 1950 to 1970.* Dissertation, University of Rochester, 1978; 296-320.

---

[14] Frank Tirro: *Jazz: A History.* New York: W.W. Norton, 1977.

[15] This autobiography is listed in the bibliography of the "Brubeck" article in *The New Grove Dictionary of American Music*, edited by H. Wiley Hitchcock. 4 volumes. London: Macmillan, 1986; however no publisher was listed and it is not catalogued in the standard book-trade references.

Brubeck, Dave: *The Genius Continues*. Hialeah, FL: CPP/Belwin, 1986.

Zirpoli, Danny Roland: *An Evaluation of the Work of Jazz Pianist/Composer Dave Brubeck*. University of Florida: Dissertation, 1990.

Light in the Wilderness (1968)

Duration: with improvisations ca. 75 minutes
without improvisations ca. 60 minutes

Text: Bible, Dave Brubeck, and Iola Brubeck (the composer's wife)

Performing Forces: *voices*: baritone soloist; SATB choir; *orchestra*: 3 flutes (flute III doubling piccolo), 2 oboes, English horn, 2 clarinets, bass clarinet, 2 bassoons, contrabassoon, 4 horns, 3 trumpets, 3 trombones, tuba, timpani, percussion (2 players - trap set (bass drum, snare drum, tom toms, cymbals, high-hat), bongos or small eastern drum, high middle eastern drum, small tom tom, tabla in D, tambourine, crash cymbals, finger cymbals, 2 hand cymbals (small and medium), gong, oriental gong, small gong, temple blocks, gourd, slapstick, 2 maracas, ratchet, wash board with thimbles, glockenspiel, crotales in E^b, G, B, and A, xylophone, vibraphone, chimes), and strings; organ soloist and jazz combo: piano soloist (with optional improvisations), drums, and double bass.

The entire accompaniment may be performed by a combo of piano, double bass, and drums.

First Performance: *with combo only*: January 1968; University of North Carolina, Chapel Hill, NC; University of North Carolina Choir; conducted by Lara Hoggard.

full orchestra: 29 March 1968; Cincinnati, OH; William Justus, baritone; Dave Brubeck, piano; Miami University (OH) *A Cappella* Singers, Cincinnati Symphony; conducted by Erich Kunzel.

Edition: *The Light in the Wilderness* is published by St. Francis Music and distributed by Shawnee Press. A reduced study score, organ excerpts, piano improvisation chart, percussion parts, and double bass parts are available for purchase; orchestral materials are available for rental.

Autograph: A copy of the composer's manuscript is in the possession of Shawnee Press.

Notes: The work is in two parts organized as follows:

Part I

I.	The Temptations	Choir and Baritone
IIa.	Forty Days	Choir
IIb.	Forty Days	optional improvisation
IIc.	Forty Days	organ solo
III.	Repent! Follow Me	baritone and optional improvisation
IVa.	The Sermon on the Mount	baritone and optional improvisation
IVb.	The Sermon on the Mount	choir and optional improvisation
Va.	Repent, Follow Me	baritone, choir, and optional improvisation
Vb.	The Kingdom of God	baritone
VI.	The Great Commandment	baritone, double choir and optional improvisation
VII.	Love Your Enemies	baritone and choir

Part II

VIIIa.	What Does it Profit a Man	baritone
VIIIb.	Where is God?	baritone and choir
IXa.	We Seek Him	choral interlude and optional improvisation
IXb.	Peace I Leave with You	baritone
X.	Let not Your Heart be Troubled	baritone, double choir and optional improvisation
XI.	Yet a Little While	baritone and choir
XII.	Praise Ye the Lord	choir

Performance Issues: The composer notes that any sections may be excerpted for performance, and that the instrumentation may be subject to the conductor's discretion. The piano improvisations are completely optional and need not be in a jazz style, but should represent the player's "musical orientation." The tenor part is written in the bass clef. The choral writing includes random imitation and free note-on-note counterpoint between parts. The part writing is primarily diatonic and shows the influence of Milhaud. Vocal dissonances are approached carefully by stepwise motion. Brubeck uses many extended non-functional tertian harmonies, which often exhibit parallel motion or contrary motion between opposing triads. There are divisi in vocal parts which are very clearly supported by the accompaniment, and at times the vocal ensemble is divided into two choirs. There are frequent descriptions of specific vocal effects such as "whining," "straight tone," "eerie," "mouth almost closed," "with the sound of the desert," etc. The combo parts are relatively difficult, requiring players well versed in the jazz idiom. The orchestra parts are straightforward and well within the abilities of an amateur ensemble. The percussion players are not technically challenged, but due to the variety of instruments used and the frequent changes, they should be experienced players. The part very clearly assigns each instrument to a specific player. *Soloist*: baritone, range: B^b-f#'; tessitura: g-e^b', powerful with long legato phrases and broad melodic leaps. *Choir*: medium easy; *Orchestra*: medium.

Discography: William Justus, baritone; Gerre Hancock, organ; Dave Brubeck, piano; University of Miami *A Cappella* Singers, Cincinnati Symphony Orchestra; conducted by Erich Kunzel. Recorded in 1968. DL-740155-56 [LP].

Selected Bibliography

Brubeck, Dave: Program Booklet for *The Light in the Wilderness*. Delaware Water Gap, PA: Shawnee Press, 1968.

Cowell, Henry Dixon (b. Menlo Park, CA, 11 March 1897 - d. Shady, NY, 10 December 1965).

Life: In addition to maintaining a productive compositional career, Cowell worked tirelessly as a promoter of contemporary music (particularly that by American composers). He decided to become a composer at age 8, beginning his first lengthy work, *Golden Legend*, in 1908. He was the child of "free thinkers" who encouraged his self-guided education and an acceptance of the sounds of the world as musically worthwhile. This included the broad range of Asian music to be heard in the San Francisco area and the Irish folk music of his family.[16] Cowell began his formal training with Charles Seeger at the University of California at Berkeley in 1914. He also pursued studies in English composition from Samuel Seward at Stanford University. Between 1923 and 1933 he made five European tours as a composer-pianist, gaining notoriety and forging many friendships with Europe's most prominent composers. He was the first American composer to be invited to the USSR (1929). Cowell's most significant role in music history was through his writing, publishing, and ceaseless championship of modern music. He founded the New Music Society, which published the quarterly, *New Music*. This unique periodical introduced editions of numerous significant composers, including Ives, Ruggles, and Varèse. He was crucial in the establishment of the Pan-American Association of Composers and founded New Music Quarterly Recordings. Cowell was one of the first composers to explore the incorporation of non-western musical techniques into his compositions.[17] He greatly accelerated the development of systematic ethnomusicology and the study of American folk music.[18] He lectured extensively, and held teaching positions at Columbia University (1949-65), Peabody Conservatory (1951-56), and the New School for Social Research (1941-1963). His pupils include John Cage, Lou Harrison, George Gershwin, and Burt Bacharach. Cowell was elected to the National Institute of Arts and Letters in 1951. He also served as president of ACA from 1951 to 1955.

Principal Writings: *American Composers on American Music* (2nd edition, New York, Frederick Ungar, 1962), *Charles Ives and his Music* (New York: Oxford University Press,1955), co-authored with his wife, Sydney.

Principal Works: His catalogued compositions number nearly 1000, encompassing all traditional genres and exploring a diversity of

---

[16] from a conversation with Vivian Fine, 1987.

[17] Harold Gleason and Walter Becker: "Henry Cowell," in *20th-Century American Composers*. Music Literature Outlines, series iv. Bloomington, IN: Indiana University Press, revised 1981.

[18] Frank McCarty: in a lecture given at the University of North Carolina at Greensboro, February 1990.

styles ranging from the wildly dissonant avant-garde to simple folk-like tunes.

Selected Composer Bibliography

Slonimsky, Nicholas: "Henry Cowell," in *American Composers on American Music: A Symposium*, edited by Henry Cowell. New York: Frederick Ungar Publishing, 1933 (Revised, 1962).

Goldman, Robert Franko: "Henry Cowell," *Inter-American Institute for Musical Research Yearbook*, ii (1966), 96.

Godwin, Joscelyn: *The Music of Henry Cowell.* Cornell University: Dissertation, 1969.

Saylor, Bruce: *The Writings of Henry Cowell: A Descriptive Bibliography.* Brooklyn: Institute for the Study of American Music Monographs, 1977.

Gleason, Harold, and Walter Becker: "Henry Cowell," *20th-century American Composers.* Music Literature Outlines, series iv, 58-77. Bloomington, IN: Indiana University Press, revised, 1981.

Mead, Rita: *Henry Cowell's New Music 1925-36: The Society, the Music Editions, and the Recordings.* Ann Arbor, MI: University of Michigan Research Press, 1981.

Manion, Martha L.: *Writings about Henry Cowell: An Annotated Bibliography.* Brooklyn: Institute for the Study of American Music Monographs, 1982.

Mead, Rita: "The Amazing Mr. Cowell," *American Music*, i/4 (1983), 63.

Lichtenwanger, William: *The Music of Henry Cowell: A Descriptive Catalogue.* Brooklyn: Institute for the Study of American Music Monographs, 1986.

Saylor, Bruce, William Lichtenwanger, and Elizabeth A. Wright: "Henry Cowell," *The New Grove Twentieth-Century American Masters*, 101-136. New York: W.W. Norton, 1986.

...If he please (1955)

Duration: ca. 18 minutes

Text: Edward Taylor, the first 30 lines of "The Preface," from *God's Determinations Touching His Elect* (ca. 1703), as found in *The Poetical Works of Edward Taylor*, ed. Thomas H. Johnson. New York: Rockland Editions, 1939.

Performing Forces: *voices*: SATB choir, boy·choir; *orchestra*: 2 flutes, 2 oboes, 2 clarinets, 2 bassoons, 2 horns, 3 trumpets, 2 trombones, tuba, timpani, percussion (1 player - suspended cymbal, 4 anvils or metal pipes [low to high], slap stick), and strings.

First Performance: 29 February 1956; Carnegie Hall, New York; Oratorio Society of New York, Choristers of St. John the Divine and St. Thomas Church; conducted by William Strickland.

Edition: *...If he please* is published by C. F. Peters; orchestral materials are available for rental.

Autograph: The ink full score and an incomplete pencil draft of the condensed score are held by the Cowell Collection at the Library of Congress, Washington, DC; an ozalid copy is in the possession of C. F. Peters

Notes: The work bears the dedication: "Written for William Strickland and the Oratorio Society of New York." The text was suggested to the composer by Strickland as one particularly appropriate in the nuclear age. Cowell states that the boy choir may be replaced by women, girls, or mixed children if preferred by the conductor.

Performance Issues: The boys divide into three parts and the adult choir divides into six women's and nine men's parts. The score is fairly diatonic with extended functional harmonies in the voices. The strings frequently exploit harmonies built from adjacent seconds. There are numerous octave doublings and unisons within the choir. The anvils could be replaced by brake drums of varied pitches. The principal oboe, horn and trumpets all have exposed solo passages. All of the orchestra writing is within the capacity of a moderately experienced amateur ensemble. The divisions in the choir suggest a large group. If the nine-part men's section is not a deterrent, this is an attractive and accessible work which has become a neglected part of the repertoire. *Choir*: medium; *Orchestra*: medium easy.

Discography: Rolf Karlsen, organ; Norwegian Choir of Solo Singers; members of the Oslo Philharmonic Orchestra; conducted by William Strickland. Recorded in 1968. CRI: CRI-165 [LP] and CRI-217 [LP].

Selected Bibliography

Schoneberg, Harold C.: "Oratorio Society gives modern program [review of premiere]," *New York Times* (1 March 1956), p. 36, col. 1.

Sabin, Robert: "Strickland Leads Contemporary Works," *Musical America*, lxxvi (March 1956), 18.

Rich, Alan: "Records; innovators new and old," *New York Times* (23 June 1963), section II, p. X12, col. 1.

Shupp, Enos E., Jr.: "Concert: Sowerby...Cowell: ...*If He Please,*" *New Records*, xxxi/4 (June 1963), 6.

Miller, Philip L.: "Cowell: ...*If He please,*" *American Record Guide*, xxix/11 (July 1963), 868.

Frankenstein, Alfred: "Cowell ...*If He please...*," *High Fidelity*, xiii/8 (August 1963), 76.

Flanagan, William: "Cowell ...*If He Please*, for chorus and orchestra (1955)...," *HiFi/Stereo Review*. xi/3 (September 1963), 75.

Miller, Philip L.: "Cowell: *If He please...*," *Library Journal*, lxxxviii/18 (15 October 1963), 3831.

The Creator, op. 919 (1963)

Duration: ca. 25 minutes

Text: Gavril Romanovich Derzhavin, from his poem "Bog," from *Sochinenya* ("Works," vol. 1, St. Petersburg, 1798); translated as "God," by John Bowring in *Specimens of the Russian Poets* (London, 1821).

Performing Forces: *voices*: soprano, alto, tenor, and bass soloists; double SATB choir; *orchestra*: 3 flutes, 3 oboes, 3 clarinets, 3 bassoons, 4 horns, 3 trumpets, 3 trombones, tuba, timpani (4), percussion (2 players - 4 suspended cymbals [low to high], 5 drums [low to high], 5 metal sounds [low to high]), and strings.

First Performance: 1 May 1964; Elizabeth Hall, Stetson University, De Land, FL; Stetson University Concert Choir, Chorus, and Symphony Orchestra; conducted by Robert L. Hause.

Edition: *The Creator* is published and distributed by C. F. Peters; vocal and orchestral materials are available for rental (full score #P66084).

Autograph: The ink full score and pencil sketches are held by the Cowell Collection at the Library of Congress, Washington, DC; an ozalid copy is in the Music Library of Stetson University and C. F. Peters. The full score is a facsimile of the composer's manuscript.

Notes: *The Creator* was "Commissioned by Stetson University. . . for Stetson's 1964 Observance of Religious Focus Week." It is in 14 movements which are to be played without pause.

Performance Issues: The choral parts divide: SSSSAAAATTTBBB. The vocal writing is strictly homophonic and uses functional harmonies. The choir is asked to speak and to use semi-pitched *Sprechstimme*. The choral and solo tenor parts are written in the bass clef. The first horn player has some exposed and expressive solos. The first trumpet is consistently high with rapid passagework above the staff. The "metal sounds" would probably be best achieved with brake drums of varied pitches. *Soloists*: soprano, range: c'-g"; tessitura: f'-e", lyric and sustained; alto, range: a-d"; tessitura: d'-b', dramatic and filled with melismas; tenor, range: c-a'; tessitura: f-e", bright and powerful; bass, range: E-d'; tessitura: G-g, declamatory with good projection in the bottom range. The divisi suggest the use of a large choir. This is a very accessible piece for singers and players alike. With the noted exceptions above this is a fine work for a community orchestra and choir. *Choir*: medium easy; *Orchestra*: medium easy.

Discography: As of January 1993, no commercial recording has been made available.

Selected Bibliography

Anderson, Owen: "New Works/New York[review]," *Music Journal*, xxiv (May 1966), 82.

Creston, Paul (b. New York, 10 October 1906; d. San Diego, CA, 24 August 1985).

Life: Creston chose a career in composition in 1932 with little previous training. He received a Guggenheim Fellowship in 1938 and the New York Critic's Circle award in 1941 for his Symphony no. 1.

Creston served as president of the National Association for American Composers and Conductors (1956-60), director of ASCAP (1960-68), and composer-in-residence at Central Washington State College (1968-.75). Creston's music is tied to tradition in its formal unity and creative methods of thematic development. His harmonic language exploits non-functional triads and pandiatonicism. It is incisive and energetic rhythms which most distinguish his music.[19] Interested in improving methods of rhythmic notation and practice, he authored *Principles of Rhythm* (1964) and *Rational Metric Notation* (1979).

Principal Works: *orchestral* - 6 Symphonies (op. 20 - 1940, op.35 - 1944, op. 48 - 1950, op. 52 - 1951, op. 64 - 1955, and op. 118 -1981), 2 Violin Concertos (op. 65 - 1956 and op. 78 - 1960), Saxophone Concerto, op. 26 (1941), Piano Concerto, op. 43 (1949), Accordion Concerto, op. 75 (1958); *choral* - Mass "Adoro te," op. 54 for choir and piano (1952), Mass "Cum jubilo," op. 97 for choir and piano (1968), *Calamus*, op. 104 for men's choir, brass, and percussion (1972).

Selected Composer Bibliography

Cowell, Henry: "Paul Creston," *The Musical Quarterly*, xxxiv (1948) 533.
Simmons, Walter: "Paul Creston: Maintaining a Middle Course," *Music Journal*, xxxiv/10 (1976), 12.
[obituary], *New York Times* (26 August 1985).
Simmons, Walter: "Paul Creston," in *The New Grove Dictionary of American Music*, edited by H. Wiley Hitchcock, i: 535-6. 4 volumes. London: Macmillan, 1986.
Slowski, Monica Justine: *Paul Creston: The Man and His Music with an Annotated Bibliography of His Works*. University of Missouri at Kansas City: Dissertation, 1987.

Isaiah's Prophecy (a Christmas Oratorio), op. 80 (1962)

Duration: ca. 30 minutes

---

[19] Gilbert Chase: *America's Music*, 535-36. New York: McGraw-Hill, 1955.

Text: Bible and traditional carols

Performing Forces: *voices*: soprano, mezzo-soprano, 2 tenor, 2 baritone, and bass soloists; narrator; SATB choir; *orchestra*: 2 flutes, 2 oboes, 2 clarinets, 2 bassoons, 2 horns, 2 trumpets, 2 trombones, timpani, percussion (1 player - tom-tom, crash cymbals, suspended cymbal, glockenspiel, chimes), harp, and strings.

First Performance: 12 December 1962; University of South Florida, Tampa, FL; University of South Florida ensembles; conducted by A. A. Beecher.

Edition: *Isaiah's Prophecy* is published by F. Colombo and distributed by Theodore Presser Company. The piano-vocal score and study score are available for purchase; orchestral materials are available on rental.

Autograph: A pencil manuscript score in in the Library of Congress (ML 96C8335, case).

Notes: *Isaiah's Prophecy* is dedicated: "To A. A. Beecher with profound thanks for a magnificent and memorable premiere of the work — and in everlasting friendship." It is in fifteen sections, many of which use traditional carols for texts and some of the music, as follows:

I.	Come near, ye nations
II.	And there shall come forth a rod
III.	O come, O come, Emmanuel
IV.	And the angel Gabriel
V.	The Salutation
VI.	Magnificat
VII.	And It Came to Pass
VIII.	While Shepherds Watched
IX.	Pastoral Night
X.	Glory to God in the Highest
XI.	Shepherd's Colloquy
XII.	Sleep, Holy Babe
XIII.	Star in the East
XIV.	We Three Kings
XV.	Alleluia

Performance Issues: This is a chromatic work which operates within the traditions of functional harmony. The choral writing is primarily homophonic with *a cappella* passages and divisi in all parts. Movement X provides the greatest challenge to the singers with eight fairly independent parts and increased contrapuntal complexity. The instrumental parts are quite straightforward. There is rapid passagework in the strings and bassoons. The trumpets and trombones have a number of exposed brass choir passages. *Soloists*: soprano, range: b♭'-g♭", tessitura: b♭'-g♭", very sustained; Mary - mezzo-soprano, range: c#'-f#", tessitura: e'-b', very articulate with sustained phrases; Evangelist - tenor, range: db-gb', tessitura: ab-eb', declamatory with some speaking; Caspar - tenor, range: f#-g', tessitura: f#-f#', small role; Prophet - baritone, range: c#-f', tessitura: f-e', lyric and articulate; Melchior - baritone, range: d-c#', tessitura: d-c#', small role; Balthazar - bass, range: F#-a, tessitura: A-a, small role. *Choir*: easy to medium easy; *Orchestra*: medium easy.

Discography: As of January 1993, no commercial recording has been made available.

Selected Bibliography

[review]: *Choral Journal* (March 1963), 7.

Delius, Frederick (b. Bradford, Yorks, 29 January 1862; d. Grez-sur-Loing, France, 10 June 1934).

Life: Delius was the son of a German-born British textile merchant who was involved with the founding of the Hallé concerts and who entertained many prominent musicians. Frederick attended Bradford Grammar School and the International College in Isleworth. The father opposed his son's pursuit of a career in music, so Frederick attempted to work in the wool trade. Showing no aptitude for this, he was sent to Jacksonville, FL to manage a citrus plantation. In Jacksonville, he studied theory with a local organist, Thomas Wood. In 1886, with his father's support, he began 18 months of study at the Leipzig Conservatory. There he studied with Sitt, Carl Reinecke, and Jadassohn. In Leipzig he also met and befriended Edvard Grieg, who convinced Delius's father to continue to support his son's career in music. Delius moved to Paris where his associations included Paul Gauguin, August Strindberg, Edvard Munch, and Maurice Ravel. He succumbed to an illness in the 1920s which led to paralysis and blindness. He had contracted syphilis in 1895. His last works were notated by his amanuensis, Eric Fenby. The first significant performance of his music in England was in 1907, after which, with Sir Thomas Beecham's support, he became regarded as a national treasure.[20] Delius's music is in the extended tonal language of Mahler, Debussy, and Strauss. His works are romantic and rhapsodic, using chromatic modes to great effect. His music exhibits the beginnings of the English mysticism that pervaded the music of Vaughan Williams and Howells.[21]

Honors: Companion of Honour (1929), the Freedom of Bradford (1932), Gold Medal of the Royal Philharmonic Society (1925).

Principal Works: *operas* - *Irmelin* (1890-2), *The Magic Fountain* (1893), *Kuanga* (1895-7), *A Village Romeo and Juliet* (1900-1), *Margot-la-Rouge* (1902), *Fennimore and Gerde* (1908-10); *orchestral*-*Florida Suite* (1886-7), Piano Concerto (1897, revised 1906), *Life's Dance* (1899), *Paris* (1898-9), *Brigg Fair* (1907), *In a Summer Garden* (1908), Dance Rhapsody No. 1 (1908), *On hearing the first cuckoo in spring* (1912), *North Country Sketches* (1913-4), Concerto for Violin and Cello (1915), Violin Concerto (1917), *Eventyr* (1917), Cello Concerto (1921), *A Song of Summer* (1930); *vocal* - *Songs of Sunset* (1906-8), *Songs of Farewell* (1930), *Idyll: Once I passed through a populous city* (1930-2).

Selected Composer Bibliography

Delius, Clare: *Frederick Delius: Memories of My Brother*. London: Ivor Nicholson and Watson, 1935.
Fenby, Eric: *Delius as I Knew Him*. London: Faber and Faber, 1936.
Mitchell, Donald: "Delius: The Choral Music," *Tempo*, special Delius edition (Winter 1952-53).
Fenby, Eric: *Delius*. London: Faber and Faber, 1971.
Jefferson, Alan: *Delius*. London: J. M. Dent and Sons, 1972.
Caldwell, Donald Graham: *The Choral Music of Frederick Delius*. University of Illinois at Urbana-Champaign: Dissertation, 1975.

---

[20] Christopher Redwood: *A Delius Companion*, 2nd edition. London: Scolar Press, 1980.

[21] Michael Kennedy: *The Oxford Concise Dictionary of Music*. Oxford: Oxford University Press, 1981.

Redwood, Christopher: *A Delius Companion*, 2nd edition. London: Scolar Press, 1980; paperback: New York: Riverrun Press, 1991.

Palmer, Christopher: *Delius: Portrait of a Cosmopolitan*. New York: Holmes and Meier, 1984.

Payne, Anthony: "Frederick Delius," *The New Grove Twentieth-Century English Masters*, 69-96. New York: W.W. Norton, 1986.

Delius Society Newsletter. London: Delius Society of Great Britain, 1963- .

Appalachia (1896-1903)

Duration: ca. 34 minutes

Text: traditional: "After night has gone comes the day"

Performing Forces: *voices*: SSAATTBarBB choir; *orchestra*: 3 flutes (flute I doubling piccolo), 3 oboes, English horn, E^b clarinet, 2 B^b clarinets, bass clarinet, 3 bassoons, contrabassoon, 6 horns, 3 C trumpets, 3 trombones, tuba, timpani, percussion (2 players - bass drum, snare drum, tam-tam), 2 harps, and strings.

First Performance: 15 October 1904; Stadthalle, Elberfeld, Germany; Elberfeld Choral and Orchestral Societies (Gesangverein); conducted by Hans Haym.

Edition: *Appalachia* is published by Boosey and Hawkes in an edition supervised by Sir Thomas Beecham. The full score and orchestral materials are available for rental. A miniature score is for sale. Kalmus publishes a reprint of the same edition for which the full score, piano-vocal score, and orchestral materials may be purchased or rented. A piano-vocal score prepared by Suchoff is for sale from Fox publishers (S PS170).

Autograph: Delius's sketches and manuscripts, and those executed by Eric Fenby are in the possession of the Delius Trust.

Notes: *Appalachia* is dedicated to Julius Buths, and subtitled, "Variations on an Old Slave Song." It was adapted in 1902-03 from Delius's purely orchestral work of the same title composed in 1896. It should be noted that this work is frequently listed for baritone soloist, choir, and orchestra. All vocal parts in this version of the piece are assigned to the choir. Some performances may assign the choral baritone division, which occurs from measures 593 to 619, to a soloist, but this is clearly not the score's indication.

Performance Issues: This composition presents seven sets of variations and a finale. It is a lushly scored work with traditional periodic phrase structures and key exploration through relationships of thirds.

> The harmony is always recognizably his own, but there is still considerable reliance on conventional melodic developments and counterpoints; regular phrase patterns are as much in evidence as the subtle flights of harmony which point forward to his maturity.[22]

The chorus occupies only the last 119 measures of this 654 measure work with texted singing. Delius uses them elsewhere for momentary orchestral color on the syllable "la." The vocal parts are aurally accessible to choirs of limited experience. The vocal harmonies explore extended tertian sets. These non-traditional chords are logically approached by linear movement and generally reinforced by the accompaniment. There is a 14 measure *a cappella* section at the beginning of the finale. The men's parts are somewhat vocally demanding due to high tessituri; however, the brevity of the choir's role in the work diminishes this challenge. The string section must be large, (Delius calls for 8 stands of first violins) as there are numerous divisi. The assignment of most string divisions is made in the score. There are a number of prolonged solos for the concert master. The individual wind parts present many technical challenges as a result of significant passagework. The overall orchestral part should present only minor challenges to successful ensemble. The scoring is very precise and practical, and while the division of the beat varies regularly within the work, Delius uses   the same division throughout the ensemble at any given time. Although there is frequent doubling of instruments throughout the piece, all parts at some point are integral and should be present including the two harp parts. *Choir*: medium; *Orchestra*: medium difficult.

---

22 Anthony Payne: "Frederick Delius," *The New Grove Twentieth-Century English Masters*, 76. New York: W.W. Norton, 1986.

Discography: Jenkins; Hallé Orchestra and Ambrosian Singers; conducted by Sir John Barbirolli. EMI: EMX 41 2081-1/4 [LP].
BBC Chorus, Royal Opera Chorus, London Philharmonic Orchestra; conducted by Sir Thomas Beecham. Volume III of the Delius Society recordings, recorded in 1938. Columbia: SDX 15/21 [78's].
Slovak Philharmonic Orchestra; conducted by Hopkins. Records International: 7012-2 [DDD]. This is a recording of the purely orchetral version of the work.

Selected Bibliography

Holland, A. K.: "Notes" for Delius Society recording, Columbia: SDX 15/21. London: Delius Society, 1938.

Sea Drift (1903-04)

Duration: ca. 25-30 minutes[23]

Text: Walt Whitman, excerpted from *Out of the Cradle Endlessly Rocking*

Performing Forces: *voices:* baritone soloist; SATB choir; *orchestra:* 3 flutes, 3 oboes, English horn, 3 clarinets in B^b, bass clarinet, 3 bassoons, contrabassoon, 6 horns, 3 trumpets in C, 3 trombones, tuba, timpani, percussion (1 player - bass drum), 2 harps, and strings.

First Performance: 24 May 1906; Essen, Germany; J. Loritz; conducted by G. Witte.

Other early performances: 1908; Sheffield; conducted by Henry Wood. 1909; London; conducted by Sir Thomas Beecham.

Edition: *Sea Drift* is published by Boosey and Hawkes. The full score, piano-vocal score, choral parts, and orchestral materials are available for rental; a study score, piano-vocal score and choral

---

[23] Farish (Margaret K. Farish: *Orchestra Music in Print.* Philadelphia: Musicdata, 1979.) lists a duration of 25 minutes, but the score indicates ca. 30 minutes.

parts are available for purchase. Kalmus publishes a reprint of this same set of which the full score and orchestral materials are available for sale or rent.

Autograph: Delius's sketches and manuscripts, and those executed by Eric Fenby are in the possession of the Delius Trust.

Notes: *Sea Drift* is dedicated to Max Schillings.

Performance Issues: There are divisi in all string parts. The double basses are asked to play down to a pedal C. There are solos for the concert master. The individual instrumental parts are not technically demanding, although the winds must be capable of soft sustained playing in high registers. This is a very tender and subtle composition which requires sensitive playing by all members of the orchestra. Challenges in rehearsal will prove to be controlling intonation and balance. The choral writing is generally homophonic with consistent doublings between choral parts and by the orchestra. The harmonic vocabulary is conservative for the voices and well within the grasp of amateur choirs. Vocal divisi are infrequent, however there is an eight-part chorale with soloist in measures 344-369. It is supposed to be *a cappella*, but there are woodwind cues which double the voices if this section proves impractical. In general this would be an excellent work for developing a keener sense of ensemble and blend for developing choirs and orchestra. *Soloist*: range: A-f#', tessitura: f-d', this is a very sustained role with frequent octave leaps. The soloist must be able to clearly carry over the entire ensemble. The role requires vocal endurance and a powerful yet lyric voice capable of sustained soft singing in the top of the range. *Choir*: medium; *Orchestra*: medium.

Discography: Bruce Boyce; Royal Philharmonic Orchestra and BBC Chorus; conducted by Sir Thomas Beecham. Recorded in 1954. English Philips: ABL 3088 [78's]. Re-released as Sony Masterworks: MPK 47680 [ADD].

Thomas Hampson; Welsh National Opera Orchestra and Chorus; conducted by Sir Charles Mackerras. Argo: 430206-2 ZH [DDD].

John Brownlee; London Select Chorus and the London Philharmonic Orchestra; conducted by Sir Thomas Beecham. Volume II of the Delius Society Recordings, recorded in 1936. Columbia: SDX8/14 [78's].

Selected Bibliography

Brennan, J. G.: "Delius and Whitman," *Walt Whitman Review*, xviii/3 (1972), 90.

Foreman, Lewis: *From Parry to Britten: British Music in Letters 1900-1945*, 52, 141, 161. Portland, OR: Amadeus Press, 1987.

Requiem (1913-16)

Duration: ca. 45 minutes

Text: Friederich Nietzsche as translated by Heinrich Simon

Performing Forces: *voices*: soprano and baritone soloists, double SATB choir; *orchestra*: 3 flutes (flute III doubling piccolo), 2 oboes, English horn, bass oboe, 3 clarinets in B^b, bass clarinets, 3 bassoons, sarrusophone (contrabassoon), 6 horns, 3 trumpets in C, 3 trombones, tuba, timpani, percussion (3 players - snare drum, bass drum, cymbals, triangle, glockenspiel), celeste, harp, and strings.

First Performance: 23 March 1922, Queen's Hall, London; Evans, Williams, Philharmonia Choir, conducted by Albert Coates.

First United States performance: 6 November 1950; New York.

Edition: *Requiem* is published and distributed by Boosey and Hawkes. The piano-vocal and study scores are for sale; orchestral materials are available for rental.

Autograph: Delius's sketches and manuscripts, and those executed by Eric Fenby are in the possession of the Delius Trust.

Notes: *Requiem* is dedicated, "To the memory of all young Artists fallen in war." Nietzsche's text addresses the mourning for those who have died. There is a singing English translation in the score. The choral writing is primarily homophonic in a harmonic style resembling French impressionism, and owing some credit to Ravel's choral writing. This combined with the modality of English folksong created the sonority associated with English nationalism which was shared by Elgar, Vaughan Williams, and

Howells.[24] Though smaller in scale Delius's work exhibits a strong influence from Brahms's Requiem. The text is pantheistic with solace being found in the predictability of the cycles of nature as symbolized in the seasons. Because of its atheistic inclinations, this work received such violent criticism upon its premiere that a second performance did not occur for over 40 years.

Performance Issues: In this work, Delius creates a mystical sound through the integration of chromaticisms and modal pitch sets. There is a great variety of contrapuntal textures, especially emphasizing exchanges between the two choirs. The choral writing moves primarily by step and third with many internal cross-rhythms. The two choirs should be spatially divided to clarify exchanges between them. Most of the choral parts are clearly supported in the accompaniment. The presence of a sarrusophone part should be noted, although it can be played on contra-bassoon. Of greater concern is the bass-oboe whose unavailability would require that a divided part be written between bassoon and English horn. Beginning 4 measures after rehearsal #14, Delius establishes a curious duel between the women on "Hallelujah" and the men on "La Allah il Allah." There are elements of bitonality in the coda. The individual instrumental parts are not particularly difficult, and the interplay between parts should present few significant challenges. The orchestration is denser than that of most of Delius's other works. This is a composition which demands an experienced choir to guarantee clarity in the eight-part sections. The orchestra's role is less challenging with many passages of only sustained harmonies. *Soloists*: soprano, range: b^b-a", tessitura: g'-e", lyric and sustained; baritone, range: A-e', with an optional A^b, tessitura: e^b-c', requiring a voice which is dramatic, powerful, and declamatory with good endurance. *Choir*: medium difficult; *Orchestra*: medium.

Discography: Heather Harper, Thomas Hemsley; Royal Liverpool Philharmonic Orchestra and Choir; conducted by Charles Groves. Recorded live in 1965. Intaglio: INCD 702-2 [ADD].

---

[24] Willi Apel, editor: *The Harvard Dictionary of Music*, second edition. Cambridge, MA: Belknap Press of Harvard University Press, 1972.

Selected Bibliography

Payne, Anthony: "Delius's Requiem," *Tempo* (Spring 1966).
Foreman, Lewis: *From Parry to Britten: British Music in Letters 1900-1945*, 97. Portland, OR: Amadeus Press, 1987.
Carley, Lionel: *Delius: A Life in Letters II, 1909-34.* Cambridge: Scolar Press, 1988.

Dello Joio, Norman (b. New York, 24 January 1913).

Life: Dello Joio began his musical career as an organist, receiving his earliest organ studies from his godfather, Pietro Yon. He pursued his formal musical education at the Institute of Musical Art, and the Juilliard Graduate School where he studied composition with Bernard Wagenaar. This was followed by post-graduate study with Paul Hindemith at Tanglewood and Yale University. He has held a number of teaching positions: Sarah Lawrence College (1945-50), Mannes College (1956-72), and Boston University (1972-). He organized and directed (1959-1973) the Contemporary Music Project for Creativity in Music Education, through which the Ford Foundation established residencies for composers within public school music programs.

Awards: Elizabeth Sprague Coolidge Award (1937) for his piano trio, 2 Guggenheim Fellowships, 2 New York Critics' Circle Awards [for the orchestra work *Variations, Chaconne, and Finale* (1948) and the opera *The Triumph of St. Joan* (1962)], Pulitzer Prize (1957) for *Meditations on Ecclesiastes* for string orchestra. Dello Joio's compositional style combines melodic qualities of Roman Catholic liturgical music and nineteenth-century harmonic language with jazz rhythms and a non-traditional approach to form.[25] His music is always tuneful and written for practical performance.[26]

Principal Works: 5 ballets; 4 operas; scores for 7 television programs including: *Air Power* (1956-57) and *The Louvre* (1965); 40 choral works including *The Mystic Trumpeter* (1943), *A Fable* (1946),

---

[25] Gilbert Chase: *America's Music*, 537-38. New York: McGraw-Hill, 1955.

[26] Robert Sabin: "It Takes a Great Strength to Remain Tender and Simple," *Musical America* (1 December 1950), 9.

A Psalm of David (1950), *Years of the Modern* (1968), *The Psalmist's Meditation* (1979); and many chamber works and songs.

Selected Composer Bibliography

Sabin, Robert: "It Takes a Great Strength to Remain Tender and Simple," *Musical America* (1 December 1950), 9.

"Dello Joio, Norman," *Current Biography Yearbook*, xviii (September 1957); New York: H. W. Wilson Company.

Downes, Edward: "The Music of Norman Dello Joio," *The Musical Quarterly*, xlviii (1962), 149.

Jackson, Richard: "Norman Dello Joio," *The New Grove Dictionary of American Music*, edited by H. Wiley Hitchcock, i: 596-98. 4 volumes. London: Macmillan, 1986.

Bumgardner, Thomas A.: *Norman Dello Joio*. Boston: Twayne Publishers, 1986.

Song of Affirmation (1952)

Duration: ca. 42 minutes

Text: Adapted from *Western Star* (1943) by Stephen Vincent Benét

Performing Forces: *voices*: soprano soloist, narrator, SATB choir; *orchestra*: 3 flutes, 2 oboes, 2 clarinets, 2 bassoons, 4 horns, 3 trumpets, 3 trombones, tuba, timpani, percussion (2 players - snare drum, bass drum, tambourine, crash cymbals, suspended cymbal, xylophone, glockenspiel, chimes), and strings.

First Performance: May 1952; Cornell College, Mount Vernon, IA; Jennie Tourel, soprano; the composer, narrator; Cornell College Choir, members of the Chicago Symphony Orchestra; conducted by Raphael Kubelik.

Edition: *Song of Affirmation* is published and distributed by Carl Fischer. The piano-vocal score (N1878) and study score (SC 20) are available for purchase. The full-score (RCO-D 36) and orchestral parts are available on rental.

Autograph: The full score is a facsimile of the composer's manuscript.

Notes: *Song of Affirmation* was commissioned by Cornell College in Mount Vernon, Iowa to commemorate their Centennial. The work is organized into three movements as follows:

I. Virginia	- Narrator and Choir
II. New England	- Soprano, Narrator, and Choir
III. The Star in the West	- Narrator and Choir

Thomas A. Bumgardner explains this work's previous incarnation:

> The *Symphony for Voices and Orchestra* was commissioned by Robert Shaw who premiered it on 28 April 1945 with the Collegiate Chorale; Eileen Farrell, soprano; Robert Merrill, baritone; Joseph Laderoute, tenor; and Frederick Hart as narrator. Dello Joio culled his text from various passages in Stephen Vincent Benét's epic poem, "Western Star." The first movement, entitled "Virginia," deals with the desire of those in England destined to become the first pioneers from that country to America. The second movement, "New England," is a Pilgrim's prayer asking that God sustain them in their attempt to build a "New Zion." The last movement, "The Star in the West," has to do with the essential restlessness and progressiveness of Americans from the earliest colonial days to the present. According to the *New York Times* review, the work was brilliantly performed and well received by the capacity crowd. Dello Joio, however, felt that it had too many weaknesses and withdrew the score from circulation.
>
> In 1953, when Dello Joio was commissioned by Cornell College in Iowa to compose a large work to be presented in the final festival concert of their centennial celebration, he took the score of *Symphony for Voices and Orchestra* and recast it into a symphonic cantata for chorus, soprano soloist, and full orchestra which he entitled *Song of Affirmation*. ...The major revisions were made in movements 1 and 3. Movement 2 was left virtually intact. Basically the latter work is a

condensation of the material from the former with some new sections added. [27]

Performance Issues: There are prominent sections of rhythmic speaking in the chorus parts in the first movement The narrator speaks in rhythm in the second movement for eight measures at rehearsal letter L; however, the rest of the narration is unaccompanied, or over a sustained harmony. The choral writing is almost exclusively homophonic with brief passages for one or two sections of the choir. There are divisi in all parts often with octave doublings between the men's and women's parts, some paired doublings, and frequent choral unisons. There are a few brief *a cappella* passages; the most dissonant of which are cued in the orchestra parts, to be played in case it should prove problematic (rehearsal letter U). The work has great rhythmic vitality; it incorporates qualities of American folk music which well underscores the patriotism of the text. Although the tonal center shifts frequently, the melodies are diatonic and tonally conceived, and the harmonies are triadic and executed via common-practice methods. The orchestral gestures resemble those found in solo piano music and not always idiomatic for the instruments used. Dello Joio also uses many octave doublings, ostinati, and motor rhythms. It is very conservatively conceived, presenting no contrapuntal complexities, and is well voiced to guarantee a good balance within the orchestra, and between the instruments and the voices. It is quite approachable by an average college-level orchestra. *Soloist*: Soprano, range: e'-a^{b}", tessitura: g'-g", the solo is not substantial, but it is sustained, and the singer should be able to project over the entire ensemble. *Choir*: medium easy; *Orchestra*: medium.

Discography: As of January 1993, no commercial recording has been made available.

Selected Bibliography

Mussulman, John A.: *Dear People...Robert Shaw: A Biography.* Bloomington, IN: Indiana University Press, 1979; 55-6.

---

[27] Thomas A. Bumgardener: *Norman Dello Joio*, 38. Boston:Twayne Publishers, 1986.

Songs of Walt Whitman (1966)

Duration: ca. 25 minutes

Text: Walt Whitman as adapted by the composer

Performing Forces: *voices*: baritone soloist; SATB choir; *orchestra*: 2 flutes (flute II doubling piccolo), 2 oboes (oboe II doubling English horn), 2 clarinets (clarinet II doubling bass clarinet), 2 bassoons (bassoon II doubling contrabassoon), 4 horns, 3 trumpets, 3 trombones, tuba, timpani, percussion (3 players - snare drum, bass drum, tambourine, crash cymbals, suspended cymbal, tam-tam, ratchet, wood block, xylophone, glockenspiel, vibraphone, chimes), celeste, harp, and strings.

In movement #4, there are **three optional brass choirs**: 3 horns, 3 trumpets, and 3 trombones in each.

First Performance: 20 August 1966; Interlochen, MI; ensembles of the National Music Camp.

Edition: *Songs of Walt Whitman* is published by E. B. Marks and distributed by Theodore Presser Company. The movements are published in separate piano-vocal scores which are available for purchase; a unified full score and orchestral materials are available for rental.

Autograph: The full score is a facsimile of the composer's manuscript.

Notes: This work was "Commissioned by and dedicated to: National Music Camp, on the occasion of the 7th International Society of Music Education, Interlochen, Michigan, August 18-26, 1966." It is in four movements as follows:

1. I Sit and Look out upon the World
2. The Dalliance of Eagles
3. Tears
4. Take Our Hand, Walt Whitman

In the full score, the composer notes for the fourth movement:

> The addition of the three brass choirs at the coda is
> optional. Their use is not a requisite for performance.
> However, if the forces are available, the following is a
> suggested placement plan: [He includes a diagram which places
> Choir I to the audience's left, Choir II to the audience's rear,
> and Choir III to the audience's right.] A man for each brass
> choir should be advantageously placed to take his cues and
> tempo from the conductor for maximum performance accuracy.
> If the placement suggested is not feasible, the discretion of the
> conductor should be relied upon.

Performance Issues: This is a spectacular work well suited for a
festival event. It is a highly chromatic but tonally oriented
composition. The choral writing is primarily homophonic with
some paired imitation and occasional free polyphony. The vocal
harmonies are almost exclusively triadic and dissonances are
approached melodically. The choral parts are rhythmically simple,
generally being an exaggeration of the natural text rhythm. The
vocal pitches are clearly supported by the accompaniment. The
orchestra parts are much more rhythmically complex. There are
unusual beat divisions and a number of levels of hemiola. The
string writing is quite conservative with many unisons between the
sections. The winds all have rapid and complex passagework
throughout the work. The tessitura of the brass parts suggests a
need for experienced players. The auxiliary brass parts for the coda
are high and difficult. The rhythmic activity exchanged between
ensembles in that portion of the score will require substantial
rehearsal, especially in a large performance space. The rest of the
score is also filled with challenges to ensemble integration. There
are many terraced and echoed entrances, as well as some hocket-like
events for the winds. The orchestra brass players are presented with
an endurance test and some potential balance problems. This is an
excellent piece deserving many performances. It should only be
attempted if substantial rehearsal time for the orchestra is available.
Soloist: baritone, range: Bᵇ-d#', tessitura: e-b, declamatory and
articulate with broad leaps. This is not a substantial solo. *Choir*:
medium; *Orchestra*: medium difficult.

Discography: As of January 1993, no commercial recording has been
made available.

Selected Bibliography

Wannamaker, John Samuel: *The Musical Settings of Walt Whitman.* Dissertation, University of Minnesota, 1975.

Del Tredici, David (b. Cloverdale, CA, 16 March 1937).

Life: A virtuoso pianist, Del Tredici studied with Bernhard Abromowitsch and Robert Helps. On the suggestion of Darius Milhaud, he turned to compostion, studying with Arnold Elston and Seymour Shifrin at the University of California, Berkeley; and Roger Sessions and Earl Kim at Princeton. He has served on the faculties of Harvard (1966-72), SUNY Buffalo (1973), Boston University (1973-84), and since 1984 at City College and Graduate School, CUNY. Del Tredici's earlier works favored the texts of James Joyce, but since 1968, virtually all of his work has been centered around the writings of Lewis Carroll, with a specific focus on *Alice's Adventures in Wonderland* and *Through the Looking Glass.* His compositions incorporate elements of theater and a good amount of humor.[28] From 1968-76 he composed for ensembles which included a rock 'n' roll combo.

Awards: Guggenheim Fellow (1966), Naumburg Award (1972), three NEA grants (1973, 1974, and 1984), Pulitzer Prize (1980 for *In Memory of a Summer Day*), Friedheim Award (1982 for *Happy Voices*).

Principal Works: *Joyce texts - Four Songs* (1961), *I Hear an Army* (1963-4), *Night Conjure-verse* (1965), and *Syzygy* (1966); *Carroll texts - An Alice Symphony* (1969), *Adventures Underground* (1971), *Vintage Alice: Fantascene on A Mad Tea Party* (1972), *Final Alice* (1976), *Child Alice* (1977-81), and *Haddocks' Eyes* (1985-6).

Selected Composer Bibliography

Del Tredici, David; et. al.: "Contemporary Music: Observations from Those Who Create It," *Music and Artists*, v/3 (1972), 12.
"Del Tredici, David," *Current Biography Yearbook*, xliv (March 1983); New York: H. W. Wilson Company.

---

[28] Robert P. Morgan: *Twentieth-Century Music*, 435. New York: W.W. Norton, 1991.

Wierzbicki, James: "Del Tredici, David" in *The New Grove Dictionary of American Music*, edited by H. Wiley Hitchcock, i: 598-600. London: Macmillan, 1986.

Pop-Pourri (1968, revised 1973)

Duration: ca. 27-28 minutes

Text: Lewis Carroll's "Turtle Soup I and II" from *Alice in Wonderland* and "Jabberwocky" from *Through the Looking Glass*; "The Litany of the Blessed Virgin Mary" from *Liber Usualis*; and "Es ist genug" from Bach's Cantata No. 60.

Performing Forces: *voices*: soprano soloist (amplified); SATB choir; *orchestra*: 2 flutes (flutes I and II doubling piccolo), 2 oboes (oboe II doubling English horn), 2 clarinets (clarinet II doubling bass clarinet), 2 bassoons (bassoon II doubling contrabassoon), 2 trumpets in C, 2 trombones, percussion (3 players - bass drum [largest possible], anvil [largest possible], tam-tam [largest possible], wind machine [largest possible, or electronic equivalent], electric bull-horn [for the soprano]), and strings; *rock group*: 2 soprano saxophones (soprano saxophone II doubling tenor saxophone), electric guitar (with "fuzz" and "wah-wah" effects), electric bass guitar (with "fuzz" and "wah-wah" effects).

The score notes that there must be a sound technician to control a mixing board for the rock group and soprano. In "Turtle Soup I and II," the solo may be performed by a mezzo-soprano or countertenor.

Edition: *Pop-Pourri* is published and distributed by Boosey and Hawkes. The piano-vocal and miniature scores are for sale; orchestral materials are available for rental.

Autograph: The full score is a facsimile of the composer's manuscript.

Notes: The work uses Bach's chorale setting "Es ist genug" throughout. It is in five movements with an introduction and subsequent interjections of the chorale as follows:

> Chorale
> I.   Turtle Soup I (A Song)

II. Litany of the Blessed Virgin Mary
     Chorale
III. Jabberwocky (A Melodrama)
     Chorale
IV. Turtle II
V.   Chorale (with fragments from Turtle Soup)

Del Tredici notes that the "Litany" may be omitted. The closing
bars have three chime parts (playable on one set of chimes), each of
which has thirteen successive notes. These are numbered in Italian,
closing the work with "*TREDICI*," which is Italian for thirteen.

Performance Issues: This score presents an interesting hodgepodge
of techniques including traditional tonality, free-atonality, and
hexachordal combinatoriality. The score is rhythmically very
complex. The choir sings in only about five minutes of the piece.
They present the "Litany" and all of the statements of the chorale.
That movement is mostly easy with mere recitations on single
pitches for each choral part. However, there are 38 measures in the
middle of that movement which are fiercely difficult. Here, Del
Tredici weaves a most complex contrapuntal fabric with much
rhythmic and pitch disparity between parts. The tenor part is
written at sounding pitch and is notated alternately between treble
and bass clef. The score is filled with lengthy instructions
regarding articulations, style, and methods of presentation. The
rock group parts are thoroughly notated using traditional staff
notation. Their parts are often serial and are rhythmically very
challenging. *Soloist*: soprano, range: e-d$^{b'''}$, tessitura: g'-g".
This is a most demanding role with broad leaps, difficult pitch
language, and complex rhythms. This is a very theatrical part with
directions for many characterizations and unusual vocal sounds. To
program this work, one must have a soloist in mind. If a separate
soloist is used in the two movements listed above, it requires,
range: d$^{b'}$-g"; tessitura: f'-g"; it is full of melodic leaps with long
sustained passages in the top of the range. *Choir*: difficult;
Orchestra: difficult.

Discography: As of January 1993, no commercial recording has been
made available.

Dett, R(obert) Nathaniel (b. Drummondsville [now
part of Niagara Falls], Ont., 11 October 1882; d. Battle Creek, MI, 2
October 1943).

Life: Dett was born into a musical family and began formal musical training at the Oliver Willis Halstead Conservatory (1901-3) in Lockport, NY. In 1908, he became the first black man to receive a BMus from Oberlin Conservatory. At Oberlin, Dett studied piano with Howard Handel Carter, theory with Arthur E. Heacox, and composition with George Carl Hastings. He pursued further studies at Columbia University, the University of Pennsylvania, the American Conservatory, and Harvard University (1919-20) where he was a composition student of Arthur Foote. In 1929, he also studied with Nadia Boulanger in Paris, and in 1932 he received a MMus from the Eastman School. He taught at Lane College (1908-11), Lincoln Institute (1911-13), and the Hampton Institute (1913-31) where he was Director of Music. At Hampton, he established a strong choral tradition with international tours of the Hampton Institute Choir. Dett moved to Rochester, NY teaching privately and conducting a choir which did weekly radio broadcasts on NBC. He joined the faculty of Bennett College (1937-42), and in 1943 he became music director of the USO in Battlecreek, MI. There he also conducted the Women's Army Corps Chorus. Dett was fundamental in the founding of the National Association of Negro Musicians (1919). His music combines the essence of African-American folk music, as well as actual quotations of it, with the structures and counterpoint of European tradition.[29]

Awards: Bowdoin Literary Prize, Francis Boott Music Award from Harvard, the Palm and Ribbon Award from the Royal Belgian Band, Harmon Foundation Award.

Principal Works: *oratorios - Music of Mine* (1916) and *The Chariot Jubilee* (1921); *piano suites - Magnolia* (1912), *In the Bottoms* (1913), *Enchantment* (1922), *Tropic Winter* (1938), *Eight Bible Vignettes* (1941-3); and many motets and spiritual arrangements.

Selected Composer Bibliography

"Dett, Nathaniel," *Current Biography Yearbook*, obituary, iv (November 1943); New York: H. W. Wilson Company.

Ewen, David: "Dett, Nathaniel," in *American Composers Today: A Biographical and Critical Guide*. New York: H. W. Wilson, 1949.

---

[29] Hildred Roach: *Black American Music: Past and Present*. Boston: Crescendo Publishing, 1973.

McBrier, Vivian: *R. Nathaniel Dett: His Life and Works: 1882-1943.* Washington DC: Associated Publishers, 1977.

Simpson, Anne Key: *Follow Me: The Life and Music of R. Nathaniel Dett. Composers of North America Series,* number 10. Metuchen, NJ: Scarecrow Press, 1993.

The Ordering of Moses (1937)

Duration: ca. 40 minutes

Text: compiled by the composer from the Bible and folklore

Performing Forces: *voices*: soprano, alto, tenor, and 2 baritone soloists; SATB choir; *orchestra*: piccolo, 3 flutes, 2 oboes, 2 clarinets, 2 bassoons, 4 horns, 2 trumpets, 3 trombones, tuba, percussion (3 players - snare drum, tenor drum, bass drum, tom tom, tambourine, cymbals, triangle, chains), harp, organ, and strings.

First Performance: 7 May 1937; May Music Festival, Cincinnati, OH.

Edition: *The Ordering of Moses* was originally published by J. Fischer and Brothers. It is now published by Belwin-Mills and distributed by Theodore Presser Company. The piano-vocal score is available for purchase; orchestral materials may be rented.

Autograph: The full score is a facsimile of the composer's manuscript.

Notes: Despite Dett's two earlier works in this genre, David Ewen states that this is "The first oratorio composed by a black man."[30] It does appear to be the oldest oratorio by an African American to be published.

Performance Issues: Although the opening section is very chromatic and tonally unstable, this is a diatonic work with

---

[30] as quoted under "Dett, Nathaniel: The Ordering of Moses" in Thurston Dox: *American Oratorios and Cantatas: A Catalogue of Works Written in the United States from Colonial Times to 1985.* 2 volumes. Metuchen, NJ: Scarecrow Press, 1986.

traditional tonal relationships. It is a rhythmically intricate composition which juxtaposes a variety of beat divisions and utilizes frequently displaced downbeats, polyrhythms, and syncopations. At times, the vocal parts quote actual African-American tunes and elsewhere imitate spirituals. The choral writing is strictly homophonic with divisi in all parts. There are passages in which melodic figures are repeated under a freely intoned text. The orchestration exhibits some sound effects including the rattling of chains upon the word "bondage." In the accompaniment, beats are frequently divided into 5, 7, 10, 12, and 14 even parts. The winds and upper strings have a considerable amount of very fast unison passagework. The notation of the full score is generally clear, but the Horn IV part often appears to be a first trumpet part. Dett labels one of the percussion parts for side drum, which probably means tenor drum. Side drum is usually synonymous with snare drum, but that is also listed in the score. There is ensemble singing for the soloists, which should be considered when selecting them. *Soloists*: Miriam - soprano, range: f'-c''', tessitura: a'-g'', lyric, high, and sustained; Voice of Israel - alto, range: f#-c'', tessitura: c'-a', rich and sustained with strength in the bottom of the range; Moses - tenor, range: e-b$^{b'}$, tessitura: a^{b}-f', powerful and sustained; bass, range: c-f', tessitura: d-d', declamatory and speech-like. The choral parts are very straight-forward and quite easy. There is little variety for the singers; however, the orchestra's music is diverse and at times very difficult. An advanced instrumental ensemble is necessary while a large choir of limited experience would be adequate. *Choir*: medium easy; *Orchestra*: medium difficult.

Discography: As of January 1993, no commercial recording has been made available.

Selected Bibliography

Bicknell, Dwight: [review of premiere], *The Cincinnati Enquirer* (8 May 1937).

Yeiser, Frederick: [review of premiere], *The Cincinnati Enquirer* (8 May 1937).

_____: "Whithorne's Symphony; Dett's Moses," *Modern Music*, xiv/4 (May/June 1937), 222.

Diamond, David Leo (b. Rochester, NY, 9 July 1915).

Life: Diamond studied composition at the Cleveland Institute and the Eastman School with Bernard Rogers. He then attended the Dalcroze School in New York (1934-6) where he studied with Roger Sessions and Paul Boepple. This was followed by study in Paris with Nadia Boulanger. In Paris, he made contacts with André Gide, Maurice Ravel, Albert Roussel, and Igor Stravinsky. Diamond served as Fulbright professor at the University of Rome in 1951. Two years later he moved to Florence where he lived until 1965. He has taught at the Harvard Seminar in American Studies, SUNY Buffalo (1961 and 1963), the Manhattan School (1967-8), and since 1973, at the Juilliard School. Of Diamond's music, Virgil Thomson writes: "His string works are idiomatic, his songs melodious, his symphonies romantically inspired. The musical style in general is harmonious, the continuity relaxed. For all its seeming emotional self-indulgence, this is music of artistic integrity and real thought."[31]

Awards: National Institute of Arts and Letters, New York Critics' Circle Award for *Rounds* (1944), 3 Guggenheim Fellowships (1938, 1942, and 1958), William Schuman Award (1985) for lifetime achievement as a composer.

Principal Works: 11 Symphonies (1940-1, 1942, 1945, 1945, 1951, 1951-4, 1959, 1960, 1985, 1987, and 1992), 3 Violin Concertos (1936, 1947, and 1967-8), *Hommage à Satie* (1934), *Elegy in Memory of Maurice Ravel* (1938), *The Enormous Room* (1948), *The World of Paul Klee* (1957), *This Sacred Ground* (1962), *A Secular Cantata* (1976), many chamber works and songs.

Selected Composer Bibliography

"Diamond, David," *Current Biography Yearbook*, xxvii (1966); New York: H. W. Wilson Company.

Peyser, Joan: "A Composer who Defies Categorization," *New York Times* (6 July 1985).

Kimberling, Victoria: *David Diamond: A Bio-Bibliography.* Metuchen, NJ: Scarecrow Press, 1987.

Diamond, David: *The Midnight Sleep* (unpublished autobiography).

---

[31] Virgil Thomson: *American Music Since 1910*, 138-39. New York: Holt, Rinehart, and Winston, 1971.

To Music (1967)

Duration: ca. 20 minutes

Text: John Masefield "Invocation to Music" as published by Macmillan (1953), and Henry Wadsworth Longfellow

Performing Forces: *voices*: tenor and bass-baritone soloists, SATB choir; *orchestra*: piccolo, 2 flutes, 2 oboes, English horn, E^b clarinet, 2 clarinets (B^b and A), bass clarinet, 2 bassoons, contrabassoon, 6 horns, piccolo trumpet in D, 3 trumpets in C, 3 trombones, tuba, timpani (2 players), percussion (3 players - snare drum, tenor drum, bass drum, cymbals, large gong, triangle, woodblock, gavel, xylophone, glockenspiel), piano, harp, and strings.

First Performance: The Golden Anniversary Celebration of the Manhattan School of Music; Manahattan School of Music Ensembles; conducted by the composer.

Edition: *To Music* is published by Southern Music Publishing and distributed by Theodore Presser Company. The piano-vocal score is for sale; orchestral materials are available for rental.

Autograph: The full score is a facsimile of the composer's manuscript. The original autograph is in the possession of the Thorne Foundation.[32]

Notes: This work is dedicated to Ann and Francis Thorne, and was "commissioned by The Thorne Music Fund Inc. for The Golden Anniversary Inauguration Ceremonies of the Manhattan School of Music in New York City." Subtitled "Choral Symphony," it is in three movements as follows:

I. Invocation to Music (Masefield)
II. Symphonic Affirmation - orchestra alone
III. Dedication (Longfellow)

---

[32] telephone interview with David Diamond, August 1992.

Performance Issues: The composer lists 4 players total for the timpani and percussion parts, but the numbers listed above are preferable. The first movement of this work is atonal although not serial. Dissonance is the result of inverted quartal/quintal harmonies and free imitation. There are frequent choral unisons and the vocal parts exploit approachable melodic intervals while remaining isolated within a dissonant accompaniment. Most vocal pitches are supported in some part of the orchestra, but this is not always evident. There are also passages for *a cappella* singing or for voices and unpitched percussion. The choral writing is generally homophonic or in close imitation and exploits quartal/quintal relationships. The final movement is triadically conceived in the manner of Debussy with free movement between triads without regard to harmonic function. This is executed through melodic lines which have awkward leaps and unexpected chromaticisms. There are no significant rhythmic difficulties; however, in the second movement there are many levels of hemiola, displaced downbeats, and some very rapid unison off-the-string passages for all strings. Diamond's string writing exhibits an intimate understanding of the instruments with thorough indications of articulation and bow use. Although practical, the string parts are not easy. It should be noted that the composer has indicated that the glockenspiel sounds an octave higher than written; it is actually two octaves above the notated pitch. *Soloists*: tenor, range: f-a', tessitura: a-f', it is sustained and lyrical; bass-baritone, range: F#-f#', tessitura: f#-d', declamatory and speech-like. This piece has considerable rhythmic vitality and is varied in style and texture. The orchestra part is challenging, but clearly conceived. The choir sings only about ten minutes of music, so while difficult, this could be learned by a choir of limited means, and could be a practical way of introducing a choir to music of this style. The text would allow for practical programming with more conservative works such as Vaughan Williams's *Serenade to Music*, or one of the St. Cecilia works, such as those by Vivian Fine, Handel, Finzi, Britten, and Dello Joio. *Choir*: medium; *Orchestra*: medium difficult.

Discography: As of January 1993, no commercial recording has been made available.

Elgar, Sir Edward (b. Lower Broadheath, Worcester, 2 June 1857; d. Worcester, 23 February 1934).

Life: As a youth, Elgar worked in his father's music store and served as assistant organist to his father at St. George's, Worcester. He also played violin in a number of regional orchestras some of which he also conducted. He began to establish a national reputation as a composer with a number of works for the 3 Choirs Festival in Worcester. His first triumph in London was the debut of the *Enigma Variations* (1899). This was followed by the oratorio *The Dream of Gerontius* (1900), which secured his fame. He is best known for his five *Pomp and Circumstance* Marches (1901-30), the first of which has virtually become Britain's second national anthem with the addition of the text, "Land of Hope and Glory."[33] Elgar was knighted in 1904, was made a member of the Order of Merit in 1911. This was followed by the title, Master of the King's Music in 1924 and a baronet in 1931. He also received several honorary doctorates, notably from Cambridge (1900) and Yale (1905). He served as conductor of the London Symphony for the 1911-12 season. After his wife's death he completed few scores. Elgar's music was surely the finest of Britain's romantic composers. His fame was instantly established by the success of the *Enigma Variations* and the oratorios. His style is one of elegance and regal grandeur. The harmonic language is that of the late nineteenth century, and Elgar's method of composition is purposefully non-provincial. Outspoken with regard to the lack of quality English music at the beginning of this century, Elgar strove to adopt the fluid musical style of the continent. One can hear an English quality in his music, but in fact one probably hears a bit of Elgar in all of the English music to follow him. He became the paradigm of English musical sound.[34] The orchestration is lush and very knowledgeable of instrumental potentials, especially in his string writing which is frequently challenging but always effective.

Principal Works: *choral-orchestral* - *The Black Knight*, op. 25 (1889-92), *Light of Life*, op. 29 (1896), *Scenes from the Saga of King*

---

[33] Michael Kennedy: *Portrait of Elgar*, revised. London: Oxford University Press, 1983.

[34] Jerrold Northrop Moore: *Spirit of England: Edward Elgar in his World*. London: Oxford University Press, 1984.

Olaf, op. 30 (1897), and *Caractacus,* op. 35 (1898); *orchestral - Variations on an Original Theme* ("Enigma"), op. 36 (1898-99), *Froissart,* op. 19 (1890), *Cockaigne,* op. 40 (1901), *The Wand of Youth* Suites 1 and 2, op. 1 (1907), 2 Symphonies, opp. 55 and 63 (1907-08 and 1903-11), Violin Concerto, op. 61 (1909-10); many songs and chamber music.

Selected Composer Bibliography

Maine, Basil: *Elgar: His Life and Works,* 2 volumes. Reprint of 1933 edition, New York: AMS Press, [no date given, but still listed in print as of January 1993].

Young, Percy, editor: *Letters of Edward Elgar and Other Writings.* London: Collins, 1956.

Moore, Elaenor Marie: *A Study of the Vocal Works of Sir Edward Elgar.* University of Rochester: Dissertation, 1961.

Redwood, Christopher, editor: *An Elgar Companion.* Ashbourne: Sequoia Publishing, 1982.

Kennedy, Michael: *Portrait of Elgar,* revised. London: Oxford University Press, 1983.

Moore, Jerrold Nórthrop: *Spirit of England: Edward Elgar in his World.* London: Oxford University Press, 1984.

Philip, Robert: "The recordings of Edward Elgar (1857-1934), authenticity and performance pracytice," *Early Music,* xii/4 (1984), 481-9.

Willets, Pamela: "The Elgar Sketch-books," *British Library Journal,* xi/1 (1985), 25.

McVeagh, Diana: "Edward Elgar," *The New Grove Twentieth-Century English Masters,* 1-68. New York: W.W. Norton, 1986.

Reed, William H.: *Elgar as I Knew Him.* Oxford: Oxford University Press, 1989.

Anderson, Robert: *Elgar in Manuscript.* Portland, OR: Timber Press, 1990.

Monk, Raymond, editor: *Elgar Studies.* Aldershot, England: Scolar Press, 1990.

The Dream of Gerontius, op. 38 (1900)

Duration: ca. 100 minutes

Text: Cardinal John Henry Newman abridged by the composer

Performing Forces: *voices*: mezzo-soprano, tenor, and 1 or 2 bass soloists; semi-chorus (5 sopranos, 5 altos, 4 tenors, 4 basses), SATB choir; *orchestra*: piccolo, 2 flutes, 2 oboes, English horn, 2 clarinets, bass clarinet, 2 bassoons, contra bassoon, 4 horns, 3 trumpets, 3 trombones, tuba, timpani, percussion (2 players - bass drum, snare drum, cymbals, tam-tam, triangle, glockenspiel, bells), 2 harps (harp II is optional), organ, and strings (an additional 3 trumpets and extra timpanists are optional between rehearsal #'s 118 and 120 - These are mislabeled as page numbers in the introduction to the full score).

First Performance: 3 October 1900; Town Hall, Birmingham, England; Marie Brema, mezzo-soprano, Edward Lloyd, tenor, Harry Plunket Greene, baritone; Birmingham Festival Chorus and Orchestra; conducted by Hans Richter.

Edition: *The Dream of Gerontius* is available from three publishers: the piano-vocal score, full score, and orchestral materials are available for rental from Novello; a study score is for sale and full score and orchestral materials are available for rental from H. W. Gray; piano-vocal score, full score and orchestral materials are for sale from Kalmus. Novello has released a critical edition of the full score as part of *Elgar Complete Edition*, prepared by Jerrold Northrop Moore and Christopher Kent, which is for sale.

Autograph: The manuscript of the full score is in the possession of the Birmingham Oratory.

Notes: The Dream of Gerontius was commissioned for the 1900 Birmingham Festival. Into the manuscript, the composer copied these lines from John Ruskins's Sesame and Lilies:

> This is the best of me; for the rest I ate, and drank, and slept, loved and hated, like another; my life was the vapour and is not, but *this* I saw and knew: this, if anything of mine, is worth your memory.

The composer notes that the tenor solo, "Santus fortis," may be sung a step lower. He indicates the locations of the cued modulation and return. This transposed section is available with the Gray and Novello materials. The four solo roles are assigned as follows: Gerontius - tenor, The Angel - mezzo-soprano, The Priest - bass, and The Angel of the Agony - bass. Elgar states that the two bass roles may be performed by the same singer. He indicates that the mezzo-soprano soloist should not be seen on-stage until Part II. Elgar also suggests that the semi-chorus be placed between the orchestra and the soloists.

Performance Issues: This work has served for many writers as the touchstone of British oratorios. There are multiple divisi in the string parts. These include solo passages for the principal cellist. The individual instrumental parts are quite challenging, but Elgar demonstrates an intimate understanding of the strengths and weaknesses of the instruments for which he has written. The string parts are consistently more ambitious than their counterparts; however, there is some very intricate passagework for the woodwinds. The greatest challenge for the orchestra is the rhythmic integration of very diverse parts. The work is harmonically dense and metrically complex. The choral writing combines the harmonic language of the late nineteenth century with the contrapuntal techniques of the Tudor period including paired and pervasive imitation. The choral parts are subtly, but consistently doubled by the orchestra. Much of the melodic motion for the choir involves intricate chromaticism which may prove troublesome for intonation. There are occasional vocal divisi, including three-part divisions in the soprano section and the presence of the semi-chorus. At times these divisions yield twelve independent choral parts. At rehearsal #64, there is a section which emulates Anglican chant. There are frequent cross-rhythms of substantial complexity. The score is filled with tempo changes and expressive indications which will require substantial rehearsal time to guarantee. This score is filled with delicate musical nuance within the framework of an emense symphonic work. These intricacies, combined with the scope of the composition, limit its performances to the major symphonic organizations. *Soloists:* The Angel - mezzo-soprano, range: b^b-f#" or a", tessitura: e'-d", sustained and lyric; Gerontius - tenor, range: e^b-a', tessitura: g-g', lyric and expressive in the tradition of Bach's Evangelists; The Priest/The Angel of Agony - bass, range: B^b-e', tessitura: g-d', declamatory and powerful. The mezzo-soprano and tenor roles are substantial requiring vocal endurtance. They also have prolonged duet sections, therefore the compatibility of their voices must be considered. *Choir:* difficult; *Orchestra:* difficult.

Discography: Yvonne Minton, Peter Pears, John Shirley-Quirk; London Symphony Orchestra and Chorus, King's College Choir;

conducted by Benjamin Britten. Recorded July 1971 in the
Maltings, Snape, England. Decca: SET 525/6 421 381-2 [LP]; re-
released as London: 421381-2 LM2 [ADD].

Felicity Palmer, Arthur Davies, Gwynne Howell; London Symphony
Orchestra and Chorus; conducted by Richard Hickox. Chandos:
CHAN-8641/42 [DDD].

Constance Shacklock, Jon Vickers, M. Nowkovski; Rome Radio
Orchestra and Chorus; conducted by Sir John Barbirolli. Recorded
from a live broadcast, 20 November 1957. Arkadia: 2 CDHP 584
[ADD].

Dame Janet Baker, Richard Lewis, Kim Borg; Ambrosian Singers,
Sheffield and Hallé Choirs, Hallé Orchestra; conducted by Sir John
Barbirolli. Recorded December 1964 in the Free Trade Hall,
Manchester, England. HMV: ALP 2101/2 [LP] and ASD 648/9
[LP]; re-released as Angel: CMS 763185-2 [ADD].

Dame Janet Baker, John Mitchinson, John Shirley-Quirk; Birmingham
Symphony Orchestra and Chorus; conducted by Simon Rattle.
Angel: C-49549-B [DDD].

Mary Thomas, Keith Lewis, John Ewen Cameron; Huddersfield Choral
Society and Royal Liverpool Philharmonic Orchestra; conducted by
Sir Malcolm Sargent. Columbia: CX 1247/8 [LP]; re-released as
Angel: 4-63376-B [ADD].

Helen Watts, Nicolai Gedda, Robert Lloyd; London Philharmonic
Orchestra, John Alldis Choir; conducted by Sir Adrian Boult.
Recorded May/July in Kingsway Hall, London. HMV: SLS 987
[LP]; re-released as Angel: C-47208-B [ADD].

Gladys Ripley, Heddle Nash, Dennis Noble, Norman Walker;
Huddersfield Choral Society and Royal Liverpool Philharmonic
Orchestra; conducted by Sir Malcolm Sargent. Recorded April 1945
in Huddersfield Town Hall. Gramophone: 3435/46 [78's]; re-
released as HMV: RLS 709 [LP].

prelude only:

BBC Symphony; conducted by Sir Adrian Boult.   Angel: H-63134
[ADD].

excerpts:

Dame Clara Butt, Maurice D'Oisly; New Queens Hall Orchestra and
Chorus; conducted by Sir Henry Wood. Recorded 1916 in Queens
Hall, London. Columbia: 7128/31 [78's]; re-released as HLM
7025 [LP].

Excerpts conducted by the composer:

Margaret Balfour, Steuart Wilson, Herbert Heyner; Royal Choral
Society, Royal Albert Hall Orchestra. Recorded February 1927
from a concert performance in the Royal Albert Hall, London.
HMV: D1242/3 [78's]; re-released on *The Elgar Edition: The
Complete Electrical Recordings of Sir Edward Elgar, 1927-1932,*
volume 1. EMI Classics: CDCC 54560 [AAD mono].

Margaret Balfour, Tudor Davies, Horace Stevens; Three Choirs Festival
Chorus, London Symphony Orchestra. Recorded September 1927
from a concert performance in Hereford Cathedral. HMV: D1348/50
[78's]; re-released on *The Elgar Edition: The Complete Electrical
Recordings of Sir Edward Elgar, 1927-1932,* volume 1. EMI
Classics: CDCC 54560 [AAD mono].

The Elgar Edition: The Complete Recordings 1914-1925. Pearl:
GEMM CDS 9951-55 [AAD mono].

Selected Bibliography

Jaeger, August Johannes: *The Dream of Gerontius: Book of Words,
with Analytical and Descriptive Notes.* London: Novello, 1901,
reprinted in 1974.

Payne, Anthony: "Gerontius Apart," *Music and Musicians,* xiii/4
(1964-5), 5.

Day, E.: "Interpreting Gerontius," *The Musical Times,* cx (1969), 607.

Foreman, Lewis: *From Parry to Britten: British Music in Letters 1900-
1945,* many entries. Portland, OR: Amadeus Press, 1987.

The Apostles, op. 49 (1903)

Duration: ca. 130 minutes

Text: adapted by the composer from the Bible

Performing Forces: *voices:* soprano (1 or 2), alto, tenor and 3
bass soloists; SSAA semi-chorus, SATB chorus; *orchestra:*
piccolo, 2 flutes, 2 oboes, English horn, 2 clarinets, bass clarinet,
2 bassoons, contrabassoon, 4 horns, 3 trumpets, 3 trombones,
tuba, timpani (3), percussion (4 players - bass drum, snare drum,
tambourine, cymbals, tan-tam, small gong in Eb, antique cymbals
{in this case finger cymbals}, glockenspiel), 2 harps (harp II is
optional), organ, and strings.

Elgar calls for an additional trumpet, preferably natural, to represent a shofar.

First Performance: 14 October 1903, Town Hall, Birmingham England; Emma Albani Gye, soprano; Muriel Foster, alto; John Coates, tenor; Robert Kennerly Rumford, Andrew Black, and David ffrangçon-Davies, basses; Birmingham Festival Chorus (prepared by R. H. Wilson) and Orchestra; conducted by the composer.

Edition: *The Apostles* is published by Novello. The piano-vocal score is available for sale or rental. The full score and orchestral materials are available for rental. Novello has released a critical edition of the full score as part of *Elgar Complete Edition*, prepared by Jerrold Northrop Moore and Christopher Kent, which is for sale. Rental materials for the Prologue are available separately.

Autograph: The composer's manuscript of the full score is in the British Library (Add. MS. 58019).

Notes: There are numerous indications which appear in the manuscript that are not present in the engraved edition. These have been meticulously presented in the frontismaterial in the *Elgar Complete Edition.* The score consists of 67 independent numbers which are organized in the following larger sections:

PART I
> Prologue
> I.   The Calling of the Apostles
>> In the Mountain–Night
>> Dawn
>> Morning Psalm
> II.   By the Wayside
> III.   By the Sea of Galilee
>> In the Tower of Magdala
>> In Cæsarea Philippi

PART II
> Introduction (orchestral)
> IV.   The Betrayal
>> In Gethsemane
>> The Temple
>> Without the Temple
> V.   Golgotha
> VI.   At the Sepulchre

VII.   The Ascension
         In Heaven
         On Earth

The soloists are assigned the roles of Jesus, Mary, Mary
Magdalene, John, Peter, and Judas, as indicated in the solo
descriptions below. Elgar states that the soprano who sings the
role of the Virgin Mary may also portray the Angel. This was in
fact done on the premiere. Elgar notes in the score that the semi-
chorus should have 24 members, six on a part. He prefers the use
of boys' voices in a group separated from and higher than the
principal choir. If the available forces prohibit an independent
ensemble, he requests that they be situated in the front two rows of
the choir.

The score incorporates a traditional Hebrew melody for the Psalm
92, using a harmonization by Ernst Pauer. Elgar also used
segments of the Gregorian chant, "Constitues eos," in which the
Apostles are promised divine power. *The Apostles* and *The
Kingdom* were to be the first and second works of a trilogy
illustrating the teaching of the apostles and the founding of the
early Christian church.[35] Elgar's first inspiration for The Apostles
was his schoolmaster:

> The idea of the work originated in this way. Mr.
> Reeve, addressing his pupils, once remarked: "The
> Apostles were poor men, young men, at the time of their
> calling; perhaps before the descent of the Holy Ghost not
> cleverer than some of you here." This set me thinking,
> and the oratorio of 1903 is the result. . . I have been
> thinking it out since boyhood, and have been selecting the
> words for years, many years.[36]

---

[35] Diana McVeagh: "Edward Elgar," *The New Grove Twentieth-
Century English Masters*, 13. New York: W.W. Norton, 1986.

[36] Robert J. Buckley: *Sir Edward Elgar*, 8, 74. London: The Bodley
Head, 1905.

Of his original intentions the composer stated:

> It was part of my original scheme to continue *The Apostles* by a second work carrying on the establishment of the Church among the Gentiles. This, too, is to be be followed by a third oratorio, in which the fruit of the whole — that is to say, the end of the world and the Judgement — is to be exemplified. I, however, faltered at that idea. . .[37]

Material for what was to be a third part of *The Apostles* was absorbed into *The Kingdom*. The last installment in Elgar's planned trilogy was to be titled *The Last Judgement*. The composer sketched sections of the text and music for many years. Portions of these musical sketches were used as source material for an unfinished third symphony.

Performance Issues: Elgar uses the symbols R, A, and L to indicate ritardando, accelerando, and largamente throughout the score. There are multiple divisi within the string sections. The orchestration is at times, very dense with substantial doublings throughout. Many of these full-ensemble passages are intended to be soft. Balance and the maintenance of a low dynamic may prove to be difficult. The score is filled with cross-rhythms and constant shifts of tempo. The strings have many intricate passages, particularly the clarinets and violins. Melodic motives are rapidly exchanged between diverse sections of the orchestra, the coordination of which will require cautious rehearsal. Throughout the score are indications for optional doubling of the wind parts. There are a number of sections which contain melismatic choral unisons which at times resemble chant; however their rhythms are fully notated. Elgar continues to combine the chromatic harmonic practice of the late nineteenth century with counterpoint modeled upon Tudor church music. However, the choral counterpoint is far less complicated than in his *Dream of Gerontius*. There are divisi in all choral parts. The soloists have a significant quantity of ensemble singing often in opposition to the choir. The presentation and content of the text is very reminiscent of the dated Passions of this same era, particularly those of Stainer and

---

[37] Interview with Robert de Cordova: *The Strand Magazine* (May 1904), 543.

Maunder; however, Elgar's work is of much greater musical sophistication. *Soloists*: The Blessed Virgin/The Angel - soprano, range: eb'-g", tessitura: a'-e", lyric and sustained; Mary Magdalene - contralto, range: b-g", tessitura: d'-b', resonant and dramatically expressive; St. John - tenor, range: c-a', tessitura: g-g', ; St. Peter - bass, range: Bb-f', tessitura: f-d', sustained and somewhat declamatory; Judas - bass, range: F#-f', tessitura: f-d', lyric and articulate; Jesus - bass, range: c-f', tessitura: g-d', expressive, very sustained and lyric. The ranges and tessituri of the solo roles compared to Elgar's indication of *fach*, suggests that his labels are indicative of timbre rather than range. Judas and Mary Magdalene are the largest and most vocally demanding of the solo roles. *Choir*: medium difficult; *Orchestra*: difficult.

Discography: Sheila Armstrong, Heather Watts, Robert Tear, Benjamin Luxon, John Carol Case; London Philharmonic Orchestra and Choir, Downe House School Choir; conducted by Sir Adrian Boult. Recorded October-December 1973 and July 1974 in Kingsway Hall, London. HMV SLS 976 EX 749742-1 [LP]; re-released as EMI Classics: CDMB-64206 [AAD).

Alison Hargan, Alfreda Hodgson, David Rendall, Stephen Roberts, Robert Lloyd; London Symphony Orchestra and Chorus; conducted by Richard Hickox. Chandos: 8875/76 [DDD].

excerpts:

D. Labbette, Harold Williams, H. Eisdell, Dennis Noble, Robert Easton; Hallé Orchestra and Chorus; conducted by Hamilton Harty. Columbia: 9343 [78's].

Selected Bibliography

Jaeger, August Johannes: *The Apostles: Book of Words with Analytical and Descriptive Notes.* London: Novello, 1903.

Gorton, Canon Charles Vincent: *The Apostles: An Interpretation of the Libretto.* London: Novello, 1903.

Powell, Dorabella M.: "The First Performances of *The Apostles* and *The Kingdom*," *The Musical Times*, ci (1960), 21.

Anderson, Robert: "Elgar and some Apostolic Problems," *The Musical Times*, cxxv (1984), 13.

Foreman, Lewis: *From Parry to Britten: British Music in Letters 1900-1945*, 141, 148, 193. Portland, OR: Amadeus Press, 1987.

The Kingdom, op. 50 (1901-06)

Duration: ca. 100-105 minutes

Text: adapted by the composer from the Bible

Performing Forces: *voices*: soprano, alto, tenor, and bass soloists; SATB choir; *orchestra*: 3 flutes (flute III doubling piccolo), 2 oboes, English horn, 2 clarinets, bass clarinet, 2 bassoons, contrabassoon, 4 horns, 3 tumpets, 3 trombones, tuba, timpani, percussion (2 players - bass drum, snare drum, cymbals), 2 harps, organ, and strings.

First Performance: 3 October 1906; Town Hall, Birmingham, England; Agnes Nicholls, Muriel Foster, John Coates, W. Higley; Birmingham Festival Chorus and Orchestra; conducted by the composer.

Edition: *The Kingdom* is published by Novello. The piano-vocal and full scores are available for purchase; the full score and orchestral materials are available for rental. Novello has released a critical edition of the full score as part of *Elgar Complete Edition*, prepared by Jerrold Northrop Moore and Christopher Kent, which is for sale.

Autograph: The composer's manuscript of the full score is in the Bodleian Library (MS. Mus.b.32)

Notes: *The Kingdom* is in 65 independent numbers which are arranged within the following larger sections:

> Prelude (orchestral)
> I. In the Upper Room
> II. At the Beautiful Gate
> The Morn of Pentecost
> III. Pentecost
> In the Upper Room
> In Solomon's Porch
> IV. The Sign of Healing
> At the Beautiful Gate
> The Arrest
> V. The Upper Room
> In Fellowship
> The Breaking of Bread

The Prayers

The soloists are assigned the roles of the Virgin Mary, Mary Magdalen, St. John, and St. Peter, but there are some narrative solos in which they are not portraying their assigned characters.

The Apostles and *The Kingdom* were to be the first and second works of a trilogy illustrating the teaching of the apostles and the founding of the early Christian church. See "notes" under *The Apostles*.

Performance Issues: Elgar uses the symbols R, A, and L to indicate ritardando, accelerando, and largamente throughout the score. Throughout the score are indications for optional doubling of the wind parts. The individual intrumental parts contain much intricate passagework, particularly the strings. The integration of diverse section of the ensemble will require significant rehearsal. The size of the instrumental forces will produce additional challenges to the creation of a well coordinated and balanced ensemble. Most of the choral writing is homophonic with tertian harmonies and stepwise preparation of dissonances. The choral parts are clearly supported by the accompaniment. There are divisi in all choral parts, the greatest division being SSSAAATTBB. At times, the choir is used to represent different groups of people in the *turba* tradition of Handelian oratorio. The soloists are often presented duets and as a quartet, which is juxtaposed with the choir. While still musically very complex, this work contains fewer cross-rhthyms and chromaticisms than its predecessor, *The Apostles*. The size of the orchestra and level of divisi within the choir suggest a very large vocal ensemble. This work is much more challenging for the orchestra than it is for the choir. The instrumental contingent will require substantial independent rehearsal. *Soloists*: The Blessed Virgin - soprano, range: c'-b♭'', tessitura: g'-e'', rich and sustained; Mary Magdalene - contralto, range: a-g#'', tessitura: c'-c'', lyric, powerful, and articulate; St. John - tenor, range: c-a', tessitura: g-f', declamatory, expressive, and must be capable sustained phrases; St. Peter - bass, range: A-f', tessitura: f-d', powerful, lyric, and sustained, with *recitativo* passages. *Choir*: medium difficult; *Orchestra*: difficult.

Discography: Yvonne Kenny, Alfreda Hodgson, Christopher Gillett, Benjamin Luxon; London Philharmonic Orchestra and Chorus; conducted by Leonard Slatkin. RCA: 7862-2 RC [DDD].

Margaret Marshall, Felicity Palmer, Arthur Davies, David Wilson-Johnson, Roderick Elms; London Symphony Orchestra and Chorus; conducted by Richard Hickox. Chandos: CHAN-8788/89 [DDD]

Margaret Price, Yvonne Minton, Alexander Young, John Shiley-Quirk; London Philharmonic Choir and Orchestra; conducted by Sir Adrian Boult. Recorded December 1968 and February 1969 in Kingsway Hall, London. HMV: SAN 244/5 [LP]; re-released as Angel: CDS 749381-2 [ADD].

Prelude only, conducted by the composer:

BBC Symphony Orchestra. Recorded April 1933 in Abbey Road Studios, London. HMV: DB 1934 [78's]; re-released as World Record Club: SH 139 [LP].

Selected Bibliography

Jaeger, August Johannes: *The Kingdom: Book of Words with Analytical and Descriptive Notes.* London: Novello, 1906.

Gorton, Canon Charles Vincent: *The Kingdom: An Interpretation of the Libretto.* London: Novello, 1906.

Powell, Dorabella M.: "The First Performances of *The Apostles* and *The Kingdom*," *The Musical Times*, ci (1960), 21.

Foreman, Lewis: *From Parry to Britten: British Music in Letters 1900-1945*, 32, 148. Portland, OR: Amadeus Press, 1987.

The Music Makers, op. 69 (1902-12)

Duration: ca. 35 minutes

Text: Arthur O'Shaughnessy "We are the Music Makers" first published in *The Athenaeum*, 30 August 1873, and then in the author's book *Music and Moonlight.*

Performing Forces: *voices*: alto soloist; SATB choir; *orchestra*: piccolo, 2 flutes, 2 oboes, English horn, 2 clarinets, bass clarinet, 2 bassoons, contrabassoon, 4 horns, 3 trumpets 3 trombones, tuba, timpani, percussion (2 players - bass drum, snare drum, triangle, cymbals), 2 harps, organ, and strings.

First Performance: 1 October 1912; Town Hall, Birmingham, England; Muriel Foster; Birmingham Festival Orchestra and Chorus; conducted by the composer.

Edition: *The Music Makers* is published by Novello. The piano-vocal score, full score, and orchestral materials are available for rental. Novello has released a critical edition of the full score as part of *Elgar Complete Edition*, prepared by Jerrold Northrop Moore and Christopher Kent, which is for sale.

Autograph: The composer's manuscript of the full score is in the Music Library of the Barber Institute of Fine Arts at the University of Birmingham, England. A number of sketches and proofs may be found at Elgar's Birthplace Museum (MS. 49a, 49b, 583608, 622, and 980). The manuscript vocal score (Add. MS. 58036) and numerous sketches (Add. MSS. 47902, 63153, 63154, 63156, 63158, 63159, and 63160) in the British Library.

Notes: The Music Makers is an ode. In the program notes to the first performance Ernest Newman wrote:

> The "motif" of the poem is the idea that the poets — the music makers and dreamers — are really the creators and inspirers of men and their deeds, and the true makers of history and of human societies. Their dreams and their visions are the foreshadowing of what the rest of mankind are predestined to work out in endless conflict.

In this work Elgar used a number of musical quotations, many from his own works. They are *The Marseillaise, Rule Britannia!*, and the composer's own: *Enigma Variations, Sea Pictures, The Apostles,* The Violin Concerto, *The Dream of Gerontius*, and Symphonies 1 and 2.

The Birmingham Festival concert upon which The Music Makers was premiered also marked the first British performance of Symphony No. 4 of Sibelius.

Performance Issues: This is a colorfully orchestrated score with technically challenging passages for all parts, particularly the strings and woodwinds. The coordination of the entire ensemble will require careful rehearsal. There are numerous tempo changes and interpretive nuances which will require sensitive and responsive playing from the orchestra. The choral writing is generally homophonic with contrapuntal independence usually occurring merely as text repetition within isolated sections. There are limited divisi in all of the choral parts and also some choral unisons. There are a few brief *a cappella* passages for the choir. This work presents a wide variety of musical textures within a relatively short time frame. This piece would be an excellent introduction to Elgar's large choral-orchestral works while remaining within the grasp of a developing oratorio society. The text is also well suited to virtually any program. This would be a fine companion piece to Ralph Vaughan Williams's *Serenade to Music*, Gerald Finzi's *For St. Cecilia*, or David Diamond's *To Music*. *Soloist*: contralto, range: b♭-g', tessitura: e♭'-e♭'', this role requires a powerful, lyric voice capable of great expression. *Choir*: medium difficult; *Orchestra*: medium difficult.

Discography: Linda Finnie; London Philharmonic Orchestra and Chorus; conducted by Bryden Thomson. Recorded April 1991. Chandos: CHAN-9022 [DDD].

Dame Janet Baker; London Philharmonic Orchestra and Chorus; conducted by Sir Adrian Boult. Recorded April 1966 in Abbey Road Studios, London. HMV: TC C2-POR 54291 [LP]; re-released as Angel: CDS 747208-8 [ADD].

Excerpts conducted by the composer:

London Symphony Orchestra and Hereford Three Choirs Festival Chorus. Recorded September 1927 in Hereford Cathedral. HMV: D 1347 and 1349 [78]; re-released as World Record Club: SH 175 [LP]; currently available on *The Elgar Edition: The Complete Electrical Recordings of Sir Edward Elgar, 1927-1932*, volume 1. EMI Classics: CDCC 54560 [AAD mono].

Selected Bibliography

Newman, Ernest: "*The Music Makers* by Edward Elgar," *The Musical Times*, liii (1912), 566.

Foreman, Lewis: *From Parry to Britten: British Music in Letters 1900-1945*, 52. Portland, OR: Amadeus Press, 1987.

The Spirit of England, op. 80 (1915-17)

Duration: ca. 21-27 minutes (I - ca. 5 minutes, II - ca. 5 minutes, III - ca. 11 minutes)

Text: (Robert) Lawrence Binyon's "For the Fallen"

Performing Forces: *voices*: soprano or tenor soloists; SATB choir; *orchestra*: piccolo (ad lib), 2 flutes, 2 oboes, English horn (ad lib), 2 clarinets, bass clarinet (ad lib), 2 bassoons, contrabassoon, 4 horns, 3 trumpets, 3 trombones, tuba, timpani (3), percussion (3 players - snare drum, bass drum, crash cymbals), 2 harps, organ, and strings.

First Performance: Part I - 4 October 1917; Birmingham, England; R. Buckman; conducted by A. Matthews. Part II and III - 3 May 1916; Leeds; Agnes Nicholls, John Booth; Leeds Choral Union; conducted by the composer. First complete performance - 31 October 1917; Agnes Nicholls, Gervase Elwes; Leeds Choral Union; conducted by the composer.

Edition: *The Spirit of England* is published by Novello and distributed by Theodore Presser Company, including a critical edition (catalogue #73 0010) prepared by Robert Anderson and Jerrold Northrop Moore (1986). The piano-vocal and full scores are for sale; orchestral materials are available for rental.

Autograph: The full-score is housed at the British Library (Add. MSS 58041, 58042, and 58043), the British Library also houses sketches (Add. MSS 63153, 63159, and 47908) and the manuscript vocal score (Add. MS 58040).

Notes: *The Spirit of England* is a Requiem to those who had fallen in the First World War (during which it was composed). It was first suggested by Sir Sidney Colvin, who also recommended Binyon's "For the Fallen." The composer was then put in touch with the poet by R. A. Streatfield. Elgar inscribed the score: "My portion of this work I dedicate to the memory of our glorious men, and with a special thought for the WORCESTERS." The completion of the first movement was delayed by Elgar's difficulty in setting the section beginning, "She fights the fraud that feeds on Lies." There is thematic material which is reworked throughout the three movements (note particularly the opening material of the soloist, which returns most conspicuously at rehearsal #21 in the final movement). For intended use at a ceremony unveiling the cenotaph machine (a device for engraving burial markers) and commemorating the second anniversary of Armistice Day, Elgar reworked the score, replacing the final movement with the new chorus, "With proud Thanksgiving," which was initially scored for choir and military band. This was intended to change the mood from funereal to festive. *The Spirit of England* is in three sections, organized as follows:

1. The Fourth of August
2. To Women
3. For the Fallen

Performance Issues: The orchestration is lush and typical of the ceremonial quality for which Elgar is famous. The power of the instrumental writing demands a very large choir. There is only one written harp part; the indication of two players is surely for audibility. The string writing is contrapuntally complex with frequent divisi best achieved with a large string section. The organ part is integral to the score; it calls for a 32' pedal stop. The choral parts are very accessible, being generally homophonic with some paired imitation. The vocal writing is consistently diatonic with frequent unison and octave passages and all parts doubled by the accompaniment. Climactic moments include divisi in all vocal parts. The choir is asked for a wide range of dynamics, the soft passages of which are intelligently scored to allow for a relaxing in the sonic intensity required by the heavy orchestration of the forte sections. This score is dramatic with constantly shifting tempi in a style reminiscent of the late nineteenth century. The sheer number of performers and the independence of the orchestra parts will obligate substantial rehearsal time. *Soloist*: range: $e^{b'}$-b", tessitura: a'-g", requiring a powerful voice, though the paucity of low notes helps the likelihood of the solos carrying over the ensemble. The part is labeled merely as "solo" without discriminating a gender preference. The title page calls for soprano or tenor. In the performances given during Elgar's life two soloists were employed, probably using tenor in I and III and soprano in II, although the tessitura of all three movements is virtually identical. *Choir*: medium easy; *Orchestra*: medium.

Discography: Teresa Cahill; Scottish National Orchestra and Chorus; conducted by Alexander Gibson. Chandos: CHAN-8428 [ADD].

Selected Bibliography

Newman, Ernest: *"The Spirit of England,* Edward Elgar's New Choral Work," *The Musical Times,* lvii (1916), 235.

_____: "Fourth of August," *The Musical Times,* lviii (1917), 295.

Finney, Ross Lee (b. Wells, MN, 23 December 1906).

Life: Finney studied composition with Donald Ferguson at the University of Minnesota, Nadia Boulanger in Paris (1927-8), Edward Burlingame Hill at Harvard (1928-9), Alban Berg in Vienna (1931-2), and Roger Sessions (1935). Finney was a faculty member at Smith College (1929-48), and he then served as composer-in-residence at the University of Michigan (1949-). There he established the electronic music studio, and established a fine reputation for his teaching, with many successful students including William Albright, George Crumb, and Roger Reynolds. Finney's compositional style is an eclectic amalgamation of folk music, tonal traditions, and intense formal organization which at times includes the serialization of rhythm, tempo, and even musical form.[38] He believes that the process of memory is an integral element in listening, and has therefore continued to expand the process of variation in his music to exploit that aspect of the musical experience.[39]

Awards: Pulitzer Fellowship (1937), 2 Guggenheim Fellowships (1937 and 1947), the Rome Prize (1960), membership in the National Institute of Arts and Letters (1962), the Brandeis Medal (1968).

---

[38] Virgil Thomson: *American Music Since 1910,* 143. New York: Holt, Rinehart, and Winston, 1971.

[39] Wilfrid Mellers: *Music in a New Found Land: Themes and Developments in the History of Amerian Music,* 2nd edition. New York: Hillstone, 1975.

Principal Writings: *The Game of Harmony* (1947) and *Time Line* (1974).

Principal Works: 4 Symphonies (1942, 1958, 1960, and 1972), 2 Violin Concertos (1933, revised 1952; and 1973), 2 Piano Concertos (1948 and 1968), Variation for Orchestra (1957), *Variations on a Memory* (1975), Concerto for Strings (1977), and 8 String Quartets (1935, 1937, 1940, 1947, 1949, 1950, 1955, and 1960).

Selected Composer Bibliography

Cooper, Paul: "The Music of Ross Lee Finney," *The Musical Quarterly*, liii (1967), 1.

"A Tribute to Ross Lee Finney," *Music at Michigan*, xv/2 (1982), 1.

Pilgrim Psalms (1945)

Duration: ca. 20 minutes

Text: Ainsworth Psalter

Performing Forces: *voices*: soprano, alto, and tenor soloists; SATB choir; *orchestra*: 2 horns, 3 trumpets, 2 trombones, timpani, percussion (1 player - cymbal), and strings.

Pilgrim Psalms may also be performed with organ or piano.

First Performance: unable to determine

Edition: *Pilgrim Psalms* is published and distributed by Carl Fischer. The piano-vocal score is for sale; orchestral materials are available for rent. There is a separate publication of the complete text and the music for the final hymn which is to be given to the audience for their participation. It is sold in packages of one hundred (0 3640 A).

Autograph: The full score is a facsimile of the composer's manuscript.

Notes: The *Ainsworth Psalter* was brought to Plymouth by the Pilgrims and the singing of these psalms was some of the first such music making in the New World. Finney's work uses the texts and tunes from this Psalter as the basis of his composition. The work is composed for amateur performers as is described by the composer in the vocal score:

> *Pilgrim Psalms* has been planned so as to distribute the performance between different school groups. There are two unison choruses (Nos. 1 and 7) so simple that they can be sung by children. The men's glee club may learn Nos. 4 and 10, and the women's glee club, No. 11. There are four *a cappella* choruses for mixed voices (Nos. 2, 4, 9, and 12). The organ [orchestra] has a prelude and an interlude in which there are no vocal parts (Nos. 6 and 13). There are two psalms for mixed chorus and organ [orchestra] (Nos. 8 and 14). A short tenor solo with organ [orchestra] may be included if a soloist is available. The whole audience may sing the simple hymn that ends the work. All of the psalms written for mixed voices, or for men's or women's voices alone may be sung, if desired, without accompaniment, in the order that they appear in this work (or, indeed in any other order) and the resulting program will be musically satisfactory.

The texts are arranged as follows:

1.	Psalm XXIV	unison choir and orchestra
2.	Psalm LXIV	mixed choir, *a cappella*
3.	Psalm CXXXVII, 1st version	tenor solo and orchestra
4.	Psalm CXXXVII, 2nd version	double choir, *a cappella*
5.	Psalm V	men's choir, *a cappella*
6.	Prelude on Psalm I	orchestra
7.	Psalm CL	unison choir and orchestra
8.	Psalm XCV	mixed choir and orchestra
9.	Psalm LI	mixed choir, *a cappella*
10.	Psalm LV	men's choir, *a cappella*
11.	Psalm I	women's choir, *a cappella*
12.	Psalm CXXXVIII	mixed choir, *a cappella*
13.	Interlude on Psalm CVIII	orchestra
14.	Psalm C	mixed choir and orchestra
15.	Psalm CXXXIX	mixed choir, audience, and orchestra

Performance Issues: See "notes" above. The choral writing is quite beautiful and it is very simple, reflecting its source. Some of the awkward prosody of the original Ainsworth settings is preserved in Finney's arrangements. The mixed choir is given divisi in all parts, including the optional double choir in No. 4. That movement is arranged for antiphonal effect. It can be performed by a single four-part choir without eliminating any music or text. The orchestral writing is within the ability of most student orchestras. *Soloist*: tenor, range: d-f', tessitura: f-f', this role can be sung by a light, young voice capable of fairly long phrases and melismatic clarity. This work would be a fine piece to close a school music concert which involved a variety of ensemble. The historic relevance of the source material should eclipse the current trend to exclude sacred texts from public school music programs. *Choir*: easy; *Orchestra*: easy.

Discography: As of January 1993, no commercial recording has been made available.

Selected Bibliography

Noss, Luther: "Ross Lee Finney: Pilgrim Psalms," *Notes*, viii (1950-1), 570.

Still are New Worlds (1962)

Duration: ca. 28 minutes

Text: Various authors (see below) as quoted by Marjorie Hope Nicholson (a 1914 graduate of the University of Michigan), in *The Breaking of the Circle*, also a brief quote from Albert Camus's *The Myth of Sisyphus* as translated by Justin O'Brien.

Performing Forces: *voices*: narrator; SATB choir; *orchestra*: 3 flutes (flute III doubling piccolo), 2 oboes, English horn, 2 clarinets, bass clarinet, 2 bassoons, contrabassoon, 4 horns, 3 trumpets in C, 3 trombones, tuba, timpani, percussion (3 players - snare drum, bass drum, cymbals, suspended cymbals, 2 tam-tams (small and large), triangle, xylophone, glockenspiel, vibraphone), harp, celeste, strings, and *electronic tape*.

First Performance: 10 May 1963; Ann Arbor May Festival, Ann Arbor, MI; University of Michigan Choral Union, Philadelphia Orchestra; conducted by Thor Johnson.

Edition: *Still Are New Worlds* is published and distributed by C. F.
Peters (P 6553). The piano-vocal score is available for purchase;
orchestral materials (including the tape) are available may be rental.

Autograph: The full score is a facsimile of the composer's
manuscript.

Notes: The score is inscribed: *"Still Are New Worlds* was
commissioned by the University Musical Society of the University
of Michigan, Ann Arbor, for the Fiftieth Anniversary of the
construction of Hill Auditorium for the first performance at the
Seventieth Annual Ann Arbor May Festival." The first work of
Earthrise: A Trilogy Concerned with the Human Dilemma, it is
"concerned with the discovery of new stars in the seventeenth
century that challenged the old concept of a finite universe." The
texts are arranged into two parts with ten movements as follows:

PART ONE

I.	The Sun	Johann Kepler
II.	The Moist Earth	Gabriel Harvey
III.	Our Soules	Christopher Marlowe
IV.	Man hath weav'd out a net	John Donne
V.	To ask or search I blame thee not	John Milton
VI.	Is Every Star	Bernard Fontenelle
VII.	Farre Aboven	Henry More

PART TWO

VIII.	Give me to learn	Mark Akenside
IX.	Here are trees	Albert Camus
X.	He... with ambitious aim	John Milton

The eighth movement closes with a quotation from Pindar.

Performance Issues: *Still Are New Worlds* is a twelve-tone
composition. The choral writing is mostly homophonic, using
dyads doubled at the octave, or harmonic tetrads of similar
construction throughout, which should prove helpful for pitch
learning. All choral entrance pitches are clearly cued by the
orchestra, and Finney has conspicuously supported most of the
choral harmonies with brass instruments. Melodic lines utilize
consistent intervallic patterns which help to establish a sense of
aural order in the vocal parts. Moreover, independent statements of
the row within the choir are organized to occasionally create

unisons between parts and to serve as reference points for the singers. The third movement is the most challenging to the vocalists because of a more polyphonic treatment of the choral parts and a sparser accompaniment. At some points in the score metric accents are indicated using the symbols from poetry for indicating strong and weak syllables. The tape is cued in the score for beginnings and endings with no apparent need for the conductor to be conscious of clock time. There is an extended *a cappella* section in the fifth movement, which is in strict homophony. The narrator is asked to speak in rhythm in one passage. The choir also has passages of rhythmic speaking. The frequent brass doublings of the voices suggests a medium to large choir. The complexity of the pitch material requires an ensemble of experienced singers. Although the musical language is difficult, the orchestral writing is not very challenging technically. Therefore it could be a good piece with which to introduce serial music to a college ensemble. *Choir*: difficult; *Orchestra*: difficult.

Discography: As of January 1993, no commercial recording has been made available.

Selected Bibliography

Amman, David D.: *The Choral Music of Ross Lee Finney.* University of Cincinnati: Dissertation, 1972.

The Martyr's Elegy (1966)

Duration: ca. 18-23 minutes

Text: Percy Byshe Shelley, from his *Adonais*

Performing Forces: *voices*: "high solo voice"; SATB choir; *orchestra*: 3 flutes (flute III doubling piccolo), 2 oboes, English horn, 2 clarinets, bass clarinet, 2 bassoons, contrabassoon, 4 horns, 3 trumpets, 3 trombones, tuba, timpani, percussion (2 players - 2 snare drums, 2 bass drums (large and small), cymbals (large, medium, and small), 2 tam-tams (large and small), gong, 2 triangles (large and small), temple blocks, glockenspiel, vibraphone, 3 tubular bells), harp, and strings.

First Performance: 23 April 1967; Ann Arbor, MI; University of Michigan Ensembles.

Edition: *The Martyr's Elegy* is published and distributed by C. F. Peters (P 66094). The piano-vocal score is for sale; orchestral materials are available for rental.

Autograph: The full score is a facsimile of the composer's manuscript.

Notes: The second work of *Earthrise: A Trilogy Concerned with the Human Dilemma*. It was commissioned by the University Musical Society of the University of Michigan, Ann Arbor to commemorate the Sesquicentennial of the University of Michigan.

Performance Issues: Like its companion work, *Still Are New Worlds*, this is a twelve-tone composition. The choral writing similarly uses dyads with octave doublings, and tetrads of like construction. Pitch learning should be enhanced by these regular harmonic patterns. All choral entrance pitches are clearly cued by the orchestra, and again Finney has supported many of the choral harmonies with brass instruments. In contrast to *Still Are New Worlds*, there are a number of arrows connecting orchestra pitches to the soloist pitches allowing the solo to immediately discern such cues. The soprano part is very high, and all vocal parts have long sustained lines. There are a number of sustained hisses for the choir to prolong "s's." The percussionists are asked to make quick changes of instruments and to use a variety of beaters which are indicated graphically throughout the score. There is intricate passagework in the woodwinds and strings. In measures 78-110 and 162-169, the conductor is to beat seconds. In these sections, quarter notes are equal to one second and there are some instances of graphic notation in the harp and vibraphone parts. *Soloist*: high voice - soprano, range: d'-a", tessitura: f'-e", very sustained and scalar. *Choir*: difficult; *Orchestra*: difficult.

Discography: As of January 1993, no commercial recording has been made available.

Selected Bibliography

Amman, David D.: *The Choral Music of Ross Lee Finney.* University of Cincinnati: Dissertation, 1972.

Finzi, Gerald (b. London, 14 July 1901; d. Oxford, 27 September 1956).

Life: Finzi was the son of a ship broker. His early composition study was with Ernest Farrar (1914-16) and Edward Bairstow (1917-22). Upon Holst's advice, Finzi took a course in counterpoint in 1925 under R. O. Morris. This led him to settle in London and to establish himself within a musical circle which included Howard Ferguson, Gustav Holst, Robin Milford, Edmund Rubbra, and Ralph Vaughan Williams. From 1930-33, Finzi taught composition at the Royal Academy of Music. In 1933, he married the artist Joyce Black, and in 1937 the two built a house in the country where Finzi composed and cultivated an orchard of rare trees. He also amassed a fine library including what was probably the finest private collection of English music from the middle of the eighteenth century. In 1939 he established the Newbury String Players which he maintained until his death. With that group he read the works of many aspiring composers and revived numerous eighteenth-century compositions to which he dedicated much editorial time. He gave the 1955 Crees lectures at the Royal College of Music in which he analyzed the history and aesthetics of English song. He died of leukemia, from which he had privately suffered for five years during which he maintained public appearances between medical treatments. His best known works are the songs which are logogenically conceived. He was an authority on English literature with a particular predilection for the works of Thomas Hardy. His music tends to be formally small, tuneful, and meticulously crafted.[40]

Principal Works: *orchestral - Severn Rhapsody*, op. 3 (1923), *Romance*, op. 11 (1928), Clarinet Concert, op. 31 (1948-9), Grand Fantasia and Toccata, op. 38 (1953), Cello Concerto, op. 40 (1951-5); *choral* - Seven Partsongs, op. 17 (1934-7), Magnificat, op. 36 (1956), *In terra pax* (1954); *solo voice with orchestra - Dies natalis*, op. 8 (1926-39), *Farewell to Arms*, op. 9 (1940), *Let us garlands bring*, op. 18 (1929-42); *song cycles with piano - A Young Man's Exhortation*, op. 14 (1926-9), *Earth and Air and Rain*, op. 15 (1929-32), *Before and After Summer*, op. 16 (1938-49), *Let Us Garlands*

---

[40] Diana McVeagh: "Finzi, Gerald," in *The New Grove Dictionary of Music and Musicians*, edited by Stanley Sadie, vi/594-7. 20 volumes. London: Macmillan, 1980.

Bring, op. 18 (1929-42); *Till Earth Outwears*, op. 19 (1929-56), *I Said to Love* (1928-56).

Selected Composer Bibliography

Rubbra, Edmund: "Gerald Finzi," *The Monthly Musical Record*, lix (1929), 14.

Ferguson, Howard: "Gerald Finzi (1901-56)," *Music and Letters*, xxxviii (1957), 130.

Hansler, George E.: *Stylistic Characteristics and Trends in the Choral Music of Five Twentieth-Century Composers: A Study of the Choral Works of Benjamin Britten, Gerald Finzi, Constant Lambert, Michael Tippett, and William Walton*. New York University: Dissertation, 1957.

McVeagh, Diane: "Gerald Finzi," *Records and Recording*, xxiii/4 (1980), 30.

_____: "Finzi, Gerald," in *The New Grove Dictionary of Music and Musicians*, edited by Stanley Sadie, vi/594-7. 20 volumes. London: Macmillan, 1980.

McCoy, Jerry Michael: *The Choral Music of Gerald Finzi: A Study of Text/Musical Relationships*. University of Texas at Austin: Dissertation, 1982.

For St. Cecilia, op. 30 (1947)

Duration: ca. 17-21 minutes

Text: Edmund Charles Blunden

Performing Forces: *voices*: tenor soloist; SATB choir; *orchestra*: 3 flutes (flute III doubling piccolo), 2 oboes, English horn, 2 clarinets, bass clarinet, 2 bassoons, contrabassoon, 4 horns, 3 trumpets in C, 3 trombones, tuba, timpani, percussion (3 players - snare drum, bass drum, tambourine, cymbal, gong, triangle, xylophone), 2 harps (harp II is optional and only doubles the harp I), celeste, and strings.

First Performance: unable to determine

Edition: *For St. Cecilia* is published and distributed by Boosey and Hawkes. The piano-vocal score is for sale; orchestral materials are available for rental.

Autograph: The full score is a facsimile of the composer's manuscript.

Notes: The score is dedicated to Howard Ferguson, an Irish pianist and composer, who was a fellow student with Finzi.

Performance Issues: This is a tonal work which uses functional harmonies and traditional voice leadings. The choral writing is strictly homophonic and very rhythmic. There are divisi in all choral parts. The orchestration is varied, with melodic exchanges between sections and a great deal of rhythmic interplay. There is intricate passagework for all winds and strings, and the brass have numerous rapidly articulated phrases. *Soloist*: tenor, range: c-b', tessitura: g-g', powerful, bright, and rhythmic. The orchestral parts are subtle and quite sophisticated, requiring an ensemble of experienced players. The choral writing is more conservative in terms of counterpoint and pitch learning, but the group must be capable of rhythmically-challenging unified declamations. The choir must also be able to effect subtle change of color and articulation. *Choir*: medium; *Orchestra*: medium difficult.

Discography: Philip Langridge; London Symphony Orchestra and Choir; conducted by Richard Hickox. Argo: ZRG 896 [LP].

Flagello, Nicolas (b. New York, 15 March 1928).

Life: Nicolas is the brother of the opera singer, Ezio Flagello. He studied at the Manhattan School (MMus 1950) and the Accademia di S. Cecilia in Rome (DMus 1956). His teachers have included Vittorio Giannini (composition) and Dmitri Mitropoulos (conducting). He has had a successful career as a conductor of orchestral and operatic repertoire including a number of recordings with the Rome Symphony Orchestra and the Chamber Orchestra of Rome. His compositional style incorporates the tunefulness and expressive dramatic sweeps of *verismo* opera and the rhythms of American popular music within concise formal structures.[41]

Principal Works: *opera - Mirra*, op. 13 (1953), *The Wig*, op. 14 (1953), *Rip Van Winkle*, op. 22 (1957), *The Sisters*, op. 25 (1958),

---

[41] Arthur Cohn and Philip Miller: "The Music of Nicolas Flagello," *American Record Guide*, xxxi (1965), 1054.

The Judgement of St. Francis, op. 28 (1959), *The Piper of Hamelin,* op. 62 (1970), and *Beyond the Horizon,* op. 76 (1983); *orchestral* - 2 Symphonies, opp. 57, 63 (1968, 1970); 3 Piano Concertos, opp. 7, 18, 36 (1950, 1956, 1960); *Missa Sinfonica,* op. 24 (1957); *Lautrec,* op. 47 (1965); *Credendum,* op. 67 (1974); *vocal - The Land,* bass-baritone and orchestra, op. 15 (1954); *Dante's Farewell,* soprano and orchestra, op. 37 (1962); and *Te Deum for all Mankind,* choir and orchestra, op. 55 (1967).

Selected Composer Bibliography

Cohn, Arthur, and Philip Miller: "The Music of Nicolas Flagello," *American Record Guide,* xxxi (1965), 1054.

Simmons, Walter: "The Music of Nicolas Flagello," *Fanfare,* ii/1 (1978), 143.

_____: "Flagello, Nicolas," *The New Grove Dictionary of American Music,* edited by H. Wiley Hitchcock. 4 volumes. ii: 136. London: Macmillan, 1986.

The Passion of Martin Luther King (1968)

Duration: ca. 35-47 minutes [42]

Text: adapted from Latin liturgical texts and speeches of Martin Luther King, Jr.

Performing Forces: *voices*: bass-baritone soloist; SSAATTBB choir; *orchestra*: 3 flutes, 3 oboes, 2 clarinets, 2 bassoons, 4 horns, 3 trumpets, 3 trombones, tuba, timpani, percussion, celeste, organ (optional), and strings.

First Performance: 19 February 1974; Washington, DC; Cathedral Society Choir.

Edition: *The Passion of Martin Luther King* is published by Belwin-Mills and distributed by Theodore Presser Company. The piano-

---

[42] The composer lists 47 minutes, but Dox lists 35 minutes. Thurston Dox: *American Oratorios and Cantatas: A Catalogue of Works Written in the United States from Colonial Times to 1985.* 2 volumes. Metuchen, NJ: Scarecrow Press, 1986.

vocal score (SB-916) is for sale; orchestral materials are available for rental.

Autograph: The full score is a facsimile of the composer's manuscript.

Notes: The work was commissioned by the London Philharmonic Orchestra. The liturgical texts are in Latin and sung by the choir, while King's texts are of course in English and presented by the soloist. The work is structured as follows:

I.	Hosanna Filio David	- Choir
II.	At the Center of Nonviolence	- Soloist
III.	Cor Jesu	- Choir
IV.	In the struggle. . .	- Soloist
V.	Et Flagellis Subditum	- Choir
VI.	Death is Inevitable	- Soloist
VII.	Stabat Mater	- Choir
VIII.	We've got some difficult days. . .	- Soloist
IX.	Finale (Jesu misere nobis)	- Choir

Performance Issues: This work is well composed for voices. The solos are written in a recitative style imitating speech rhythms throughout. The harmonic language is highly chromatic frequently utilizing non-functional seventh and ninth chords. Most dissonances are created through traditional and logical linear means. The choral parts are fairly easy, being made almost exclusively of triadic and scalar figures and never departing far from language of the common practice period. Flagello uses a good deal of imitation. One difficulty arises from an inconsistent use of enharmonic spellings within vocal lines: some diatonic scales include diminished thirds. Divisi within parts occur only in homophonic/chordal passages and then only in 17 measures (I-eleventh and twelfth measures of rehearsal #1, last 3 measures; III - first five measures of rehearsal #5; VII - last five measures; IX - first two measures of rehearsal #3) to add density to the voicing of triads. The tessitura of the alto part is rather high, although in some passages the composer offers the alternative of the lower octave. The orchestra is very accompanimental though rhythmically active. Flagello creates an energized background with an accompaniment built from ostinati and sequences, none of which presents a substantial challenge to the ensemble. *Soloist*: baritone, range: A^b (of which there is but one) - e$^{b'}$, tessitura: e -

d'; the role requires a good control of sustained, legato singing. *Choir*: medium easy; *Orchestra*: medium easy.

Discography: As of January 1993, no commercial recording has been made available.

Selected Bibliography

Hume, Paul: [review of the premiere], *The Washington Post* (20 February 1974).

Foss [Fuchs], Lukas (b. Berlin, Germany, 15 August 1922).

Life: Foss's music studies began in Berlin with Julius Herford, and continued in Paris (1933-7) where his teachers were Noël Gallon (composition), Felix Wolfes (orchestration), Lazare Levy (piano), and Louis Moyse (flute). His family emigrated to the U.S. in 1937, and Lukas continued his studies at the Curtis Institute, studying conducting with Fritz Reiner and composition with Rosario Scalero and Randall Thompson. At Tanglewood (1939-42) he studied conducting with Serge Koussevitsky and composition with Paul Hindemith. He served as pianist for the Boston Symphony from 1944-50. From 1950 to 1952, he worked under a Fulbright grant as a Fellow of the American Academy in Rome. Foss joined the faculty of UCLA (1953-63) where he founded the Improvisation Chamber Ensemble, and directed the Ojai Festival. He then took the music directorship of the Buffalo Philharmonic (1963-70) and founded the Center for Creative and Performing Arts at SUNY, Buffalo. In 1971, he became conductor of the Brooklyn Philharmonic, and from 1981 to 1986 added the directorship of the Milwaukee Symphony to his duties. He retired as conductor laureate from the Brooklyn Philharmonic to dedicate himself to guest conducting and composition. Foss's style is that of a chameleon: his works up to about 1960 are neoclassical with elements of American popular music; after 1960 his music utilizes aleatoric devices and controlled improvisation. Throughout his compositional career, he has maintained a wry sense of humor using frequent quotations of familiar music, and musical jokes such as Armageddon being announced by a toy pop-gun, and the attempt to mock electronic sounds with acoustic instruments.[43]

---

[43] Gilbert Chase and David Wright: "Foss, Lukas," in *The New Grove Dictionary of American Music*, edited by H. Wiley Hitchcock, ii: 155-57. 4 volumes. London: Macmillan, 1986.

Awards: 3 New York Critics' Circle Awards (1944 for *The Prairie*, 1954 for Piano Concerto no. 2, and 1961 for *Time Cycle*), a Guggenheim Fellowship (1945 - the youngest recipient in the award's history), membership in the Institute of Arts and Letters (1962), and membership in the Academy the American Academy and Institute of Arts and Letters (1983).

Principal Works: *operas* - *The Jumping Frog of Calaveras County* (1950), *Griffelkin* (1955); *ballets* - *The Heart Remembers* (1944), *Within these Walls* (1944), *The Gift of the Magi* (1945); *orchestral* - *Recordare* (1948), 2 Piano Concertos (1944, 1949, revised 1953), *Symphony of Chorales* (1956-8), *Baroque Variations* (1967), *Geod* (1969), *Night Music for John Lennon* (1979-80), *200 Cellos, a Celebration* (1982); *chamber music* - *Echoi* (1961-3), *Paradigm* (1968), *Curriculum Vitae with Time Bomb* (1980); *vocal* - *Cool Prayer* (1944), *Behold I build an House* (1950), *A Parable of Death* (1952), *Fragments of Archilochos* (1965), *American Cantata* (1976).

Selected Composer Bibliography

Mellers, Wilfrid: "Today and Tomorrow: Lukas Foss and the Younger Generation," *Music in a New Found Land*, 220. New York: A.A. Knopf, 1965.

"Foss, Lukas," *Current Biography Yearbook*, xxvii (June 1966); New York: H. W. Wilson Company.

Salzman, Eric: "The Many Lives of Lukas Foss," *Saturday Review*, 1/8 (1967), 73.

Browne, Bruce Sparrow: *The Choral Music of Lukas Foss*. University of Washington: Dissertation, 1975.

Chase, Gilbert and David Wright: "Foss, Lukas," in *The New Grove Dictionary of American Music*, edited by H. Wiley Hitchcock, ii: 155-157. 4 volumes. London: Macmillan, 1986.

Perone, Karen L.: *Lukas Foss: A Bio-Bibliography*. New York: Greenwood Press, 1991.

The Prairie (1943)

Duration: ca. 48-54 minutes

Text: Carl Sandburg's opening poem in *Cornhuskers*, published by Henry Holt and Co.

Performing Forces: *voices*: soprano, alto, tenor, and bass soloists; SATB choir; *orchestra*: flute, oboe, English horn, clarinet, bass clarinet, bassoon, horn, trumpet, trombone, percussion (1 player - timpani, snare drum, bass drum, crash cymbals, suspended cymbal, triangle, xylophone), piano, and strings.

First Performance: 14 May 1944; Town Hall, New York; Patricia Neway, Alice Howland, Lucius Metz, Elwyn Carter; Collegiate Chorale, members of the NBC and CBS Orchestras; conducted by Robert Shaw.

Edition: *The Prairie* is published and distributed by G. Schirmer. The piano-vocal score is for sale (publisher's plate #40798; publisher's edition #1793); orchestral materials are available for rental. "Cool Prayers" is published separately (G. Schirmer # 9605).

Autograph: The full score is a facsimile of the composer's manuscript.

Notes: *The Prairie* received the 1944 New York Critics' Circle Award for best new American work. *The Prairie Symphonic Suite* based on the cantata for orchestra alone was premiered first (15 October 1943; Boston, MA; Boston Symphony Orchestra; conducted by Serge Koussevitsky). Compare to the setting by Normand Lockwood. The work is divided into 7 sections as follows:

I.	I was Born on the Prairie	- tenor
II.	Dust of Men	- soloists and choir
III.	They Are Mine	- soprano, alto, and choir
IV.	When the Red and the White Men Met	- choir
V.	In the Dark of a Thousand Years	- bass and men's choir
VI a.	Cool Prayers	- choir
VI b.	O Prairie Girl	- soprano

VI c. Songs Hidden in Eggs   - soprano and alto
VII. To-morrow   - soloists and choir

Performance Issues: This is a tonal work in the American mold of
Aaron Copland and Roy Harris. The scoring is practical,
remaining light during vocal passages and written well for the
respective instruments. This is a rhythmically active piece with
constantly changing meters and varied groupings of the
subdivision. The choral writing is mostly homophonic with some
inventive harmonies which are approached from tertian harmonies
by stepwise motion. There are some passages for *a cappella* choir
and some divisi for 6-part choir. The third movement calls for one
off-stage voice, which should be soprano. The small wind section
of this work suggests a small to medium sized choir and string
section. Each wind player has numerous exposed passages which
will require soloistic tone and confidence, but which should present
no significant technical demands. The less-exposed piano part is
well conceived, but technically challenging. Melodic elegance may
be prohibited by regular shifts in meter and a constant interchange
of instruments. Although at first contact the score appears to be
vertically conceived, focussing on its inherent linear momentum
should be an important part of the initial rehearsal process.
Soloists: soprano, range: c'-g", tessitura: e'-e", lyric and fairly
low; alto, range: b-f", tessitura: e'-b', should be warm and lyric;
tenor, range: e-a', tessitura: a-f#, declamatory, rhythmically active,
and speech-like; bass, range: F-e', tessitura: c-c', declamatory, crisp,
and not very demanding. Of the "Americana" works examined in
this study, Foss's is the most inventive and interesting. It is well
crafted and logically organized while remaining tuneful and
sonorous. The vocal writing is accessible to choirs of moderate
experience and size and the orchestra is fairly small. *Choir:*
medium easy; *Orchestra:* medium difficult.

Discography: Jeanne Distell, Ani Yervanian, Jerold Norman, Harlan
Foss; Gregg Smith Singers, Long Island Symphonic Choral
Association, Brooklyn Philharmonic; conducted by Foss. Recorded
in 1976. Turnabout TV-S 34649 [LP].

Selected Bibliography

Thomson, Virgil: "Music [review of the premiere]," *New York Herald
Tribune* (16 May 1944), 14.

Downes, Olin: [review of the premiere], *New York Times* (16 May 1944).

Berger, Arthur: "Scores and Records," *Modern Music*, xxii (March/April 1945), 200.

Foss, Lukas: "The Prairie, A Parable of Death, and Psalms," in *The Composer's Point of View: Essays on Twentieth-Century Music By Those Who Wrote It*, edited by Robert Stephan Hines, 3-13. Norman, OK: University of Oklahoma Press, 1963.

Pisciotta, Louis Vincent: "Texture in the Choral Works of Lukas Foss," in *Texture in the Choral Works of Selected Contemporary American Composers*, 200-33. Indiana University: Dissertation, 1967.

Browne, Bruce Sparrow: *The Choral Music of Lukas Foss*, 26-58. University of Washington: Dissertation, 1976.

Mussulman, John A.: *Dear People. . . Robert Shaw: A Biography*, 52-53. Bloomington, IN: Indiana University Press,1979.

Foulds, John (b. Manchester, 2 November 1880; d. Calcutta, 25 April 1939).

Life: Largely a self-taught composer, Foulds played cello in the Hallé Orchestra under Richter. As early as 1898, he was playing music which used quarter-tones. He traveled to Essen in 1906 where he met Gustav Mahler, Frederick Delius, and Engelbert Humperdinck. He began to study Greek modes and Indian instruments about the time of the First World War. He served as conductor of the London University Musical Society (1921-7), and also conducted a number of London theatrical productions. Foulds moved to Paris in 1927, returning to London three years later. In 1935 he moved to India to collect folk-music, study Indian musical practices, and to write. He became director of European Music for All-India Radio in Delhi (1937). Foulds died of cholera in 1939. He presented numerous lectures on the role of music in society in which he expressed his populist beliefs. Foulds published many articles on ethnic musics (mostly Greek and Indian). In the book, *Music To-day*, op. 92 (London, 1934), he presented his concepts about music and described his musical development and influences. Foulds was known mostly for semi-popular music during his lifetime, but in his serious music he created a unique musical style which integrated Western music traditions with Eastern styles, particularly elements of Indian music and some use of microtones. There has been a recent rekindling of interest in Foulds's serious works. Unfortunately, many of his manuscripts are lost, but since 1980 over a dozen of his works have been recorded with more scheduled for release.[44]

Principal Works: *opera* - The Vision of Dante, op. 7 (1905-8); *orchestral* - *Epithalamium* (1906), 2 Cello Concertos (1908-9, 1910), *Keltic Melodies* (1911), *Dynamic Triptych* (1929), *Mantras* (1930), *Keltic Overture* (1930), *April-England* (1926-32), *3 Pasquinades* (1935) *Chinese Suite* (1935); incidental music for 27 plays; 12 short film scores; 9 String Quartets, and many other works for varied ensembles.

Selected Composer Bibliography

Foulds, John: *Music To-day*, op. 92. London: Ivor Nicholson and Watson, Ltd., 1934.
MacDonald, Malcolm: *John Foulds and His Music: An Introduction.* White Plains, NY: Pro/Am Music Resources, 1989.

A World Requiem, op. 60 (1919-21)

Duration: ca. 125 minutes

Text: Bible, Requiem Mass, "Benedicite," Kabir, and Maud MacCarthy

Performing Forces: *voices*: soprano, alto, tenor, and bass soloists, SATB choir, children's choir; *orchestra*: organ, extra brass and percussion in the corners of the hall; *distant ensemble*: 2 harps, celeste, sistrum, and 4 solo violins.

First Performance: 11 November 1923; Royal Albert Hall, London to benefit the British Legion; Ida Cooper, Olga Haley, William Heseltine, Robert Heyner; Festival Choir of 1200 and Orchestra; C. H. Kempling, organ; Maud MacCarthy, concert-mistress; conducted by Foulds.

Edition: A piano-vocal score was published for sale by Novello which is now represented in the United States by Theodore Presser Company. These piano-vocal scores could be reprinted upon

---

[44] Malcolm MacDonald: *John Foulds and His Music: An Introduction.* White Plains, NY: Pro/Am Music Resources, 1989.

request. A copy of the manuscript full-score and orchestral materials are available for rental.

Autograph: A copy of the composer's manuscript is in the possession of Novello and Company.

Notes: The premiere performance was repeated annually for three more years. In the style of Granville Bantock, Frederick Delius and Havergal Brian, it has never been performed since and has not been reissued by the publisher. It is included in this catalogue because of its relevance to Britten's *War Requiem* and Howells's *Hymnus Paradisi*, and in anticipation of its possible revival. The work was a failure in the press, but gained lavish praise from audiences and composers of the time. The *World Requiem's* text certainly speaks to modern audiences and many of its musical devices are suggestive of things which were to come.

Performance Issues: The publisher possesses a single copy of the full score and parts. Piano-vocal scores were published for the performances noted above, but these scores are no longer held by Novello. The publisher has stated that performance materials could be made if a performance were scheduled.[45] The following remarks are based upon decriptions by Robertson[46] and excerpts published in MacDonald's[47] biography. The work contains many non-functional ninth, eleventh, and thirteenth chords. There are occasional uses of microtones in the strings and voices. Most of these are relegated to solo passages for the concertmaster. Most of the choral writing is homophonic with divisi in all parts. The orchestrational style is reminiscent of Delius. Instruments are treated idiomatically, and in general the orchestra parts are not very challenging. The choir often sings unusual harmonies which are approached by stepwise motion. The majority of the vocal

---

[45] via a letter to this writer from Theodore Presser and Company

[46] Alec Robertson: *Requiem: Music of Mourning and Consolation.* London: Praeger Press, 1985.

[47] Malcolm MacDonald: *John Foulds and His Music: An Introduction.* White Plains, NY: Pro/Am Music Resources, 1989.

material is supported by the instruments. *Choir*: difficult; *Orchestra*: medium.

Discography: As of January 1993, no commercial recording has been made available.

Selected Bibliography

Foreman, Lewis: *From Parry to Britten: British Music in Letters 1900-1945*, 166. Portland, OR: Amadeus Press, 1987.

Hanson, Howard (b. Wahoo, NE, 28 October 1896; d. Rochester, NY, 26 February 1981).

Life: In addition to possessing superior musical skills, Hanson was a master academic administrator and a significant voice in the development of music education in the twentieth century. He attended Luther College in Wahoo, receiving a diploma in 1911. He was a pupil of Percy Goetschius at the Institute of Musical Art (1914) and Northwestern University (BA 1916). As the first American recipient of the Rome Prize (1921) to establish a residency in Rome, Hanson continued his studies with Ottorino Respighi. He taught composition and music theory at the College of the Pacific in California (1916-19) and was made dean of the Conservatory of Fine Arts in 1919. From 1924 to 1964, Hanson served as the director of the Eastman School. Under his leadership, the school flourished. He also became involved with the administration of NASM, MENC, MTNA, and the National Music Council. In 1964, he founded the Institute of American Music of the Eastman School. As a conductor, he built the Eastman Philharmonia into a top-flight ensemble, with whom he made the premiere recordings of many American compositions. He was a frequent guest conductor throughout the US and Europe.

Awards: 36 honorary degrees, Pulitzer Prize (1944 for Symphony no.4, "The Requiem," op. 34), George Foster Peabody Award, Oliver Ditson Award, membership in the Institute of Arts and Letters (1935), and the Academy of the American Academy and Institute of Arts and Letters (1979).

Principal Writing: *Harmonic Materials of Modern Music* (New York: Appleton-Century-Crofts, 1960).

Principal Works: *opera - Merry Mount* op. 31 (1933); *ballet - California Forest Play of 1920,* op. 16 (1919); *symphonies* - no.1 "The Nordic," op. 21 (1922), no. 2 "The Romantic," op. 30 (1930), no. 3, op. 33 (1937-8), no. 4 "The Requiem," op. 34 (1944), no. 5 "Sinfonia sacra," op. 43 (1954), no. 6 (1967), no. 7 "A Sea Symphony," (1977); *vocal - Hymn for the Pioneers* (1938), *Song of Democracy,* op. 44 (1957), *The Mystic Trumpeter* (1970), *Lumen in Christo* (1974), *New Land, New Covenant* (1976).

Selected Composer Bibliography

Royce, Edward: "Howard Hanson," in *American Composers on American Music: A Symposium,* edited by Henry Cowell, 97. New York: Frederick Ungar Publishing, 1933 (revised, 1962).

Alter, Martha: "American Compoers, XVI: Howard Hanson," *Modern Music,* xviii/2 (January/February 1941), 84.

"Hanson, Howard," *Current Biography Yearbook,* ii (October 1941); xxvii (September 1966); obituary, lxii (April 1981); New York: H. W. Wilson Company.

Watanabe, Ruth T.: "Howard Hanson's Manuscript Scores," *University of Rochester Library Bulletin,* v/2 (1950), 21.

_____: *Music of Howard Hanson.* Rochester: University of Rochester Press, 1966.

Monroe, Robert C.: *Howard Hanson: American Music Educator.* Florida State University: Dissertation, 1970.

Carmine, Albert Junior: *The Choral Music of Howard Hanson.* University of Texas: Dissertation, 1977.

Gleason, Harold and Walter Becker: "Howard Hanson," *Twentieth-Century American Composers,* second ed., Music Literature Outlines, series iv. Bloomington, IN: Frangiapani Press, 1981; 74.

The Lament for Beowulf, op. 25 (1925)

Duration: ca. 19-20 minutes

Text: *Beowulf* as translated by William Morris and A. J. Wyatt

Performing Forces: *voices*: SATB choir; *orchestra*: 3 flutes, 2 oboes, 2 clarinets, 3 bassoons, 4 horns, 3 trumpets, 3 trombones, tuba, 2 timpanists (4 timpani each), percussion (1 player - snare drum, bass drum), harp, and strings.

First Performance: May 1926; Ann Arbor May Festival, Ann Arbor, MI; conducted by the composer.

Edition: *The Lament for Beowulf* is published and distributed by Carl Fischer. The piano-vocal score is for sale; orchestral materials are available for rental.

Autograph: The composer's manuscript is in the Sibley Library of the Eastman School of Music.

Notes: *Beowulf* is dedicated to the Leeds Festival Chorus.

Performance Issues: The choral writing is tonal with dissonances carefully prepared through melodic motion of independent parts. Terraced entrances are frequent with the imitation of parts being more rhythmic than pitch oriented. The vocal parts are consistently declamatory and rhythmically rigid. Much of the accompaniment is built from ostinato figures which are constructed from non-functional seventh chords, or other extended tertian harmonies in various inversions. The string parts are energetic, but not difficult. The winds and brass are presented with no technical snares, but the powerful dynamic level required throughout most of the piece may expose limits of endurance. This composition has great rhythmic drive and power and is short enough to maintain a successful level of frenetic excitement. *Choir*: medium easy; *Orchestra*: medium.

Discography: Eastman School of Music Chorus, Eastman-Rochester Symphony Orchestra; conducted by Hanson. Mercury (Living Presence): SRI-75007 [LP]; re-released as 434302-2 [ADD].
Seattle Symphony Orchestra and Chorale; conducted by Gerard Schwarz. Recorded on 15 and 18 February 1991. Delos: DE 3105 [DDD].

Selected Bibliography

Lieberson, Goddard: "Spring Fancies, 1937," *Modern Music*, XIV/4 (May/June 1937), 220.
Ewen, David: *The Complete Book of Twentieth-Century Music*, revised edition, 162. New York: Prentice-Hall, 1967.

Three Songs from "Drum Taps," op. 32
(1935)

Duration: ca. 16-18 minutes

Text: Walt Whitman from "Drum Taps"

Performing Forces: *voices*: SATB choir; *orchestra*: 3 flutes, 3 oboes, 3 clarinets, 3 bassoons, 4 horn, 3 trumpets, 3 trombones, tuba, timpani (2 players), percussion (3 players - snare drum, tenor drum, bass drum, crash cymbal, suspended cymbal, gong, xylophone, glockenspiel, chimes), 2 harps, and strings.

First Performance: 1935 May Festival; Ann Arbor, MI; conducted by the composer.

Edition: *Songs from "Drum Taps"* was published by J. Fischer and Brother (6925-52) and then Belwin-Mills; it is distributed by Theodore Presser Company. The piano-vocal score is for sale; orchestral materials are available for rental.

Autograph: A copy of the composer's manuscript is in the special collections of the Sibley Library of the Eastman School of Music. As of August 1992 it had not been catalogued.

Notes: This composition is dedicated to the composer's mother and father. Compare with the setting by William Schuman (*A Free Song*). Hanson's work is in three movements as follows:

    I.   Beat! beat! drums! (text - 1861)
   II.   By the bivouac's fitful flame (text - 1865)
  III.   To thee old cause (text - 1871)

Performance Issues: This is a rhythmically charged and tonally oriented work. The metric drive of the piece is guaranteed by Hanson's use of rhythmic and melodic ostinati juxtaposing varied divisions of the beat. The harmonic language is very static, exploiting quartal-quintal relationships and pedal points. The choral writing is generally homophonic with occasional interplay between the men's and women's sections of the choir and substantial choral unisons. Hanson also gives the tune and text to one section of the choir while the remaining parts sing "ah" behind it. The most contrapuntal activity occurs in the third movement where there a number of imitative textless phrases for the singers. There are divisi in all of the choral sections. The orchestration is very straightforward, presenting no ensemble challenges. The orchestra's endurance, however, is tested. The players, particularly the brass, are asked to play at a full dynamic throughout most of the work. Two confident players are needed for the percussion parts, which have many exposed drum solos. The final eight measures require an additional percussionist to play the chime part. There are also very challenging gestures in all of the woodwinds in the final movement. This is a very exciting and dramatic work with a text well suited to many programs. It would make a fine companion piece to Vaughan ·Williams's *Dona Nobis Pacem* or Delius's *Requiem*. *Soloist*: baritone, range: c-e', tessitura: e-b, powerful and declamatory with sustained phrases. *Choir*: medium; *Orchestra*: medium difficult.

Discography: Eastman School of Music Chorus, Eastman-Rochester Symphony Orchestra; conducted by Hanson. Mercury: MG-50073 [LP], and Eastman-Rochester Achives: ERA-1010 [LP].

Selected Bibliography

[review], *Musical America*, lv/11 (1935), 24.
Tuthill, Burnet C.: "Howard Hanson," *The Musical Quarterly*, xxii (1936), 146.
Lieberson, Goddard: "Rochester's Sixth Festival," *Modern Music*, xiii/4 (May/June 1936), 50.

Harris, Roy [LeRoy] (b. near Chandler, OK, 12 February 1898; d. Santa Monica, CA, 1 October 1979).

Life: Harris received his early musical training from his mother. He was a student at the University of California, Berkeley (1919) and UCLA (1921). He studied privately (1924-5) with Arthur Farwell (theory) and Modest Altschuler (orchestration). On the advice of Aaron Copland, Harris traveled to Paris where he was a pupil of Nadia Boulanger (1926-8). He joined the summer faculty of the Juilliard School (1932) and then served on the faculties of Westminster Choir College (1934-8), Princeton University (1938), Cornell University (1941-3), Colorado College (1943-8), the University of Utah (1948-9), the George Peabody College for Teachers (1949-51), Pennsylvania College for Women (1951-6), Southern Illinois University (1956-7),

Indiana University (1957-60), the Inter-American University (1959-61), UCLA (1961-73), the University of the Pacific (1963-4), and California State University, Los Angeles (1969-76). Among his many pupils were George Lynn, Peter Schickele, and William Schuman. Harris was very active in the formation and administration of organizations for the promotion of new music and young composer. The most notable of these were the Composers' Forum-Laboratory (1935), the Pittsburgh International Festival of Contemporary Music (1952), and the International Congress of Strings (1958). Harris's music is often complex, using many imitative and developmental devices from the Baroque and Renaissance eras including fugue, quodlibet, variations, passacaglias, and sixteenth-century imitative processes. His works are characterized by broad gestures, a vastness of orchestration, use of folk materials, and expansive forms. He used a single-movement form in four of his symphonies and a number of chamber works.[48]

Awards: 3 Guggenheim Fellowships (1927, 1928, 1975), Elizabeth Sprague Coolidge Medal (1942), Naumburg Award (1956), several honorary degrees, membership in the Institute (1944) and Academy (1978) of the American Academy and Institute of Arts and Letters, Composer Laureate of the State of California in 1975.

Principal Works: orchestral - 15 symphonies: no. 1, "Symphony 1933" (1933), no. 2 (1934), no. 3 (1938), no. 4, "Folk Song Symphony" (1940), no. 5, op.55 (1942), no. 6, op. 60, "Gettysburg Address Symphony" (1944), no. 7 (1951), no. 8, "St. Francis" (1962), no. 9 (1962), no. 10, "Abraham Lincoln Symphony" (1965), no. 11 (1967), no. 12, "Pere Marquette" (1969), no. 13 (1969), no. 14 (1974), no. 15 (1978), *Ode to Truth* (1941), *Acceleration* (1941), *Children's Hour* (1942), *Memories of a Child's Sunday* (1945), *Kentucky Spring* (1949), *Elegy and Dance* (1958), *Epilogue to Profiles in Courage: J. F. K.* (1962); 9 concertos; and many chamber and vocal pieces.

Selected Composer Bibliography

Farwell, Arthur: "Roy Harris," *The Musical Quarterly*, xviii (1932), 117.

---

[48] Harold Gleason and Walter Becker: "Roy Harris," *20th-Century American Composers*. Music Literature Outlines, series iv. Bloomington, IN: Indiana University Press, revised 1981.

Cowell, Henry: "Roy Harris," in *American Composers on American Music: A Symposium*, edited by Henry Cowell, 64. New York: Frederick Ungar Publishing, 1933 (revised, 1962).

Piston, Walter: "Roy Harris," *Modern Music*, xii (1943-5), 73.

Harris, Roy: "Folk Song: American Big Business," *Modern Music*, xviii (1940), 8.

"Harris, Roy," *Current Biography Yearbook*, i (August 1940); obituary, lx (November 1979); New York: H. W. Wilson Company.

Slonimsky, Nicholas: "Roy Harris," *The Musical Quarterly*, xxxiii (1947), 17.

Plinkiewisch, Helen E.: *A Contribution to the Understanding of the Music of Charles Ives, Roy Harris, and Aaron Copland*. Columbia University: Dissertation, 1955.

Brookhart, Charles E.: *The Choral Music of Aaron Copland, Roy Harris, and Randall Thompson*. George Peabody College for Teachers: Dissertation, 1960.

Stehman, Dan: *The Symphonies of Roy Harris: An Analysis of the Linear Materials and Related Works*. University of Southern California: Dissertation, 1973.

Gleason, Harold and Walter Becker: "Roy Harris," *Twentieth-Century American Composers*, second ed., Music Literature Outlines, series iv. Bloomington, IN: Frangiapani Press, 1981; 92.

Stehman, Dan: *Roy Harris: An American Musical Pioneer*. Boston: Twayne Publishers, 1984.

_____: "Harris, Roy," in *The New Grove Dictionary of American Music*, edited by H. Wiley Hitchcock, ii: 331-337. 4 volumes. London: Macmillan, 1986.

_____: *Roy Harris: A Bio-Bibliography*. Westport, CT: Greenwood Press, 1991.

Symphony No. 4, *Folk Song* (1940)

Duration: ca. 44 minutes

Text: traditional folk songs as listed below in "notes"

Performing Forces: *voices*: SATB choir; *orchestra*: 3 flutes, 3 oboes, 4 clarinets, 3 bassoons, 4 horns, 3 trumpets, 3 trombones, tuba, timpani, percussion (7 players - snare drum, bass drum, Indian drum, tambourine, cymbals, gong, triangle, temple blocks, wood block, marimba, vibraphone, chimes), piano, and strings.

First Performance: 25 April 1940; American Spring Festival, Rochester, NY; Eastman School of Music Choir, Eastman-Rochester Orchestra; conducted by Howard Hanson.

Edition: Symphony No. 4 is published and distributed by G. Schirmer. The piano-vocal score is for sale; orchestral materials are available for rental.

Autograph: The full score is a facsimile of the composer's manuscript.

Notes: Harris has used traditional folk songs as the basis for each movement they are as follows:

1. "The Girl I Left Behind Me"
2. Western Cowboy - "O Bury Me Not On the Prairie"
3. Interlude: Dànce Tunes for Strings and Percussion
4. Love Song - "I'm Goin' Away for to Stay a Little While"
5. Interlude (2): Dance Tunes for Full Orchestra
6. Negro Fantasy - "De Trumpet Sounds It In My Soul"
7. Finale - "When Johnnie Comes Marching Home Again"

Performance Issues: This is a very large work both in terms of duration and the number of performers, but it is written very idiomatically for all of the participants. The choral writing is either in unison or homophonic in four-part spelling of triads. A large choir is desirable because of the size of the orchestra; however, the orchestration is generally thin during the sung sections. The familiarity of the melodic material and accessibility of the writing make this an ideal work for an amateur choral society or large student ensemble. In the second and fourth movements the choral parts taken turns singing isolated melodic lines providing a good opportunity to work on unifying the sound between sections of the choir. It is also a good piece for developing internal rhythmic skills. The first movement has no tempo indication, but ca. 144 quarter notes per minute is appropriate for the original folk song. One issue which will consume rehearsal time is that Harris changes the level of division of the beat constantly. The accuracy of these changes must be maintained, since this is the feature which keeps this piece from being square and unvital. Rhythmic clarity and strictness of beat are mandatory to success although many triplets and sextuplets in the accompaniment seduce the ensemble into unwarranted rubati.

The introduction of the sixth movement is the most contrapuntally complex section for the orchestra and may be difficult to integrate. This movement also has the most complex choral writing with divisi in the women's parts and terraced entrances. With the likely exception of his Symphony No. 3, this Harris's most popular work. It contains many of his trade-mark devices including perpetually overlapping figures in the winds and extensive use of pedal point. However, there are none of the typical extended slow sections with prolonged tune spinning to provide a static tonal fabric behind slower melodic material. This work is more consistently direct than most of his other music, and therefore has excellent audience appeal. The "Negro Fantasy" utilizes a magnificent spiritual, but it is surely prudent to de-ethnicize the text. The style and content make it an ideal feature piece for a concert of Americana or of lighter works. *Choir*: medium easy; *Orchestra*: medium.

Discography: American Festival Chorus and Orchestra; conducted by Vladimir Golschmann. Released in 1960. Vanguard: VRS-1064 [LP].

Utah Chorale, Utah Symphony Orchestra; conducted by Maurice Abravanel. Recorded 6 May 1975. Angel: S-36091 [LP].

Selected Bibliography

Elwell, Herbert: "Harris's Folk Song Symphony," *Modern Music* xviii/2 (1940-41), 113.

Diether, Jack: "What the Real Roy Harris Sounds Like," *American Record Guide*, xxvii (July 1961), 866.

Hindemith, Paul (b. Hanau, 16 November 1895; d. Frankfurt, 28 December 1963).

Life: Hindemith studied composition with Arnold Mendelssohn and Bernhard Sekles. He established a reputation for his virtuosity on the viola (He premiered a number of solo works, including Walton's Viola Concerto.) and as an important chamber musician. Hindemith left Germany in 1937 following pressure from the Nazi party which forbade the performance of his works (most notably the cancellation of the premiere of *Mathis der Mahler* in 1933). He emigrated to the United States where he taught at Yale University and Tanglewood (where his students included Lukas Foss and Leonard Bernstein); he became a citizen in 1945. As the 1949-50 Norton Professor of Poetry at Harvard

University, he presented *A Composer's World*. In 1953, he moved his permanent residence to Zürich while maintaining an international career. He mastered all of the orchestral instruments and wrote very practical sonatas and concertos for all of them. His music is always masterfully crafted and practical in its orchestration.[49]

Principal Works: opera - *Cardillac*, op. 39 (1926), *Mathis der Mahler* (1933-5), *Die Harmonie der Welt* (1956-7); **ballets** - *Nobilissima Visione* (1938), *The Four Temperaments* (1940); **oratorios** - *Das Unaufhörliche* (1931), *Ite, angeli veloces* (1955); **vocal** - *Das Marienleben*, op. 27 for soprano and piano (1922-3), 12 *Madrigals* for choir (1958); **orchestral** - *Mathis der Mahler Symphony* (1934), *Symphonic Metamorphosis of Themes by Carl Maria von Weber* (1940-3), *Pittsburgh Symphony* (1958); as well as a number of significant educational books for developing musicians and composers.

Selected Composer Bibliography

Kemp, Ian: *Hindemith*. Oxford: Oxford University Press, 1970.

Monroe, Robert C.: *Compositional Techniques in the Choral Works of Stravinsky, Hindemith, Honegger, and Britten*. Northwestern University: Dissertation, 1953.

Skelton, Geoffrey: *Paul Hindemith: The Man Behind the Music*. Taplinger Publishing Company, 1978.

Kemp, Ian: "Paul Hindemith," *The New Grove Modern Masters*, 229-282. New York: W.W. Norton, 1984.

Neumeyer, David: *The Music of Paul Hindemith*. New Haven: Yale University Press, 1986.

Noss, Luther: *Paul Hindemith in the United States*. Champaign-Urbana: University of Illinois Press, 1989.

When Lilacs Last in the Dooryard Bloom'd
(1946)

Duration: ca. 65 minutes

Text: Walt Whitman's poem of the same title; it is one of four poems in *Leaves of Grass* dedicated to the memory of Abraham Lincoln;

---

[49] Ian Kemp: "Paul Hindemith," *The New Grove Modern Masters*, 229-282. New York: W.W. Norton, 1984.

the other three of which are: "O Captain! My Captain!" "Hush'd be the Camps To-day," and "This Dust Was Once the Man."[50]

Performing Forces: *voices*: mezzo-soprano and baritone soloists; SATB choir; *orchestra*: piccolo, flute, oboe, English horn, clarinet, bass clarinet, bassoon, contrabassoon, 3 horns, 2 trumpets, 2 trombones, tuba, timpani (3), percussion (3 players - snare drum, parade (tenor) drum, bass drum, cymbal, gong, triangle, glockenspiel, chimes), organ, army bugle in B^b, and strings.

First Performance: 14 May 1946; New York; Mona Paulee, George Burnson (later to be George London); Collegiate Chorale with orchestra; conducted by Robert Shaw.

Edition: *When Lilacs...* is published by B. Schott's Söhne including a critical edition prepared by Charles Jacobs which includes critical notes, nine pages of facsimile, and an excellent corrected score. It is in English and German. The German translation is by Hindemith. A standard piano-vocal score and study score are for sale; orchestral materials are available for rental. All materials are distributed by European-American Music.

Autograph: Located in the Beinecke Rare Book and Manuscript Library at the Yale University Library, New Haven, CT. It is catalogued as "Music Deposit No. 7." Sketches are held by the Hindemith-Institut, Frankfurt, Germany.

Notes: Subtitled "A Requiem for Those We Love," *When Lilacs...* was commissioned by Robert Shaw and the Collegiate Chorale in memory of Franklin D. Roosevelt and the Americans fallen in World War II. Compare this to Sessions's setting of the same text. Hindemith had previously set Whitman's texts: *Three Hymns*, op. 14 (no. 2 is "Sing on, there in the swamp"), and "Sing On," from *Nine English Songs*. Upon receiving U.S. citizenship, he presented the manuscript of the latter to the Judge presiding over his naturalization. Unlike Sessions, Hindemith

---

[50] George and Barbara Perkins and Phillip Leininger: *Benét's Reader's Encyclopedia of American Literature*. New York: Harper Collins, 1991.

divides the three sections of the poem into smaller movements as
follows:

	Prelude	- orchestra alone
I.	When lilacs last in the dooryard bloom'd	- baritone and choir
II.	Arioso, In the swamp	- mezzo-soprano
III.	March, Over the breast of spring	- baritone and choir
IV.	O western orb	- baritone and choir
V.	Arioso, Sing on, there in the swamp	- mezzo-soprano
VI.	Song, O how shall I warble	- baritone and choir
VII.	Introduction and Fugue, Lo! body and soul	- choir
VIII.	Sing on! you gray-brown bird	- mezzo-soprano
	Recitative, Now while I sat in the day	- baritone
	Hymn "For Those We Love"	- baritone
	Duet, I fled forth	- baritone and mezzo-soprano
IX.	Death Carol, Come, lovely and soothing death	- choir
X.	To the tally of my soul	- baritone and choir
XI.	Finale, Passing the visions	- all

Performance Issues: The orchestral prelude introduces the theme of
A-C-F-E over a C# pedal, which outlines the tonal centers to be
used throughout the entire piece. The coda of X. includes an
offstage bugle playing *Taps*. The orchestra is never "flashy," but
presents challenges to successful ensemble playing, including rapid
chromatic passagework in the strings, isolated and varied rhythmic
patterns with alternating single and double dotting, cross rhythms,
and sudden silences. The instrumental textures are constantly
shifting with melodic lines being passed between sections of the
orchestra. The double bass requires a low C' extension. The string
parts are quite challenging throughout, individually and in terms of
ensemble, whereas the wind parts, though not technically
demanding, require sensitive soft playing and intonation challenges
within the section. The linear construction of the choral parts is so
finely crafted, that although Hindemith's harmonic language is
challenging, they should be practically learned.   The chorus
contains some contrapuntal writing and many unaccompanied
passages. Rhythmic accuracy is of particular concern. Strong
dynamic contrasts, including sustained, soft tutti sections are

required throughout the entire work. *Soloists*: Mezzo-Soprano, range: c'-f#", tessitura: e'-c", the arioso movements are lyric and rhythmically facile; Baritone, range: B^b-f', tessitura: e-e', this role is extensive, it requires firm control of sustained singing and exploits the top of the voice. *Choir*: medium; *Orchestra*: medium difficult.

Discography: Louise Parker, George London; Schola Cantorum of New York, New York Philharmonic; conducted by Hindemith. Columbia: MS-6573 [LP], reissued on Odyssey: Y-33821 [LP]; re-released (July 1990) as CBS Masterworks (Portrait): MPK-45881 [ADD].
Burmeister, Leib; Berlin Radio Chorus and Symphony Orchestra; conducted by Koch. Recorded in 1966. Deutsche Gramophon: DG 2543 825 [LP].
Jan DeGaetani, William Stone; Atlanta Symphony and Chorus; conducted by Robert Shaw. Telarc: CD-80132 [DDD].
Brigitte Fassbaender, Dietrich Fischer-Dieskau; Vienna Symphony and State Opera Chorus; conducted by Wolfgang Sawallisch. Recorded live: 1 November 1983, in English. Orfeo: C-112851 [DDD].

Selected Bibliography

Mize, Lou Stem: *A Study of Selected Choral Settings of Walt Whitman's Poems.* Florida State University: Dissertation, 1967.
Wannamaker, J. S.: *The Musical Settings of Walt Whitman.* University of Minnesota: Dissertation, 1975.
Mussulman, John A.: *Dear People. . . Robert Shaw: A Biography*; 64-7, 77, 107. Bloomington, IN: Indiana University Press, 1979.

Holst, Gustav (b. Cheltenham, 21 September 1874; d. London, 25 May 1934).

Life: The son of a pianist, Holst learned the instrument from his father and began to compose while a student at the Cheltenham Grammar School where he was virtually self-taught. At 17, he studied counterpoint for a few months at Oxford and entered the Royal College of Music in 1893. There he studied composition with Charles Villiers Stanford. In that same year he made the acquaintance of Ralph Vaughan Williams. The two became life-long friends and regularly criticized each other's sketches. While in London, Holst guest directed the Hammersmith Socialist Choir in the home of William Morris where he was introduced to Hindu philosophy and literature. This led to his later study of Sanskrit at University College in London. He worked for a number of years as an orchestral trombonist. Holst began teaching at James Allen's Girls' School in Dulwich (1903), continuing at St. Paul's Girls' School in Hammersmith (1903-34), the Royal College of Music (1919-25), University College at Reading (1919-25), and he took over the music program at Morley College (1907-24). He remained active in the direction of amateur music ensembles and hosted annual 3-day festivals on Whitsunday in Thaxted. He led the English premieres of a number of Bach cantatas, and the first performance of Purcell's *The Fairy Queen* since 1697. He suffered from ill health most of his life, but particularly after a fall from a podium in 1923. He was ordered to spend the entire year of 1924 at rest in the country. The works which followed this hiatus are marked by a new sparseness and a keener awareness of his Hindu influences. He served as a visiting lecturer at Harvard in 1932, but fell ill the following March and had to return to England where he never truly recovered (although he was able to compose until his death). Like Vaughan Williams, Holst refused official titles of honor including knighthood. Holst's music combines the contrapuntal elegance of Byrd and Weelkes (whose revivals he championed) with the harmonic palette of Stanford and Elgar. His music is imbued with a mystical sense, but is always direct in its approach to the listener. The last decade of his work is marked by an increased presence of Eastern philosophy (compare with John Foulds).[51]

Awards: Fellowship of the Royal College of Music, the Gold Medal of the Royal Philharmonic Society (1930), and the Yale University Howland Memorial Prize for distinction in the Arts.

Principal Works: *operas* - *Savitri*, op. 25 (1908), *The Perfect Fool*, op. 39 (1920-1), *At the Boar's Head*, op. 42 (1924), *The Wandering Scholar*, op. 50 (1929-30); *orchestral* - *Beni Mora*: oriental suite in E minor, op. 29, no. 1 (1910, revised. 1912), *St. Paul's Suite*, op. 29, no. 1 (1912-3), *The Planets*, op. 32 (1914-6), *Egdon Heath*, op. 47 (1927), *A Moorside Suite* (1928), *Brook Green Suite* (1933); *band* - Suite No. 1 in Eb, op. 28a (1909), Suite No. 2 in F, op. 28b (1911), *Hammersmith*, op. 52 (1930-1); *vocal* - *The Mystic Trumpeter*, op. 18 (1904, revised 1912), *3 Choral Hymns from*

---

[51] Imogen Holst: *The Music of Gustav Holst*, third edition; and *Holst's Music Reconsidered*. 1 volume. Oxford: Oxford University Press, 1986.

the Rig Veda, op. 26 (1908-10), *The Cloud Messenger*, op. 30 (1910, revised 1912), *Dirge for 2 Veterans* (1914), *Ode to Death*, op. 28 (1919), Seven Partsongs, op. 44 (1925-6), and *Choral Fantasia*, op. 51 (1930).

Selected Composer Bibliography

Kröne, Max Thomas: *The Choral Works of Gustav Holst*. Northwestern University: Dissertation, 1940.

Boult, Sir Adrian: "Gustav Holst," *Royal College of Music Magazine*, lxx (1974), 52.

Holst, Imogen, and C. Matthews, eds.: *Gustav Holst: Collected Facsimile Edition of Autograph Manuscripts of the Published Works*. 4 volumes. London: Faber, 1974-83.

Holst, Imogen: *A Thematic Catalogue of Gustav Holst's Music*. London: Faber and Faber, 1974.

_____: *The Music of Gustav Holst*, third edition; and *Holst's Music Reconsidered*. 1 volume. Oxford: Oxford University Press, 1986.

_____: "Gustav Holst," *The New Grove Twentieth-Century English Masters*, 145-174. New York: W.W. Norton, 1986.

Short, Michael: *Gustav Holst: The Man and His Music*. Oxford: Oxford University Press, 1990.

Hymn of Jesus, op. 37 (1917)

Duration: ca. 20 minutes

Text: Holst's translation of the "dancing hymn" from *The Apocryphal Acts of St. John*

Performing Forces: voices: double SATB choir, women's SSA semi-choir; **orchestra:** 3 flutes (flute III doubling piccolo), 2 oboes, English horn, 2 clarinet, 2 bassoons, 4 horns, 2 trumpets, 3 trombones, timpani, percussion (1 player - snare drum, bass drum, tambourine, cymbals), celeste, piano, organ, and strings.

First Performance: 25 March 1920; Queen's Hall, London; Royal Philharmonic Society; conducted by the composer.

Edition: *The Hymn of Jesus* is published by Stainer and Bell and distributed by Galaxy. The piano-vocal and study scores are for sale; orchestral materials are available for rental.

Autograph: An incomplete autograph full score is in the British Museum (Add. MS 57885). The original sketch (some words in another hand) is in the Edwin Evans collection of the Central Music Library, Westminster, London. There is an arrangement for strings, piano, and organ made by Jane Joseph (preparer of the piano-vocal edition), which has many details in the composer's hand, in the British Museum (Add. MS 57886).[52]

Notes: This work is dedicated to Ralph Vaughan William. It was immediately heralded as a masterpiece and secured Holst's unsought fame. In it, Holst quotes the plainchants "Pange lingua" and "Vexilla regis." There is a footnote on the title-page which states:

> I wish to express my thanks to Mr. G.[eorge] R. S. Mead, Mr. Clifford Bax, and Miss Jane Joseph [Holst's former pupil] for kindly helping me to make my version of the words of this Hymn.

Here, the composer also states:

> The two choruses should be of fairly equal strength, and if possible, should be well separated. The semi-chorus should be placed above them and well apart. If too far from the orchestra, it can be supported by a soft harmonium. . . The following instruments may be dispensed with: flute III, oboe II, bassoon II, horns III and IV, all 3 trombones, percussion celeste and organ. With performances by small choirs it may be found preferable to omit the trombones. In any case, either all three should be used or none. When there is no celesta, the part may be played on the piano, by using two pianists, excepting in one place in the Prelude where it must be omitted. When an orchestra is not available, the piano accompaniment will be greatly improved by the addition of the special *ad lib.* string parts (These are quite different from the orchestral string parts and must not be confused with the latter.). The organ is to be used whenever possible.

---

[52] Imogen Holst: *A Thematic Catalogue of Gustav Holst's Music.* London: Faber and Faber, 1974.

Performance Issues: The choir is given chant which occurs either over sustained harmonies in the orchestra or independently from ostinato figures in the accompaniment which are to be repeated until the chant is ended. The Prelude is in Latin' using the traditional "Vexilla regis" and "Pange lingua" texts. The subsequent Hymn is in English. There are passages of terraced imitation, sung and spoken, which create the effect of glossolalia. The choral writing is tonal/modal and emphasizes triadic harmonies. Preparation of the vocal material should present few pitch or rhythm problems, but emphasis will need to be placed upon stylistic presentation of the plainchant portions and a freedom from the barline in many of the traditionally notated sections. The singers must strive for a powerful symphonic sound and careful matching of timbre between the choirs. The frequent phrase exchanges between the two choirs will be most effective when these choirs are well distanced from each other. The trombones and English horn present the plainsong material at the opening of the piece. The composer notes that these players should seek the guidance of a singer experienced in such work to learn the proper nuances indigenous to chant. Holst has also indicated the slide positions for the trombones stating that these should eliminate "smears" between pitches and that the horns should be substituted for this passage if the trombonists cannot execute it cleanly. There are cued parts throughout the score to allow for the absence of the instruments listed as optional in "notes" above. The complete orchestration is dense and powerful requiring a full string section and large choirs. The sonority of the complete ensemble is so dramatic that a large ensemble is far preferable to the optional reduced forces. The most significant performance problem is the integration of the large ensemble and coordination of music from four different areas within the performance space. *Choir*: medium; *Orchestra*: medium difficult.

Discography: BBC Symphony and Chorus; conducted by Sir Adrian Boult. Released in 1962. London: CM 9324 [LP mono]. Re-released as London: 421381-2 LM2 [ADD].

London Symphony Orchestra and Chorus; conducted by Richard Hickox. Recorded in May 1991. Chandos: CHAN 8901 [DDD].

Selected Bibliography

Boyer, Daniel Royce: *Gustav Holst's* "The Hymn of Jesus." University
of Texas at Austin, 1968.
_____:"Holst's *The Hymn of Jesus*: An Investigation into
Mysticism in Music," *The Music Review*, xxxvi (1975), 272.

First Choral Symphony, op. 41 (1923-24)

Duration: ca. 50-53 minutes

Text: John Keats from *Endymion* and *Ode to Apollo*. Two passages
are from Francis Beaumont and John Fletcher.

Performing Forces: *voices*: soprano soloist; SATB choir;
orchestra: 3 flutes (flute III doubling piccolo), 2 oboes, English
horn, 2 clarinets, bass clarinet, 2 bassoons, contrabassoon, 4
horns, 3 trumpets, 3 trombones, tuba, timpani, percussion (2
players - bass drum, tambourine, cymbals, gong, triangle, sleigh
bells, xylophone, glockenspiel), celeste, harp, organ (ad lib.), and
strings.

First Performance: 7 October 1925; Town Hall, Leeds; Dorothy
Silk; Leeds Festival Chorus, London Symphony Orchestra;
conducted by Albert Coates.

Edition: *First Choral Symphony* is published by Novello and
distributed by Theodore Presser Company. The piano-vocal and
study scores are for sale; orchestral materials are for rental.

Autograph: The full score is in the Parry Room Library of the Royal
College of Music, London (MS 4237); sketches are in the British
Library (Add. MS 47830); a partially autograph vocal score is in
the British Museum (Add. MS 57893); and a partially autograph
arrangement of the Scherzo for two pianos is in the Parry Room
Library (MS 4562).[53]

---

[53] Imogen Holst: *A Thematic Catalogue of Gustav Holst's Music.*
London: Faber and Faber, 1974.

Notes: This work was commissioned for the Leeds Festival. It is Holst's longest choral work setting a variety of Keats's poems which were selected and arranged by the composer. The title, *First Choral·Symphony*, is due to Holst's intent to compose a "Second Choral Symphony" on texts of Meredith; however, this project was never completed. The piece is arranged as follows:

	Prelude: Invocation to Pan	"O Thou, whose mighty palace roof"
I.	Song and Bacchanal	"Beneath my palm trees"
II.	Ode on a Grecian Urn	"Thou still unravish'd bride of quietness"
III.	Scherzo: Fancy	"Ever let the Fancy roam"
	Folly's Song	"When wedding fiddles are a-playing"
IV.	Finale	"Spirit here that reignest"

Each of the movements can be performed separately: the Scherzo may be with or without choir, and the first movement may be done with or without the prelude. The texts: "Spirit here that reignest" and "Bards of Passion and Mirth" are from blank pages in the works of Beaumont and Fletcher. Holst sent a letter to W. G. Whittaker (19 March 1926) saying: "I think the work as a whole is the best thing I have written and, like you, I prefer the two middle movements."

Performance Issues: Much of the choral writing is chant-like and the vocal rhythms imitate those of speech. Most of it is homophonic, in paired doubling, or close imitation. The choir sings throughout the work. Dissonances are approached logically and notated in an accessible manner. The rapid text declamation in "Folly's Song" in the third movement presents the choir's greatest challenge. A large choir is recommended and the number of strings should be at the very least 8 first violins, 7 second violins, 6 violas, 5 cellos, and 3 double basses. One of the basses should have 5 strings or an extension. The score calls for divisi in all strings, and a pedal B from one of the double basses. There are unmeasured string solos and many sections which are metrically ambiguous contrasted with odd-legged rhythmic ostinati, particularly 7/8. There is a freely repeated measure over an unmeasured solo immediately before #14. The density of orchestration is highly varied with rapid shifts between sparse textures and tutti writing. There are few distinctively difficult instrumental passages; the writing is practical and direct while maintaining a sense of mysticism. The third movement deserves special attention because of its speed. *Soloist*: Soprano, range: c#'- b", tessitura: f'- e", the role is substantial requiring endurance, a control of long lines, and an awareness of the style of Anglican chant. This is an unusual work in terms of its musical variety, and one which would be accessible to most large choral societies. *Choir*: medium; *Orchestra*: medium.

Discography: Felicity Palmer, soprano; London Philharmonic Choir (prepared by John Alldis), London Philharmonic Orchestra; conducted by Sir Adrian Boult. Recorded in 1974, re-released in 1988. EMI: CDC 7 49638 2 [ADD].

Selected Bibliography

[review of the London premiere], *The Musical Times* (1 December).

Holst, Imogen, and C. Matthews, editors: *Gustav Holst: Collected Facsimile Edition of Autograph Manuscripts of the Published Works*, iv. 4 volumes. London: Faber, 1983.

Hovhaness, Alan (b. Somerville, MA, 8 March 1911).

Life: Hovhaness began composing as a child. He studied with Frederick Converse at the New England Conservatory and Bohuslav Martinu at Tanglewood (1943). During the 1950s, Hovhaness enjoyed considerable success and traveled extensively. In 1977, he was elected to the American Institute of Arts and Letters. He is one of a very few American composers to devote his entire career solely to composition. At Tanglewood, his works were sharply criticized by Aaron Copland and Leonard Bernstein; he destroyed many works, and re-evaluated his compositional style, which had been a conservative combination of sixteenth-century counterpoint and eighteenth-century harmonic practice. He began to incorporate Armenian (the nationality of his father) folk music and elements of mysticism into his music. For the next thirty years, he adopted a gamut of non-Western musical devices. Since the early 1970s, Hovhaness has returned to a more consistently Western style. These later works are lush, harmonically static, full of ostinati, and generally on a larger scale than his previous music. Hovhaness's music is contrapuntally rich, while avoiding devices of development and traditional formal structures. A sense of a sequential musical unwinding is often achieved via the use of Indian rhythmic *talas*. Most of his music is instrumental with mystical, religious themes.

Principal Works: Hovhaness is one of the most prolific of modern composers. Among his 400+ works are: 11 operas, 4 ballets, 56 symphonies, 12 concerti for various instruments, and hundreds of other pieces.[54]

Selected Composer Bibliography

Daniel, Oliver: "Alan Hovhaness," *American Composers' Alliance*, ii/3 (1952), 3.

Wade, James: "Alan Hovhaness: Pilgrimage to the Orient," *Musical America* (September 1963), 56.

"Hovhaness, Alan," *Current Biography Yearbook*, xxvi (April 1965); New York: H. W. Wilson Company.

Rosner, Albert: *An Analytical Survey of the Music of Alan Hovhaness.* University of Buffalo: Dissertation, 1972.

Cox, Dennis Keith: *Aspects of the Compositional Styles of Three Selected Twentieth-Century American Composers of Choral Music: Alan Hovhaness, Ron Nelson, and Daniel Pinkham.* University of Missouri at Kansas City: Dissertation, 1978

_____: "Hovhaness, Alan," in *The New Grove Dictionary of American Music*, edited by H. Wiley Hitchcock, ii: 431-4. 4 volumes. London: Macmillan, 1986.

Easter Cantata, no. 3 from Choral Triptych, op. 100 (1953)

Duration: ca. 16 minutes

Text: traditional texts adapted by the composer

Performing Forces: *voices*: soprano soloist; SATB choir; *orchestra*: 2 oboes, 2 horns, 3 trumpets, percussion (1 player - tam tam), harp, celeste, and strings.

---

[54] Albert Rosner: "Hovhaness, Alan," in *The New Grove Dictionary of American Music*, edited by H. Wiley Hitchcock, ii: 431-4. 4 volumes. London: Macmillan, 1986.

First Performance: 11 May 1955; Boston, MA; Boston University Chorus; conducted by the composer.

Edition: *Easter Cantata* is published by American Music Publishers and distributed by G. Schirmer. The piano-vocal score and full score may be purchased; orchestral materials are available by rental.

Autograph: The full score is a facsimile of the composer's manuscript.

Notes: This is the third work of Choral Triptych; the other pieces are *Ave Maria* and *The Beatitudes.* The composer has arranged *Easter Cantata* into five parts:

     I. Prelude
     II. O Lord
     III. Mourn, Mourn Ye Saints
     IV. The Lord Now is Risen
     V. Jesus Christ is Risen Today

Performance Issues: The score includes an errata list which must be consulted. It should be acquired if not sent with the score. This work is almost exclusively diatonic and is approachable by virtually any amateur choir. The choral part represents only about 120 measures of the entire piece. The choral writing is mostly in a homophonic, block-chord style. Divisi are called for in all parts, but often there are only six different pitches with the alto I and soprano II doubling each other, and likewise bass I and tenor II. This is a simple and not very sophisticated work which would be best presented in a church service rather than a concert. The orchestra parts are not demanding although special attention will be required to guarantee proper intonation of consecutive major and minor seconds in the strings in the final movement where crossing scalar passages create varied dissonances. In a concert situation it is advised to include the other works of op. 100. Soloist: soprano - range: e'- a", tessitura: b'- g", this is a very easy part. Almost no notes occur below the indicated tessitura. The part is slow and sustained and made up of diatonic scalar passages. *Choir:* easy; *Orchestra:* medium easy.

Discography: "Ave Maria" and "Easter Cantata" - Benita Valente; Bayerischer Rundfunk Singers; Bamberg Symphony; conducted by Alfredo Antonini. Released in 1968. CRI: CRI-221 [LP].

Selected Bibliography

Rogers, Harold: [review of the premiere], *Christian Science Monitor* (12 May 1955).

Magnificat, op. 157 (1958)

Duration: ca. 28 minutes

Text: Luke, 1: 46-55 in the Latin of the Vulgate Bible or in English adaptation by Hugh Ross

Performing Forces: *voices*: soprano, alto, tenor, and bass soloists; SATB choir; *orchestra*: 2 oboes, 2 horns, 2 trumpets, trombone, percussion (1 player - tam-tam, bell in C), harp, and strings.

First Performance: 26 January 1959, Wichita Falls, TX; Charlyn Balabanis, Juanita Teal, David Dodds, David Beckwitt; Midwestern University Choir (prepared by William V. Boland),Wichita Falls Symphony; conducted by Erno Daniel.

Edition: *Magnificat* is published and distributed by C. F. Peters. The piano-vocal score (P6107) is for sale; orchestral materials are available for rental.

Autograph: The full score is a facsimile of the composer's manuscript.

Notes: The composer has included the following comments in the full score:

> The *Magnificat* for four solo voices,—soprano, alto, tenor, and bass—chorus and orchestra, Opus 157, was composed in 1958. It was commissioned by the Koussevitsky Foundation in the Library of Congress and is dedicated to the memory of Serge and Natalie Koussevitsky.
>
> The music opens with a *Celestial Fanfare*, an introduction beginning with a murmuring passage in the basses which rises to a climax and recedes again. The

brass solo instruments—trombone, horn, and trumpet—
sound a long melodic line of religious mood.

No. 2 *Magnificat* is for chorus. The organum for all
voices leads to a brief fugato, ending again in an
organum.

No. 3 *Et exsultavit* is a tenor solo accompanied by a
murmuring pizzicato passage in the violas. The mode
alternates between two forms of the scale—D, C#, B^b, A,
G or D, C, B, A, G. An accompaniment of mysterious
sounds in rhythmic cycles is heard.

No. 4 *Quia respexit* is a soprano solo leading to a
women' chorus in three parts (No. 5 *Omnes generationes*).
The chorus is accompanied by rhythmless murmuring in
the lower strings and harp.

No. 6 *Quia fecit mihi magna* is for bass solo and
chorus, accompanied by free rhythm in the basses. A
brief fugato in the chorus leads to a wild and stormy
rhythmless passage in the strings which rises to a
thunderous climax and recedes to a pianissimo.

No. 7 *Et misericordia* for soprano solo. Violas and
cellos hold a four-note cluster throughout. The oboes
play a rapid melody which is taken up by the soprano
voice.

No. 8 *Fecit potentiam* for alto solo. Based on the
meter 3/4 plus 4/4 plus 3/4. A solemn trombone solo
sounds the prelude and postlude.

No. 9 *Esurientes implevit bonis* for tenor solo and
men's chorus. A free-rhythm passage in the strings from
fortissimo to pianissimo leads to the held A in the men's
chorus. In Byzantine style the tenor sings a florid melody
over the held A. The end is a free rhythmless passage in
cellos and basses.

No. 10 *Suscepit Israel*, for four-part women's chorus.
Oboe, strings, and harp accompany the voices.

No. 11 *Sicut locutius est.* Bass solo and chorus. An introduction for oboes and horns leads to a free-rhythm passage in the strings. The chorus enters in free rhythm, every voice chanting in its own time, like the superstitious murmuring of a great crowd coming from the distance, rising like a wave of sound and receding again into the distance. A similar passage in the lower strings becomes a background to the brass solo. Later, oboes and horns lead to a similar rhythmless passage in the violins. Again the murmuring chorus rises to a fortissimo climax in free rhythm and diminishes to pianissimo. This is unmeasured music.

No. 12 *Gloria Patri.* An introduction for trombone solo accompanied by murmuring basses leads to a rhythmless climax in the strings. *Gloria* is sounded by the sopranos and then the entire chorus. A heroic melody in the style of a noble galliard is sounded by the first and second trumpets and is taken up later by chorus. The music builds to a final climax.

I have tried to suggest the mystery, inspiration, and mysticism of early Christianity in this work.

The "Senza Misura" passages are free rhythm rapid collision passages in strings which cannot be performed by one player on the piano. The pianist must try to create a sound of confusion, mystery, sometimes rising to a thunderous climax.

Performance Issues: For a description of the performance techniques used in this piece, see "notes" above. The "senza misura" passages are unmeasured ostinati. The vocal writing is modal and scalar with regular harmonic support in the accompaniment. The orchestral parts are very accessible, with the coordination of measured and unmeasured music presenting the only significant challenge to the ensemble. There are divisi in all of the choral parts. The strings also divide and there are solos for the principal players of each string section. A strong double bass section with good solo abilities is required. *Soloists*: soprano, range: d'-a", tessitura: g'-f"; alto, range: g-c", tessitura: c'-a'; tenor, range: f-g', tessitura: g-d'; bass, range: A-d', tessitura: f-c'; all of the solos are fairly short and slow requiring control of long lyric phrases. Members of the choir should be considered for these solos. This work is attractive and quite accessible to a choir of limited experience while offering them contact with a number of modern compositional devices. The orchestra parts are within the reach of an average college or community orchestra, but some extra time might be needed to establish the sense of style demanded by a work of such temporal freedom. The premiere featured a 65-member college choir, which seems to be an appropriate size considering the orchestration. *Choir*: medium easy; *Orchestra*: medium easy.

Discography: Audrey Nossman, Elizabeth Johnson, Thomas East, Richard Dales; University of Louisville Chorus, Louisville Orchestra; conducted by Robert Whitney. Released in 1961. Louisville Orchestra First Edition Records: LOU-61-4 [LP]; re-released on Poseidon: 1018.

Selected Bibliography

[review of the premiere], *Wichita Falls Times* (27 January 1959).

Underwood, W. L.: [review of the premiere], *Wichita Falls Record News* (27 January 1959).

Carapetyan, Caro M.: [review of the premiere], *Musical Courier* (February 1959).

Sabin, Robert: "Hovhaness Writes Unusual Magnificat," *Musical America* (May 1959), 26.

Kastendieck, Miles: "Magnificat Bow is Magnificent," *New York Journal-American* (27 January 1964).

Dailey, William A.: *Techniques of Composition Used in Contemporary Works for Chorus and Orchestra on Religious Texts—as Important Representative Works of the Period from 1952 through 1962. The Following Works will be Considered: "Canticum Sacrum"—Stravinsky, "Prayers of Kierkegaard"—Barber, "Magnificat"—Hovhaness.* Catholic University of America: Dissertation, 1965.

Cantata: Praise the Lord with Psaltery, op. 222 (1968)

Duration: ca. 21 minutes

Text: Psalms 33: 2-3, 146: 1-2, and 150: 3 and 6

Performing Forces: *voices*: SATB choir; *orchestra*: 3 flutes, 2 oboes, 2 clarinets, bass clarinet, 2 bassoons, contrabassoon, 4 or 5 horns, 3 trumpets, 3 trombones, tuba, percussion (tam-tam [as large as possible], chimes), harp, celeste, and strings.

First Performance: unable to determine

Edition: *Praise the Lord with Psaltery* is published and distributed by C. F. Peters (P 66194). The piano-vocal score is for sale; orchestral materials are available by rental.

Autograph: The full score is a facsimile of the composer's manuscript.

Performance Issues: The choral writing is generally polyphonic, while occasionally introducing choral unisons and paired doublings. The choir divides into eight parts. In the score, Hovhaness asks for a large string section. There are four-part divisi in all of the string parts. This is a fairly diatonic work with thick modally related triads moving between the strings. There are very simple polymetric instances in which measured ostinati repeat at a rate unequal to the length of the bar. There are a number of unmeasured ostinati which are to be repeated freely within sustained sections. The scoring for horns is generally in unison and never divides into more than four parts. The freely repeated figures create a spectacular effect very similar to those in Hovhaness's *Magnificat*. The orchestra parts are well within the grasp of moderately experience college student or a skilled youth orchestra. The greatest limitations are the frequent 20-part string writing and facile passagework for the double basses. The choral writing is intelligent, sophisticated, and a good training piece for introducing twentieth-century techniques to developing choirs. *Choir*: medium easy; *Orchestra*: medium easy.

Discography: As of January 1993, no commercial recording has been made available.

Howells, Herbert (b. Lydney, Gloucestershire, 17 October 1892; d. Oxford, 24 February 1983).

Life: Howells decided upon a career in composition at an early age beginning his studies with Herbert Brewer at the Gloucester Cathedral (1910-12) and then entering the Royal College of Music on an open scholarship. There his teachers included Charles Villiers Stanford (composition) and Charles Wood (counterpoint). After a nearly fatal illness, Howells joined the composition faculty of the RCM in 1920, remaining there until 1972. From 1936 to 1962, he served as director of music at St. Paul's Girls' School, Hammersmith (succeeding Holst). He was also made the King Edward VII Professor of Music at London University in 1950. His music in the modal and aurally mystical style of his associates, Holst and Vaughan Williams. However, his harmonic language is more expansive and his counterpoint and metrical usage are more complex than that of his peers. Like Vaughan Williams, Howells was a professed agnostic. He stated that his many church compositions were "inspired by the buildings and people associated with the musical establishments for which they were composed."[55]

Awards: Collard Life Fellow (Worshipful Company of Musicians), Carnegie Award (1916 for the Piano Quartet), Cobbett Prize (1918 for Phantasy String Quartet), Commander, Order of the British Empire (1953), and Companion of Honour (1972).

Principal Works: *orchestral* - Piano Concerto, No. 1 (1913), Pastoral Rhapsody (1923), Piano Concerto, No. 2 (1924), Concerto for Strings (1939), Suite for Strings (1944), Music for a Prince (1949); *band* - Pageantry (1934), *Triptych* (1960); *choral* - 3 Carol Anthems (1918-20), *A Kent Yeoman's Wooing Song* (1933), *Requiem* (1936), 4 Anthems (1941), *Collegium regale* canticles (1944), Gloucester canticles (1946), *Missa sabrinensis* (1954), St. Paul's canticles (1954), *An English Mass* (1956), *Collegium Sancti Johannis Cantabrigiense* canticles (1958), *A Hymn for St. Cecilia* (1961), *Stabat Mater* (1963), *Take him, earth, for cherishing* (Motet on the Death of President Kennedy, 1964), *The Coventry Mass* (1968), Winchester canticles (1968), *The Fear of the Lord* (1976); many songs, organ, and chamber works.

Selected Composer Bibliography

Finzi, Gerald: "Herbert Howells," *The Musical Times*, xcv (1954), 180.

---

[55] as quoted in Hugh Ottaway: "Howells, Herbert (Norman)," in *The New Grove Dictionary of Music and Musicians*, edited by Stanley Sadie, viii: 756-57. 20 volumes. London: Macmillan, 1980.

Ottaway, Hugh: "Herbert Howells and the English Revival," *The Musical Times*, cliii (1967), 897.

Hodgson, Peter John: *The Music of Herbert Howells*. University of Colorado: Dissertation, 1970.

Palmer, Christopher: "Herbert Howells at 80: a Retrospect," *The Musical Times*, cxiii (1972), 967.

_____: *Herbert Howells: A Study*. London: Novello, 1978.

Hymnus Paradisi (1938)

Duration: ca. 45-48 minutes

Text: Requiem Mass, Psalms 23 and 121, Burial Service from the Book of Common Prayer, Salisbury Diurnal as translated by George Herbert Palmer.

Performing Forces: *voices*: soprano and tenor soloists, double SATB choir; *orchestra*: 2 flutes (optional flute III doubling piccolo), 2 oboes (optional oboe III doubling English horn), 2 clarinets (optional clarinet III doubling bass clarinet), 2 bassoons (optional bassoon III doubling contrabassoon), 4 horns, 3 trumpets, 3 trombones, tuba, timpani, percussion (2 players - bass drum, cymbals), Piano and Celeste (optional with one player for both), organ, harp, and strings.

First Performance: September 1950; Gloucester Three Choirs Festival; conducted by the composer.

Edition: *Hymnus Paradisi* is published by Novello and distributed by Theodore Presser Company. The piano-vocal is for sale; orchestral materials are available for rent.

Autograph: The full score is a facsimile of the composer's manuscript.

Notes: *Hymnus Paradisi* and Howells's *Requiem* (1936, for 8-part *a cappella* Choir) were composed as a cathartic reaction to the death of the composer's son, Michael Kendrick Howells. Many portions of the *Requiem* have been incorporated into the later work and it should be consulted in preparation for performance. The composer has arranged a variety of Latin and English liturgical and biblical texts in the following outline:

I   Preludio (orchestra alone)
II   Requiem aeternam (Requiem Mass)
III The Lord Is My Shepherd (Psalm 23)
IV   Sanctus (Mass)
     I Will Lift Up Mine Eyes (Psalm 121)
V   I Heard a Voice from Heaven
     (Burial Service - Book of Common Prayer)
VI   Holy Is the True Light (Salisbury Diurnal)
     Requiem aeternam

Of the work's history the composer states:

> The requiem I call *Hymnus Paradisi,* for two solo
> voices, chorus, and orchestra, although first performed in
> 1950, was actually called into being much earlier. The
> sudden loss in 1935 of an only son, a loss essentially
> profound and, in its very nature, beyond argument, might
> naturally impel a composer, after a time, to seek release
> and consolation in language and terms most personal to
> him. Music may well have power beyond any other
> medium to offer that release and comfort. It did so in my
> case, and became a personal, private document. For text, I
> sought immemorial prose; but I used only two sentences
> from the Latin Requiem Mass, at the beginning and the
> end, knowing that one of them—"et lux perpetua luceat
> eis"—would govern the work—especially that one word
> "lux," "light." Light indeed touches all but one of the six
> movements. "Blessed are the dead" alone stands outside—
> and yet is inside of—that same light. Even the gravest
> verse of the 23rd Psalm reflects it: and the movement in
> which I combine the "Sanctus" and the words of the 121st
> Psalm—"I will lift up mine unto the hills"—blazes with
> it. For an ending I had to summon, if I could, an even
> more intense degree of the work's pervasive radiance. I
> searched a long time for a verbal text that would serve my
> purpose; and for a long time I was baffled. Then my
> friend Sir Thomas Armstrong found what I had been
> looking for. Gratefully I still read again the letter in
> which Sir Thomas, in his beautiful handwriting, wrote
> out the text of "Holy is the true light," found in the
> Salisbury Diurnal and again at the end of Robert Bridges's
> *The Spirit of Man.*

> *Hymnus Paradisi* was finished in 1938. For 12 years it remained what I had always wished it to be—a personal, almost secret document. But in 1950 Ralph Vaughan Williams asked to see the work, and he insisted on my releasing it; and in September 1950 I conducted the first performance at the Three Choirs Festival in Gloucester.
> 56

Performance Issues: This is a spectacular and most difficult score. The choir, orchestra, and solo parts are all challenging. The work is thoroughly contrapuntal with an aggressive independence of parts. This independence is so profound that the performers are provided with few points of aural reference in performance. The effect however, is magnificent; and the occasional tutti sections become striking events. A large double choir is required in the second movement, which should be divided left and right. There are semi-choir sections for various configurations throughout the piece, most notably a four-part women's choir in the fourth movement. There are a number of *a cappella* passages, the more complex of which are provided with optional string doublings. Beyond the issue of dense textures and polyphony, the orchestra parts are not individually difficult with the exception of the harp and strings. The harp part has many rapid ostinato figures with some awkward pedal changes. These parts are fortunately more coloristic than functional, but nonetheless may present some trouble in rhythmic integration. The string parts are rhythmically complicated and much of the first violin part is exceptionally high. A large string section is required and there are divisi in all string parts. There are important cello solos throughout. The final two movements will require the most preparation of the total ensemble. For the choir the second and fourth movements will present the greatest problems for pitch learning. Each line is melodically conceived, but the resulting harmonic fabric is very dense,

---

56 as quoted in Christopher Palmer: Notes for Herbert Howells's *Hymnus Paradisi.* Performed by Heather Harper, Robert Tear; The Bach Choir, Choir of King's College, and New Philharmonia Orchestra; conducted by Sir David Willcocks. EMI CDM 7 63372 2, 1990.

with four to eight parts exercising rhythmic and text independence. *Soloists*: Soprano, range: d'-a", tessitura: b'-g"; Tenor, range: d-a', tessitura: g-g'; both roles demand a voice which can carry over the entire ensemble. The solo writing is high, legato, and sustained. This is a magnificent and unusually beautiful work which will require significant rehearsal time, a professional-level orchestra and an experienced choir. *Choir*: difficult; *Orchestra*: difficult.

Discography: Heather Harper, Robert Tear; The Bach Choir, Choir of King's College, New Philharmonia Orchestra; conducted by Sir David Willcocks. Recorded in 1970. EMI: CDM 7 63372 2 [ADD].

Julie Kennard, John Mark Ainsley; Royal Liverpool Philharmonic Orchestra and Choir; conducted by Vernon Handley. Hyperion: CDA 66488 [DDD].

Judith Siirila, Daniel Plaster; Estonian National Symphony Orchestra, Pacific Chorale; conducted by John Alexander. Bay Cities: BCD 1035 [DDD].

Selected Bibliography

Jacques, Reginald: "Howells's *Hymnus Paradisi*," *Music and Letters*, xxxi (1952), 193.

Foreman, Lewis: *From Parry to Britten: British Music in Letters 1900-1945*, 302. Portland, OR: Amadeus Press, 1987.

Kay, Ulysses Simpson (b. Tucson, AZ, 7 January 1917).

Life: Kay graduated from the University of Arizona, and received an MA in composition from the Eastman School. He did further study at Tanglewood and Yale with Paul Hindemith. Following service in the Second World War, Kay continued his studies at Columbia University. He served as a consultant for BMI and as a musical envoy for the US State Department travelling to England, France, Italy, Yugoslavia, and the USSR. He joined the faculty of Lehman College, CUNY, in 1968, and was made Distinguished Professor of Music in 1972. His compositions are neoclassical and melodic, displaying elegant craftsmanship.[57]

---

[57] Virgil Thomson: *American Music Since 1910*, 155. New York: Holt, Rinehart, and Winston, 1971.

Principal Works: *opera - The Boor* (1955), *The Juggler of Our Lady* (1956), *The Capitoline Venus* (1971), *Jubilee* (1976), *Frederick Douglass* (1983); *orchestral - Brief Elegy* (1946), *Fantasy Variations* (1963), *Umbrian Scene* (1963), *Markings* (1966), *Scherzi musicali* (1968), *Southern Harmony* (1975), *Chariots: Orchestral Rhapsody* (1979); *choral - Phoebus Arise* (1959), *Inscriptions from Whitman* (1963), and *Stephen Crane Set* (1967).

Selected Composer Bibliography

Slonimsky, Nicholas: "Ulysses Kay," *American Composers' Alliance Bulletin*, vii/1 (1957), 3.

Hadley, Richard Thomas: *The Published Choral Music of Ulysses Simpson Kay—1943 to 1968.* University of Iowa: Dissertation, 1972

Baker, David N., Lida M. Belt, and Herman C. Hudson, editors: *The Black Composer Speaks*, 139-171. Metuchen, NJ: Scarecrow Press, 1978.

James, Shaylor Lorenza: *Contribution of Four Selected Twentieth-Century Afro-American Classical Composers: William Grant Still, Howard Swanson, Ulysses Kay, and Olly Wilson.* Florida State University: Dissertation, 1988.

Inscriptions from Whitman (1963)

Duration: ca. 25 minutes

Text: Walt Whitman's "O Swift Wind," "On the Beach at Night," "I Hear America Singing," and "Poets to Come."

Performing Forces: *voices*: SATB choir; *orchestra*: 2 flutes, 2 oboes, 2 clarinets, 2 bassoons, 4 horns, 3 trumpets, 3 trombones, tuba, timpani, percussion, harp, and strings.

First Performance: 1964, Women's Chorus of Douglass College, New Jersey Oratorio Society Male Chorus of Atlantic City, New Jersey Symphony Orchestra; conducted by Kenneth Schermerhorn.

Edition: *Inscriptions from Whitman* is published by Pembroke Music and distributed by Carl Fischer. The piano-vocal scores may be purchased; orchestral materials are available by rental.

Autograph: The full score is a facsimile of the composer's manuscript.

Notes: This work was commissioned by the New Jersey Symphony and the New Jersey State Tercentenary Commission to commemorate the New Jersey Tercentenary. The score is in two movements.

Performance Issues: This is a serial work, but Kay is very successful in his treatment of the vocal parts to facilitate their accessibility. He is not strict with his use of serial technique, allowing for deviations including motivic repetition and retrogression, and some use of incomplete statements of the row. Through the use of choral unisons, paired doublings, motivic imitation and melodic inversion, he provides the singers numerous patterns and devices which should prove useful in learning of their parts. However, this is still a very challenging work to sing. It requires an experienced choir and substantial rehearsal time. Choral pitches are generally supported by the harmony of the accompaniment, but these accompanimental pitches are not aurally conspicuous. The rhythms are straightforward and often imitative of dance music of the eighteenth century. The orchestral material is not very technically demanding, but the complexity of the pitch language demands an ensemble of reasonable musical sophistication. For no logical reason, both movements use a combination of rehearsal letters and numbers. A medium-sized choir will effectively balance the instrumental forces, and may be better suited to the melodic subtleties of the score than a large choir. This is a difficult and dissonant score, which is melodically elegant and consistently sensitive to the text. *Choir*: medium difficult; *Orchestra*: medium difficult.

Discography: As of January 1993, no commercial recording has been made available.

Selected Bibliography

Herrema, R.: "The Choral Works of Ulysses Kay," *Choral Journal*, xi/4 (December 1970), 5.
Hadley, Richard Thomas: *The Published Choral Works of Ulysses Kay*. University of Iowa: Dissertation, 1972.

Lambert, Constant (b. London, 23 August 1905 - d. London, 21 August 1951).

Life: Lambert was educated at Christ's Hospital (1915-22) and the Royal College of Music (1922-26). At the latter, his teachers included Ralph Vaughan Williams and Reginald Morris. In 1926, his *Romeo and Juliet* was the first work of a British composer to be performed on a commission from Diaghilev and the Ballet Russe. The focus of his career became and remained conducting. He conducted the Camargo Society (1930-31), Vic-Wells Ballet (1931-47, artistic director 1949-51). He also led performances of Puccini and Purcell at Sadler's Wells and Covent Garden. He made over fifty radio broadcasts, championing the works of Liszt, Weill, Chabrier, Purcell, Satie, and Walton. As a cunning writer, Lambert contributed a regular column to the *Nation* and *Athenaeum* and the *Sunday Referee*. He also authored a book on music, *Music Ho! A Study of Music in Decline* (1934). Lambert's music is distinguished by a unique blend of jazz and concert styles, which he molds into elegant forms with strong forward momentum. The most prominent influences in his music are Frederick Delius and Duke Ellington.[58]

Principal Works: *ballets* - Romeo and Juliet (1924-25), *Pomona* (1926), *Tiresias* (1937); *orchestral* - The Bird Actors (1925), *Champêtre* (1926), *Elegiac Blues* (1927), *Music for Orchestra* (1927), Piano Concerto (1930-31), *Aubade héroïque* (1942); *choral* - Dirge from Cymbeline (1940); many chamber works and arrangements.

Selected Composer Bibliography

Foss, Hugh: "Constant Lambert," *The Musical Times*, xcii (1951), 449.

Hansler, George E.: *Stylistic Characteristics and Trends in the Choral Music of Five Twentieth-Century Composers: A Study of the Choral Works of Benjamin Britten, Gerald Finzi, Constant Lambert, Michael Tippett, and William Walton*. New York University: Dissertation, 1957.

Palmer, Christopher: "Constant Lambert — a Postscript," *Music and Letters*, lii (1971), 173.

---

58 Ronald Crichton: "Lambert, Constant," in *The New Grove Dictionary of Music and Musicians*, edited by Stanley Sadie, ix: 394-96. 20 volumes. London: Macmillan, 1980.

Shead, Richard: *Constant Lambert*. London: Simon Publications of Butterworth Press, 1973.

Crichton, Ronald: "Lambert, Constant," in *The New Grove Dictionary of Music and Musicians*, edited by Stanley Sadie, ix: 394-96. 20 volumes. London: Macmillan, 1980.

The Rio Grande (1927)

Duration: ca. 14-16 minutes

Text: Sachereverell Sitwell from *The Thirteenth Caesar and Other Poems*

Performing Forces: *voices*: SATB choir; *orchestra*: 2 trumpets in C, 2 cornets in A, 3 trombones, tuba, percussion (5 players - xylophone, keyboard glockenspiel, triangle, castanets, small cowbell, tambourine, snare drum (with brushes), tenor drum, Chinese tom-tom, temple block, cymbals, suspended cymbal, bass drum, tam tam, 3 timpani), and strings; solo pianist.

First Performance: 1928; BBC Broadcast; Hamilton Harty, piano; conducted by the composer.

Edition: *The Rio Grande* is published and distributed by Oxford University Press. The piano-vocal score, solo piano part, and study score are for sale; orchestral materials are available for rent.

Autograph: Copies of the composer's manuscript are in the possession of Oxford University Press and the BBC.

Notes: *The Rio Grande* is dedicated to Angus Morrison. Lambert was an experienced conductor and skilled orchestrator. The performance indications (particularly the percussion parts) are more thorough than most works of this era. The score contains the following note from the composer:

> A large chorus is not necessary for this work and, indeed if more than a hundred voices are used I recommend subdividing the choir into semi-chorus, medium chorus, and tutti, using the whole choir only for the more strenuous sections. The chorus is only a part of the work and no more important than, say, the piano part and it is essential that the singers should have absolute rhythmic

precision as the least lagging behind will ruin the ensemble. The chorus should aim at a rather more theatrical and pungent style of singing than is usual with most choral societies. All instructions concerning the method of playing the percussion instruments should be meticulously followed and a separate rehearsal of the cadenza is recommended. There is a special arrangement of the percussion part (without timpani) for 3 players which may be used when absolutely necessary. When there are only 4 players this arrangement should be used with the addition of the timpani part. It is undesirable, though, that the original 5 player version should be used. The cornet parts should not be played by trumpets. Fibre mutes in the brass instruments will be found to yield better results than brass mutes.

Of the work, Lyndon Jenkins writes:

It was the success of *The Rio Grande* during 1928-29 that first gave Lambert a place alongside William Walton in the roster of up-and-coming English composers at that time. Composed in 1927 when he was just 22 and dedicated to the pianist Angus Morrison, this setting of a poem by Sacheverell Sitwell was heard from a BBC studio in 1928; the following year its first public performances in Manchester and London created quite a furore and brought Lambert overnight fame. At both the conductor of the Hallé Orchestra, Sir Hamilton Harty, surrendered the baton to the composer and despatched the important piano part brilliantly (as the famous old recording made at the time confirms). Nearly 20 years later Lambert conducted the work again for the gramophone: this time the soloists were the pianist sister [Hyla] of the conductor Hyam Greenbaum and Gladys Ripley, whose career was cut short by cancer two years afterwards when she was only 47. Although in later life Lambert was inclined to value others of his works, such as *Summer's Last Will and Testament* and the Piano Concerto, above *The Rio Grande*, it has remained in musicians' estimations the most significant of all his original works, and it has achieved the greatest popularity with the public.[59]

Performance Issues: This is a charming and remarkably well crafted work which is the epitome of the melding between the European elite and the jazz age. It is truly a piano concerto with chorus. The score requires intense reinforcement of rhythmic precision. All parts present some rhythmic difficulties, but there are certain repeated dance figures which form the basis of most of the work. The harmonic language is tonal with occasional chromatic passages. The borrowed pitches are not used functionally (as in modulations or tonicizations), but instead are used to imitate jazz styles. There are frequent dissonances in the choir which are always prepared effectively, but may present problems in intonation. The choral parts also exercise a good amount of rhythmic independence which may be prohibitive to the clarity of the text if this is not stressed. The first trumpet has a demanding and somewhat high part. It is important to use both cornets and trumpets as their timbres are contrasted in the score. All of the percussion parts need experienced players, since the parts call for a variety of playing methods on each instrument. The strings present no particular difficulties. *Soloists*: there is a 12-measure alto solo, range: d'- e", tessitura: g'- d", it is not difficult and requires a "torch-singer" style. The solo piano part is featured throughout in a bravura jazz-like role which includes substantial, notated, cadenzas. It is an extremely demanding part requiring a first-rate player with a good understanding of the style of Gershwin and Porter. This piece has fallen into neglect despite its quality of composition and nostalgic charm. It would ideally be placed on a program of similar choral works or as a companion to another short piano-orchestra work such as Richard Addinsell's *Warsaw Concerto*, or as a witty pairing with Beethoven's *Choral Fantasy*. *Choir*: medium difficult; *Orchestra*: medium difficult.

Discography: Hamilton Harty, piano; St. Michael's Singers, Hallé Orchestra; conducted by the composer. Columbia Masterworks: X52 [78].

---

[59] Lyndon Jenkins: notes for *Constant Lambert Conducts*. EMI Classics Great Recordings of the Century series, 1992. EMI: CDH 7 63911 2.

Cristina Ortiz, piano; London Madrigal Singers, London Symphony Orchestra; conducted by André Previn. HMV: ASD 2990 [LP].

Kyla Greenbaum, piano; Gladys Ripley, contralto; BBC Chorus, Philharmonia Orchestra; conducted by the composer. Recorded: 13 January 1949. Columbia: CAX 10427-30 [78], DX 1591-2 [LP]; re-released as EMI: CDM 7 63911 2 [ADD mono].

S. Burgess, J. Gibbons; English Northern Philharmonia; conducted by David Lloyd-Jones. Hyperion: CDA 66565 [DDD].

Della Jones, Kathryn Scott; BBC Concert Orchestra and BBC Singers; conducted by Barry Wordsworth. Argo: 436118-2 ZH [DDD].

Selected Bibliography

McPhee, Colin: "Winter Chronicle New York," *Modern Music*, VIII/3 (March/April 1931), 42.

Mills, Charles: "Over the Air," *Modern Music*, XVII/1 (November/December 1940), 65.

Foreman, Lewis: *From Parry to Britten: British Music in Letters 1900-1945*, 103, 303. Portland, OR: Amadeus Press, 1987.

Summer's Last Will and Testament (1932-35)

Duration: ca. 53 minutes

Text: Thomas Nashe, from the play of the same title (1593)

Performing Forces: *voices*: baritone soloist; SATB choir; *orchestra*: 3 flutes (flute III doubling piccolo), 2 oboes, English horn, 2 clarinets, bass clarinet, 2 bassoons, contrabassoon, 4 horns, 3 trumpets in C, 2 Cornets in B^b, 3 trombones, tuba, timpani, percussion (3 players - snare drum, tenor drum, bass drum, tambourine, suspended cymbal, crash cymbal, gong, triangle, cowbell, rattle, xylophone), 2 harps, and strings.

First Performance: 29 January 1936; London; BBC Symphony Orchestra and Chorus; conducted by the composer.

First performance in the United States: 6 May 1951; Ann Arbor, MI; University of Michigan Choral Union, Philadelphia Orchestra; conducted by Thor Johnson.

Edition: *Summer's Last Will and Testament* is published and distributed by Oxford University Press. The piano-vocal score is for sale; orchestral materials are available for rent. There was a limited edition score with illustrations by Michael Ayrton.

Autograph: The full score is a facsimile of the composer's manuscript.

Notes: The work is divided into seven sections as follows:

1. Intrata
2. "Fair Summer Droops"
3. "Spring the Sweet Spring is the Year's Pleasant King"
4. "Trip and Go, Heave and Ho!"
5. "Autumn Hath All the Summer's Fruitful Treasure"
6. "King Pest" (rondo burlesca for orchestra)
7. Sarabande - "Adieu! Farewell Earth's Bliss"

Performance Issues: This is a chromatic yet tonally oriented work. It is very well orchestrated, treating each instrument idiomatically; Lambert introduces many coloristic effects. There are many indications regarding the methods of playing various passages. The choral writing is generally homophonic with three-part divisi in the men's parts and two-part divisi for the women. Only about a third of the work has singing. The choral parts are quite accessible; however, a large ensemble is required. Likewise, a full string section will be needed to balance the rest of the orchestra. As in Lambert's *Rio Grande*, cornets and trumpets must be used as indicated. The full score is very difficult to read, but the parts have been commercially extracted. The score order is inconsistent throughout the work. Most of the percussion parts were added to the ink score in pencil. The reproduction of those lines is particularly unclear. The lack of clarity is compounded by some shorthand marking in these parts. There are prominent solos for the concertmaster, timpanist, and tuba player. All of the wind parts have intricate passagework. There are few challenges to good ensemble integration. The string writing is fairly conservative. The lowest string of each harp is to be tuned down to C. This work is ideal for a symphonic chorus as the focal work of an orchestra program. *Soloist*: baritone, range: A-e', tessitura: e-c', lyric with long phrases. The solo is only in the final movement and involves only about three minutes of singing. *Choir*: medium; *Orchestra*: medium difficult.

Discography: W. Shimmel, English Northern Philharmonia; conducted by David Lloyd-Jones. Hyperion: CDA 66565 [DDD].

Selected Bibliography

Copland, Aaron: "Scores and Records," *Modern Music* (March/April 1938), 179.

Cutler, Helen Miller: "Ann Arbor Celebrates Fifty-Eighth Anniversary of Its May Festival," *Musical America* (June 1951), 34.

Lees, Benjamin (b. Harbin, China, 8 January 1924).

Life: As an infant, Lees moved with his family to the US. He studied at the University of Southern California (1945-8) with Halsey Stevens, Ernst Kanitz, and Ingolf Dahl. This was followed by four years of private study with George Antheil. From 1954 to 1961, Lees devoted his full attention to composition, residing in various European cities under a series of grants. Since returning to the US he has taught at the Peabody Conservatory (1962-4, 1966-8), Queens College, CUNY (1964-6), the Manhattan School (1972-4), and the Juilliard School (1976-7). Lees's musical style is fairly conservative, having developed in reasonable seclusion. His music is modally chromatic and highly rhythmic, with frequent changes of meter, betraying the influence of Bartok and Prokofieff.[60]

Awards: Fromm Foundation Award (1953), Guggenheim Fellowship (1954), NEA Award (1981).

Principal Works: *opera - The Oracle* (1956); *orchestral* - 4 symphonies (1953, 1958, 1968, 1985), 2 piano concertos (1955, 1966), Violin Concerto (1958), Oboe Concerto (1963), Concerto for String Quartet and Orchestra (1964), Concerto for Woodwind Quintet and Orchestra (1976), Concerto for Brass Choir and Orchestra (1983), *Portrait of Rodin* (1984); *vocal - Medea of Corinth*, S, Mez, Bar, B, wind quintet and timpani (1970), *The Trumpet of the Swan*, narrator and orchestra (1972); many songs and chamber pieces.

---

[60] Niall O'Loughlin: "Lees, Benjamin" in *The New Grove Dictionary of American Music*, edited by H. Wiley Hitchcock, iii: 25. 4 volumes. London: Macmillan, 1986.

Selected Composer Bibliography

Cooke, Derryck: "The Music of Benjamin Lees," *Tempo*, no. 51 (1959), 20.

O'Loughlin, Niall: "Lees, Benjamin" in *The New Grove Dictionary of American Music*, edited by H. Wiley Hitchcock, iii: 25. 4 volumes. London: Macmillan, 1986.

Visions of Poets (1961)

Duration: ca. 40 minutes

Text: Walt Whitman

Performing Forces: *voices*: soprano and tenor soloists; SATB choir; *orchestra*: 3 flutes (flute III doubling piccolo), 3 oboes (oboe III doubling English horn), 3 clarinet (clarinet III doubling bass clarinet), 3 bassoons (bassoon III doubling contrabassoon), 4 horns, 3 trumpets, 3 trombones, tuba, timpani, percussion (3 players - snare drum, tenor drum, bass drum, tambourine, cymbals, tam-tam, whip, triangle, woodblock, xylophone, glockenspiel), harp, celeste, and strings.

First Performance: 15 May 1962; Seattle Opera House; Seattle Symphony Orchestra and Chorus; conducted by Milton Katims.

Edition: *Visions of Poets* is published and distributed by Boosey and Hawkes. Piano-vocal scores may be purchased; orchestral materials are available by rent.

Autograph: The full score is a facsimile of the composer's manuscript.

Notes: *Visions of Poets* was commissioned by the Seattle Symphony Orchestra for the Formal Dedication of the Seattle Opera House. It is in ten sections as follows:

I.	Introduction	orchestra alone
II.	Song of the Exposition	soprano solo
III.	O Sun of Real Peace	tenor solo
IV.	Old Age's Lambent Peaks	choir
V.	Song of Myself	soprano solo
VI.	Soon Shall the Winter's Foil Be Here	tenor solo

VII.	Song of the Broad-Axe	choir
VIII.	Scherzo	orchestra alone
IX.	from Song of Myself	soprano solo
X.	The Mystic Trumpeter	tenor, soprano, and choir

Performance Issues: This is a dramatic and challenging work. It is very chromatic with a pronounced emphasis upon half-step relationships. All of the frequent trills are of a semitone and there is frequent exploitation of the cross-relation of major and minor thirds within triads. There are frequent metric changes and constant shifts in rhythmic stress. Lees establishes many polyrhythmic devices which will prove difficult to execute. These relationships include 7 against 4, 5 against 4, and 5 against 3. The choral writing is strictly homophonic with clear doublings of the vocal parts in the orchestra. There are some peculiar enharmonic spellings in the solo and ensemble vocal parts which should perhaps be noted for more efficient reading. There are divisi in all parts. Not only are the choral parts significantly simpler than the remainder of this work, but they represent only about ten minutes of music. Although there are many extreme dissonances in the choral portion, the preparation of the choir will not require a great amount of rehearsal. The instrumental difficulties are mostly the awkward integration of rhythmically diverse material. There is an exposed and fairly high trumpet solo in the final movement. *Soloists*: soprano, range: c#'-b", tessitura: g'-g", sustained and powerful with long phrases; tenor, range: d-a', tessitura: a-f', lyric and sustained with broad melodic leaps. *Choir*: medium difficult; *Orchestra*: difficult.

Discography: As of January 1993, no commercial recording has been made available.

Selected Bibliography

Guzzo, Louis R.: [review of premiere], *Seattle Times* (16 May 1962).
Cooke, Derryck: "Benjamin Lees's Visions of Poets," *Tempo*, lxviii (1964), 25.

Lockwood, Normand (b. New York, 19 March 1906).

Life: Lockwood's father Samuel was head of the violin department at the University of Michigan, where his uncle, Albert, was head of piano

studies. Lockwood studied composition in Rome with Ottorino
Respighi (1924-5), and in Paris with Nadia Boulanger (1925-8),
returning to Rome (1929-32) as a fellow of the American Academy. He
returned to the U.S. where he has taught at Oberlin Conservatory
(1932-43), Columbia University (1945-53), Trinity University, San
Antonio (1953-5), and the University of Denver (1961-75) with brief
residencies at Yale University, Westminster Choir College, the
University of Oregon, and the University of Hawaii.

Awards: Swift Prize, 2 Guggenheim Fellowships (1943, 1944), an
Alice M. Ditson commission (1945), National Institute of Arts and
Letters award (1947), Colorado Council on the Arts and Humanities
grant (1971), the Marjorie Peabody Waite Award (1981).

Principal Works: *opera - The Scarecrow* (1945), *Early Dawn*
(1961), *The Wizards of Balizar* (1962), *The Hanging Judge* (1964),
Requiem for a Rich Young Man (1964); *orchestral - A Year's
Chronicle* (1934), 2 symphonies (1934, 1979), Oboe Concerto (1968),
Organ Concerto (1973), Piano Concerto (1974), *Panegyric* (1979),
Prayers and Fanfares (1982); *vocal - Out of the Cradle endlessly
Rocking* (1938), *The Birth of Moses* (1947), *Elegy for a Hero* (1951),
Children of God (1956), *Light Out of Darkness* (1957), *Choreographic
Cantata* (1968), *For the Time Being* (1971),.*Mass for Children and
Orchestra* (1976), *Donne's Last Sermon* (1978), *A Child's Christmas in
Wales* (1984).

Selected Composer Bibliography

Lynn, G.: "Normand Lockwood and Choral Music," *American
    Composers' Alliance Bulletin*, vi/4 (1957), 3.
Sprenger, Curtis Donald: *A Study of the Text-Music Relationships in
    the Choral Works of Jean Berger, Cecil Effinger, and Normand
    Lockwood.* University of Northern Colorado: Dissertation, 1969.
Davis, Tony Max: *A Study of Stylistic Characteristics in Selected
    Major Choral Works of Normand Lockwood.* University of
    Missouri at Kansas City: Dissertation, 1980.
Porter, Susan J.: "Lockwood, Normand," in *The New Grove Dictionary
    of American Music*, edited by H. Wiley Hitchcock, iii: 96-7. 4
    volumes. London: Macmillan, 1986.
Norton, Kay: *Normand Lockwood: His Life and Music.* Metuchen, NJ:
    Scarecrow Press, 1993.

The Prairie (1952)

Duration: ca. 25 minutes

Text: Carl Sandburg

Performing Forces: *voices*: SATB choir; *orchestra*: 3 flutes (flute III doubling piccolo), 2 oboes, English horn, 2 clarinets, bass clarinet, 2 bassoons, 4 horns, 3 trumpets, 2 trombones, tuba, timpani, percussion, and strings.

First Performance: May 1953; sixtieth Annual May Festival, Ann Arbor, MI; University of Michigan Choirs, Philadelphia Orchestra; conducted by Thor Johnson.

Edition: *The Prairie* is published as a special festival edition for the University Musical Society of the University of Michigan by Broude Brothers. The piano-vocal score is for sale; orchestral materials are available for rental.

Autograph: The piano-vocal score is a facsimile of the composer's manuscript most of the text is set with a typewriter.

Notes: *The Prairie* was commissioned by the University Musical Arts Society of the University of Michigan, Ann Arbor for their annual May Festival. Compare with the setting by Lukas Foss. The score is performed without pauses, but it is organized into ten sections as follows:

      I. I Was Born on the Prairie
     II. Here the Water Went Down
    III. After the Sunburn of the Day
   IV. The Overland Passenger Train
     V. I Am Dust of Men
    VI. Towns on the Soo Line
   VII. I Am the Prairie, Mother of Men
  VIII. Look at Six Eggs
    IX. Any New Songs
     X. O Prairie Mother

Performance Issues: There was no copy of the full score in the possession of the publisher when this entry was written. However, in the event of a scheduled performance, they have a blueprint master and will generate a score.[61] For this reason, this entry is based upon the piano-vocal score. The work is diatonic with frequent key changes. The choral writing is conservative and generally homophonic. Lockwood at times establishes one vocal line (usually the basses) as a solo part while the remaining vocal parts accompany it. There is paired doubling between the tenor and sopranos, and the altos and basses. There is excellent rhythmic organization with most figures occurring on at least one, and often more, level of augmentation. The score is also filled with hemiolas. There are frequent choral unisons and divisi in all parts. The movements are to be performed successively without pause. Most of the melodic material emulates folk song which is appropriate for Sandburg's text, and also fitting because of his lifelong association with folk music. The ensemble for which this piece was composed (University Choral Union) had about 300 members, but it would be appropriate for a moderate sized ensemble. The music is very accessible and would be well suited for an amateur choral society. A large and confident bass section is definitely in order since that section has the majority of the melodic material, and presents the greatest portion of the text. From the piano-reduction, the accompaniment appears to be quite simple. It is an attractive piece which would be well paired with a work like Roy Harris's *Folk Song Symphony*. *Choir*: medium; *Orchestra*: apparently, medium.

Discography: As of January 1993, no commercial recording has been made available.

Selected Bibliography

Davis, Tony Max: *A Study of Stylistic Characteristics in Selected Major Choral Works of Normand Lockwood*. University of Missouri: Dissertation, 1980.

Mennin, Peter (b. Erie, PA, 17 May 1923; d. New York, 17 June 1983).

Life: Mennin was the brother of the composer, Louis Mennini. After brief study with Normand Lockwood at the Oberlin Conservatory and subsequent military service, he attended the Eastman School (BMus and

---

[61] telephone conversation with Broude Bros., Publishers

MMus 1945, and PhD 1947) where he studied composition with Howard Hanson and Bernard Rogers. He taught composition at the Juilliard School (1947-58), served as director of the Peabody Conservatory (1958-62), and was president of the Juilliard School (1962-83). His compositional style is contrapuntal, rhythmic, and exhibits a keen sense for large formal organization.[62]

Awards: Joseph Bearns Prize (1945), Gershwin Memorial Award (1945), National Institute of Arts and Letters award (1946), 2 Guggenheim Fellowships (1949, 1957), Naumburg Award (1952), membership in National Institute of Arts and Letters (1965).

Principal Works: Symphony no. 1 (1941), Symphony no. 2 (1944), Symphony no. 3 (1946), Symphony no. 4, "The Cycle" (1948), Symphony no. 5 (1950), Symphony no. 6 (1953), Symphony no. 7, "Variation-Symphony" (1963), Symphony no. 8 (1973), Symphony no. 9 (1981), Flute Concertino (1944), Concertato "Moby Dick" (1952), Cello Concerto (1956), Piano Concerto (1958), Flute Concerto (1983), *Voices* for voice, piano, percussion, harp, and harpsichord (1975), and *Reflections of Emily* for boy choir, harp, piano, and percussion (1978).

Selected Composer Bibliography

Hendl, Walter: "Music of Peter Mennin," *The Juilliard Review*, i/2 (1954), 18.

"Mennin, Peter," *Current Biography Yearbook*, xxv (November 1964); obituary, lxvim (August 1983); New York: H. W. Wilson Company.

Mayer, M.: "Peter Mennin of Juilliard," *New York Times* (28 September 1969), 17.

Owens, D.: "Composer: Peter Mennin: An Interview," *Christian Science Monitor* (29 and 30 July 1981).

Ayers, Mary Jane Bowles: *The Major Choral Works of Peter Mennin*. University of Miami: Dissertation, 1982.

[obituary], *New York Times* (18 June 1983).

Simmons, Walter G.: "Mennin, Peter," in *The New Grove Dictionary of American Music*, edited by H. Wiley Hitchcock, iii: 208-9. 4 volumes. London: Macmillan, 1986.

---

[62] Joseph Machlis: *Introduction to Contemporary Music*, 527-30. New York: W.W. Norton, 1961.

Symphony No. 4, The Cycle (1948)

Duration: ca. 23 minutes

Text: by the composer

Performing Forces: *voices*: SATB choir; *orchestra*: 3 flutes, 2 oboes, 2 clarinets, 2 bassoons, 4 horns, 3 trumpets, 3 trombones, tuba, timpani, percussion (2 players - snare drum, bass drum, cymbals), and strings.

There is a concert reduction of the full score for two pianos.

First Performance: 18 March 1949; New York; Collegiate Chorale and Orchestra; conducted by Robert Shaw.

Edition: *The Cycle* is published and distributed by Carl Fischer. The piano-vocal score (3647) and is available for purchase; orchestral and two-piano performance sets are available for rental (RCO-M42).

Autograph: The full score is a facsimile of the composer's manuscript.

Notes: This work was commissioned by the Collegiate Chorale and conductor Robert Shaw. The work is a three-movement symphony (fast, slow, fast). The choir sings throughout most of the piece, but the orchestra's most interesting and difficult music occurs in the non-vocal interludes. Mennin's text is concerned with the cycle of time and the earth's action of continually reclaiming itself from past destruction.

Performance Issues: Mennin's rhythmic language creates multimetric groupings which cross the bars in varied configurations. He clarifies these with beaming, dotted inner-barlines, or square brackets over groupings. One curious problem for the singers is the occurrence of two syllables assigned to a single note. The vocal writing is diatonic and always rhythmically simple. The majority of the choir's music is homophonic with many of the polyphonic passages still resembling chordal writing, but with a displacement of the text between parts. There are brief *a cappella* passages, which are cued in the orchestra in case support is required. The second movement has frequent changes of meter which are not particularly evident due to a slow tempo. The third movement is the most challenging for the singers and orchestra because of the quantity and speed of the music. The woodwind writing includes some intricate unison passage work which demands good facility and a well coordinated wind section. This work is accessible to a choir of limited experience, but the orchestration requires that the choir be fairly large. The orchestra parts are within the grasp of an ensemble of moderate ability. The solemnity of the text and heaviness of this score suggest that it be programmed with dissimilar works, such as Beethoven's *Choral Fantasia*, or a liturgical composition. *Choir*: medium; *Orchestra*: medium difficult.

Discography: Camerata Singers and Symphony Orchestra; conducted by Abraham Kaplan. Released in 1974. Desto: DC-7149 [LP]; re-released as Phoenix: PHCD-107 [AAD].

Christmas Story (1949)

Duration: ca. 24-25 minutes

Text: Bible

Performing Forces: *voices*: soprano and tenor soloists; SATB choir; *orchestra*: 2 trumpets in C, 2 trombones, timpani, and strings.

Also arranged for two pianos

First Performance: 24 December 1949; American Broadcasting Network; Collegiate Chorale; conducted by Robert Shaw.

Edition: *The Christmas Story* is published and distributed by Carl Fischer. The piano-vocal score may be purchased (3700); orchestral materials are available for rental (RCO-M38).

Autograph: The full score is a facsimile of the composer's manuscript.

Notes: This work was commissioned by the Protestant Radio Commission. It is in 9 movements as follows:

I.	Arise, shine	unaccompanied choir
II.	The people that walked in darkness	choir
III.	For unto us a child is born	choir
IV.	Now it came to pass	tenor solo and choir
V.	And there were shepherds	soprano solo and choir
VI.	For there is born to you this day	soprano and tenor solos
VII.	Glory to God	choir
VIII.	And it came to pass	choir
IX.	I will greatly rejoice	choir

Performance Issues: The first movement is *a cappella* and filled with alternating meters which include a shift in the value of the beat between the quarter note and dotted quarter. There is a broad variety of contrapuntal styles including strict homophony and diverse method of imitation. The vocal writing is scalar and generally diatonic, with the majority of accidentals reflecting a migration of the tonic. The harmonic language is functionally triadic. Virtually all of the choral lines are supported by the accompaniment. The brass parts are well paced between playing and resting. All of the parts require rapid passagework and rhythmic flexibility. The first trumpet demands a player capable of clean entrances at the top of the range. The string parts are well within the range of an amateur ensemble. *Soloists*: Neither solo role is substantial nor difficult. Soprano, range: d'- a'', tessitura: g'- e'', rhythmical and diatonic, consistently legato; tenor, range: e- a', tessitura: a- f', sustained and lyric, in the manner of a recitative. This is an ideal piece to be used as a Christmas or Advent (although the birth of Christ occurs in the eighth movement) cantata within a church setting. The music is attractive, varied, and well written. The solos and choruses are well within the ability of a moderate church music program, and the accompanying ensemble is small enough to be within the fiscal and space confines of many such churches. *Choir*: medium easy; *Orchestra*: medium easy.

Discography: As of January 1993, no commercial recording has been made available.

Selected Bibliography

Smith, Cecila: "For Christmas and All Seasons," *Musical America*, lxx (December 1950), 28.
[review], *Notes*, viii/4 (1951), 747-8.

Cantata de virtute: Pied Piper of Hamelin
(1969)

Duration: ca. 40 minutes

Text: Robert Browning, Psalm 117, and two thirteenth-century poems which are adaptations of the *Missa pro defunctis*.

Performing Forces: *voices*: narrator, tenor and bass soloists; SSAATTBB choir; children's choir; *orchestra*: 4 flutes, 3 oboes, 3 clarinets, 3 bassoons, 4 horns, 3 trumpets, 3 trombones, tuba, timpani, percussion (4 players - 2 snare drums, tenor drum, bass drum, suspended cymbal, crash cymbals, hand cymbals, tam-tam, bells), and strings.

First Performance: 2 May 1969; Annual May Festival, Cincinnati, OH.

Edition: *Cantata de Virtute* is published and distributed by Carl Fischer. The piano-vocal score is for sale; orchestral materials are available on rental (RCO-M36).

Autograph: The full score is a facsimile of the composer's manuscript. The original autograph is in the possession of Carl Fischer, Inc.

Notes: This work was commissioned for the Cincinnati May Festival. Mennin combines Browning's poem with liturgical Latin texts. The tenor soloists portrays the Mayor of Hamelin, and the bass plays the part of the Pied Piper. The score is in four sections which are to be performed without pause.

Performance Issues: This is an atonal composition which combines free atonality with serial procedures. The serial treatment utilizes more than one row; these are integrated with elements of whole-tone and chromatic scales. One of the most dramatic features of the piece is its conclusion in E^b major, the first stable harmony in the entire work. The children's choir is divided into two soprano parts of equal range, and at [R] they divided into four-part harmony. They must be capable of executing atonal passages without support from the orchestra. There are also divisi in each of the choral parts and a division into two choirs. The choral writing is contrapuntally complex and very dissonant, with particular emphasis upon tritone and augmented octaves. There are a variety of choral textures which include paired doubling, some imitation, and occasionally ten independent parts. The narrator must occasionally speak in rhythm. Nearly half of the choral part is for speaking choir. For them, Mennin indicates high, medium, and low, within the range of each part. He also uses glissandi for the speaking voices and laughter with approximated pitches and rhythms. At [W] choir II and the children's choir are to clap, cheer, and whistle freely as choir I sings a Latin prayer in unison. The orchestration is varied with demands put upon all of the players, exploiting extremities of range, glissandi in all sections and complex passagework. The pitch language and rhythmic complexity necessitate an orchestra of professional players. *Soloists*: Mayor - tenor, range: d-a'; tessitura: f#-f#', declamatory and requiring vocal flexibility; Pied Piper - bass, range: A#-f'; tessitura: e-d', must be flexible and capable of rapid melismas. The composer lists the role of the Pied Piper for bass; however, it seems better suited for a lyric baritone. To balance with the ensemble, the narration will require amplification. *Choir*: difficult; *Orchestra*: difficult.

Discography: As of January 1993, no commercial recording has been made available.

Menotti, Gian Carlo (b. Cadegliano, Italy, 7 July 1911).

Life: Menotti was first taught music by his mother. He had already composed two operas before entering the Milan Conservatory (1924-7). Upon Arturo Toscanini's recommendation, he entered the Curtis Institute (1927-34) where he studied composition with Rosario Scalero. It was there that he established a lifelong friendship with fellow student, Samuel Barber. A gifted writer, he authored most of his own librettos, as well as the libretto for Barber's *Vanessa*. His works combine the essence of contemporary theater with the melodic vocal style of Puccini and the orchestration of Mussorgsky.[63]

Award: New York Critics' Circle Award and the Pulitzer Prize (1950 for *The Consul*), and a Kennedy Center Honor for lifetime achievement in the arts.

Principal Works: *opera - Amelia Goes to the Ball* (1936), *The Old Maid and the Thief* (1939), *Sebastian* (1944), *The Medium* (1945), *The Telephone* (1946), *The Consul* (1949), *Amahl and the Night Visitors* (1951), *The Saint of Bleeker Street* (1954), *Maria Golovin* (1958), *Help, Help, the Globolinks!* (1968), *The Hero* (1976), *La loca* (1979), *The Boy who Grew too Fast* (1982); *ballet* - Sebastian (1944), Errand into the Maze (1947); *orchestral* - Piano Concerto (1945), *Apocalypse* (1951), Violin Concerto (1952), *Triplo Concerto a tre* (1976), Doublebass Concerto (1983); *choral - The Unicorn, the Gorgan and the Manticore, or The Three Sundays of a Poet* (1956), *Landscapes and Remembrances* (1976), and *Muero porque no muero* (1982).

Selected Composer Bibliography

Tricoire, Robert: *Gian Carlo Menotti: l'homme et son oeuvre.* Paris: Seghers, 1966.

Gruen, John: *Menotti: A Biography.* New York: Macmillan, 1978.

"Menotti, Gian Càrlo," *Current Biography Yearbook,* viii (December 1947); lx (January, 1979); New York: H. W. Wilson Company.

Ardoin, John: *The Stages of Menotti.* Garden City, NY: Doubleday, 1985.

Archibald, Bruce: "Menotti, Gian Carlo," in *The New Grove Dictionary of American Music,* edited by H. Wiley Hitchcock, iii: 209-12. 4 volumes. London: Macmillan, 1986.

The Death of the Bishop of Brindisi (1963)

Duration: ca. 30 minutes

Text: Menotti

---

[63] John Ardoin: *The Stages of Menotti.* Garden City, NY: Doubleday, 1985.

Performing Forces: *voices*: mezzo-soprano and baritone soloists; SATB choir, children's choir; *orchestra*: 2 flutes (flute II doubling alto flute), 2 oboes, 2 clarinets (clarinet II doubling bass clarinet), 2 bassoons, 4 horns, 3 trumpets, 3 trombones, tuba, timpani, percussion (3 players - bass drum, snare drum, suspended cymbal, gong, triangle, anvil, xylophone, bells, chimes), harp, 2 pianos (piano II doubling celeste), and strings.

First Performance: 18 May 1963; Rosalind Elias, Richard Cross; Cincinnati May Festival Chorus and Orchestra; conducted by Thomas Schippers.

First Staged Performance: 11 January 1968; University of New Mexico, Albuquerque, NM.

Edition: *The Death of the Bishop of Brindisi* is published and distributed by G. C. Schirmer. Piano-vocal scores may be purchased; orchestral materials are available by rental.

Autograph: A copy of the manuscript is in the possession of G. Schirmer.

Notes: The mezzo-soprano plays the role of a Nun, the baritone portrays the Bishop, and the choirs represent townspeople and children. There have been many staged and semi-staged productions of this work. However, the composer has stated that he regards it strictly as a concert piece. The composer derived his text from a passage in Adolf Waas's *History of the Crusades*. It takes place just prior to the Fifth Crusade (1218-21) with what was known as the Children's Crusade in which children from Germany and France traveled to the Holy Land. At Brindisi, they had to sail across the Mediterranean Sea. The Bishop of Brindisi intervened in an attempt to stop their futile journey. The children who did sail either died at sea, or were sold as slaves upon their arrival on the southern shore.[64] The story is told through a series of flashbacks by the Bishop from his deathbed.

Performance Issues: There may be a missing measure in the vocal score immediately preceding rehearsal #15. The composer lists 2

---

[64] Will and Ariel Durant: *The Story of Civilization*. 11 volumes. New York: Simon and Schuster, 1975.

players for the percussion parts, but 4 are necessary. The SATB choir sings only twice in the piece: the first time for 44 measures and the second time portraying townspeople for 34 measures. The children's choir sings throughout the work, usually in two parts which move in parallel thirds and sixths or in pervasive imitation at the unison. There is a section of three-part divisi in parallel motion at the fifth and octave. Menotti uses ostinati to create a sonic fabric behind solo materials. He also imitates Gregorian chant in his accompaniments to create the historic and dramatic backdrop of the story. The score is very operatic in its conception and content. The choral writing for the mixed choir is strictly homophonic and triadic. The one challenge is an alternation between 8/8, 9/8, and 12/8 in a fairly fast tempo with the quarter or dotted quarter designated as the beat while the eighth remains constant. The orchestra parts are not notably difficult with the exception of the two piano parts which are technically difficult and which present challenges to ensemble integration. There are some polyrhythmic passages including an overlap of divisions of 2, 3, and 4, and 4 against 5. There is a storm scene between rehearsal #40 and 45 which is difficult because of its speed. *Soloists*: mezzo-soprano, range: b$^{b'}$-e$^{b'''}$, tessitura: e'-c''; baritone, range: A-f', tessitura: g-d'; both roles are declamatory and very dramatic. The Bishop's role is particularly demanding with consistent exploitation of the upper range and it is requiring of endurance. *The Death of the Bishop of Brindisi* is a very effective piece of music drama which by the composer's nature seems to demand some degree of staging. *Choir*: medium; *Orchestra*: medium difficult.

Discography: Lili Chookasian, George London; New England Conservatory Chorus, Catholic Memorial High School Glee Club, St. Joseph's High School Glee Club, Boston Symphony Orchestra; conducted by Erich Leinsdorf. Released in 1965. RCA: SC-2785 [LP].

Selected Bibliography

Humphreys, Henry: [review of the premiere], *The Cincinnati Enquirer* (20 May 1963), 33.

Persichetti, Vincent (b. Philadelphia, PA, 6 June 1915; d. Philadelphia, PA 13 August 1987).

Life: At the age five, Persichetti entered the Combs Conservatory (BMus 1936) studying composition with Russell King Miller. After his graduation, he chaired the theory/composition department at Combs while attending the Philadelphia Conservatory (MMus 1941, DMus 1945). There he studied piano with Olga Samaroff and composition with Paul Nordoff. He also studied conducting with Fritz Reiner at the Curtis Institute. He served as head of the theory/composition department of the Philadelphia Conservatory (1941-47), he then joined the faculty of Juilliard (1947-87). While at Juilliard, he chaired the composition department (1963-70) and the literature and materials department from 1970. His compositional style is eclectic in its acceptance of all contemporary techniques. Persichetti was a very prolific composer who tried to use all of the techniques available to him. Each piece shows an unwavering commitment to quality and musical sincerity.[65] This same lack of musical prejudice is evidenced by the quantity of his instructional music and works for congregational church use.

Awards: 3 Guggenheim Fellowships, an award from the National Institute of Arts and Letters, 2 awards from the National Foundation on Arts and Humanities, membership in Institute of the American Academy and Institute of Arts and Letters (1965).

Writings: *Twentieth-Century Harmony* (New York: W.W. Norton, 1961), and with Flora R. Schreiber, *William Schuman* (New York: G. Schirmer, 1954).

Principal Works: *opera - The Sibyl: Parable XX*, op. 135 (1976); *orchestral* - 9 symphonies, *Fables*, op. 23 (1943), *The Hollow Men*, op. 25 (1944), *Fairy Tale*, op. 48 (1950), Piano Concerto, op. 90 (1962), *Introit*, op. 96 (1964), *Night Dances*, op. 114 (1970), *A Lincoln Address*, op. 124 (1972), English Horn Concerto, op. 137 (1977); *band - Pageant*, op. 59 (1953), *O Cool is the Valley*, op. 118 (1971); *choral - Spring Cantata*, op. 94 (1963), *Winter Cantata*, op.

---

[65] Walter Simmons: "Persichetti, Vincent," in *The New Grove Dictionary of American Music*, edited by H. Wiley Hitchcock, iii: 539-41. 4 volumes. London: Macmillan, 1986.

97 (1964), *Celebrations* for choir and wind ensemble, op. 103 (1966); and 24 "Parables" for various solos instruments and ensembles.

Selected Composer Bibliography

Evett, Robert: "The Music of Vincent Persichetti," *Juilliard Review*, ii/2 (1955), 15.

Schuman, William: "The Compleat Musician," *The Musical Quarterly*, xlvii (1961), 379.

Barnhard, Jack Richard: *The Choral Music of Vincent Persichetti: A Descriptive Analysis*. Florida State University: Dissertation, 1974.

Simmons, Walter: "A Persichetti Perspective," *American Record Guide*, xl/6 (1977), 6.

Ashiazawa, Theodore Fumio: *The Choral Music of Vincent Persichetti*. University of Washington: Dissertation, 1977.

Barham, Terry Joe: *A Macroanalytic View of the Choral Music of Vincent Persichetti*. University of Oklahoma: Dissertation, 1981.

Shackleford, Ruth: "Conversation with Vincent Persichetti," *Perspectives in New Music*, xx/1-2 (1981-2), 104-34.

Simmons, Walter: "Persichetti, Vincent," in *The New Grove Dictionary of American Music*, edited by H. Wiley Hitchcock, iii: 539-41. 4 volumes. London: Macmillan, 1986.

Stabat Mater, op. 92 (1963)

Duration: ca. 28 minutes

Text: Jacopone da Todi, with a singing English translation by Persichetti

Performing Forces: *voices*: SATB choir; *orchestra*: 2 flutes, 2 oboes, 2 clarinets, 2 bassoons, 4 horns, 2 trumpets, 3 trombones, tuba, timpani, and strings.

First Performance: 1 May 1964; Carnegie Hall, New York; Collegiate Chorale; conducted by Abraham Kaplan.

Edition: *Stabat Mater* is published by Elkan-Vogl and distributed by Theodore Presser Company. The piano-vocal score is for sale; orchestral materials are available for rent.

Autograph: The composer's manuscript is in the possession of Theodore Presser Company.

Notes: This works was commissioned by the Collegiate Chorale, Abraham Kaplan, conductor. It is in five sections as follows:

I. *Stabat Mater Dolorosa* / Sorrow Laden
II. *O Quam Tristis* / O How Saddened
III. *Eia Mater* / Blessed Mother
IV. *Sancta Mater* / Holy Mother
V. *Fac ut Portem* / Grant that I May Bear

Performance Issues: This is a tonally oriented work which features regular exploitation of simultaneous presentations of the major and minor versions of the same triad. The choral writing is primarily homophonic with frequent octave doublings between the tenor and soprano, and the bass and alto. There are some unison canonic portions between the male and female voices. The choral pitches are consistently supported in the accompaniment although there are some interesting enharmonic spellings for the singers which do not simplify their parts in any way. Some of the harmonic language is extended beyond traditional function; however, conventional voice-leading is maintained whereby dissonances are carefully and logically approached. The vocal parts are rich with melismatic passages. It is apparent that the work was initially composed with the Latin text, but the prosody of Persichetti's translation is very well suited to the music. The orchestration is diverse with many fine coloristic combinations. The individual parts should be accessible to players of moderate experience. There are some prominent and technically challenging solos for the principal oboe and clarinet. The orchestration allows for a small to medium choir of experienced singers. This is an excellently crafted setting of this text which should be considered as focal work within a Good Friday service or program. *Choir*: medium; *Orchestra*: medium difficult.

Discography: As of January 1993, no commercial recording has been made available.

Selected Bibliography

Weisgall, Hugo: "Current Chronicle: New York," *The Musical Quarterly*, 1 (1964), 379.

The Creation, op. 111 (1969)

Duration: ca. 60 minutes

Text: Persichetti from mythology, poetry, the Bible, and scientific sources.

Performing Forces: *voices*: soprano, alto, tenor, and baritone soloists; SATB choir; *orchestra*: piccolo, 2 flutes, 2 oboes, English horn, 2 clarinets, bass clarinet, 2 bassoons, 4 horns, 3 trumpets in C, 3 trombones, tuba, timpani, percussion (3 players - bass drum, snare drum, tenor drum, 2 timbales, large suspended cymbal, medium suspended cymbal, suspended sizzle cymbal, tam-tam, triangle, wood block, crotales (B^b, E, A), xylophone), and strings.

First Performance: 17 April 1970; Alice Tully Hall, New York; ensembles of the Juilliard School of Music; conducted by the composer.

Edition: *The Creation* is published by Elkan-Vogel and distributed by Theodore Presser Company. Piano-vocal scores may be purchased; orchestral materials are available by rental.

Autograph: The manuscript is in possession of Theodore Presser Company. The full score is a facsimile of that manuscript.

Notes: This work was commissioned by the Juilliard School. It is in seven sections, organized as follows [() indicate minor solo sections]:

I.	Darkness and Light	Bar, S, and Choir
II.	Let There Be a Firmament	A, T, and Choir
III.	I Will Multiply Your Seed	S, (T, B), and Choir
IV.	Light for Seasons	B, (S, A), and Choir
V.	Of Sea and Air	A, (S, T), and Choir
VI.	After His Kind	S, A, T, B, and Choir
VII.	Behold the Glory	S, A, T, B, and Choir

Performance Issues: This is an erudite undertaking in terms of music and text. The compositional textures are complex and varied exploiting secundal harmonies, notated accelerandi, unusual subdivisions, cross-rhythms, and spiky melodic lines. There are three-part divisi in all choral parts. The choral writing is homophonic and the part-writing emulates tonal practice while not using actual functional harmonies. Persichetti places non-triadic pitch sets within a framework of traditional part-writing procedures and tonal voicings. The first entrance of the choir is a tone-cluster containing all twelve discrete pitches. There are many subsequent tone-clusters which are approached via traditional part-writing procedures. The orchestral writing is idiomatic for each instrument; it is however rhythmically challenging and nearly all parts have exposed solo passages. The horns and oboes are particularly exposed, and there is some rapid passagework for the piccolo, flutes, clarinets, bassoons, and trumpets. Persichetti uses orchestration to clarify an often dense contrapuntal texture. There is a prolonged quartet for the soloists in the sixth movement. The text, which combines concepts from science and the mythologies of numerous cultures, is at once dated and timely. It is certainly an inviting work to coordinate with academic programs exploring the history of myth. The pitch language and the rhythmic complexity make this work accessible to only the most experienced choirs. The orchestral textures are dense enough to require significant rehearsal time even for experienced ensembles. The integration of choir and orchestra will also need more practice than would usually be allocated for a work of this length. *Soloists*: soprano, range: c#'-b", tessitura: e'-e", powerful with sustained phrases and awkward leaps; alto, range: f-e", tessitura: b^b-f", lyric with broad melodic leaps; tenor, range: c-a', tessitura: a-f', lyric and sustained; baritone, range: B^b-e', tessitura: e-b, dramatic and articulate. *Choir*: difficult; *Orchestra*: difficult.

Discography: As of January 1993, no commercial recording has been made available.

Selected Bibliography

Ericson, Raymond: [review of premiere], *New York Times* (18 April 1970).

Riegger, Wallingford (b. Albany, GA, 29 April 1885; d. New York, 2 April 1961).

Life: Born into a musical family, Riegger was a member of the first graduating class of the Institute of Musical Art (1907). There he studied cello with Alvin Schroeder and composition with Percy

Goetschius. He then spent three years at the Berlin Hochschule für Musik, studying cello with Robert Haussman and Anton Hekking, and composition with Max Bruch and Edgar Stillman-Kelley. He became principal cellist of the St. Paul Orchestra (1911-4), returning to Germany in 1914 as assistant conductor at the Stadttheater of Würzburg and then in Königsberg. Upon the US entry into the First World War he returned to his homeland. Riegger then taught at Drake University (1919-22), the Institute of Musical Art (1925-6), and Ithaca College (1926-8). In 1928, he returned to New York where he would remain for the rest of his life, supporting himself through editing and commercial arrangements of folk songs and carols under pseudonyms. Although his teaching career was brief, his student legacy includes Henry Brant, Michael Colgrass, Morton Feldman, and Elie Siegmeister. He became a part of the New York avant-garde with Henry Cowell, Carl Ruggles, Carlos Salzédo, Edgar Varèse, and Charles Ives. He was active in the administration of the Central Music Committee of Yaddo, the League of Composers, and the Pan American Association of Composers. His music is highly contrapuntal, often combining a fairly simple 12-tone technique with terse free atonality.[66]

Awards: Paderewski Prize (1922), Coolidge Prize (1924), Alice Ditson Fund award (1946), New York Critics' Circle Award (1948 for Symphony no. 3), Naumberg Recording Award.

Principal Works: *dance* - *Evocation* (1932), *The Cry* (1935), *With my Red Fires* (1936), *Four Chromatic Eccentricities* (1936), *Machine Ballet* (1938), *Pilgrim's Progress* (1941); *orchestral* - 4 symphonies (1944, 1945, 1946-7, 1956), *Dichotomy* (1931-2), *Music for Orchestra* (1952), Variations for Piano and Orchestra (1952-3), Variations for Two Pianos and Orchestra (1952-4), *Dance Rhythms* (1954), *Quintuple Jazz* (1959); *vocal* - La *belle dame sans merci* (1921-4), *Who can revoke?* (1948, text by C. R. Harris), and *The Dying of the Light* (1954).

Selected Composer Bibliography

Riegger, Wallingford: "Materials and Musical Creation," in *American Composers on American Music: A Symposium*, edited by Henry

---

66 Harold Gleason and Walter Becker: "Wallingford Riegger," *20th-Century American Composers*. Music Literature Outlines, series iv. Bloomington, IN: Indiana University Press, revised 1981.

Cowell, 180. New York: Frederick Ungar Publishing, 1933 (revised 1962).

Cowell, Henry: "Wallingford Riegger," *Musical America*, lxviii/14 (1948), 9.

Carter, Elliott: "Wallingford Riegger," *American Composers' Alliance Bulletin*, ii/1 (1952), 3.

"Wallingford Riegger: List of Works and Discography," *American Composers' Alliance Bulletin*, ix/3 (1960), 19.

Ardoin, John: "Wallingford Riegger Dies at 75," *Musical America* (May 1961), 65.

Gatwood, Dwight D., Jr.: *Wallingford Riegger: A Biography and Analysis of Selected Works*. George Peabody College for Teachers: Dissertation, 1970.

Rosenfeld, Paul: *Discoveries of a Music Critic*, 344. New York: Harcourt and Brace, 1936, revised 1972.

Savage, Newell Gene: *Structure and Cadence in the Music of Wallingford Riegger*. Stanford University: Dissertation, 1972.

Gleason, Harold, and Walter Becker: "Wallingford Riegger," *Twentieth-Century American Composers*. Music Literature Outlines, series iv, 148-57. Bloomington: Indiana University Press, revised 1981.

Spackman, Stephen: *Wallingford Riegger: Two Essays in Musical Biography*. Brooklyn, NY: Institute for Studies in American Music, monograph, xvii, 1982.

Cantata, In Certainty of Song, op. 46 (1950)

Duration: ca. 21 minutes

Text: Catherine R. Harris

Performing Forces: *voices*: soprano, alto, tenor, and baritone soloists; SATB choir; *orchestra*: flute, oboe, clarinet, bassoon, horn, trumpet, trombone, percussion (1 player - timpani, snare drum, bass drum, cymbals), and strings.

First Performance: 23 April 1952; Northwestern University, Chicago, IL; Northwestern University Ensembles; conducted by George Howerton.

Edition: *In Certainty of Song* is published and distributed by Peer International. Piano-vocal scores may be purchased; all materials are available by rental.

Autograph: The full score is a facsimile of the composer's manuscript.

Notes: This work is in six movements which may be played without pause.

Performance Issues: This is a tonal work with diatonic melodies and functional harmonies. However, Lowens describes the fluent use of the twelve-tone method. The single winds and a delicate orchestration allow for a small string section (as small as 3 violins I, 3 violins II, 2 viola, 2 cellos, and 1 double bass) and a small to medium-sized choir. Much of the choral writing is unison or paired doubling at the octave between the soprano with tenor, and alto with bass. In some sections the composer has notated only two parts with basses and altos on the bottom and soprano and tenor on the top. There are occasional sections of pervasive imitation and rhythmic speaking. The beginning pitches of each choral passage are anticipated by the accompaniment, and the orchestra continually supports the harmonies of the vocal parts. In contrapuntally complex sections each melodic line of the choir is doubled in the orchestra. There are divisi in all sections and some hummed and spoken passages. There is an optional piano part to reinforce the cellos and basses (movement III, from D to K). There are also optional instrumental cues to double vocal parts in the same movement. The orchestra parts are very accessible for amateur players. All of the instruments are treated conservatively and the orchestration is generally sparse. *Soloists*: soprano, range: f'-$b^{b''}$, tessitura f'-f', speech-like with some high sustained vocalises; alto, range: c'-a', tessitura c'-a', only sings in three measures; tenor, range: c-f', tessitura f-d', sustained and gentle; bass, range: A^b-$e^{b'}$, tessitura e-b, lyrical and rhythmically involved. Each soloist has freely spoken sections. This is an ideal introduction to twentieth-century music for inexperienced ensembles. The small orchestra makes the programming of this work reasonably affordable. *Choir*: medium easy; *Orchestra*: medium easy.

Discography: As of January 1993, no commercial recording has been made available.

Selected Bibliography

[review]: *Musical Courier*, cxliv (1 December 1951), 34.

Lowens, Irving: [review of the score], *Notes*, ix (1951-52), 325-26.
Goldman, Richard F.: "Current Chronicle," *Music Quarterly*, xxxviii (1952), 438.

Rogers, Bernard (b. New York, 4 February 1893; d. Rochester, NY, 24 May 1968).

Life: Rogers began composing in 1909, and between 1915 and 1918, studied music theory with Hans van den Berg and composition with Arthur Farwell. At the Institute of Musical Art (1919-20), he was a composition student of Percy Goetschius. He moved to Cleveland where he studied with Ernst Bloch (1920-22). On a Guggenheim Fellowship (1927-9), he studied in London with Frank Bridge, and in Paris with Nadia Boulanger. He had been in the service of an architectural firm, and later did editorial work for *Musical America* (1915-22, 1923-5) and the *Cleveland Commercial* (1920-23). He taught at the Hartt School of Music (1926-7), and then at the Eastman School (1929-67). At Eastman, he was chairman of the composition department, and taught composition and orchestration. His many distinguished pupils include Dominick Argento, Wayne Barlow, David Diamond, Peter Mennin, Burrill Phillips, Robert Stern, Vladimir Ussachevsky, and Robert Ward. Rogers's music shows the influence of his love for poetry (notably Whitman) and Japanese prints. He was one of America's most skillful orchestrators with an acute sense of instrumental color, textural variety.[67]

Awards: Pulitzer Travel Scholarship (1918), 2 Guggenheim Fellowships (1927, 1928), David Bishpam Medal (1931), Alice M. Ditson Award (1946), 2 honorary doctorates, Lillian B. Fairchild Award (1963), elected to the National Institute of Arts and Letters (1947).

Principal Works: *operas* - *Dierdre* (1922), *The Marriage of Aude* (1931), *The Warrior* (1944), *The Veil* (1950), *The Nightingale* (1954); *orchestral* - Symphony, no.1, "Adonais," (1926), Symphony, no. 2 (1928), Symphony, no. 3 "On a Thanksgiving Song," (1936), Symphony, no. 4 (1940), Symphony, no. 5, "Africa," (1959), *To the Fallen* (1918), *Fuji in Sunset Glow* (1925), *3 Japanese Dances* (1933), *Colors of War* (1939), *The Silver World* (1949), *Colors of Youth*

---

[67] Ruth Watanabe: "Rogers, Bernard," in *The New Grove Dictionary of American Music*, edited by H. Wiley Hitchcock, iv: 74-75. 4 volumes. London: Macmillan, 1986.

(1951), *New Japanese Dances* (1961), *Apparitions* (1967); *choral - The Light of Man* (1964), *Dirge for Two Veterans* (1967).

Selected Composer Bibliography

Hanson, Howard: "Bernard Rogers," *Modern Music*, xviii (1941), 259.

Diamond, David: "Bernard Rogers," *The Musical Quarterly*, xxxiii (1947), 207.

_____: "Bernard Rogers," *Proceedings of the National Institute of Arts and Letters*, second series, xix (1968), 119.

Dersnah, Susan Jane: *Orchestration in the Orchestral Works of Bernard Rogers*. Eastman School of Music at the University of Rochester: Dissertation, 1975.

Intili, Dominic Joseph: *Text-Music Relationships in the Large Choral Works of Bernard Rogers*. Case Western Reserve University: Dissertation, 1977.

Gleason, Harold, and Walter Becker: "Bernard Rogers," *Twentieth-Century American Composers*. Music Literature Outlines, series iv, 158-64. Bloomington: Indiana University Press, revised 1981.

Watanabe, Ruth: "Bernard Rogers," in *The New Grove Dictionary of American Music*, edited by H. Wiley Hitchcock, iv: 74-5. 4 volumes. London: Macmillan, 1986.

The Passion (1942)

Duration: ca. 65 minutes [68]

Text: Charles Rodda

Performing Forces: *voices*: tenor and baritone soloists, incidental solos from the choir; SATB choir; *orchestra*: 3 flutes (flute III doubling piccolo), 3 oboes (oboe III doubling English horn), 3 clarinets (clarinet III doubling bass clarinet), 3 bassoons (bassoon III doubling contrabassoon), 4 horns, 3 trumpets in C, 3 trombones, tuba, timpani, percussion (4 players - snare drum, tenor drum, bass drum, small oriental drum (or tom-tom piccolo pitched acutely), tambourine, triangle, tam-tam, large gong, small gong,

---

[68] Farish (Margaret K. Farish: *Orchestra Music in Print*. Philadelphia: Musicdata, 1979.) lists a duration of 45 minutes, but the score indicates ca. 65 minutes.

suspended cymbal, large crash cymbals, glockenspiel, xylophone, 1
chime - g'), piano (doubling celeste), harp, and strings.

First Performance: 12 May 1944; Annual May Music Festival,
Cincinnati, OH; Cincinnati Symphony and Chorus; conducted by
Eugene Goosens.

Edition: *The Passion* is published from manuscript by Elkan-Vogl
and distributed by Theodore Presser Company. Piano-vocal scores
may be purchased; orchestral materials are available by rental.

Autograph: The full score is a facsimile of the composer's
manuscript. The original autograph is in the special collections of
the Sibley Library of the Eastman School of Music in Rochester,
NY.

Notes: *The Passion* is dedicated to Anne, Betty, and Charles. It is in
six scenes as follows:

1. The Entry into Jerusalem
2. The Temple
3. Gethsemane
4. Pilate
5. Calvary
6. The Triumph

Of this work, Joseph Machlis states:

> [Rogers's] most important work is The Passion, for
> solo voices, mixed chorus, and organ, an impressive,
> deeply felt version of the last hours and death of Christ.[69]

Performance Issues: This is a remarkably complex composition
with constantly changing meters, plentiful chromaticism, and
highly involved contrapuntal and orchestrational textures. The
vocal writing is tonally conceived and clearly supported by the
accompaniment. The choral passages are generally homophonic or
in paired doublings with divisi in all parts. Vocal dissonances are
cautiously prepared by step or cued by other parts. The vocal

---

[69] Joseph Machlis: *Introduction to Contemporary Music*, 547. New
York: W.W. Norton, 1961.

rhythms are derived from the natural text declamation, but the prosody of the text is often at odds with the implied stress of the indicated meters. There is an unmeasured recitative for the baritone soloist. At times the men's section is divided to portray the Scribes and Money Changers, the Priests, the Pharisees, Elders, and the Disciples. There are also a variety of women's semi-choirs. Rogers gives thorough indications regarding articulation and quality of sound. His indications for octave transpositions are unusual: one octave higher marked - 1^8, and two octaves higher - 2^8. All of the instrumental parts have difficult passage work. The string writing is particularly challenging with divisi, cross-rhythms within the sections, and rapid chromatic passagework. Virtually every wind player has conspicuous solo sections. The percussion parts are detailed in the manner of playing and prominent throughout the piece. There are a number of changes made to the full score in the composer's hand which should be checked against the parts. The score order of the piano, harp, and percussion is inconsistent. Some of the double basses must have an extension to C'. The list of percussion instruments at the beginning of the score is incomplete; however, the listing above is accurate. The timpanist must be adjacent to the percussion section. The opening page of the score lists the two principal solo roles as Pilate and Jesus; however, the latter role is labeled "The Voice" throughout the score. Some confusion may arise in that there is one soloist labeled "The Voice," two labeled "a Voice," and two labeled "a Man." The latter pairs are distinguished only by a difference of clef. The various choral and string divisi, as well as the depth of the general orchestration, require a large choir and string section. This is a profound and impeccably crafted composition which is within the ability of a choir of medium experience, but the level of the orchestra parts demands an ensemble of professional players. This is probably the most sophisticated setting of the Passion story in English. *Soloists*: Pilate - tenor, range: d#-f#', tessitura: a-f', declamatory with rapid articulation; Jesus - baritone, range: A-f', tessitura: e-d', this is a large role requiring power and textual clarity. *Incidental solos*: soprano, range: d'-b", tessitura: f'-f"; a Young Voice - soprano, range: b♭'-g#", tessitura: c#"-g#"; a voice - soprano, range: f#", tessitura: f#"; alto, range: d'-f', tessitura: f'-c"; a Woman, range: c#'-f#", tessitura: d'-b"; a Man - tenor, range: db-a', tessitura: b-e'; a Man - baritone, range: c-e', tessitura: g-c'; a Voice - baritone, range: g-c', tessitura: g-c'. *Choir*: medium difficult; *Orchestra*: difficult.

Discography: As of January 1993, no commercial recording has been made available.

Selected Bibliography

Leighton, Mary: [review of the premiere], *Cincinnati Enquirer* (13 May 1944), 18.
Bruno, Anthony: "Rogers's Passion at Juilliard," *Musical America*, lxix (March 1949), 7.

Letter from Pete (1947)

Duration: ca. 24 minutes

Text: Walt Whitman

Performing Forces: *voices*: soprano and tenor soloists; SATB choir; *orchestra*: 2 flutes, 2 oboes, 2 clarinets, 2 bassoons, 4 horns, 2 trumpets, 3 trombones, tuba, timpani, percussion (3 players - bass drum, snare drum, tenor drum, triangle, cymbals, tam-tam), harp, and strings.

Also arranged for *chamber orchestra*: flute, clarinet, horn, trumpet, trombone, percussion (1 or 2 players* - timpani, snare drum, bass drum, triangle, cymbals, tam-tam), piano, and strings.

* Where there are two percussion parts, the composer has indicated which part may be omitted.

First Performance: unable to determine

Edition: *A Letter from Pete* is published by Southern Music Publishing and distributed by Peer International. Piano-vocal scores may be purchased; orchestral materials are available by rental.

Autograph: The full scores are facsimiles of the composer's manuscripts.

Notes: The score is subtitled, "A Cantata of the Civil War on a Poem by Whitman." Throughout this work, the orchestra imitates military drum cadences. The two orchestrations contain the same music, but the reduction is available for ensembles of limited size.

Performance Issues: The choral writing is very conservative, exploiting pervasive imitation and melodic motion by step or third. There are divisi in each choral section. The size of the choir is variable and the choice of orchestration should reflect the choir's size. At some points, the score calls for only a few members of each section to sing and there are limited *a cappella* passages. The choir must sometimes sing pitches in opposition to those in the orchestra. Dissonances are frequent and well prepared. As with the bulk of Rogers's music, the most striking characteristics of this work are the rhythmic vitality and the orchestration. The instruments are effectively used for their color and yet the writing remains very practical for each instrument. The most challenging instrumental passage is the ten measures following rehearsal number 45. *Soloists*: soprano, range: f#'-a'', tessitura: b'-f''; tenor, range: f-g', tessitura: b-e', sustained and lyrical; both solo roles are minimal and would well be assigned to members of the choir. This work requires an experienced choir. Although the part-writing is impeccable, beginning pitches of choral sections are often difficult to find and have limited conformation in the accompaniment. The orchestra parts are less difficult and could be performed by an ensemble of moderate ability. The instrumental writing will present limited rehearsal challenges. The freed-up orchestra rehearsal time will be needed for extra tutti rehearsals to give the choir a chance to find their pitches. It is well advised that a piano cue the choral pitches at the first tutti rehearsal. This is a fine piece deserving of the extra preparation time needed for a successful performance. *Choir*: medium easy; *Orchestra*: medium.

Discography: As of January 1993, no commercial recording has been made available.

Selected Bibliography

[review of the score], *Notes*, x/4 (September 1953), 680.
Flanagan, William: "New Cantata and Suite by Bernard Rogers," *Musical America*, lxxiii (15 December 1953), 24.

The Prophet Isaiah (1950)

Duration: ca. 32 minutes

Text: The Book of Isaiah from the Bible

Performing Forces: *voices*: 2 soprano, tenor, and bass choral soloists; SATB choir; *orchestra*: 3 flutes, 2 oboes, 2 clarinets, 2 bassoons, 4 horns, 3 trumpets, 3 trombones, tuba, timpani, percussion (3 players - bass drum, tenor drum, triangle, cymbals, suspended cymbal, small gong, small tam-tam, xylophone, glockenspiel), piano, harp, and strings.

First Performance: unable to determine

Edition: *The Prophet Isaiah* is published by Southern Music Publishing and distributed by Peer International. Piano-vocal scores may be purchased; orchestral materials are available by rental.

Autograph: The full score is a facsimile of the composer's manuscript. A photocopy of the manuscript is in the Sibley Library of the Eastman School of Music in Rochester, NY.

Notes: This is a through-composed work with many contrasting sections.

Performance Issues: This is a very sophisticated and complex work. It is tonal and presents few rhythmic challenges, but it contains varied and complex textures which will require substantial rehearsal time to coordinate. The choral writing is vocally demanding, but musically accessible with scalar melodies and pitch support from the orchestra. There are divisi in all of the choral parts and small groups are called for from within the choir. The instrumental writing is very complex with numerous details regarding methods of playing. Rogers was one of this century's most gifted orchestrators and this is reflected throughout the piece through his knowledgeable treatment of individual instruments and his coloristic use of instrumental sounds within the ensemble. A large string section is required to balance with the rest of the ensemble and to accommodate a variety of divisi. *Soloists*: soprano I, range: e'-g#", tessitura: g'-e", at rehearsal number 10 she is asked to sing slightly sharp; soprano II, range: g#'-a", tessitura: a'-f#"; tenor, range: f#-d', tessitura: f#-d'; bass, range: Ab-f'; tessitura: d-eb'. The solos are minimal and appropriate for members of the ensemble. The bass and soprano I parts are larger than the other two roles. The orchestra part is substantially more difficult than the choral part, making this an ideal work for a collaboration between a community chorus and professional orchestra. It is particularly appropriate for the Advent and Christmas seasons. Although it is quite difficult for the performers, it is a beautiful work which is accessible to general audiences. *Choir*: medium; *Orchestra*: medium difficult.

Discography: As of January 1993, no commercial recording has been made available.

Selected Bibliography

Smith, Cecil: [review of the score], *Musical America*, lxxxii (July 1962), 31.

Rorem, Ned (b. Richmond, IN, 23 October 1923).

Life: Rorem had early music theory training (1938-9) with Leo Sowerby. He attended the Curtis Institute (1943), and the Juilliard School (BS 1946, MS 1948). He studied privately with Virgil Thomson, for whom he was a copyist. It is Thomson whom he claims as his primary influence. He also studied with Arthur Honegger (1950) in France, living in Paris and Morocco for eight years. Returning to the US in 1958, Rorem held occasional teaching posts: the University of Buffalo (1959-60), the University of Utah (1965-6), and the Curtis Institute (1980-6). Among composers, Rorem is one of the most prolific essayists, and like his mentor Thomson, Rorem has been entwined with words, becoming a most prolific song composer. Even his instrumental works are often comprised of brief movements which depend on short epigrammatic titles.[70] His music is tuneful and diatonic with a cosmopolitan quality not unlike that of Poulenc.[71] The songs vary from terse and biting to sublime and elegant.

Awards: Fulbright scholarship (1950), 2 Guggenheim Fellowships (1956, 1978), Pulitzer Prize (1976 for *Air Music*), Grammy Award (1977 for *String Symphony*), American Guild of Organists Musician of

---

[70] James Holmes: "Rorem, Ned," in *The New Grove Dictionary of American Music*, edited by H. Wiley Hitchcock, iv: 87-90. 4 volumes. London: Macmillan, 1986.

[71] Joseph Machlis: *Introduction to Contemporary Music*, 561. New York: W.W. Norton, 1961.

the Year (1977), elected to the Institute of the American Academy and Institute of Arts and Letters (1979).

Principal Writings: *The Paris Diaries* (New York: George Braziller, 1966), *The New York Diaries* (New York: George Braziller, 1967), *Music from Inside Out* (New York: George Braziller, 1967), *Music and People* (New York: George Braziller, 1969), *Critical Affairs: A Composer's Journal* (New York: George Braziller, 1970), *Pure Contraption* (New York: George Braziller, 1973), *The Final Diary* (New York: George Braziller, 1974), *An Absolute Gift* (New York: Simon and Schuster, 1978), *Setting the Tone: Essays and a Diary* (New York: Simon and Schuster, 1983), and *The Nantucket Diary of Ned Rorem, 1973-1985* (San Francisco: North Point Press, 1987).

Principal Works: *opera* - *A Childhood* (1952), *The Robbers* (1956), *Miss Julie* (1964-5), *Three Sister who are not Sisters* (1968), *Bertha* (1968), *Fables* (1970), *Hearing* (1976); *orchestral* - 3 symphonies (1950, 1956, 1957-8), 2 piano concertos (1948, 1950), *Eagles* (1958), *Pilgrims* (1958), *Lions* (1963), *Water Music* (1966), *Air Music* (1974), Organ Concerto (1984), Violin Concerto (1984); *choral* - *A Sermon on Miracles* (1947), *Laudemus tempus actum* (1964), *An American Oratorio* (1983), *A Whitman Cantata* (1983); and over 400 songs.

Selected Composer Bibliography

Anderson, G.: "The Music of Ned Rorem," *Music Journal*, xxi/4 (1963), 34, 71.

Rivers, Earl G.: *The Significance of Melodic Procedures in the Choral Works of Ned Rorem*. University of Cincinnati: Dissertation, 1976.

Griffiths, Richard Lyle: *Ned Rorem: Music for Chorus and Orchestra*. University of Washington: Dissertation, 1979.

Davis, Deborah: "An Interview About Choral Music with Ned Rorem," *The Musical Quarterly*, lxviii (1982), 390.

Holmes, James: "Rorem, Ned," in *The New Grove Dictionary of American Music*, edited by H. Wiley Hitchcock, iv: 87-90. 4 volumes. London: Macmillan, 1986.

McDonald, Arlys L., and Donald L. Hixon: *Ned Rorem: A Bio-Bibliography*. Westport, CT: Greenwood Press, 1989.

The Poet's Requiem (1954-55)

Duration: ca. 22-28 minutes

Text: Franz Kafka, Rainer Maria Rilke, Jean Cocteau, Stéphane Mallarmé, Sigmund Freud, Paul Goodman, and André Gide, as collected and translated by Paul Goodman in *Dead of Spring* (1950).

Performing Forces: *voices*: soprano soloist; SATB choir; *orchestra*: 2 flutes, 2 oboes, 2 clarinets in A, 2 bassoons, 2 horns, trumpet in C, trombone, timpani (3), percussion (2 players - snare drum, large gong, cymbals, triangle), piano, harp, and strings.

First Performance: 15 February 1957; Town Hall, New York; Ellen Faull; The American Concert Choir and Orchestra; conducted by Margaret Hillis.

Edition: *The Poet's Requiem* is published and distributed by Boosey and Hawkes. The piano-vocal score is for sale; orchestral materials may be rented.

Autograph: A copy of the manuscript is in the possession of Boosey and Hawkes.

Notes: This work is in eight movements as follows:

I. Kafka   from "Reflections on Sin, Death, and the True Way"
              soprano, SATB choir
II. Rilke   from "Duino Elegies"
              SATB choir
III. Cocteau from "Les chevaliers de la table ronde"
              2 men's voices, soprano, and SSATBB choir
IV. Mallarmé from "Toast funèbre"
              SSATBB choir
V. Freud   from "Reflections on the War"
              man speaking
VI. Goodman   from "Sentences and Prayers"
              soprano, TBB choir
VII. Gide   from "Les nouvelles nourritures"
              SSATBB choir
VIII. Rilke   from "Duino Elegies"

soprano, SATB choir

Performance Issues: This is a very effective setting of a fine collection of texts. It is an eloquent non-sectarian tribute to the beloved passed. The harmonic language is mostly functional tertian with some influence from early twentieth-century French music, exploring parallel octaves and fifths and unresolved pedal tones. The choral writing exploits elements of pervasive imitation and motivic development. Rorem neatly contrasts the contrapuntal sections with passages of unison choral singing. There are numerous melismas, and all choral parts are melodically and vocally conceived. The vocal pitches are consistently doubled in the accompaniment except for an *a cappella* section in the final movement. The fifth movement contains no singing, but there is text for a man to read over the orchestra. The orchestral writing is pianistic in conception with spiky leaping accompanimental chords and chord voicing reflective of keyboard music. There is difficult passagework for all of the wind and string players, while the brass parts are quite conservative. *Soloist*: soprano, range: d'-c'''; tessitura: g'-g", powerful and very dramatic. There are some *incidental solos* for members of the choir: tenor, range: d-a', tessitura: a-e', sustained and lyric; baritone, range: d-d', tessitura: f#-b, lyric. This is a fine work for an experienced small choir. The orchestration is thin and also allows for a small string section. Rorem uses many contrapuntal devices reminiscent of Renaissance music. It may be ideally programmed opposite a large sixteenth-century work. *Choir*: medium difficult; *Orchestra*: medium.

Discography: As of January 1993, no commercial recording has been made available.

Letters from Paris (1966)

Duration: ca. 22-25 minutes

Text: Janet Flanner from her "Letters from Paris," which appeared in *The New Yorker* between 1945 and 1965 under the name Genêt, and were published as the collection in *Paris Journal* by Athenaeum in 1965.[72]

---

[72] George and Barbara Perkins and Phillip Leininger: *Benét's Reader's Encyclopedia of American Literature.* New York: Harper Collins, 1991.

Performing Forces: *voices*: SATB choir; *orchestra*: flute (doubling piccolo), oboe (doubling English horn), clarinet in B^b and A (doubling E^b alto saxophone), bassoon, horn, trumpet, trombone, timpani, percussion (players - snare drum, tenor drum, bass drum, triangle, cymbals, 2 bongos, castanets, anvil, tam tam, ratchet, police whistle, chimes, xylophone, vibraphone, glockenspiel), harp, harmonium, celeste, piano, and strings.

First Performance: 25 April 1966; Hill Auditorium, University of Michigan, Ann Arbor; University of Michigan Ensembles; conducted by Thomas Hilbish.

Edition: *Letters from Paris* is published and distributed by Boosey and Hawkes. The piano-vocal score is for sale; orchestral materials are available for rent.

Autograph: The full score is a facsimile of the composer's manuscript.

Notes: Rorem includes the following notes in the score:

> Janet Flanner's letters from Paris, signed Genêt, first appeared in *The New Yorker* between 1945 and 1965. In 1966 they were collected in *Paris Journal* from which my friend Robert Phelps extracted the following fragments expressly for me to set to music. The nine texts, in choice and organization, are close to my heart, not only for their clean nostalgic style, but for their subject of a place and periods I inhabited long ago.

> The Koussevitsky Foundation in the Library of Congress commissioned the music, which was begun March 3rd, 1966 in Salt Lake City. The orchestration...was completed on July 30th of that same year.

Letters from Paris is dedicated to the memory of Serge and Natalie Koussevitsky. It is in nine sections as follows:

1. Spring
2. The French Telephone
3. Summer

4. Colette
5. Autumn
6. The Sex of the Automobile
7. Winter
8. Mistinguett
9. Spring Again

Performance Issues: This piece is a virtual song cycle for choir. The choral writing is melodic in all parts with a balance between homophonic textures and paired imitation. Rorem has obviously made text declamation the most important feature of his setting. Both the prosody of the text and its inflection are carefully outlined by the rhythm and melodic contour of each vocal part. The vocal pitches are clearly supported by the accompaniment although there are some *a cappella* passages. The orchestra's part is very pianistic and completely accompanimental. In fact most of the instrumental role of the second movement is a piano solo. The piano part is consistently challenging and calls for limited playing from the inside of the piano. These inner-piano ventures are very clearly explained in the score. The tempo of the fourth movement is notated as a half-note equalling 44; however, the rhythmic content of the movement will be better served with the quarter-note receiving the beat. That same movement has some difficult rhapsodic passages for the clarinets and strings. Throughout the composition, there are some very difficult flourishes for piccolo, flute, bassoon, and mallets. There are frequent cross-rhythms and unusual divisions of the beat including 7, 9, 10, 12 and 13. This is a witty and charming piece which poignantly presents a variety of sentimental and provocative texts. The transparency of the orchestration and the lightness of the vocal scoring make this an ideal piece for a small choir of experienced singers. There are some four-part divisi in the string parts which would require strong players throughout the section if a reduced string section were used. The pianistic qualities of the score cause the solo woodwind parts to be very difficult. However, there are only limited challenges to ensemble cohesion. *Choir*: medium; *Orchestra*: medium difficult.

Discography: As of January 1993, no commercial recording has been made available.

Rubbra, Edmund (b. Northampton, 23 May 1901; d. Gerrards' Cross, 13 February 1986).

Life: Rubbra gave a concert of Cyril Scott's piano music as a youth. This caught Scott's attention, and he invited Rubbra to be his pupil in piano and composition. He attended Reading University (1920-21) and then entered the Royal College of Music (1921-1925). There his teachers were Gustav Holst (composition), Evlyn Howard-Jones (piano), and R. O. Morris (counterpoint and harmony). Rubbra taught at Oxford University (1947-68) and the Guildhall School of Music (1961-1986). He also served as a critic of new music for the *Monthly Musical Record*. His music is melodically conceived using motivic germs which generate complete movements through a organic process of development. The majority of his works are through composed using a harmonic language and contrapuntal devices similar to those of Holst and Vaughan Williams.[73]

Awards: Collard Fellowship (1938), Cobbett Medal (1955), Commander, Order of the British Empire (1960), two honorary doctorates, Fellow of Worcester College, Oxford; Fellow of the Guildhall School of Music, Member of the Royal College of Music.

Principal Works: *orchestral* - Symphony No. 1, op. 44 (1935-37), Symphony No. 2, op. 45 (1937), Symphony No. 3, op. 49 (1939), *Improvisation on Virginal Pieces by Giles Farnaby*, op. 50 (1939), Symphony No. 4, op. 53 (1941), *Soliloquy*, op. 57 (1943-44), Symphony No. 5, op. 63 (1947-48), Viola Concerto, op. 75 (1952), Symphony No. 6, op. 80 (1950), Piano Concerto, op. 85 (1956), Symphony No. 7, op. 88 (1957), Violin Concerto, op. 103 (1959), Symphony No. 8, op. 132 (1966-68), Symphony No. 9, "Sinfonia Sacra," op. 140 (1971-71), Symphony No. 10, "Sinfonia da Camera," op. 145 (1974), Symphony No. 11, op. 153 (1978-79); *choral - The Dark Night of the Soul*, op. 41/1 (1935), *The Morning Watch*, op. 55 (1941), *Missa cantuariensis*, op. 59 (1945), *Missa in honorem Sancti Dominici*, op. 66 (1948), *Festival Gloria*, op. 94 (1957), *Cantata di camera*, op. 111 (1961), *Nocte surgentes*, op. 123 (1964); and many chamber works.

---

[73] Andrew Lamb: "Rubbra, Edmund," in *The New Grove Dictionary of Music and Musicians*, edited by Stanley Sadie, xvi: 292-94. 20 volumes. London: Macmillan, 1980.

Selected Composer Bibliography

Mellers, Wilfrid H.: "Rubbra and the Dominant Seventh," *The Music Review*, iv (1943), 145.

Evans, Edwin: "Edmund Rubbra," *The Musical Times*, lxxxvi (1945), 41, 75.

Ottaway, Hugh: "Edmund Rubbra and His Recent Works," *The Musical Times*, cvii (1966), 765.

Lyne, Gregory Kent: *Edmund Rubbra: The Man and His Choral Works*. University of Northern Colorado: Dissertation, 1976.

Lamb, Andrew: "Rubbra, Edmund," in *The New Grove Dictionary of Music and Musicians*, edited by Stanley Sadie, xvi: 292-94. 20 volumes. London: Macmillan, 1980.

Inscape, op. 122 (1964-65)

Duration: ca. 20 minutes

Text: Gerard Manley Hopkins

Performing Forces: *voices*: SATB choir; *orchestra*: harp (optionally substituted by piano), and strings.

First Performance: 1965; Stroud Festival for the Arts.

Edition: *Inscape* is published by Lengneck and distributed by Theodore Presser Company. The piano-vocal score is for sale; orchestral materials are available for rental.

Autograph: The full score is a facsimile of the composer's manuscript.

Notes: *Inscape* was composed for the Stroud Festival of Religious Drama and the Arts in 1965. It is in Five sections as follows:

      I. Pied Beauty
     II. The Lantern Out of Doors
   III. Spring
   IV. God's Grandeur
    V. Epilogue (fragment labeled "Summa" by the poet)

Performance Issues: This is a tonal work obeying the traditional part-writing procedures of the common-practice period. The contrapuntal treatment of the inner voices of the strings creates a modal flavor which is easily associated with the works of Ralph Vaughan Williams. The choral writing is linear in conception and mostly homophonic with occasional divisi in all parts. There are some passages of paired imitation, but in general, imitative processes are left to the instruments. There are many unusual harmonies in the voices which are the result of clear and logical stepwise motion. The majority of the vocal pitches is well defined in the accompaniment. The delicacy and constituency of the orchestration suggest the use of a small choir and reduced strings. One minor problem in the preparation of this piece involves the apparent absence of a true full score. The substitution is a copy of the engraved piano-vocal score which has been "enlightened" with numerous hand-written cues and additional notes. This score adequately presents all of the necessary information, but in a less than ideal format. This is an exceptionally well-crafted score which betrays an apparent influence from the music of Brahm's as well as its English contemporaries. *Choir*: medium; *Orchestra*: medium easy.

Discography: As of January 1993, no commercial recording has been made available.

Advent Cantata, op. 136 (1968)

Duration: ca. 22 minutes

Text: Unidentified English and Latin Texts

Performing Forces: *voices*: baritone soloist; SATB choir; *orchestra*: 2 flutes, 2 oboes, 2 clarinets, 2 bassoons, 2 horns, bells, harp, and strings.

First Performance: unable to determine

Edition: *Advent Cantata* is published by Lengnick and distributed by Theodore Presser Company. The piano-vocal score is for sale; orchestral materials are available for rental.

Autograph: The full score is a facsimile of the composer's manuscript.

Notes: The arrangement of the text divides this single-movement work into four sections. The opening section is labeled "recitative." The next section is labeled "aria." Both of the sections are in English. The middle portion is a setting of an acrostic Latin poem. As each of its seven stanzas begins on the successive letter of the alphabet, the starting pitch of each climbs diatonically from a to g. The final chorale is again in English.

Performance Issues: This is a chromatic modal piece. The choral writing is melodically scalar with non-functionally triadic and harmonies. Most of the choral sections are homophonic with occasional contrapuntal exchanges in the inner voices and a few passages of pervasive imitation. The singers have many unisons and some paired doublings. There are many unusual harmonies which are approached by step. There are divisi in all choral and string parts. The score contains many unusual enharmonic spellings causing ordinary triads to become visually unrecognizable. The orchestral writing is very conservative and idiomatic for each instrument. There are many octave doublings in the winds which may present intonation problems. The orchestra parts are accessible to amateur players of moderate experience. This is an excellent work for use within an advent service. *Soloist*: baritone, range: B$^\flat$-e', tessitura: c#-c#', declamatory with long phrases, must be capable of powerful singing at the extremes of the indicated range. *Choir*: medium; *Orchestra*: medium.

Discography: As of January 1993, no commercial recording has been made available.

Schuller, Gunther (b. New York, 22 November 1925).

Life: Schuller attended the St. Thomas Choir School (1938-44). He played horn in the New York City Ballet orchestra (1943). He then was principal horn in the Cincinnati Symphony (1943-5) and the Metropolitan Opera (1945-59). He gave up the horn in 1962 to dedicate more of his time to composition. He taught horn at the Manhattan School (1950-63), and was professor of composition at Yale University (1964-7). From 1967 to 1977, he served as president of the New England Conservatory. He was also on the composition faculty of Tanglewood, where he was artistic co-director (1969-74) and artistic director (1974-84). He has since dedicated himself to composing, lecturing and conducting. He is the founder of publishing companies: Margun Music (1975), Gunmar Music (1979); and the recording company, GM Recordings (1980); all of which are dedicated to the dissemination of American music. He has lectured and written on early jazz music, and prepared scholarly editions of the music of Joplin (including the orchestration of Treemonisha). His writings include: *Horn Technique* (London and New York: Oxford University Press, 1962), *Early Jazz: Its Roots and Musical Development* (London and New York: Oxford University Press, 1968), and *Musings: The Musical Worlds of Gunther Schuller* (London and New York: Oxford University Press, 1986). Schuller's musical output is vast and diverse. He has used most of the techniques common in the twentieth century (free atonality, serialism, and combinatoriality), as well as devices from modern jazz. He also has attempted to use elements from the visual arts as technical models for his music.[74]

Awards: 3 Grammy Awards (1973, 1976, 1985), membership in the Institute (1967) and Academy (1980) of the American Academy and Institute of Arts and Letters, Rodgers and Hammerstein Award (1971), 7 honorary degrees, a Letter of Distinction from American Music Center (1985), and a MacArthur Foundation Award (1991).

Principal Works: *opera - The Visitation* (1966), *The Fisherman and his Wife* (1970); *ballet - Variants* (1960); *orchestral - 2* horn concertos (1944, 1976), Cello Concerto (1945), *Symphonic Tribute to Duke Ellington* (1955), *Contours* (1958), *Spectra* (1958), *Seven Studies on Themes of Paul Klee* (1959), Contrasts (1960), 2 piano concertos (1962, 1981), *Threnos* (1963), Doublebass Concerto (1968), *Shapes and Designs* (1969), *Four Soundscapes* (1974), Violin Concerto (1975-6), Trumpet Concerto (1979), Alto Saxophone Concerto (1983), *Farbenspiel* (1985), Viola Concerto (1985), Bassoon Concerto (1985); *vocal - O Lamb of God* (1941), *Meditations* (1960), *Poems of Time and Eternity* (1972).

Selected Composer Bibliography

Rich, Alan: "Gunther Schuller," *HiFi/Musical America*, xxvi/4 (1976), 6.
Battisti, Frank: "Gunther Schuller and His Many Worlds of Music: An Interview," *The Instrumentalist*, xxxii/11 (1978), 38.

---

[74] Norbert Carnovale: *Gunther Schuller: A Bio-Bibliography*. New York: Greenwood Press, 1987.

Hasse, John Edward: "An Interview with Gunther Schuller," *Jazz Studies*, i (1982), 39.

Tassel, Janet: "Gunther Schuller: Composer, Conductor and Musical Conscience," *Ovation*, vi/10 (1985), 23.

Clarkson, Austin: "Schuller, Gunther," in *The New Grove Dictionary of American Music*, edited by H. Wiley Hitchcock, iv: 164-6. 4 volumes. London: Macmillan, 1986.

Carnovale, Norbert: *Gunther Schuller: A Bio-Bibliography*. New York: Greenwood Press, 1987.

The Power Within Us (1971)

Duration: ca. 25 minutes

Text: H. Long translation of "La relación de Alvar Nuñez Cabeza de Vaca."

Performing Forces: *voices*: narrator, baritone soloist; SATB choir; *orchestra*: 3 flutes (flute III doubling piccolo), 3 oboes (oboe III doubling English horn), 3 bassoons (bassoon III doubling contrabassoon), 4 horns, 3 trumpets, 3 trombones, tuba, timpani, percussion (5 players - vibraphone, celeste, triangle, glockenspiel, chimes, sizzle cymbal, suspended cymbal, guiro, claves, bass drum, 3 tom-toms, marimba, medium gong, large tam-tam, maracas, castanets), harp, piano, organ (pedals only), and strings.

First Performance: 11 March 1972; Atlanta, GA; Larry Bogue, baritone, John D. Burke, narrator; Georgia Senior High School All-State Chorus and Orchestra; conducted by Schuller.

Edition: *The Power Within Us* is published by Associated Music Publishers and distributed by G. Schirmer. The piano-vocal score is for sale; orchestral materials are available for rental.

Autograph: Copies of the manuscript are at the Library of Congress, and the American Music Center.

Notes: *The Power Within Us* is composed in a single movement. In the text, Nuñez Cabeza de Vaca describes his remarkable experiences on a failed sixteenth-century expedition to the New World. He was one of four who survived from an expedition of 580. These four survivors spent eight years among the Indians healing the sick through prayer and an apparent supernatural inner strength which was summoned by their hardship. It is also a story about overcoming prejudice. The concluding text describes his realizations upon re-entering European culture:

> If one lives where all suffer and starve, one acts on one's own impulse to help, but where plenty abounds we surrender our generosity. The power of maintaining life in others lives within each of us to render life and happiness, and from each of us does it recede when unused.

Performance Issues: The choral parts are difficult, but logically written and supported by the accompaniment. The pitch language of this work betrays Schuller's involvement with jazz. He has combined the harmonic language of jazz from the 1950s and 1960s (ninth, eleventh, and thirteenth chords) with the quartal/quintal and chromatic melodic languages of concert music of the same era. The choir must execute frequent leaps, tight dissonant clusters and numerous glissandi. They must also perform *Sprechstimme* with approximate pitches (measures 349-367). The organ part occurs only in measures 503-521 and could be deemed optional, since its pitches are doubled by other instruments although not always in the correct octave. All instrumental parts are notated at sounding pitch. A large choir and string section are suggested since there are substantial divisi. These include a 5-part division in violin I, 4-part in Violin II, 4-part in the violas and cellos; the double basses have a divisi for six solo players. All of the choral parts have 3-part divisi. The percussion parts demand experienced players familiar with a broad range of playing techniques. There are sections of free repetition of ostinato patterns in the voices and the orchestra (note measures 116-119). The harpist is asked to re-tune during the works to effect certain rapid scalar passages. The indications for articulation are thoroughly labeled and always clear. The orchestration is diverse and coloristically conceived. The individual instrumental parts are not excessively difficult, but the integration of parts is quite intricate. There are a number of extended techniques for singers and players which may require explanation, but which should present no significant challenge to the performers. *Soloist*: baritone, range: F#-f', tessitura: f-d'; this role is declamatory including some *Sprechstimme*; it is full of large and awkward leaps. The lowest fourth of the range is used in only one phrase, which is sparsely accompanied and marked piano. The narrator, who speaks throughout most of the piece, is occasionally asked to speak in rhythm and to integrate his reading with certain musical events. The fact that this work was composed for a festival of high school students should not lead one to believe that it is an easily performed piece. *The Power Within Us* is a most sophisticated work requiring strong musical skills by all involved. The patchwork quality of the instrumentation demands a sensitivity for ensemble playing. This moving narrative becomes almost a theatrical work in the tradition of the Baroque cantata. It is very effectively written with great variety and excellent dramatic momentum. *Choir*: difficult; *Orchestra*: difficult.

Discography: As of January 1993, no commercial recording has been made available.

Schuman, William (b. New York, 4 August 1910; d. 15 February 1992).

Life: Schuman began his musical career writing popular songs and playing in dance bands. Upon hearing his first symphony concert in 1930 (the New York Philharmonic under Toscanini), he immediately decided to pursue a career in music. He studied harmony with Max Persin, and counterpoint with Charles Haubiel. In 1933, he entered Columbia Teacher's College (BS 1935, MA 1937). He studied at Juilliard School during the summers with Bernard Wagenaar and Adolf Schmid and then privately with Roy Harris (1936-8). He attended the Mozarteum in Salzburg during the summer of 1935, returning to teach at Sarah Lawrence College (1935-45). In 1945, Schuman was appointed consultant to G. Schirmer publishers. He simultaneously was made president of the Juilliard School (1945-62), and then president of Lincoln Center for the Performing Arts (1962-9). He retired in 1969 to dedicate himself fully to composition. He was elected to the Institute (1946) and the Academy (1973) of the American Academy and Institute of Arts and Letters. Columbia University established the William Schuman Award in his honor (1981). Schuman's music is melodically conceived and firmly rooted in diatonicism. He has a fine sense of musical architecture sometimes overlapping layers of varied melodic material to create a constantly changing sonic fabric. His harmonic language is triadic and often static with some added pitches and frequently using triads which simultaneously contain major and minor thirds.[75]

Awards: 2 Guggenheim Fellowships (1939, 1940), the first New York Critics' Circle Award (1941 for Symphony no. 3), the first Pulitzer Prize in music (1943 for *A.Free Song*) and another special Pulitzer Prize for lifetime achievement, the first Brandeis University Creative Arts Award in music (1957), a Kennedy Center Award (1989), and over 25 honorary degrees.[76]

Principal Writings: Schuman's pedagogical views are expressed in the *Juilliard Report* (New York: W.W. Norton, 1953).

Principal Works: *opera - The Mighty Casey* (1951-3); *ballet - Undertow* (1945), *Night Journey* (1947), *Judith* (1950); *orchestral -* 10 symphonies: no. 1 (1935), no. 2 (1937), no. 3 (1941), no. 4 (1941), no. 5, "Symphony for Strings" (1943), no. 6 (1948), no. 7 (1960), no. 8 (1962), no. 9, "Le fosse ardeantine" (1968), no. 10, "American Muse" (1975); Piano Concerto (1938), *American Festival Overture* (1939), *Circus Overture* (1944), Violin Concerto (1947), *Credendum* (1955), *New England Triptych* (1956), *In Praise of Shahn* (1969), *Voyage for Orchestra* (1972); *vocal - Pioneers* (1937), *Requiescat* (1942), *Truth shall Deliver* (1946), *The Young Dead Soldiers* (1975), *Time to the Old* (1979), *On Freedom's Ground* (1985).

Selected Composer Bibliography

Bernstein, Leonard: "William Schuman," *Modern Music*, xix (1942), 97.

Broder, Nathan: "The Music of William Schuman," *The Musical Quarterly*, xxxi (1945), 17.

Schreiber, Flora R., and Vincent Persichetti: *William Schuman*. New York: G. Schirmer, 1954.

Eyer, Ronald: "William Schuman: A Profile," *Musical America* (September 1962), 26.

---

[75] Harold Gleason and Walter Becker: "William Schuman," *Twentieth-Century American Composers*. Music Literature Outlines, series iv, 170-84. Bloomington, IN: Indiana University Press, revised, 1981.

[76] Bruce Lambert: "William Schuman Is Dead at 81; Noted Composer Headed Juilliard," *New York Times* (16 February 1992), 48-L.

"Schuman, William (Howard)," *Current Biography Yearbook*, iii (January 1942); xxiii, (December 1962); New York: H. W. Wilson Company.

Griffin, Malcolm Joseph: *Style and Dimension in the Choral Works of William Schuman*. University of Illinois at Urbana-Champaign: Dissertation, 1972.

Rouse, C.: *William Schuman: Documentary*. New York: Boosey and Hawkes, 1980.

Gleason, Harold, and Walter Becker: "William Schuman," *Twentieth-Century American Composers*. Music Literature Outlines, series iv, 170-84. Bloomington: Indiana University Press, revised, 1981.

Hall, David: "A Bio-Discography of William Schuman," *Ovation*, vi (1985), vii, p. 4 and viii, p. 18.

Lambert, Bruce: "William Schuman Is Dead at 81; Noted Composer Headed Juilliard," *New York Times* (16 February 1992), 48-L.

This is Our Time
(Secular Cantata no. 1) (1940)

Duration: ca. 30 minutes

Text: Genevieve Taggard

Performing Forces: *voices*: SATB choir; *orchestra*: 3 flutes, 3 oboes, 3 clarinets, 2 or 3 bassoons, 4 horns, 3 trumpets, 3 trombones, tuba, timpani, percussion, piano, and strings.

First Performance: 4 July 1940; Lewisohn Stadium, New York; People's Philharmonic Choral Society [a workers' ensemble]; conducted by Alexander Smallens.

Edition: *This is Our Time* is published and distributed by Boosey and Hawkes. The piano-vocal scores is (reduction by Paul Weissleder) for sale; orchestral materials are available for rental.

Autograph: There is a holograph in pencil in the Library of Congress (M1522. S 392 T5).

Notes: This work is written for a workers' chorus and the text and music reflect this intent. The poetry addresses the needs and aspirations of the working class with many socialist undertones. The music is logically very accessible with frequent choral unisons. The piece is in five sections as follows:

1. Celebration
2. Work
3. Foundations
4. Questions
5. Fanfares

Performance Issues: This is an easily accessed work for performers of limited skill and experience. The vocal writing employs frequent choral unisons and paired doublings. The rhythms are reflective of the natural text declamation. *Work* is for four-part men's choir and *Questions* for four-part women's choir. The orchestra parts are generally within the abilities of amateur players. The brass parts should be covered by secure players. There are prominent solos for flute and English horn. This is an example of American "socialist realism," which could be effectively programmed in association with some work or industry related event or anniversary. *Choir*: medium easy; *Orchestra*: medium easy.

Discography: As of January 1993, no commercial recording has been made available.

Selected Bibliography

Strauss, Noel: [review of the premiere], *New York Times* (5 July 1940).
"New Schuman Work Heard," *Musical America*, lx (July 1940), 27.

A Free Song
(Secular Cantata no. 2) (1942)

Duration: ca. 22 minutes

Text: adaptations of Walt Whitman's "Drum Taps"

Performing Forces: *voices*: baritone soloist (minor); SATB choir; *orchestra*: 3 flutes, 5 oboes, 4 clarinets, 4 bassoons, 4 horns, 3 trumpets, 3 trombones, tuba, timpani, percussion, and strings. The composer lists the following instruments as "optional but very desirable": oboe III, clarinet III, bassoon III, and contrabassoon.

There is an arrangement of the orchestra part for two pianos.

First Performance: 26 March 1943; Boston, MA; Boston Symphony Orchestra; conducted by Serge Koussevitsky.

Edition: *A Free Song* is published and distributed by G. Schirmer. The piano-vocal scores are for sale; orchestral materials are available for rental.

Autograph: There is a holograph ink score in the Library of Congress.

Notes: This work received the very first Pulitzer prize in music. Compare with Howard Hanson's setting of the same text. Schuman has divided his work as follows:

> I   a.   Long, Too Long America
> b.   Look Down, Fair Moon
> II   Song of the Banner

Performance Issues: This is a very approachable score for singers and players alike. It presents no great demands upon any of the parts. The choral writing is reminiscent of the socialist choral music of the 1930s. However, Schuman's score is much more technically intricate than most of those populist works. He utilizes some interesting effects, including overlapping repetition of a single word or phrase in close imitation between four parts in three octaves and the exploitation of choral unisons. This work is very accessible for amateur choirs and would be a good vehicle with which to introduce some basic twentieth-century techniques including ostinati, and some unusual rhythmic figures. The harmonic language is diatonic with occasional shifts of mode and explorations of quartal/quintal harmonies. The orchestra parts are suitable for a student or amateur ensemble. There is an oboe and English horn duet at the end of the first movement which is not difficult, but is exposed. The orchestral introduction to the second movement is very contrapuntal and opens with a quartet for clarinets. This work is vitally rhythmic in the tradition of American concert music of that era. It is filled with displaced downbeats, accent shifts, and rapidly varying articulations. *Soloist*: baritone, range: d-f#', tessitura: g-e'; this solo is only 11 measures long and should be given to a member of the choir (probably a tenor). It is very sustained, but low in dynamic level and thinly accompanied. *Choir*: easy to medium easy; *Orchestra*: medium easy.

Discography: As of January 1993, no commercial recording has been made available.

Selected Bibliography

[review of the premiere]: *Boston Daily Globe* (27 March 1943).

"Schuman Wins First Pulitzer Prize in Music," *Musical America*, lxiii (May 1943), 25.

McGlinchee, Claire: "American Literature in American Music," *The Musical Quarterly*, xxxi (1945), 108.

Mize, Lou Stem: *A Study of Selected Choral Settings of Walt Whitman's Poems*. Florida State University: Dissertation, 1967.

Wannamaker, John Samuel: *The Musical Settings of Walt Whitman*. University of Minnesota: Dissertation, 1975.

Sessions, Roger (b. Brooklyn, 28 December 1896; d. Princeton, NJ, 16 March 1985).

Life: Sessions spent his youth between Hadley, MA and New York. He entered Harvard in 1914 (BMus 1917) where he studied composition with Horatio Parker. In 1919, he began private study with Ernst Bloch. Sessions joined the faculty of Smith College (1917-21) where he taught music theory. He then became Bloch's assistant at the Cleveland Institute of Music. A series of fellowships allowed him to study throughout Europe (Berlin, Florence, Paris, and Rome) from 1926 to 1933. In 1933, he began to teach at the Dalcroze School and the New School for Social Research. Two years later, he joined the faculty of Princeton University (1935-1944, and 1953-65 as the Conant Professor of Music). From 1959 to 1965, he served as co-director, with Milton Babbitt, of the Columbia-Princeton Electronic Music Center in New York. He taught at the University of California, Berkeley (1944-53, and 1966-67 as Bloch Professor of Music). He was the Norton Professor at Harvard (1968-69) at which time he authored *Questions About Music*. He continued his academic career until his death through a part-time appointment at Juilliard.[77]   Sessions's music is very

---

[77] Harold Gleason and Walter Becker: "Roger Sessions," *Twentieth-Century American Composers*. Music Literature Outlines, series iv, 170-84. Bloomington, IN: Indiana University Press, revised 1981.

complex, exhibiting an affection for intricate textures, multi-fold contrapuntal techniques, and jagged yet precisely planned formal structures. The majority of his pieces are freely atonal, although there are eloquent passages of harmonic stability. Sessions's works are dramatic, often rhapsodic, with powerful tutti passages and spiky rhythms.[78]

Awards: 2 Guggenheim Fellowships (1926, 1927), Rome Prize (1928), Carnegie Foundation Award (1931), elected to the National Institute of Arts and Letters (1938), New York Critics' Circle Award (1950, for Second Symphony), elected to the American Academy of Arts and Letters (1953, Gold Medal in 1961), Brandeis Creative Arts Medal (1958), honorary life member of ISCM (1959), elected to the American Academy of Arts and Sciences (1961), Akademie der Kuenste (1961), MacDowell Medal (1968), the first Pulitzer Prize for lifetime achievement (1974), and another Pulitzer Prize (1982, for Concerto for Orchestra).

Principal Works: *opera - The Trial of Lucullus* (1947), *Montezuma* (1947-63); *incidental music - The Black Maskers* (1923); *orchestral* - Symphony No. 1 (1926-27), Symphony No. 2 (1944-46), Symphony No. 3 (1957), Symphony No. 4 (1958), Symphony No. 5 (1964), Symphony No. 6 (1966), Symphony No. 7 (1966-67), Symphony No. 8 (1968), Symphony No. 9 (1975-78), Violin Concerto (1930-35), Piano Concerto (1955-56), Divertimento (1959-60), Rhapsody for Orchestra (1970), Concerto for Violin, Cello, and Orchestra (1970-71), Concertino for Chamber Orchestra (1971-72), Concerto for Orchestra (1981); *vocal - Turn, O Libertad* (1944), *Idyll of Theocritus* (1954), *Mass for Unison Choir* (1955), Psalm cxl (1963), Three Choruses on Biblical Texts (1971-72).

Selected Composer Bibliography

Slonimsky, Nicholas: "Roger Sessions," in *American Composers on American Music: A Symposium*, edited by Henry Cowell, 75. New York: Frederick Ungar Publishing, 1933 (revised 1962).

---

[78] John Harbison and Andrea Olmstead: "Roger Sessions," *The New Grove Twentieth-Century American Masters*, 81-101. New York: W.W. Norton, 1986.

Sessions, Roger: *Questions About Music.* Cambridge, MA: Harvard University Press, 1970.

_____: *Sessions on Music: Collected Essays,* edited by Edward T. Cone. Princeton, NJ: Princeton University Press, 1979.

"Sessions, Roger," *Current Biography Yearbook,* xxxvi (January 1975); obituary, xlvi (May 1985); New York: H. W. Wilson Company.

Gleason, Harold, and Walter Becker: "Roger Sessions," *Twentieth-Century American Composers.* Music Literature Outlines, series iv, 185-195. Bloomington: Indiana University Press, revised 1981.

"In Memoriam Roger Sessions (1896-1985)," *Perspectives in New Music,* xxiii/2 (1985), 110.

Olmstead, Andrea: *Roger Sessions and His Music.* Ann Arbor, MI: UMI Research Press, 1985.

"An Appreciation: Roger Sessions, 1896-1985," *Kent Quarterly,* v/2 (1986).

Harbison, John, and Andrea Olmstead: "Roger Sessions," *The New Grove Twentieth-Century American Masters,* 81-101. New York: W.W. Norton, 1986.

When Lilacs Last in the Dooryard Bloom'd
(1964-70)

Duration: ca. 45 minutes

Text: Walt Whitman's poem of the same title; it is one of four poems in *Leaves of Grass* that are dedicated to the memory of Abraham Lincoln; the other three of which are: "O Captain! My Captain!" "Hush'd be the Camps To-day," and "This Dust Was Once the Man."[79]

Performing Forces: *voices*: soprano, alto, and baritone soloists, SATB choir; *orchestra*: piccolo, 2 flutes (flute II doubling alto flute), 2 oboes, English horn, E^b clarinets, 2 clarinets, bass clarinets, 2 bassoons, contrabassoon, 4 horns, 2 trumpets, 3 trombones, tuba, percussion (timpani, vibraphone, xylophone, marimba), and strings.

---

[79] George and Barbara Perkins and Phillip Leininger: *Benét's Reader's Encyclopedia of American Literature.* New York: Harper Collins, 1991.

First Performance: 23 May 1971, Berkeley, CA; Helene Joseph, Stephanie Friedman, Allen Shearer; University of California Choirs and Orchestra; conducted by Michael Senturia.

Edition: *When Lilacs. . .* is published by Merion and distributed by Theodore Presser Company. The piano-vocal score (facsimile of the composer's manuscript) is for sale; orchestral materials are available for rental.

Autograph: Sketches and manuscript are in the Princeton University Library. The piano-vocal score and rental full score are both facsimiles of the composer's manuscript.

Notes: This work was commissioned by the University of California to commemorate its centennial in 1964; it is dedicated, "To the memory of Martin Luther King, Jr. and Robert F. Kennedy." Compare with Hindemith's setting of the same text. Three elements of the poem are of particular significance: lilacs, representing spring; the star, symbolizing Lincoln; and the hermit thrush, representing the American countryside. The work is organized into three sections as follows:

I.	When lilacs last in the door-yard bloom'd	- S, Bar, and choir
II.	Over the breast of the Spring	- S, A, Bar, and choir
III.	Now while I sat in the day	- S, A, Bar, and choir

Performance Issues: All vocal and instrumental parts are musically very difficult. Sessions has indicated strict metrical modulations and performance markings. There are choral notes written in the manner of string harmonics for which no explanation is given. The score contains very complex cross-rhythms. The orchestra usually doubles the choral parts, but these doublings frequently do not occur in accompaniment of the piano-vocal score. It is interesting that the piano-vocal score is a facsimile of the composer's manuscript containing many orchestral labels. Unfortunately, it is a copy of a manuscript executed in free-hand. The vocal parts and rehearsal accompaniment are of such complexity that the clearest of editions would be likely to present frustration to the performers. Use of this edition results in futility, and the ability of the rehearsal accompanist to double the choral parts which are lacking in this reduction is greatly inhibited. The horn and trumpet parts are consistently demanding, requiring endurance and fine control of the high range. The double bass part is unusually active with much fast passagework. The piccolo and flute writing in measures 297-315 needs particular attention. There are some additional optional passages if the singers require additional support. Measure 474 to the end (m. 600) is riddled with ensemble problems, including complex passages from offstage winds. *Soloists*: All of the soloists are required to exploit the extremes of their ranges frequently. The solos are consistently angular and rhythmically erratic. Soprano, range: b^b-b", tessitura: e'-e"; alto, range: g^b-g", tessitura: b-d'; baritone, range: A-g', tessitura: d-d'. Mr. Sessions has constructed a very personal and dramatic work of great technical and emotional power. It is, however, fiercely difficult throughout for all performers, instrumental and vocal; and should only be considered if premiere ensembles are to be involved and a great deal of rehearsal time is available. It is a work deserving high-quality performances, but it does not invite them. *Choir*: difficult; *Orchestra*: difficult.

Discography: Esther Hinds, Florence Quivar, Dominic Cossa; Boston Symphony, and Tanglewood Chorus; conducted by Seiji Ozawa. First released in 1978. New World: NW-296-2 [AAD].

Selected Bibliography

Hamilton, David: "Music," *The Nation* (19 April 1975).

Kerner, Leighton: "Sessions Blooms in Chicago," *The Village Voice* (16 February 1976).

Porter, Andrew: "An American Requiem," *New Yorker*, liii (16 May 1977), 17.

Henahan, Donald: "A Soothing Sessions Leads off Contemporaries at Tanglewood," *New York Times* (15 August 1977).

Porter, Andrew: "Sessions's Passionate and Profound Lilacs," *HiFi*, xxviii/2 (1978), 17.

Swan, Annalyn: "Sessions: *When Lilacs Last in the Dooryard Bloom'd*," *Time* (26 June 1978).

Gorelick, Brian: *Movements and Shapes in the Choral Music of Roger Sessions.* University of Illinois, Champaign-Urbana: Dissertation, 1985.

Siegmeister, Elie (b. New York, 15 January 1909; d. Manhasset, NY, 10 March 1991).

Life: Siegmeister attended Columbia College (BA 1927) where he studied composition with Seth Bingham. He studied counterpoint privately with Wallingford Riegger. He studied composition with Nadia Boulanger in Paris (1927-31), and conducting with Arthur Stoessel in New York (1935-8). Siegmeister has served on the faculties of Brooklyn College (1934), the New School for Social Research (1937-8), the University of Minnesota (1948), and Hofstra University (1949-76). He was active in the organization and administration of many artistic organizations including ASCAP, the American Composers' Alliance, the American Ballad Singers, Council of Creative Artists, Libraries and Museums, the Black Music Colloquium, and the American Music Center. His music employs qualities of jazz and quotations of folk music combined with an acute awareness of melodic line. He creatively uses ostinati and songlike tunes to create very accessible yet sophisticated works. It is of primary importance that his music be relative to social issues and for consumption by the populace.[80]

Awards: Ford Foundation (1971), National Endowment for the Arts (1974, 1980), American Academy and Institute of Arts and Letters (1978), Library of Congress (1983), United States Information Agency (1985).

Principal Writings: *The New Music Lover's Handbook* (Irvington-on-Hudson, NY: 1973), *Work and Sing* (New York: 1944), *Invitation to Music* (Irvington-on-Hudson, NY: 1961), *Harmony and Melody* (1965-6).

Principal Works: *opera* - *Darling Corie* (1952), *Miranda and the Dark Young Man* (1955), *The Mermaid in Lock no. 7* (1958), *The Plough and the Stars* (1963-9), *Night of the Moonspell* (1976), *The Marquesa of O* (1982), *Angel Levine* (1984-5), *The Lady of the Lake* (1985); *orchestral* - 6 symphonies (1947, 1950, 1957, 1967-70, 1971-5, 1983), *American Holiday* (1933), *Abraham Lincoln Walks at Midnight* (1937), *Prairie Legend* (1944), *Wilderness Road* (1944) *Lonesome Hollow* (1946), *From My Window* (1949), Clarinet

---

[80] Nicholas Slonimsky: *Baker's Biographical Dictionary of Musicians,* eighth edition. New York: Schirmer Books, 1991.

Concerto (1956), Flute Concerto (1960), *Shadows and Light* (1975), Violin Concerto (1977-83), *Fantasies in Line and Color* (1981); *vocal - John Henry* (1935), *Johnny Appleseed* (1940), *A Tooth for Paul Revere* (1945), *The New Colossus* (1949), *American Folk Song Choral Series* (1953), *The Face of War* (1966), *Songs of Experience* (1966), *A Cycle of Cities* (1974), *Cantata for FDR* (1981).

Selected Composer Bibliography

Rothstein, E.: "Music: Works by Siegmeister," *New York Times* (17 January 1984).

Mandel, Alan: "Siegmeister, Elie," in *The New Grove Dictionary of American Music*, edited by H. Wiley Hitchcock, iv: 224-5. 4 volumes. London: Macmillan, 1986.

I Have a Dream (1967)

Duration: ca. 25 minutes

Text: Edward Mabley, based on Martin Luther King, Jr.'s "I have a dream. . ." speech, which crowned a major march on Washington, DC that he led in 1963.

Performing Forces: *voices*: narrator and baritone soloist; SATB chorus; there are two orchestrations depending upon the size of the choir:

small orchestra: flute (doubling piccolo), oboe, 2 clarinet (clarinet II doubling alto saxophone), bassoon, 2 horns, 2 trumpets, tenor trombone, bass trombone, percussion (1 Player - 2 timpani, snare drum, large tom-tom, 2 cymbals, wood block, 2 bongos, cowbell, xylophone, glockenspiel, tambourine), piano, and strings.

large orchestra: 2 flutes (flute II doubling piccolo), 2 oboes, 2 clarinets (clarinet II doubling alto saxophone), 2 bassoons, 4 horns, 2 trumpets, 3 trombones, tuba, percussion (2 Players - 2 timpani, snare drum, large tom-tom, 2 cymbals, wood block, 2 bongos, cowbell, xylophone, glockenspiel, tambourine), piano, and strings.

First Performance: 16 April 1967; Temple Beth Sholom, Long Beach, NY; William Warfield, narrator; Cantor Solomon

Mendelson, baritone; Ronim Choir and Cornerstone Baptist Church Choir; conducted by Herbert Beattie.

Edition: *I Have a Dream* is published by MCA Music and distributed by Theodore Presser Company. The piano-vocal score (14781-049) is available for purchase; orchestral materials are available for rental.

Autograph: There is a photocopy of the holograph in the American Music Center (M1533. 3. S5 I2).

Notes: *I Have a Dream* was commissioned by the Men's Club of Temple Beth Sholom, Long Beach, NY.

Performance Issues: The composer requests that whenever possible, the two solo roles should be performed by people of differing races. The work is tonally conceived, although it uses many non-functional seventh and ninth harmonies and imposed dissonances of diminished and augmented octaves. The choral writing is mostly homophonic with brief elements of imitation. The fifth movement begins with an unaccompanied and very chromatic fugue. With the exception of this section, the pitches of the choir are consistently doubled in the orchestra. The choral parts have a combination of rhythmic speaking and sung passages in movements 3 and 8. In movement 9, narrator's text is set in rhythm. *Soloist*: baritone, range: c-f#', tessitura: g-e', the role demands a powerful and dramatic voice. *Choir*: medium; *Orchestra*: medium.

Discography: As of January 1993, no commercial recording has been made available.

Starer, Robert (b. Vienna, 8 January 1924).

Life: Starer began his musical studies at the Vienna Conservatory (1937). He continued his education at the Jerusalem Conservatory where his teachers were Oedoen Partos, Solomon Rosowsky, and Josef Tal. He entered Juilliard in 1947 where he studied with Frederick Jacobi. In 1948, he studied with Copland at Tanglewood. The following year, he joined the faculty of Juilliard (1949-74) and later taught at Brooklyn College, CUNY (1965-). Starer's music is a unique combination of Arabic scales, jazz rhythms, and very complex contrapuntal procedures. His use of chromaticisms and modality reflect his dedication to the Jewish musical culture of his youth.[81]

Awards: 2 Guggenheim Fellowships (1957, 1963), a Fulbright grant (1964), 3 NEA grants (1976, 1978, 1983), and an award from the American Academy and Institute of Arts and Letters (1979).

Principal Works: *opera - The Intruder* (1956), *Pantagleize* (1967), *Apollonia* (1978); *ballets - The Story of Esther* (1960), *The Dybbuk* (1960), *Samson Agonistes* (1961), *Phaedra* (1962), *The Touch* (1967), *Holy Jungle* (1974); *orchestral -* 3 Symphonies (1950, 1951, 1969), 3 Piano Concertos (1947, 1953, 1972), *Journals of a Songmaker* (1975), *Violin Concerto* (1979-80), *Hudson Valley Suite* (1984), Serenade (1984); *vocal - Joseph and his Brothers* (1966), *Sabbath Eve Service* (1968), *The People, Yes* (1976), *Anna Margherita's Will* (1979), *Transformations* (1980), and *Voices of Brooklyn* (1980-84). His writings include *Rhythmic Training for Musicians* (New York: MCA Books, 1969).

Selected Composer Bibliography

Dreier, Robert: "Robert Starer," *HiFi/Musical America*, xxxiii/10 (1983), 10.
Lewis-Griffith, Dorothy: "Starer, Robert," in *The New Grove Dictionary of American Music*, edited by H. Wiley Hitchcock. London: Macmillan, 1986.

Ariel (Visions of Isaiah) (1959)

Duration: ca. 27 minutes

Text: Isaiah as arranged by the composer

Performing Forces: *voices*: soprano and baritone soloists; SATB choir; *orchestra*: 2 flutes (flute II doubling piccolo), 2 oboes, 2 clarinets, 2 bassoons, 2 horns, 2 trumpets, tenor trombone, bass trombone, percussion (2 players - timpani [2], snare drum, tenor

---

[81] Dorothy Lewis-Griffith: "Starer, Robert," in *The New Grove Dictionary of American Music*, edited by H. Wiley Hitchcock. London: Macmillan, 1986.

drum, bass drum, tambourine, crash cymbals, large suspended cymbal, large tam-tam, triangle, wood block), celeste, and strings.

First Performance: 15 May 1960; Town Hall, New York; Interracial Fellowship Choir; conducted by Harold Aks.

Edition: *Ariel* is published by MCA and distributed by Theodore Presser Company. The piano-vocal score is for sale; orchestral materials are available for rental.

Autograph: The full score is a facsimile of the composer's manuscript.

Notes: This work was commissioned by the Interracial Fellowship Chorus, Harold Aks, conductor. Ariel means "Lion of God," which is a symbolic name for Jerusalem. It is in six movements as follows:

     I. Woe to Ariel
    II. The Earth Mourneth
   III. The Daughters of Zion are Haughty
   IV. Fear, and the Pit, and the Snare
    V. The Lord Shall Give Thee Rest
   VI. Break Forth into Joy

Performance Issues: This is a highly chromatic work which follows the traditions of functional harmony. Much of the choral writing is homophonic with extended passages of unison singing and some paired doubling. There are two extended sections for two soprano parts. The vocal rhythms reflect the inherent rhythm of the text and the vocal pitches are very clearly supported by the accompaniment. The score has many vocal dissonances, many of which are approached by step, but some of which occur on entrances. There is a particularly evident exploitation of the tritone. Starer uses some passages of rhythmically notated choral speaking, the first of which is for, "and thy speech shall whisper out of the dust." There are occasional spoken passages for the baritone soloist, some of which are said over the entire ensemble. The orchestration is very pianistic in voicing and gesture. The individual orchestral parts are of moderate difficulty with few exceptional challenges to ensemble integration. The clarinet part has some difficult solos in the final movement. The choral parts present substantial pitch difficulties suggesting the need for an advanced vocal ensemble. The transparent orchestration would allow for a small string section and a fairly small choir. The fifth movement features an SATB semi-choir of solo voices or a quarter of the full choir. This group and the remaining singers are set against each other. *Soloists*: soprano, range: f'-g", tessitura: a'-f", lyric and sustained; baritone, range: c-e', tessitura: e-c', powerful, declamatory, and very rhythmic. *Choir*: medium difficult; *Orchestra*: medium.

Discography: Roberta Peters, J. Patrick; Camerata Orchestra and Singers; conducted by Abraham Kaplan. Recorded in 1972. CRI: CD 612 [ADD].

Stevens, Halsey (b. Scott, NY, 3 December 1908; d. Long Beach, CA, 20 January 1989).

Life: Stevens attended Syracuse University (BMus 1931, MMus 1937) where he was a composition student of William Berwald. He also studied with Ernst Bloch at the University of California, Berkeley (1944). He had a long and successful teaching career, including appointments at Syracuse University (1935-7), Dakota Wesleyan University (1937-41), Bradley Polytechnic Institute (1941-6), University of the Redlands (1946-7), and from 1948, the University of Southern California where he was professor emeritus until his death in 1989. He was also a guest faculty member at Yale University (1960-1) and Williams College (1970). Stevens is the recipient of 2 Guggenheim Fellowships (1964, 1971). His music is neoclassical and tonal with great rhythmic vitality and a good sense of orchestrational color. He was one of the most important authorities on Bartok, whose music has had a significant influence on Stevens's work. This can be heard in his striking rhythms and the modal chromaticisms of his melodic writing.[82]

Principal Writing: *The Life and Music of Béla Bartók* (New York: 1953, revised, 1964).

Principal Works: *orchestral* - 3 symphonies (1945-6), *A Green Mountain Overture* (1948), *Triskelion* (1953), *Sinfonia Breve* (1957), Cello Concerto (1964), *Threnos: in memoriam Quincy Porter* (1968),

---

[82] Nicholas Slonimsky: *Baker's Biographical Dictionary of Musicians*, eighth edition. New York: Schirmer Books, 1991.

Viola Concerto (1975); *choral - When I am dead, my dearest* (1938),
Go lovely rose (1942), *Like as the culver on the bared bough* (1954),
Weepe o mine eyes (1959), *The Way of Jehovah* (1963), *The Amphisbaena* (1972), *Songs from the Paiute* (1976).

Selected Composer Bibliography

Pisk, P.: "The Music of Halsey Stevens," *American Composers' Alliance Bulletin*, iv/2 (1954), 2.
Somerville, Thomas: "Some Aspects of the Choral Music of Halsey Stevens," *Choral Journal* (January 1974), 9.
Murphy, James Lawson: *The Choral Music of Halsey Stevens*. Texas Technical University: Dissertation, 1980.
Vanderkoy, P. A.: *A Survey of the Choral Music of Halsey Stevens*. Ball State University: Dissertation, 1981.

A Testament of Life (1959)

Duration: ca. 23-24 minutes

Text: Bible

Performing Forces: *voices*: tenor and bass soloists; SATB choir; *orchestra*: 2 flutes, 2 oboes, 2 clarinets, 2 bassoons, 4 horns, 3 trumpets in C, 3 trombones, tuba, timpani, percussion (3 players - snare drum, bass drum, tambourine, crash cymbals, suspended cymbals, triangle, xylophone), piano, harp, and strings.

First Performance: unable to determine

Edition: *A Testament of Life* is published and distributed by Mark Foster. The piano-vocal score is for sale; orchestral materials are available for rent.

Autograph: The full score is a facsimile of the composer's manuscript.

Notes: This work was commissioned by the Almand Memorial Fund of Stetson University in memory of Claude M. Almand.

Performance Issues: This is a very accessible composition for inexperienced performers. There are frequent short anacruses in the orchestra juxtaposed with long sustained accompanimental harmonies. The vocal writing is much more conservative than its instrumental counterpart. Most of the choral passages are homophonic with only minor imitative statements. The vocal parts are almost exclusively diatonic, and there are many choral unisons. The few strong dissonances for the singers are clearly reinforced by the orchestra. There are some simple metric modulations. The orchestra parts are generally quite easy. Stevens is careful to use very thin scoring so that a small vocal ensemble, or a young one, would be well suited to this piece. The choral portion of this piece is well within the ability of most amateur vocal ensembles and might be a good introduction to the choral orchestral repertoire for high school ensembles. The orchestra parts are accessible to a strong high school group. *Soloists*: tenor, range: c-a', tessitura: a-e', sustained and lyric; bass, range: E-e', tessitura: e-d', powerful and sustained. *Choir*: easy; *Orchestra*: easy to medium.

Discography: As of January 1993, no commercial recording has been made available.

Thompson, Randall (b. New York, 21 April 1899; d. Boston, MA, 9 July 1984).

Life: Thompson attended Harvard University (BA 1920, MA 1922) where he studied with Archibald T. Davison, Edward Burlingame Hill, Walter Spalding, and Ernst Bloch. He continued his studies at the Eastman School (1929-33). He taught at Wellesley College (1927-9, 1936-7), the University of California, Berkeley (1937-9), the Curtis Institute (1939-41), the University of Virginia (1941-6), Princeton University (1946-8), and Harvard University (1948-65). His pupils include Samuel Adler, Leonard Bernstein, Lukas Foss, Leo Kraft, and Ivan Tcherepnin. Thompson conducted an investigation of collegiate music programs under the auspices of the Association of American Colleges which produced the book *College Music* (1935). Thompson's compositional output is marked by a large quantity of fine choral works. They show a keen understanding of the singing voice and a respect for the techniques of previous centuries. He has a masterful control of imitative counterpoint and vocal color.[83]

---

[83] Harold Gleason and Walter Becker: "Randall Thompson," *Twentieth-Century American Composers*. Music Literature Outlines, series iv, 196-202. Bloomington, IN: Indiana University Press, revised 1981.

Awards: 2 Guggenheim Fellowships (1929, 1930), Fellowship from the American Academy in Rome, Elizabeth Sprague Coolidge Award for Service to Chamber Music (1941), medals from the Signet Society and Glee Club of Harvard, 4 honorary doctorates, elected to the National Institute of Arts and Letters (1938), named "Cavaliere ufficiale al merito della Repubblica Italiana" by the Italian Government (1958), and laureate of the Contemporary Composers Festival at the University of Bridgeport (1983).

Principal Works: *opera - Solomon and Balkis: The Butterfly that Stamped* (1942), *The Nativity According to St. Luke* (1961); *orchestral -* 3 symphonies (1929, 1931, 1947-9), *A Trip to Nahant* (1953-4); *choral - Five Odes of Horace* (1924), *Pueri hebraeorum* (1928), *Tarantella* (1937), *The Testament of Freedom* (1943), *The Last Words of David* (1949), *Requiem* (1957-8), *Frostiana* (1959), *The Best of Rooms* (1963), *A Psalm of Thanksgiving* (1967), *A Hymn for Scholars and Pupils* (1973), *A Concord Cantata* (1975), and *Five Love Songs* (1978). Thompson's most performed work is the *a cappella* "Alleluia" (1940), which was commissioned for the opening ceremonies of the Tanglewood Festival.

Selected Composer Bibliography

Porter, Quincy: "American Composers, XVIII, Randall Thompson," *Modern Music*, xix (1942), 237.

_____, James Haar, Alfred Mann, and Randall Thompson: "The Choral Music of Randall Thompson," *American Choral Review*, xvi/4 (1974), 1-61.

McGilvray, B. W.: *The Choral Music of Randall Thompson: An American Eclectic.* University of Missouri, Kansas City: Dissertation, 1979.

Thompson, Randall: "On Choral Composition: Essays and Reflections," edited by D. F. Urrows, *American Choral Review*, xxii/2 (1980), entire issue.

Gleason, Harold, and Walter Becker: "Randall Thompson," *Twentieth-Century American Composers*. Music Literature Outlines, series iv, 196-202. Bloomington: Indiana University Press, revised 1981.

Americana (1932)

Duration: ca. 24 minutes

Text: from the "Americana" feature of *The American Mercury* which was a collection of unusual excerpts culled from publications from throughout the country.

Performing Forces: *voices*: SATB Choir; *orchestra*: 2 flutes, 2 oboes, 2 clarinets, 2 bassoons, 2 horns, 2 trumpets in C, percussion (1 player - timpani, bass drum, cymbals, tam-tam, xylophone), harp, and strings.

First Performance: *piano-vocal*: 3 April 1932; French Institute, New York, NY; The *A Cappella* Singers of New York, conducted by the composer. This was the final work on a concert of contemporary music sponsored by the League of Composers.

orchestral: (concert) 7 and 9 March 1941; Pittsburgh, PA; Bach Choir and the Pittsburgh Symphony, conducted by Fritz Reiner.

The first actual performance with orchestra was as a special radio broadcast by the Los Angeles Symphony under the direction of Alfred Wallenstein.

Edition: *Americana* is published and distributed by E. C. Schirmer. The piano-vocal score is for sale; orchestral materials are available for rental.

Autograph: A copy of the composer's manuscript appears to be in the special collections of the Harvard University Library.

Notes: *Americana* was commissioned by the League of Composers and later orchestrated at the request of Alfred Wallenstein. This is a piece filled with humor and irony. The work is in five movements which are described by the composer in the introduction to the score as follows:

> I. *May Every Tongue* [Washington—Christian sentiment of Rev. Dr. Mark Matthews, veteran instrument of the Lord in Seattle, as reported by the *Post-Intelligencer*.] is the impassioned anathema of the preacher, discrediting science. It is vehemently chanted by the chorus, the accompaniment supplying a hymn-like background to heighten the effect.

II. *The Staff Necromancer* [New York—*The Staff Necromancer* of the *Evening Graphic* comes to the aid of troubled readers of that great family newspaper.] treats each question and answer according to the character of the questioner. Desperate, misguided humanity seeking the Delphic Oracle, the Sybils, sooth-sayers!

III. *God's Bottles* [Leaflet issued by the N.W.C.T.C.U.], suitably enough, is set for women's voices. Dare one hope that this music will do for Prohibition what *Uncle Tom's Cabin* did for slavery?

IV. *The Sublime Process of Law Enforcement* [Arkansas—*The Sublime Process of Law Enforcement* described by Joseph B. Wirger, deathhouse reporter of Little Rock *Gazette*, in *Startling Detective Adventures*.] is for mixed voices, mostly in unison. This is not 'pleasant' music. It is a short, one-act opera, deliberate and macabre — intentionally so.

V. *Loveli-lines* [California—Literary intelligence: Announcing *Loveli-lines* by Edna Nethery] is a glorification of our love of Beauty and Uplift in poetry—and advertising. The words 'Each one will lift you to heights of Consciousness,' and those following, are set as a round with chorus divided into seven parts.

Performance Issues: The orchestra score and parts have rehearsal numbers which correspond to the first measure of each page of the piano-vocal score. The vocal writing frequently utilizes choral unisons and homophonic writing, with some imitative passages in the second and last movements. The orchestration is quite transparent, allowing for a small vocal ensemble. Although this work is tonal and rhythmically concise, it demands an experienced choir because of the subtleties of texture and the need for clarity in inner voices. The singers are required to execute their material with dramatic verve and with precise ensemble rubati. There are divisi in all parts. The accompaniment consistently supports the melodic and harmonic material of the voices. The accompaniment is sparse and puts few demands upon the players beyond coordinating within an ensemble which is full of tempo changes. However, in the final movement, Thompson creates a series of displaced downbeats; and in the fourth movement, he interjects some interesting polymetric devices to heighten the emotional instability associated with the execution. This is an ideal work for a small chorus and chamber orchestra. It is musically accessible to choirs of limited experience, but it is interpretively sophisticated. This makes it a good work for training a choir to react to subtleties of text, tempo and nuance. With sufficient rehearsal time, this could provide a fine learning experience for a developing choir. It is a very witty work which would be appropriate on a program of light yet substantial works like those of Constant Lambert. *Choir*: medium easy; *Orchestra*: medium.

Discography: No. 3 only: Randolph Singers; conducted by David Randolph. Released in 1950. Concert Hall: CHC-52 [LP].
University of Michigan Choir and Symphony Orchestra; conducted by Thomas Hilbish. Recorded in 1977. New World: NW-219 [LP].

Selected Bibliography

Forbes, Eliot: "The Music of Randall Thompson," *The Musical Quarterly*, xxxv (1949), 12.

The Passion According to St. Luke (1964-65)

Duration: ca. 92 minutes

Text: *The Gospel According to St. Luke*; chapters: 19, 22, and 23.

Performing Forces: *voices*: tenor and baritone soloists; SATB choir; *orchestra*: 2 flutes (flute II doubling piccolo), 2 oboes (oboe II doubling English horn), 2 clarinets, 2 bassoons, 4 horns, 2 trumpets in C, 3 trombones, tuba, timpani, percussion (3 players - bass drum, cymbals, triangle, tenor drum, large wooden mallet), and strings.

First Performance: 28 March 1965; Symphony Hall, Boston, MA; Boston Handel and Haydn Society; conducted by Edward Gilday.

Edition: *The Passion According to St. Luke* is published and distributed by E. C. Schirmer. The piano-vocal score is for sale; orchestral materials are available for rental.

Autograph: The full score is a facsimile of the composer's manuscript.

Notes: This work was composed in honor of the sesquicentennial of the Boston Handel and Haydn Society. It is comprised of ten scenes which are organized into two parts. An intermission should divide these sections. The baritone soloist portrays Jesus, and the tenor portrays Peter and Pilate.

Performance Issues: The choir functions as the narrator and represents crowds. The choral writing is generally homophonic in a tertian harmonic language comprised mostly of non-functional seventh and ninth chords. Thompson uses choral unisons and frequent paired doublings between the sopranos and tenors, and the altos and basses. Much of Thompson's vocal music is strictly diatonic, a feature which he exploits to great effect in his shorter works, but one which seems less successful in a work of this length. Six tenors and six basses are to sing the text of the apostles, which is scored for four-part male choir. This is a dramatically-conceived work involving many elements of theater, but there are a number of extended instrumental passages which seem to have no significance to the surrounding texts. The orchestra parts are very conservatively written and well within the grasp of moderately experienced players. There are a number of small *choral solos*: a Maid - soprano (range: e'-f#"), first Owner - mezzo (range: e'-c#"), first Disciple - tenor (range: f#-f#'), second Malefactor - tenor (range: c-f'), second Owner - baritone (range: e-c#'), John - baritone (range: B-b^b), a Man - baritone (range: c#-d#'), first Malefactor - baritone (range: g-e^b'), Another Man - bass (range: F#-c#'), Roman Centurion - bass (d-g), second Disciple - bass (range: f#-a). *Principal Soloists*: Peter/Pilate - tenor, range: d-b^b', tessitura: g-f', this role is fairly small and would be best served by a bright voice; Jesus - baritone, range: G#-f", tessitura: c-c', this is a role of substantial size, requiring endurance and a lyrical voice with fine text declamation. This work is in the mold of the *Crucifixions* of Maunder and Stainer. This is probably Thompson's longest work and it suffers from a lack of musical variety which cannot sustain interest over such a long time in a concert situation. There are many lovely sections within the piece, but in this case the sum is weaker than its parts. However, this is a much better crafted work than many of the compositions featured in contemporary Passion services and would be well suited to such use. *Choir*: medium easy; *Orchestra*: medium easy.

Discography: As of January 1993, no commercial recording has been made available.

Selected Bibliography

Rogers, Harold: [review of the premiere], *Christian Science Monitor* (1 April 1965).
[review], *Notes*, xxiv/2 (December 1967).

Tippett, Sir Michael Kemp (b. London, 2 January 1905).

Life: Tippett studied at the Royal College of Music (composition with Charles Wood, conducting with Adrian Boult and Malcolm Sargent). In 1930, he studied counterpoint and fugue with Reginald Morris. The influence of Renaissance and Baroque models is evident throughout much of his music. Tippett served as a schoolmaster and conductor of a Choral Society. From 1940-51, he was music director of Morley College, and from 1971-4 he was director of the Bath Festival. He was jailed in 1943 for failure to comply with the regulations of his conscientious objection to military service. His commitment to peace has remained a focal point of his career.[84]

Awards: Commander, Order of the Order of the British Empire (1959), knighthood (1966), and Companion of Honour in (1979).

Principal Works: *operas* - *The Village Opera* (1929), *Robin Hood* (1934), *Robert of Sicily* (1938), *The Midsummer Marriage* (1952), *King Priam* (1961), *The Knot Garden* (1970), *The Ice Break* (1976); *instrumental* - four symphonies (1945, 1957, 1972, 1977); three piano sonatas (1937, 1962, 1973); four string quartets (1935, 1942, 1946, 1978), Concerto for Double String Orchestra (1939); Concerto for Piano and Orchestra (1955); Concerto for Orchestra (1963); Concerto for Violin, Viola, Cello and Orchestra (1979); *choral* - *Crown of the Year* (1958), Magnificat and Nunc Dimittis for Choir and Organ (1961), *The Mask of Time* (1984).

---

[84] Meirion Bowen: *Michael Tippett*. London: Robson, 1982.

Selected Composer Bibliography

Hansler, George E.: *Stylistic Characteristics and Trends in the Choral Music of Five Twentieth-Century Composers: A Study of the Choral Works of Benjamin Britten, Gerald Finzi, Constant Lambert, Michael Tippett, and William Walton.* New York University: Dissertation, 1957.

Tippett, Michael: *Moving Into Aquarius.* St. Albans, England: Paladin, 1974.

"Tippett, Sir Michael Kemp," *Current Biography Yearbook,* xxxv (September 1974); New York: H. W. Wilson Company.

Matthews, David: *Michael Tippett - An Introductory Study.* London: Faber and Faber, 1980.

Bowen, Meirion (ed.): *Music of the Angels - Essays and Sketchbooks of Michael Tippett.* London: Eulenberg, 1980.

_____: *Michael Tippett.* London: Robson, 1982.

Kemp, Ian: "Michael Tippett," *The New Grove Twentieth-Century English Masters,* 201-36. New York: W.W. Norton, 1986.

Theil, Gordon: *Michael Tippett: A Bio-Bibliography.* New York: Greenwood Press, 1989.

Whittall, Arnold: *The Music of Britten and Tippett: Studies in Themes and Techniques,* second edition. Cambridge: Cambridge University Press, 1990.

A Child of Our Time (1939-41)

Duration: ca. 65-70 minutes

Text: Tippett and traditional spirituals, see "notes" below

Performing Forces: *voices:* soprano, alto, tenor, and bass soloists; SATB choir; *orchestra:* 2 flutes, 2 oboes, English horn, 2 clarinets, 2 bassoons, contrabassoon, 4 horns, 3 trumpets, 3 trombones, timpani, percussion (1 Player - cymbals), and strings.

First Performance: 19 March 1944; Adelphi Theater, London; Joan Cross, Margaret McArthur, Peter Pears, Roderick Lloyd; London Region Civil Defense Choir, Morley College Choir, London Philharmonic Orchestra; conducted by Walter Goehr.

Edition: *A Child of Our Time* is published by Schott and distributed by European-American Music. The piano-vocal score (#10065) and study-score (#10899) are available for sale; orchestral materials are available for rental.

Autograph: The ink score is held in possession of the composer; a pencil copy is in the British Library (Add. MS 61754).

Notes: Tippett asked his friend T.S. Eliot to author the text, but under Eliot's advice and guidance, he wrote it himself. The work was composed in reaction to the monstrous *Krystallnacht* and the particular plight of Herschel Feibel Grynspan whose desperate assassination of German diplomat, Ernst von Rath, led to the Nazi pogroms of November 1938 in the Jewish Ghettos of Germany. Tippett describes the work as a Passion of a man, rather than a God.[85] Instead of the chorales of Bach's tradition, Tippett used African-American spirituals. These spirituals are published separately as *Five Negro Spirituals* (1958) for unaccompanied choir (Schott # 10585).

Performance Issues: Tippett's work is a provocative amalgamation of styles ranging from Handelian counterpoint to jazz-influenced harmonies and rhythms. The five spirituals ("Steal away"; "Nobody knows the trouble I've seen, Lord"; "Go down, Moses"; "O, by and by"; and "Deep River") are the choral highlights of the piece, creating a complex web of solo and choral passages. No. 11 is written for double choir. The orchestra writing is very approachable; only the trumpet parts present a significant challenge. They are high and sustained, but there is adequate recovery time between difficult passages (see nos. 18-21). Contrapuntally complex choral passages are generally doubled by instrumental lines. Narrative sections are vocally difficult in terms of pitch learning (see nos. 1, 13, 19, and 26). *Soloists*: The solo roles are all demanding, especially that of the soprano, who must have a strong low register and control of a soft high $b^{b''}$. Soprano, range: $e'\text{-}b^{b'''}$, tessitura: $g'\text{-}g''$, very dramatic with sustained forte passages; Alto, range: $b^b\text{-}f''$, tessitura: $e'\text{-}c''$, lyric, not very demanding, but requiring a flexible top range; Tenor, range: $c\text{-}b^{b'}$, tessitura: $e\text{-}g'$, declamatory, requiring power and clarity throughout the entire range; Bass, range: $B\text{-}e'$, tessitura: $c\text{-}c'$, legato and

---

[85] Gordon Theil: *Michael Tippett: A Bio-Bibliography.* New York: Greenwood Press, 1989.

narrative in quality, although rhythmically complex, particularly in no.28. *Choir*: difficult; *Orchestra*: difficult.

Discography: Elsie Morison, Pamela Bowden, Richard Lewis, Richard Standen; Royal Liverpool Philharmonic Orchestra and Choir; conducted by John Pritchard. Recorded March 1957. Argo: ZDA 19-20 [LP], re-released as London (British Collection): 425158-2 LM [ADD].

Jessye Norman, Dame Janet Baker, Richard Cassilly, John Shirley-Quirk; BBC Singers, Choral Society, and Symphony Orchestra; conducted by Colin Davis. Philips: 420 075-2 [ADD].

Sheila Armstrong, Felicity Palmer, Philip Langridge, John Shirley-Quirk; Brighton Festival Chorus, Royal Philharmonic Orchestra; conducted by André Previn. MCA Classics: MCAD-6202 [DDD], re-released as RPO Records: RPO 7012 [DDD].

Selected Bibliography

Amis, John: "New Choral Work by Michael Tippett," *The Musical Times*, lxxxv (1944), 41.

Evans, Edwin: "A Child of Our Time," *The Musical Times*, lxxxv (April 1944), 124.

Long, N.G.: "*A Child of Our Time*; a Critical Analysis of Michael Tippett's Oratorio," *The Music Review*, viii (1947), 120.

Amis, John: "A Child of Our Time," *The Listener*, xliv (1951), 436.

Cowell, Henry: "Review of M. Tippett: *A Child of Our Time*," *The Musical Quarterly*, xxxviii (1952), 443.

Mason, Colin: "Tippett and his Oratorio," *The Listener*, xxxviii (1955), 129.

Tippett, Michael: "*A Child of Our Time*: Michael Tippett," in *The Composer's Point of View: Essays on Twentieth-Century Choral Music by Those Who Wrote It*, edited by Robert Stephan Hines, 111-22. Norman, OK: University of Oklahoma Press, 1963.

Foreman, Lewis: *From Parry to Britten: British Music in Letters 1900-1945*, 255, 256. Portland, OR: Amadeus Press, 1987.

Vision of St. Augustine (1963-65)

Duration: ca. 35 minutes

Text: The Bible and St. Augustine (Tippett uses St. Augustine's vision of eternity as described in his *Confessions* as the focal point of the work.)

Performing Forces: *voices*: baritone soloist, SATB choir; *orchestra*: 2 flutes (both doubling piccolo), oboe, English horn, clarinet, bass clarinet, bassoon, contrabassoon, 4 horns, 2 trumpets (trumpet II doubling piccolo trumpet in D), 3 trombones, tuba, timpani, percussion (5 players - xylophone/marimba, tenor drum, snare drum, tambourine, bass drum, tam tam, glockenspiel, cymbals, chimes, whip, 2 wood blocks, temple blocks, metal sheet), harp, celeste, piano, and strings.

First Performance: 19 January 1966, Royal Festival Hall, London; Dietrich Fischer-Dieskau, BBC Symphony and Chorus; conducted by Tippett.

Edition: *The Vision of St. Augustine* is published by Schott and distributed by European-American Music. The piano-vocal score (#10898) and study score (#10897) are for sale; orchestral materials are available for rental.

Autograph: Both manuscripts are in the British Library: ink (Add. MS 61792) and pencil (Add. MS 61791).

Notes: This work was commissioned by the BBC and is dedicated to the memory of Tippett's parents. The text is based upon two visions of St. Augustine which Tippett describes in the preface to the full score as follows:

> In a garden near Milan, with Alypius his dearest friend, at 33 years of age, he had his first vision (if we may call it that, being only auditory)—of a child singing: *tolle lege* (take up and read). Of course there was no real child, as Augustine realized. Such a vision, whereby something apparently real appears to someone under extreme mental stress, is relatively common. In Augustine's case it led to his final submission to Christianity and to the extreme asceticism that was regarded as necessary in that period.
>
> Some months later he decided to return with his mother [Monica] to Africa. They travelled overland to Ostia, the port of Rome, and rested there before the sea voyage. Here, five days before Monica's death, Augustine

had a second vision, which Monica shared—of Eternity. This experience, known to mystics, is much rarer.

For all his rhetoric Augustine was a priest, not a poet. He should be compared with Dante; who in *The Divine Comedy* pursues finally the same vision. The composer setting Augustine's text is in this sense a poet. Apart from the music, I have had to amplify the text by other Latin quotations from the *Confessions* and from the Latin Bible.

There is one ancient musical tradition that needs mention: the belief that ecstasy forces from us a jubilation beyond words, beyond sense, expressed by melismata of vowel sounds only. The technical name is glossolalia. I have used such glossalalia in various forms, from the traditional *alleluia* (Praise-be-to-Ja, i. e. Jehovah), to the set of Greek vowels iaw, awi, wia, taken from *Pistis Sophia*, from a supposed prayer of Christ to his father...

In the text which follows and in the score itself, all bible quotations are printed in italics to distinguish them from Augustine's own words and the hymn of St. Ambrose.

Performance Issues: Nearly all of this piece is in Latin, with a few passages in Greek and only the final phrase (which is spoken in rhythm) is in English. The choral parts often outline dense tone clusters and are rhythmically independent and very complex. The choir is divided into two to eight parts. Tippett aligns the parts into opposing groups in rhythmic counterpoint. There are frequent melismas of great complexity, and regular repetitions of a single vowel sound at a given pitch on successive staccato sixteenth notes. Vocal lines are not consistently reinforced in the accompaniment and in fact are often dissonantly opposed to the instrumental parts. There are numerous glissandi for the voices and strings. All of the instrumental parts are ridden with intricate passagework and formidable rhythms. Of especial difficulty are the flutes, clarinets, mallets, and harp parts. Between [78] and [83], there is a prominent and challenging horn quartet. The integration of the ensemble is an issue of legitimate concern. The score has constant changes in meter and tempo. It also exploits the interplay between diverse and independently complicated rhythms. The orchestration is fairly thin throughout, suggesting a small choir. This composition includes many unusual vocal sounds based upon vowel repetition and vocal pulses which appear in no other works in this study. The rhythmic and pitch complexities of the choral parts, as well as the physical demands on the voices, limit the performance of this work to the most elite of choirs. It is a dramatic and musically provocative piece which is unfortunately beyond the means of most ensembles. *Soloist*: baritone, range: A^b-f#', tessitura: g-e', this is a very demanding role, both musically and vocally. It is rhythmic, melodically jagged, and requires vocal stamina. There is a three-measure soprano solo, range: d^b'-b^b". *Choir*: difficult; *Orchestra*: difficult.

Discography: John Shirley-Quirk; London Symphony Orchestra and Chorus; conducted by Tippett. Recorded at Walthamstow Town Hall, June 1971. RCA: Red Seal RL 89498 [LP].

Selected Bibliography

Rubbra, Edmund: "The Vision of St. Augustine," *The Listener*, lxxvi (1966), 74.

Mellers, Wilfrid: "Tippett's Vision," *New Statesman*, lxxi (28 January 1966), 138.

Lambert, J. W.: "Tippett's *Vision* Premiere," *Christian Science Monitor* (2 February 1966).

Souster, Tim: "Michael Tippett's Vision," *The Musical Times*, cvii (1966), 20.

Warrack, John: "The Vision of St. Augustine," *The Musical Times*, cvii (1966), 228-9.

Kemp, Ian: "Michael Tippett," *The New Grove Twentieth-Century English Masters*. New York: W.W. Norton, 1986. 218, 226-8.

Shires Suite (1965-70)

Duration: ca. 20 minutes

Text: various, see below

Performing Forces: *voices*: SATB choir; *orchestra*: 3 flutes (flutes II and III doubling piccolo), 2 oboes, English horn, 2 clarinets, bass clarinet, 2 bassoons, contrabassoon, 4 horns, 3 trumpets, 3 trombones, tuba, timpani, percussion (5 players - tam tam, chimes, claves, iron bar, glockenspiel, xylophone, bongos, castanets, trap set, wood blocks, whip, tambourine, sleigh bells, rattle, cymbals, suspended cymbal, metal plates, bass drum, military drum), harp, piano, celeste, electric-guitar, and strings.

First Performance: 8 July 1970; Cheltenham Town Hall; Schola Cantorum of Oxford, Leicestershire Schools Symphony Orchestra; conducted by Tippett.

Edition: *Shires Suite* is published by Schott and distributed by European-American Music. There are separate piano-reduction editions of the Prologue #10911 and Epilogue #10912; and a piano-vocal score of the Cantata #10852, all of which are for sale; orchestral materials may be rental.

Autograph: The ink score of Interludes I and II, and Cantata are in the British Library (Add. MS 61793). The manuscripts of the Prologue and Epilogue are lost.

Notes: The following is extracted from the composer's notes in the full score:

> The *Shires Suite* has been written for the Leicestershire Schools Senior Orchestra over the past few years: Prologue and Epilogue 1965; Interlude II 1969; Interlude I and Cantata 1970. The members of the orchestra (which changes annually as the older members leave school) playing on the same instruments as professional use, can produce an astonishing virtuosity. School choirs of the same age group, on the other hand, cannot produce a comparable quality of sound as they have not the necessary adult chest resonance. The singing in the *Shires Suite* was therefore always intended to be reasonably easy, and based on well-known canons. The orchestra was put clearly first.

> The Prologue is a setting of 'soomer is i-coomen in.'

> The orchestral Interlude I is the slow one, somewhat on the lines of a chorale prelude. It is based on the canon "The Silver Swan." The three melodic lines of the canon are presented at different speeds as between: Trumpet and Trombone (plain, normal speed); Strings (decorated and

much transformed, twice as slow); bells and woodwind (clusters, one-and-a-half times as slow).

The Cantata is a setting of three canons, before each of which the choir sing "Come let us sing you a song in canon." First a hunting canon by Byrd to the words: "Hey, ho, to the Greenwood..." Second a drinking catch by Purcell to the words: "Fie, nay prithee, John..." Third a canon by Alexander Goehr to an epigram of William Blake, presented to me on my sixtieth birthday. The words [begin]: "The sword sung on the barren heath..."

The orchestral Interlude 2 is very fast, of considerable virtuosity and occasionally jazzy. The canon "Great Tom is Cast" appears three times.

The Epilogue is a setting of Byrd's canon "Non nobis, Domine." This beautiful canon is sung in the Leicestershire State Schools as a Grace. The words are: "Non nobis, Domine, non nobis, Sed nomini tuo, da gloriam."

Performance Issues: This work is composed very knowledgeably for student ensembles. A number of special considerations have been made to accommodate young players of varied abilities. As the composer explains:

Violins can be used to play suitable portions of the viola part. There is no essential need for viola colour. The opening bar to the Cantata (for piano) is only to be played when the Cantata is performed separately (to give the choir a pitch note). The tiny hunting horns are single note instruments which sound at the pitch written. With the chorus megaphones, i. e. loud-hailers, the effect is momentarily also visual. The same goes for figure 26 where the pop-pop can be done with the finger in the cheek (or actual corks and bottles), and the clinks with real drinking glasses. The ff crash can be metal trays of cutlery dropped. The loud laughter must continue ff and suddenly cease. The extended horn part in Interlude II is written under the system that the whole group of horns present produces the single part by combination, according to abilities. In the same way, the violin parts are not so much to be thought of as divided first and second, but divided between those who can bow at speed and those who can't. With professional players this system of obtaining virtuosity from young performers does not apply, but the score and parts are nevertheless left as originally written.

The choral writing is very accessible with canonic writing and many unisons. Some of the alto parts are unusually high, but the exchange of parts in these sections is practical. Most of the orchestra parts could be mastered by a typical municipal youth orchestra, but there are some very difficult polyrhythms in the first interlude which are aided by the slow tempo, but which require the execution of some awkward arrangements of 12 against 16. That is by far the most difficult movement and could be logically left out if above the level of the ensemble. Much of the Cantata is *a cappella* and the remainder very lightly accompanied. The Cantata movement is a very witty arrangement of three independent canons. The choir must divide into six parts. This work should not be the victim of prejudice from professional ensembles because of its supposed technical accessibility. It is excellent music and is actually quite challenging. The presentation of a wide selection of traditional canons and the inclusion of well conceived musical humor is delightfully refreshing. Of the wide array of quality *Gebrauchsmusik* written in this century, this is the most notable for mixed choir and orchestra in English. *Choir*: easy to medium easy; *Orchestra*: medium easy.

Discography: Leicestershire Schools Symphony Orchestra and Chorale; conducted by Peter Fletcher. Recorded at De Montfort Hall, Leicester, April 1980. Unicorn: UNS 267 [LP].

Selected Bibliography

Oliver, Michael: "Tippett: *Shires Suite*," *Gramophone*, lix (June 1981), 44.
Freed, Richard: "Tippett: *Shires Suite*," *Stereo Review*, xlvii (April 1982), 100-1.

Vaughan Williams, Ralph (b. Down Ampney, Gloucestershire, 12 October 1872; d. London, 26 August 1958).

Life: Vaughan Williams received his early training in piano, figured bass, and harmony from his aunt. He attended Charterhouse preparatory school where he took up the viola. He then enrolled in the Royal College of Music (1892-4) and Trinity College, Cambridge (BMus 1894, BA in Music Theory 1895). He then returned to the RCM for an additional year's study. During this six-year period, RVW's composition teachers included Alan Gray, Charles Wood, Hubert Parry, and Charles Villiers Stanford. He received additional tutelage from Max Bruch in Berlin (1897) and Maurice Ravel (1908). He met Holst at the RCM in 1895, the two composers collegially criticized each other's sketches regularly until Holst's death in 1934. RVW taught composition at the RCM (1915-40), conducted the Leith Hill Festival (1905-53), and was director of the London Bach Choir (1920-8). He wrote extensively on issues of musical nationalism, history, and current trends. He also did substantial work in folk-song research collecting and cataloguing over 800; and he edited Jacobean and Elizabethan music, all of this helped to crystalize the "English" quality in his music. RVW served as editor for the *English Hymnal* (1906) for which he composed a number of original hymns and made adaptations of about 40 folk songs. This constant connection with religious themes was, for Vaughan Williams, a recognition of his history and the aspirations of his culture. For this he had profound respect while remaining an agnostic throughout his adult life. His music is personal and distinctive combining the regal quality of Elgar with native folk song and an orchestration reflecting the influence of Ravel and Delius. He was politically outspoken and involved in many public issues. This sense of community involvement and sincere concern for his fellowman can be heard in his works which speak directly to the listener.[86]

Awards: The Order of Merit (1935), Cobbett Medal (1930), Gold Medal of the Royal Philharmonic Society (1930), Collard Life Fellow (1934, succeeding Elgar), Shakespeare Prize (1937), and the Albert Medal of the Royal Society of Arts (1955). He also refused numerous official titles and knighthood.

---

[86] Ursula Vaughan Williams: *R.V.W.: A Biography*, revised. London: Oxford University Press, 1985.

Principal Works: *opera - Hugh the Drover* (1910-14), *Sir John in Love* (1925-9), *Riders to the Sea* (1925-32), *The Poisoned Kiss* (1927-9), *The Pilgrims' Progress* (1925-36, 1944-51); *film scores - The 49th Parallel* (1940-1), *The Loves of Joanna Golden* (1946), *Scott of the Antarctic* (1947-8), *The England of Elizabeth* (1955), *The Vision of William Blake* (1957); *orchestral* - 9 Symphonies: *Sea Symphony* (1906-9), *London Symphony* (1911-14), *Pastoral Symphony* (1916-21), No. 4 in F Minor (1931-5), No. 5 in D Major (1938-43), No. 6 in E Minor (1944-7), *Sinfonia Antartica* (1949-52), No. 8 in D Minor (1953-5), No. 9 in E Minor (1956-8); *In Fen Country* (1904), *Norfolk Rhapsody* (1906), *The Wasps* (1909), *Fantasia on a Theme of Thomas Tallis* (1910), *English Folk Song Suite* (band - 1923), *Fantasia on Greensleeves* (1934), *Five Variants on "Dives and Lazarus"* (1939), Concerto Grosso for String (1950); *choral - Five Mystical Songs* (1911), Mass in G (1920-1), *Benedicite* (1929), *Choral Songs in Time of War* (1940), *A Vision of Aeroplanes* (1955), and many songs and chamber works.

Selected Composer Bibliography

Kimmel, William: "Vaughan Williams's Choice of Words," *Music and Letters*, xix (1938), 132.

"Vaughan William, Ralph," *Current Biography Yearbook*, xiv (December 1953); obituary, xix (November 1958); New York: H. W. Wilson Company.

Willetts, Pamela J.: "The Vaughan Williams Collection," *British Museum Quarterly*, xxiv (1961), 3.

Day, James: *Vaughan Williams*. London: J. M. Dent, 1961.

Ottaway, Hugh: *Vaughan Williams*. London: Novello, 1966.

Kennedy, Michael: *A Catalogue of the Works of Ralph Vaughan Williams*. London: Oxford University Press, 1982.

Vaughan Williams, Ursula: *R. V. W.: A Biography* revised. London: Oxford University Press, 1985.

Ottaway, Hugh: "Ralph Vaughan Williams," *The New Grove Twentieth-Century English Masters*, 97-144. New York: W.W. Norton, 1986.

Vaughan Williams, Ralph: *National Music and Other Essays*, second edition. London: Oxford University Press, 1987.

Butterworth, Neil: *Ralph Vaughan Williams: A Guide to Research*. New York: Garland Publishing, 1990.

A Sea Symphony (1903-09, rev. 1924)

Duration: ca. 60-67 minutes

Text: Walt Whitman, specific poems are listed under "notes."

Performing Forces: *voices*: soprano and baritone soloists; SATB choir; *orchestra*: 3 flutes (flute II doubling piccolo, flute III is optional), 2 oboes (oboe II is optional), English horn, 2 clarinets in A, clarinet in E^b (optional), bass clarinet (optional), 2 bassoons, contrabassoon (optional), 4 horns, 3 trumpets, 3 trombones, 1 tuba, timpani, percussion (3 or 4 players - bass drum, snare drum, triangle, suspended cymbal, crash cymbals), 2 harps (harp II is optional), organ (optional), and strings.

First Performance: 12 October 1910; Town Hall, Leeds; Cecily Gleeson-White, soprano; Campbell McInnes, baritone; Edward Bairstow, organ; Leeds Festival Orchestra and Chorus; conducted by the composer.

Edition: The 1909 version of *A Sea Symphony* was published by Breitkopf and Härtel. The 1924 edition is published by Stainer and Bell. Piano-vocal, choral, and study scores may be purchased; the full score, orchestral materials, and choral scores are available for rental.

Autograph: The composer's manuscripts of *A Sea Symphony* are in the British Library (Add. MSS. 50361, 50362-3, 50364, 50365, 50366).

Notes: This work is in four movements using the indicated Whitman texts and organized as follows:

I.	A Song for All Seas, All Ships	"Songs of the Exposition"
		"Songs for All Seas, All Ships"
II.	On the Beach at Night	"On the Beach at Night, Alone" from "Clef Poems"
III.	Scherzo (The Waves)	"After the Sea-Ship" from "Two Rivulets"
IV.	The Explorers	from "Passage to India"

Performance Issues: The trumpet parts are in F. When reduced forces are to be utilized, there are cues throughout the score to assure the presence of all of the pitches. In the event that a bass clarinet is unavailable, there is a special part written out for the bassoon II. Virtually all of the instrumental parts are technically demanding with particularly fierce passagework in the woodwinds. Although the composer has authorized an optional reduction of parts, this should be considered undesirable. Not only would the orchestrational palette be diminished, but not all of the optional instruments' inner melodic lines are doubled elsewhere. Therefore, such a reduction impinges upon the counterpoint as well as the timbre of the work. The orchestration owes much to Ravel's influence. The work was begun before his tutiledge with the French master, and completed shortly after RVW returned to England. There is a good deal of imitative counterpoint in the vocal parts. Here, paired imitation is the norm with a regular variation of the pairings of vocal parts. Cross-rhythms are abundant in this work with many simutaneous divisions of the beat occurring throughout. The choral writing is well conceived for the voices, particularly the manner in which the text has been rhythmically interpreted. The choral harmonies are generally tertian and dissonances are achieved through step-wise motion. There are divisions in all choral parts. There are also sections for semi-chorus, which is intended to be a section of the principal choir. The breadth of the orchestration and the quantity of sustained singing required from the choir suggest a very large vocal ensemble. The clarity of diction will prove to be problematic due to the contrapuntal overlapping of text and the neccesary size of the choir. The quantity of singing will prove a challenge to vocal endurance and also presents a large portion of music to be learned by the choir. This is a massive work of the highest quality. It is within the grasp of only the finest symphonic ensembles, but is deserving of frequent hearings. *Soloists*: soprano, range: a-b", tessitura: g'-g", very sustained and dramatic, requiring clarity in the low register and freedom in the top; baritone, range: B-f', tessitura: d-d', this role is declamatory with sustained singing in the upper range, a resonant and powerful voice is needed. The accompaniment is generally thinner under the soprano than it is for the baritone. *Choir*: difficult, *Orchestra*: difficult.

Discography: Yvonne Kenny, Brian Rayner-Cook; London Symphony Órchestra and Chorus; conducted by Bryden Thomson. Chandos: CHAN 8764 [DDD]. This recording is also included in a boxed set of all nine of Vaughan-Williams symphonies as Chandos: CHAN 9087-91 [DDD].

Sheila Armstrong, John Carol Case; London Philharmonic Orchestra and Chorus; conducted by Sir Adrian Boult. Angel: CDM-64016 [ADD]. This recording is also included in a boxed set of all nine of Vaughan-Williams symphonies as Angel: CDM-63098 [ADD].

Dame Isobel Baillie, John Ewen Cameron; London Philharmonic Orchestra and Chorus; conducted by Sir Adrian Boult. Recorded in the early 1950's. Decca: LXT 2907/8 [LP]; re-released as London: 425658-2 LM [ADD mono].

Helen Bickers, Randi Blooding; Communauté Française de Belgique Youth Orchestra, The Choral Guild of Atlanta; conducted by W. Noll. Newport Classics: NCD 60134 [DDD].

Heather Harper, John Shirley-Quirk; London Symphony Orchestra and Chorus; conducted by André Previn. RCA: 60580-2-RG [ADD].

Felicity Lott, Jonathan Summers; London Philharmonic Orchestra and Chorus; conducted by Bernard Haitink. Angel: CDC-49911 [DDD].

Joan Rodgers, William Shimell; Royal Liverpool Philharmonic Orchestra and Chorus; conducted by Vernon Handley. Angel: CDM-69867 [DDD].

Smoryakova, Vasiliev; USSR Ministry of Culture Symphony Orchestra and Leningrad Choruses; conducted by Gennady Rozhdestvensky. Recorded live: 30 April 1988 in Leningrad Philharmonic Grand Hall. Melodiya: SUCD 10-00234 [DDD].

Selected Bibliography

Abraham, Gerald: "Vaughan Williams and his Symphonies: 1. The *Sea Symphony*," *The Musical Standard*, xxvii (20 February 1926), 56.

Blom, Eric: "Vaughan Willams: *A Sea Symphony*," *The Music Teacher*, viii/11 (November 1930), 661-62.

Brian, Havergal: "The Music of Ralph Vaughan Williams," *Musical Opinion*, lxiii/752 (May 1940), 345-46; and lxiii/753 (June 1940), 391.

Goddard, Scott: "Vaughan Williams' *Sea Symphony*," *The Listener*, liii (3 February 1955), 217.

Hurd, Michael: "Vaughan Williams' *Sea Symphony*," *Music in Education*, xxix/311 (January/February 1965), 27-28; and xxix/312 (March/April 1965), 83-84.

Sutton, W.: "Music and the Sea," *Musical Opinion*, xciv (June 1971), 445-46.

Clarke, F. R.: "The Structure of Vaughan Williams' *Sea Symphony*," *The Music Review*, xxxiv/1 (1973), 58-61.

Hurd, Michael: *The Ordeal of Ivor Gurney*. London: Oxford University Press, 1978.

Foreman, Lewis: *From Parry to Britten: British Music in Letters 1900-1945*, 2, 41-2, 43, 86, 280. Portland, OR: Amadeus Press, 1987.

Sancta Civitas (1923-25)

Duration: ca. 31-32 minutes

Text: Authorized version of The Revelation of St. John: XVIII, XXI, and XXII; and Taverner's Bible.

Performing Forces: *voices*: tenor and baritone soloists; SATB choir, semi-choir, distant choir; *orchestra*: 4 flutes, 2 oboes, English horn, 3 clarinets, 2 bassoons, contrabassoon, 4 horns, 3 trumpets, 3 trombones, tuba, timpani, percussion (snare drum, bass drum cymbals), harp, piano, organ, and strings.

First Performance: 7 May 1926; Sheldonian Theater, Oxford; Arthur Cranmer, Trefor Jones; Oxford Bach Choir, Oxford Orchestral Society; conducted by Hugh P. Allan.

Edition: *Sancta Civitas* was published by J. Curwen and Sons (London, 1925), and reissued by Faber Music (London, 1975). It is distributed by Educational Music. The piano-vocal score (prepared by Havergal Brian) is for sale; orchestral materials are available for rental.

Autograph: The ink manuscript is in the British Library (Add. MS #50445-45), a preliminary score is in the Bodleian Library

Notes: This is Vaughan Williams's first oratorio. It is a remarkably fiery work, full of spicy dissonances and biting rhythms.[87] In the score composer states:

> The semi-chorus should sit behind the full chorus and consist of about 20 singers (6. 6. 4. 4.). The distant choir should if possible be out of sight and must have a special conductor. It should consist of boys' voices if possible. The distant trumpet must be placed with the distant choir.

---

[87] James Day: *Vaughan Williams*. London: J. M. Dent, 1961.

Performance Issues: This is a very dramatic work. The harmonic language is diatonic with frequent modal inclinations. The choral writing is contrapuntally complex, combining the harmonic language of Stanford and Delius with imitative procedure from the renaissance. There are divisi in the soprano parts of all three choirs, and all of the parts of the full choir occasionally divide. The vocal pitches are consistently supported by the accompaniment. The orchestra parts are well within the abilities of a moderately experienced amateur ensemble. The string parts may require sectional rehearsals to clarify beat divisions between parts. The distant trumpet solo requires a strong player. It is high and very sustained. A large vocal ensemble is necessary because of the many divisions called for in the score. The complex interplay between these choirs calls for an experiences vocal contingent. *Soloists*: tenor, range: b-a', tessitura: b-a', simple and only five measures long; baritone, range: B-f', tessitura: g-d', articulate and powerful. *Choir*: medium difficult; *Orchestra*: medium.

Discography: San Francisco Bach Choir; conducted by H. Mueller. Mercury: MLR 7049 [LP].

Ian Partridge, Tenor, John Shirley-Quirk, baritone; King's College Choir, Bach Choir, London Symphony Orchestra; conducted by Sir David Willcocks. Recorded 1968, re-released 1989. EMI: CDM 7 69949 2 [ADD].

Selected Bibliography

Fox-Strangways, Arthur Henry: "*Sancta Civitas*: Ralph Vaughan Williams," *The British Musician*, xxi (October 1927), 165-7.

Five Tudor Portraits (1935)

Duration: ca. 42 minutes

Text: John Skelton

Performing Forces: *voices*: alto/mezzo-soprano and baritone soloists, SATB choir; *orchestra*: 3 flutes (flute III doubling piccolo), 2 oboes (oboe II doubling English horn), 2 clarinets, 2 bassoons, contrabassoon, 4 horns, 2 trumpets, 3 trombones, tuba, timpani, percussion (3 Players - cymbal, snare drum, bass drum, triangle, xylophone), harp, and strings.

The composer notes that the following parts may, if unavoidable, be omitted: flute II, oboe II, contrabassoon, horns III and IV, tuba, percussion II. The harp part should be played on piano rather than omitted.

There is an arrangement of the orchestra for piano and strings.

First Performance: 25 September 1936; St. Andrew's Hall, Norwich; Astra Desmond, Roy Henderson; Festival Chorus, London Philharmonic Orchestra; conducted by the composer.

Edition: *Five Tudor Portraits* is published and distributed by Oxford University Press. The study score and piano-vocal score are available for purchase; orchestral materials are available for rental.

Autograph: British Library (50455, 50456, and 50457); This includes sketches for an incomplete sixth movement, "Margery Wentworth."

Notes: Each movement may be performed separately. The five portraits are are arranged as follows:

1. Ballad   The Tunning of Eleanor Rumming
2. Intermezzo Pretty Bess
3. Burlesca   Epitaph for John Jayberd of Diss
4. Romanza   Jane Scroop (Her Lament for Philip Sparrow)
5. Scherzo   Jolly Rutterkin

In the full score the composer notes:

> In making a choral suite out of the poems of Skelton I have ventured to take some liberties with the text. In doing this I am aware that I have laid myself open to the accusation of cutting out somebody's "favourite bit." If any omissions are to be made this, I fear, is inevitable. On the whole I have managed to keep all my own "favourite bits," though there are certain passages which I have omitted unwillingly. The omissions are due partly to the great length of the original, partly because some passages did not lend themselves to musical treatment, and partly because certain lines which would look well when read cannot be sung.

I have occasionally, for musical reasons, changed the order of the lines. This seemed to me legitimate as there does not appear to be an inevitable sequence in Skelton's original order.

In "Jolly Rutterkin" I have interpolated a song from "Magnificence." I hope that this is justified by the fact that "Courtly Abusion," who sings the song in the play, has immediately before quoted a line from "Jolly Rutterkin."

The spelling has been modernized except where the final e is to be sounded.

Performance Issues: The choral writing incorporates unisons, paired imitation, and free counterpoint. There are divisi in all choral sections. The vocal lines move by scale or triadic leap. Most of the vocal material is supported by the accompaniment. The fourth movement is for women's choir and the third movement is for men's choir and includes Latin text. This is a chromatic work with many modal leanings. Vaughan Williams adds to the rhythmic momentum by using hemiolas, displaced downbeats, polymeters, and accent shifts. The score calls for two percussion players, but three are required for a few passages if everything is to be played. All of the orchestra parts are individually challenging with solos for all principal players. There is some especially intricate passagework in the winds and rapid fanfare between the winds and brass. The orchestration demands a large choir. The choral parts are well within the ability of a choir of moderate experience, but the orchestra writing requires a professional-level ensemble. *Soloists*: mezzo-soprano, range: b-f'; tessitura: f'-e^b", lyric and articulate; baritone, range: B^b-f'; tessitura: g-d', rhythmic and light. *Choir*: medium; *Orchestra*: medium difficult.

Discography: Bach Choir; New Philharmonia Orchestra; conducted by Sir David Willcocks. EMI: SLS 5082 [LP]. Also found in Set - soloists including: Dame Janet Baker, Sheila Armstrong, Heather Harper, Helen Watts, Richard Lewis, Ian Partridge, and John Shirley-Quirk; various choirs and orchestras; conductors including: Sir Adrian Boult, Sir David Willcocks, and Meredith Davies. HMV: SLS-5082 [7 LP's].

Pittsburgh Mendelssohn Choir, Pittsburgh Symphony Orchestra; conducted by William Steinberg. Capitol: P 8218 [LP].

Selected Bibliography

Frank, Alan: "Reincarnating Skelton," *The Listener*, xvii (20 January 1937), 141-2.
Howes, Frank: "Five Tudor Portraits," *The Listener*, xxiv (15 August 1940), 249.
Colles, Henry Hope: "Five Tudor Portraits," in *Essays and Lectures*, 104-6. London: Oxford University Press, 1945.
Dorian, Frederick: "Five Tudor Portraits," *The Musical Quarterly*, xxxix/3 (July 1953), 432-5.
Yaqub, Hanan: *"Five Tudor Portraits" by Ralph Vaughan Williams: Introduction to the Poetry and the Music*. University of Southern California: Dissertation, 1988.

Dona Nobis Pacem (1936)

Duration: ca. 36 minutes

Text: The Bible, John Bright's Angel of Death Speech given in the House of Commons 23 February 1855 during the Crimean War, Walt Whitman's *Drum Taps*.

Performing Forces: *voices*: soprano and baritone soloists; SATB choir; *orchestra*: 3 flutes (flute III doubling piccolo), 2 oboes, 2 clarinets, 2 bassoons, contrabassoon, 4 horns, 4 trumpet (trumpets III and IV optional), 4 trombones (trombones III and IV optional), tuba, timpani, percussion (4 players - snare drum, tenor drum, triangle, tambourine, cymbals, bass drum, tam-tam, glockenspiel, chimes), harp, organ (optional), and strings.

There is an optional version of the orchestra for piano and strings.

First Performance: 2 October 1936; Huddersfield Town Hall, England; R. Flynn, Roy Henderson; Huddersfield Choral Society, Hallé Orchestra; conducted by Albert Coates.

Edition: *Dona Nobis Pacem* is published and distributed by Oxford University Press. The study score and piano-vocal score are for sale; orchestral materials are available for rental.

Autograph: The ink manuscript is in the British Library (Add. MS #50453).

Notes: *Dona Nobis Pacem* is an anti-war piece composed in reaction to the anticipated Second World War. Vaughan Williams was fond of Whitman and used his texts in a number of works including: *A Sea Symphony, Toward the Unknown Region,* and *Three Nocturnes.*[88] It was commissioned to commemorate the centenary of the Huddersfield Choral Society. The work is organized into five sections as follows:

I. "Agnus Dei"
II. "Beat! Beat! Drums! " from *Drum Taps*
III. Reconciliation from *Drum Taps*
IV. "Dirge for Two Veterans," from Drum Taps.
[This was composed twenty-five years earlier]
Va. "Angel of Death"
Vb. "We look for peace" Jeremiah, VIII:15-22
Vc. "O Man, greatly beloved" Daniel, X:19
Vd. "The glory of this latter house" Haggai, II:9
Ve. "Nation shall not lift up sword against nation"
Micah, IV:3; Leviticus, XXVI:6; Psalms,
XC:10 and CXVIII:19; Isaiah, XLIII:9 and
LXVI: 18-22; and Luke, II:14

Performance Issues: This is a chromatic and rhythmically-charged composition. Vaughan Williams exploits parallel motion at the fourth or fifth. Cross-rhythms are featured throughout the piece, including: 8, 7, 4 and 2 against 3, and 7 against 4. Most of the choral writing is homophonic with occasional sections of internal imitation. The choral material is consistently supported by the accompaniment. There are brief divisi in all vocal parts. The orchestral writing is challenging for all players. The principal brass parts are consistently high, and all of the brass parts have unison sections and require great stamina. The orchestration demands a large string section and a large choir. The choral parts are not particularly difficult, but the orchestra portion is very sophisticated, requiring an ensemble of professional players. The principal challenges to the instrumental ensemble are the constant

---

[88] Michael Kennedy: *A Catalogue of the Works of Ralph Vaughan Williams.* London: Oxford University Press, 1985.

interplay of inner rhythms and the demands put upon the endurance of the brass players. *Soloists*: soprano, range: c'-a^{b}", tessitura: c"-g", requiring rhythmic clarity and sustained control of the upper range; baritone, range: c-e', tessitura: g-c', requires a powerful voice which is articulate and capable of sustained phrases. *Choir*: medium; *Orchestra*: difficult.

Discography: Set - soloists including: Dame Janet Baker, Sheila Armstrong, Heather Harper, Helen Watts, Richard Lewis, Ian Partridge, and John Shirley-Quirk; various choirs and orchestras; conductors including: Sir Adrian Boult, Sir David Willcocks, and Meredith Davies. HMV: SLS-5082 [7 LP's].

R. Flynn, Roy Henderson; BBC Symphony and Chorus; conducted by Vaughan Williams. Recording of a live radio broadcast, November 1936. Pearl: GEMM CD-9342 [AAD mono].

Utah Symphony Orchestra; conducted by Maurice Abravanel. Vanguard 71159 [LP].

London Symphony Orchestra; conducted by Sir Adrian Boult. EMI: CDM 769820.2 [AAD].

Wiens, Brian Rayner-Cook; London Philharmonic Orchestra and Chorus; conducted by Bryden Thompson. Chandos: CHAN-8590 [DDD].

Selected Bibliography

Terry, Sir Richard: "Dona nobis pacem," *The Listener*, xvi (1936), 879.

Baker, Norma: *Concerning the Dona Nobis Pacem of Ralph Vaughan Williams and the War Requiem of Benjamin Britten.* University of Southern California: Thesis, 1969.

Kranovsky, Paul Joseph: *Ralph Vaughan Williams's "Don Nobis Pacem" a Conductor's Analysis.* Indiana University: Dissertation, 1984.

Foreman, Lewis: *From Parry to Britten: British Music in Letters 1900-1945*, 153, 206, 220. Portland, OR: Amadeus Press, 1987.

Serenade to Music (1938)

Duration: ca. 14-15 minutes

Text: Shakespeare from *The Merchant of Venice*; Act V, scene 1.

Performing Forces: *voices*: 16 soloists*: 4 each of SATB; *orchestra*: 2 flutes, oboe, English horn, 2 clarinets, 2 bassoons,

4 horns 2 trumpets, 3 trombones, tuba, timpani, percussion (1 player - bass drum, triangle), harp, and strings.

Orchestral version: 2 flutes, oboe, English horn, 2 clarinets, 2 bassoons, 4 horns 2 trumpets, 3 trombones, tuba, timpani, percussion (1 player - bass drum, triangle), harp, solo violin, and strings.

* The composer notes in the score that the work may be performed by 4 soloists and choir, or by a choir singing all of the parts.

First Performance: 5 October 1938; Royal Albert Hall, London; Stiles Allen, Dame Isobel Baillie, Elsie Suddaby, Eva Turner, Margaret Balfour, Muriel Brunskill, Astra Desmond, Mary Jarred, Parry Jones, Heddle Nash, Frank Titterson, Walter Widdop, Norman Allen, Robert Easton, Roy Henderson, Harold Williams; BBC Symphony Orchestra, London Symphony Orchestra, London Philharmonic Orchestra, Queen's Hall Orchestra; conducted by Sir Henry Wood.

Premiere of Orchestral version: 10 February 1940; Queen's Hall, London; London Symphony Orchestra; conducted by Sir Henry Wood.

Edition: *A Serenade to Music* is published by Oxford University Press. The piano-vocal score and study score are for sale; the full score and orchestral materials are available for rental.

Autograph: The composer's manuscript is in the possession of the Royal Academy of Music in London.

Notes: *A Serenade to Music* was composed in honor of Sir Henry Woods's golden jubilee as a conductor. It was composed with voices of the soloists listed above for the premiere in mind. Their initials appear throughout the full score indicating their intended passages.

Performance Issues: In general, the individual instrumental parts are not technically demanding; however, the solo violin part requires fluid and accurate playing in very high registers. The harp part is also technically challenging and an integral part of the score. The cello and viola parts may prove difficult to integrate rhythmically with the remaining parts. The most challenging aspect of the piece for the orchestra is balance and clarity of inner contrapuntal parts. The entire ensemble must be capable of very soft sustained playing. This work is frequently performed with four soloists and choir; this vocal commentary will address that configuration. The tutti passages generaly assigned to the choir are divided differently throughout the work, the greatest number of parts being twelve (SSSAAATTTBBB). The choral writing is strictly homophonic, and despite modal inclinations, Vaughan Williams wholly honors common-practice part-writing rules. The basses must be capable of sustained singing of D. The choral parts are very accessible to amateur vocal ensemble. Much of the harmonic material is dense, but doubled between male and female section of the choir and elsewise reinforced by the orchestra. The quality of choral sound will prove to be of greater issue than the learning of notes. *Soloists*: soprano, range: f'-a", tessitura: d"-a", lyric and sustained, must be capable of very soft singing in the top of the range; alto, range: a-f', tessitura: e$^{b'}$-c", declamatory, but must be capable of legato singing in the upper passages; tenor, range: e^b-a', tessitura: a-g', florid with long sustained phrases; bass, range: A^b-e', tessitura: d-d', must be capable of articulate singing in the lower range. *Choir*: medium easy; *Orchestra*: medium to medium difficult.

Discography: Stiles Allen, Dame Isobel Baillie, Elsie Suddaby, Eva Turner, Margaret Balfour, Muriel Brunskill, Astra Desmond, Mary Jarred, Parry Jones, Heddle Nash, Frank Titterson, Walter Widdop, Norman Allen, Robert Easton, Roy Henderson, Harold Williams; BBC Symphony Orchestra; conducted by Henry Wood. Recorded: 15 October 1938, one week after the premiere, by those who first performed it. Columbia: LX 757/8 [78's]; re-released as Pearl: GEMM CD-9342 [AAD mono].

English Chamber Orchestra, Corydon Singers; conducted by Matthew Best. Hyperion: CDA 66420 [DDD].

Norma Burrowes, Sheila Armstrong, Susan Longfield, Marie Hayward, Alfreda Hodgson, Gloria Jennings, Shirley Minty, Meriel Dickinson, Ian Partridge, Wynford Evans, Kenneth Bowen, Bernard Dickerson, Richard Angas, John Carol Case, John Noble, Christopher Keyte; London Philharmonic Orchestra; conducted by Sir Adrian Boult. Angel (British Composers): CDM-66420 [ADD], and EMI: CDC 7 47218 2 [ADD].

Royal Festival Chorus and Orchestra; conducted by Sir Adrian Boult. HMV: DA 7040/1 [78's].

BBC Singers and BBC Symphony Orchestra; conducted by Sir Charles Groves. BBC: CD 580 [DDD].

Soloists, London Symphony Orchestra; conducted by Sir Malcolm Sargent. Angel: S.35564 [LP].

Royal Liverpool Philharmonic; conducted by Vernon Handley. Angel (Classics for Pleasure): CDM 64034 [DDD].

Schola Cantorum, New York Philharmonic Orchestra; conducted by Leonard Bernstein. Columbia: MS 7177 [LP].

Mary Shearer, Karen Williams, Carlotta Wilsen, Andrea Matthewa, Karen Brunssen, Trudy Weaver, Melissa Thorburn, Virginia Dupuy, Grayson Hirst, Marcus Haddock, Frederick Urrey, Ronald Naldi, Thomas Stallone, Stephen Owen, Nickolas Karousatos, Herbert Eckoff; New York Virtuosi Chamber Orchestra; conducted by K. Klein. Vox Unique: VU 9023 [DDD].

Arranged for four soloists, chorus, and orchestra:

Norma Burrowes, Alfreda Hodgson, Ian Partridge, Richard Angas; London Philharmonic Orchestra; conducted by Sir Adrian Boult. Angel: CDM-63098 [ADD].

Elsie Morrison, Marjorie Thomas, Duncan Robertson, Trevor Anthony; London Symphony Orchestra and Chorus; conducted by Sir Malcolm Sargent. Angel: CDM-63382 [ADD].

Orchestra only:

New York Virtuosi Chamber Symphony; conducted by L. William Kuyper. ASV: DCA-655 [DDD].

London Philharmonic Orchestra; conducted by Vernon Handley. Chandos: CD-8330 [DDD].

Northern Sinfonia; conducted by Richard Hickox. Angel: DS 38129 [LP].

Selected Bibliography

Manning, Rosemary: "Vaughan Williams" in *From Holst to Britten: A Study of Modern Choral Music*, 20-36. London: Workers' Music Association, 1946.

Sackerville-West, Edward, and Desmond Shawe-Taylor: *The Record Guide*, 359-61. London: Collins, 1951.

Warburton, Annie Osborn: "Serenade to Music" and "Toward the Unknown Region," *The Music Teacher*, li (October 1972), 22-23

Gammond, Peter, and Burnett James: *Music on Record 4*, 206-09. London: Hutchinson, 1963; reprinted Westport, CT: Greenwood press, 1978.

An Oxford Elegy (1949)

Duration: ca. 25 minutes

Text: Matthew Arnold, from "The Scholar Gypsy" and "Thirsis"

Performing Forces: *voices*: speaker; small SATB choir; *orchestra*: flute, oboe, English horn, 2 clarinets, bassoon, horn, and strings.

There is an arrangement of the orchestra for piano and strings, prepared by Denis Williams.

First Performance: *private*: 20 November 1949; The White Gates, Dorking; Stueart Wilson, speaker; Tudor Singers, Schwiller String Quartet, Michael Mulliner, piano; conducted by Vaughan Williams.

public: 19 June 1952; Queen's College, Oxford; Stuart Wilson, speaker; Eglesfield Musical Society, Chamber Orchestra; conducted by Bernard Rose.

Edition: *Oxford Elegy* is published and distributed by Oxford University Press. The study score and piano-vocal score are for sale; orchestral materials are available for rental.

Autograph: Some materials are in the British Library (Add. MSS 50473, 50474, and 50475). A manuscript full score is in the Bodleian Library.

Performance Issues: The score is rhythmically varied with numerous cross-relations and a variety of borrowed divisions. Half of the choir's music is textless, either hummed or on prescribed vowels. It is quite reminiscent of RVW's *Flos Campi*. The sections with text are strictly homophonic, while those without text are more contrapuntal. The choral writing is tuneful and logically conceived, but it is not conspicuously supported by the accompaniment. The string parts are rhythmically varied with rapid chromatic passagework. The wind parts are less challenging, but still require players of experience. The narrator speaks throughout most of the work. *Choir*: medium; *Orchestra*: medium difficult.

Discography: Set - soloists including: Dame Janet Baker, Sheila Armstrong, Heather Harper, Helen Watts, Richard Lewis, Ian Partridge, and John Shirley-Quirk; various choirs and orchestras; conductors including: Sir Adrian Boult, Sir David Willcocks, and Meredith Davies. HMV: SLS-5082 [7 LP's].
King's College Choir, Jacques Orchestra; conducted by Sir David Willcocks. Angel: S 36590.
Jack May, narrator; Christ Church Cathedral Choir, English String Orchestra; conducted by Stephen Darlington. Recorded at Leominster Priory, 12-14 January 1989. Nimbus: NI 5166 [DDD].

The Sons of Light (1950)

Duration: ca. 25 minutes

Text: Ursula Wood (soon to be Mrs. Vaughan Williams)

Performing Forces: *voices*: SATB choir; *orchestra*: 2 flutes, 2 oboes (oboe II doubling English horn), 2 clarinets, 2 bassoons, contrabassoon, 4 horns, 3 trumpets, 3 trombones, tuba, timpani, percussion (2 players - bass drum, snare drum, suspended cymbal, gong, triangle, xylophone, glockenspiel), celeste, harp, and strings.

alternate orchestration: 2 flutes, 2 oboes, 3 clarinets, 3 saxophones (optional), 2 bassoon, 2 horns, 3 trumpets, 3 trombones, tuba, timpani, celeste (optional), percussion (optional), piano, and strings.

Arranged for Piano and Strings by Arnold Foster.

First Performance: 6 May 1951; Royal Albert Hall, London; Schools Music Association massed choirs (1,150 voices); conducted by Sir Adrian Boult.

Edition: *The Sons of Light* is published and distributed by Oxford University Press. The study score and piano-vocal score are for sale; orchestral materials are available for rental.

Autograph: The ink manuscript is in the British Library (Add. MS #50471-72); manuscripts of *Sun, Moon, Stars, and Man* which is a selection of four songs from *The Sons of Light* are in the British Library (Add. MS #50478) and the Library of Congress.

Notes: *Sons of Light* was commissioned by the Schools Music Association. It is dedicated to Bernard Shore who was "His Majesty's Staff Inspector in Music, Ministry of Education. The work is in three movements:

      I. Darkness and Light
     II. The Song of the Zodiac
    III. The Messengers of Speech

The composer notes that the alternate orchestration is "for emergency use," and that the tuba is essential but may be replaced by euphonium with some necessary octave shifts. There is a special piano-part which should be added to cover missing instruments if the reduced orchestration is used.

Performance Issues: There are numerous cues within the orchestra to cover missing parts if the ensemble is reduced. Use of these should be clarified before rehearsal. The vocal writing is scalar and homophonic. Much of the choral parts are in unison. The vocal rhythms are reflective of the inherent rhythm of the text. The choir's music is quite easy and clearly supported in the accompaniment. There are a series of cuts made in the full-score between [18] and [23], and between [29] and [30]; be sure that the parts agree with these changes. The orchestra parts are not individually difficult, but a variety of inner rhythms and heavy scoring will require an experienced ensemble, or a lot of rehearsal time to achieve clarity in performance. The brass parts are a challenge to endurance and the mallets part are very active. There are frequent, full-brass doublings of the choir, and many tutti passage at full dynamics demanding a large vocal ensemble. This is an attractive and exciting work which would be a rewarding piece for an inexperienced choir with strong orchestral resources. *Choir*: medium easy; *Orchestra*: medium difficult.

Discography: Bach Choir, London Philharmonic Orchestra; conducted by Sir David Willcocks. Lyrita: SRCS 125 [LP].

Selected Bibliography

Martin, William R.: "The Choral Music of Vaughan Williams," *Repertoire* (October 1951), 15-22.

Hodie (1953-54)

Duration: ca. 50-55 minutes

Text: varied, see "notes" below

Performing Forces: *voices*: soprano, tenor, and baritone soloists; SATB choir, children's choir; *orchestra*: 3 flutes (flute III doubling piccolo, flute II is optional), 2 oboes (Oboe II is optional), English horn, 2 clarinets, 2 bassoons, contrabassoon (optional), 4 horns (horns III and IV are optional), 3 trumpets (trumpet III is optional), 3 trombones, tuba, timpani, percussion (4 players - snare drum, tenor drum, bass drum, cymbals, suspended cymbal, triangle, glockenspiel, chimes), celeste, harp (optional), piano, organ (optional), and strings.

First Performance: 8 September 1954; Worcester Cathedral; Evans, E. Greene, Gordon Clinton, Three Choirs Festival Chorus, London Symphony; conducted by Vaughan Williams.

Edition: *Hodie* is published and distributed by Oxford University Press. The study score and piano-vocal score are for sale; orchestral materials are available for rental.

Autograph: The ink manuscript is in the British Library (Add. MS # 50477).

Notes: *Hodie* is dedicated to Herbert Howells:

> Dear Herbert, I find that in this cantata I have inadvertently cribbed a phrase from your beautiful "Hymnus Paradisi." Your passage seems so germane to my context that I have decided to keep it (RVW).

In the narrations, the tenor is labeled, "The Angel." The cantata tells the story of the nativity using a combination of Biblical texts and British poetry. It is organized as follows:

I.	Prologue	- Choir
	(Vespers for Christmas Day)	
II.	Narration	- T, Treb, Choir
	(Matthew I:18-21, Luke I: 32)	
III.	Song	- S, SA-Choir
	(Milton - Hymn on the Morning	
	of Christ's Nativity)	
IV.	Narration (Luke II: 1-7)	- Treb
V.	Chorale	- Choir
	(Coverdale after Martin Luther)	unaccomp.
VI.	Narration	- Treb, T, S, and
	(adapted from Luke II: 8-17 and the	Choir
	Book of Common Prayer)	
VII.	Song - The Oxen (Thomas Hardy)	- Bar
VIII.	Narration (Luke II: 20)	- Treb, SA-Choir*
IX.	Pastoral (George Herbert)	- Bar
X.	Narration (Luke II: 19)	- Treb
XI.	Lullaby (William Ballet)	- S, SA-Choir
XII.	Hymn (William Drummond)	- T
XIII.	Narration (adapted from	- Treb, Choir
	Matthew II: 1, 2, and 11)	
XIV.	The March of the Three Kings	- S, T, Bar, and
	(Ursula Vaughan William)	Choir
XV.	Chorale (Anon. and Ursula	- Choir
	Vaughan Williams)	unaccomp.
XVI.	Epilogue (John I:1-14 and Milton -	- S, T, Bar, and
	Hymn of the Morning of	Choir
	Christ's Nativity)	

*   The score calls for a few rows of the choir to sing.

Performance Issues: The treble choir should be separated from the adult choir. Vaughan Williams has indicated that the organ is optional; however, the treble choir is intended to be accompanied by organ (string cues are provided). The choral and orchestral parts require very precise rhythmic articulation, particularly in the first and last movements which are riddled with hemiolas and bi-rhythmic elements. There are occasional divisi in all choral parts except for the alto part which only divides in SA sections and chorales. In III, the composer has set textless women's choral music to the syllable "er." A British dialect should be remembered, or better yet, [u] should be substituted. The orchestration is unusually practical, allowing for a variety of combinations of instruments as can be seen in the listing above. The score is full of doublings, including almost constant support of the choral parts in the orchestra. There are also considerable cues. Most of the orchestra parts are quite accessible. The first horn and first trumpet parts demand flexible and sustained playing in the high range in XIV and XVI. The tuba part is substantial and requires melodic, legato playing throughout its range. The harp and piano parts are demanding throughout the work. *Soloists*: Soprano, range: c'-g", tessitura: g'-f', must be able to maintain smoothness throughout the middle of the voice and have a strong low range, a lyric mezzo-soprano could be well suited to the role; Tenor, range: d^b-a$^{b'}$, tessitura: g-g', requires control of coloratura writing and exceptionally long phrases, notably in XII; Baritone, range: d^b-f#', tessitura: e-d', consistently lyric, must have a free and beautiful upper range. *Choir*: medium; *Orchestra*: medium difficult.

Discography: Set - soloists including: Dame Janet Baker, Sheila Armstrong, Heather Harper, Helen Watts, Richard Lewis, Ian Partridge, and John Shirley-Quirk; various choirs and orchestras; conductors including: Sir Adrian Boult, Sir David Willcocks, and Meredith Davies. HMV: SLS-5082 [7 LP's].

Dame Janet Baker, Richard Lewis, John Shirley-Quirk; London Bach Choir, Choristers of Westminster Abbey, London Symphony Orchestra; Sir David Willcocks. Angel: S-36297 [LP], EMI: CDM 769872.2 [AAD].

Selected Bibliography

Butler, E.: "Hodie: This Day by Vaughan Williams," *The Church Musician*, xii (September 1970), 18-20.

Epithalamion (1957)

Duration: ca. 37 minutes

Text: Edmund Spenser's *Epithalamion*, as selected by Ursula Vaughan Williams

Performing Forces: *voices*: baritone soloist; SATB choir; *small orchestra*: flute (doubling piccolo), piano, and strings.

First Performance: 30 September 1957; Royal Festival Hall, London; Gordon Clinton, baritone; Goldsmiths' Choral Union

Cantata Singers, Royal Philharmonic Orchestra; conducted by Richard Austin.

Edition: *Epithalamion* is published and distributed by Oxford University Press. The study score and piano-vocal score are for sale; orchestral materials are available for rental.

Autograph: The ink manuscript in in the British Library (Add. MS 50479)

Notes: This work is an adaptation of Vaughan Williams's masque *The Bridal Day* (1938). It is in eleven movements as follows:

I.	Prologue	orchestra
II.	"Wake Now"	baritone and choir
III.	The Calling of the Bride	choir
IV.	The Minstrels	choir
V.	Procession of the Bride	choir
VI.	The Temple Gates	choir
VII.	The Bellringers	choir
VIII.	The Lover's Song	baritone and choir
IX.	The Minstrel's Song	baritone and choir
X.	Song of the Winged Loves	women's choir
XI.	Prayer to Juno	baritone and choir

In 1989, Ursula Vaughan Williams wrote the following introduction for the 1990 edition of *Epithalamion*:

> Edmund Spenser wrote Epithalamion to celebrate his own marriage on 11 June 1594, to a girl called Elizabeth, after a year of somewhat stormy courtship. It is one of the few entirely happy love poems in the English langûage. Mortals and immortals are called upon to take part in the ceremonies. The poet summons Hymen, god of marriage, nymphs of the sea, and the woods to wake and adorn the bride, her friends, and his, to to escort her to the church. Bacchus, the god of wine, the Graces, and the town bellringers join in the revels until the Evening Star at last heralds the 'night so long expected,' and Juno, Queen of Heaven, is called upon for her blessing on the enchanted lovers.

In 1938 I made a scenario for a Masque based on the poem. RVW wrote the music during the winter of 1938-9 while he was also working on his Fifth Symphony. He wrote for a string quartet, piano and flute, and narrator, with one song for a baritone solo, and a small part for chorus. A performance was planned for the autumn of 1939 but was cancelled because of the war. A televised performance took place in 1953 for which two more songs were added for the baritone. The narrator was the poet C. Day Lewis, an incomparable verse reader.

It became clear that the number of performers needed for so short a work made it unlikely that there would be many performances, so the composer re-arranged the work, setting the verses he had originally designed tunes for dancers. He had followed the poem so exactly that the words fitted the tunes with almost no alteration, and the chamber group was also enlarged to balance a choir. For the Masque we had taken our title, *The Bridal Day*, from Spenser's other marriage poem, written for a double wedding, *Prothalamion*, with its well known refrain: "Against their bridal day, which was not long, Sweet Thames run softly, till I end my song." For the Choral work we returned to Spenser's own title, *Epithalamion*.

Performance Issues: This piece evidences the influence of folk songs and Tudor church music. The choral writing is mostly homophonic with some paired doublings. It incorporates renaissance dance rhythms and modal melodic material. This work is more consistently diatonic than most of Vaughan Williams's music. There are brief divisi in all choral parts. The flute part is prominent and virtuosic, but very idiomatic to the instrument. The piano and string parts are conservative and lightly scored. *Soloist*: baritone, range: d-f', tessitura: f-d'. The accompanying textures and lilting dance rhythms suggest a light and lyric voice. All of the vocal material is tuneful and easily learned. The only challenge to an inexperienced choir is the quantity of music for them (about 35 minutes). The scoring is ideal for a small choir and a chamber orchestra of twelve players. The scoring of this work makes it an ideal companion to Bliss's *Pastoral: Lie Strewn the White Flocks*. *Choir*: easy to medium; *Orchestra*: medium easy.

Discography: Bach Choir, London Philharmonic Orchestra; conducted by Sir David Willcocks. EMI: CDC 7477692 [AAD].

Walton, William (b. Oldham, 29 March 1902; d. Ischia, Italy, 8 March 1983).

Life: Walton was the son of a choirmaster and a singer. He was a chorister at Christ Church Cathedral, Oxford (1912-18). He was admitted as a special undergraduate student at Christ Church in 1918, but failed to complete a required exam for his degree. In 1918, he became a companion to Osbert, Sacheverell, and Edith Sitwell, touring England and Italy with them (1920-30). This allowed him free time for composition and introduced him to many aspects of European culture. His first commercial success in music came from film composition, which he began in 1934. His later works were all commissioned pieces. In 1948, he married Susana Gil and moved to Ischia, Italy. Walton maintained a busy schedule of guest conducting appearances and performances of of his works throughout the world. His music is characterized by a balance between spiky rhythms, broad melodic leaps, and biting dissonances and an Elgar-like melancholy filled with lush and languid passages.[89]

Awards: 7 honorary doctorates, the Gold Medal of the Royal Philharmonic Society (1947), knighthood (1951), Order of Merit (1967), Benjamin Franklin Medal (1972), and the Ivor Novello Award (1982), honorary member of the American Academy and Institute of Arts and Letters (1978).

Principal Works: *operas* - *Troilus and Cressida* (1948-54, revised 1972-6), *The Bear* (1967); *film scores* - *As You Like It* (1930), *Major Barbara* (1940), *Next of Kin* (1941), *The Foreman Went to France* (1941), *The First of the Few* (1942), *Went the Day Well?* (1942), *Henry V* (1944), *Hamlet* (1947), *Richard III* (1955), *The Battle of Britain* (1969), *Three Sisters* (1970); *orchestral* - Symphony No. 1 (1931-5), Symphony No. 2 (1959-60), *Façade* (1921, many revisions), *Portsmouth Point* (1925), Viola Concerto (1928-9), *Crown Imperial* (1937, revised 1963), Violin Concerto (1938-9, revised 1943), *Scapino* (1940, revised 1950), *Orb and Sceptre* (1953), Cello Concerto (1956),

---

[89] Carolyn J. Smith: *William Walton: A Bio-Bibliography*. Westport, CT: Greenwood Press, 1988.

Variations on a Theme of Hindemith (1962-3), *Capriccio Burlesco* (1968), *Façade 2* (1979); *choral - In Honour of the City of London* (1937), *Set Me as a Seal Upon Thy Heart* (1938), *Coronation Te Deum* (1952-3), *Gloria* (1960), *Missa Brevis* (1966), *Cantico del Sol* (1973-4), and *Magnificat and Nunc Dimittis* (1975).

Selected Composer Bibliography

"Walton, Sir William," *Current Biography Yearbook*, i (March 1940); obituary, xliv (May 1983); New York: H. W. Wilson Company.

Hansler, George E.: *Stylistic Characteristics and Trends in the Choral Music of Five Twentieth-Century Composers: A Study of the Choral Works of Benjamin Britten, Gerald Finzi, Constant Lambert, Michael Tippett, and William Walton*. New York University: Dissertation, 1957.

Craggs, Stewart R.: *William Walton: A Thematic Catalogue of His Musical Works*. London: Oxford University Press, 1977.

Fulton, W. K.: *Selected Choral Works of William Walton*. Texas Technical College: Dissertation, 1981.

Tierney, Niel: *William Walton: His Life and Music*. London: Robert Hale, 1984.

Ottaway, Hugh: "William Walton," *The New Grove Twentieth-Century English Masters*, 175-200. New York: W.W. Norton, 1986.

Smith, Carolyn J.: *William Walton: A Bio-Bibliography*. Westport, CT: Greenwood Press, 1988.

Kennedy, Michael: *Portrait of Walton*. Oxford: Oxford University Press, 1989.

Belshazzar's Feast (1929-31)

Duration: ca. 35 minutes

Text: After the Bible (Daniel, and Psalms 81 and 137) by Sir Osbert Sitwell

Performing Forces: *voices*: baritone soloist; SSAATTBB choir; *orchestra*: 2 flutes, 2 oboes, English horn (only if no saxophone is available), 3 clarinets (clarinet II doubling E^b clarinet, clarinet III doubling bass clarinet), alto saxophone, 2 bassoons, contrabassoons, 4 horns, 3 trumpets, 3 trombones, tuba, timpani (4), percussion (4 players - snare drum, tenor drum, triangle, tambourine, castanets, cymbals, bass drum, gong, xylophone, glockenspiel, wood block, slapsticks, anvil), 2 harps, piano (ad.

lib.), organ, and strings; *two brass bands* (optional): one to the conductor's left and one to the conductor's right, each consisting of 3 trumpets, 3 trombones, and a tuba.

First Performance: 8 October 1931; Leeds Town Hall; Dennis Noble; Leeds Festival Chorus, London Symphony Orchestra; conducted by Sir Malcolm Sargent.

Edition: *Belshazzar's Feast* is published and distributed by Oxford University Press. The full score and piano-vocal score are for sale; orchestral materials are available for rental.

Autograph: The composer had been unable to trace, and it has remained lost since his death.

Notes: The presence of the additional brass forces was suggested to the composer by Sir Thomas Beecham, who was preparing a performance of the Berlioz *Requiem* at the time. It was commissioned by the BBC, and is dedicated to Lord Berners. Most of the research for Sitwell's preparation of the text was done by Lady Christabel Aberconway. The composer made changes in the scoring between #74 and #77 between the first performance and the London premiere. Portions of the revisions can be found in manuscripts in the Walton Trust.[90] The three movements are labeled thus:

1. Maestoso
2. Allegro molto
3. Allegro giocoso

Performance Issues: This is a highly chromatic work which is tonally founded and achieves dissonance through logical voice-leading procedures. Harmonic stability is enhanced by regular use of pedal point. The choral writing is contrapuntally varied and keenly balances long melodic phrases with sections of choral recitative. There are optional cues for instruments to double the choir in some of the *a cappella* sections if pitch stability becomes a problem. Walton maintains a high tessitura and dynamic level in all of the choral parts. It is therefore a very physically demanding

---

[90] Stewart R. Craggs: *William Walton: A Thematic Catalogue of His Musical Works.* London: Oxford University Press, 1977.

work for the singers. The choir has some phrases which are almost hocketed between sections of the group. Since a large choir is needed, care must be taken to guarantee that such sections do not slow down. The orchestral parts are individually difficult, but the greater challenge is the integration of the ensemble. There are intricately entwined motives between displaced sections of the orchestra. This is made more complicated by the addition of the antiphonal brass bands. There is some elaborate passagework for the winds and upper strings, some in unison and some contrapuntally diverse. The score also calls for a variety of timbral effects from the instruments which may present some problems in balance and clarity. The physical separation of the brass bands on either side of the audience is quite crucial to the overall effect of the piece. This is a magnificently exciting work requiring a large and experienced vocal ensemble, a fine orchestra, and much rehearsal time to coordinate them. *Soloist*: baritone, range: B^b-f', tessitura: f-d', this role requires a large voice with great clarity. There is an unaccompanied recitative between [14] and [15]. *Choir*: difficult; *Orchestra*: difficult.

Discography: Dennis Noble; Huddersfield Choral Society and Brass Bands, Liverpool Philharmonic Orchestra; conducted by Walton. Recorded in 1943. Victor: Set 974 [78]; EMI -The HMV Treasury: ED 29 0715 1 [LP mono].

Unlisted soloist and ensemble; conducted by Sir Adrian Boult. Nixa: NLP904.

Donald Bell; Philharmonia Choir and Orchestra; conducted by Walton. Recorded in 1959. Columbia: CX1679 [LP mono], SAX 2319 [LP stereo].

Benjamin Luxon; Choirs of Salisbury, Winchester, and Chichester Cathedrals; London Philharmonic Orchestra; conducted by George Solti. London: 26525 [LP].

Benjamin Luxon; Royal Philharmonic and Chorus; conducted by André Previn. MCA Classics: MCAD-6187 [DDD], and RPO Records: RPO 7013 [DDD].

Sherrill Milnes; Scottish National Orchestra and Chorus, Scottish Festival Brass Bands; conducted by Alexander Gibson. Recorded in 1977. Chandos: CHAN 6547 [ADD/DDD].

John Shirley-Quirk; London Symphony Orchestra and Chorus; conducted by André Previn. Angel: CDC-47624 [ADD].

Thomas Allen; St. Louis Symphony Orchestra and Chorus; conducted by Leonard Slatkin. RCA (Red Seal): 60813-2 [DDD].

G. Howell; Bach Choir, Philharmonia Orchestra; conducted by Sir David Willcocks. Recorded in February 1990. Chandos: CHAN-8760 [DDD].

William Stone; Atlanta Symphony Orchestra and Chorus; conducted by Robert Shaw. Telarc: CD-80181 [DDD].

Selected Bibliography

[review of the premiere] anon., *Yorkshire Post* (9 October 1931), 5.

Cardus, Neville: [review of the premiere], *Manchester Guardian* (10 October 1931), 13.

Elliot, J. H.: [review], *Sackbut*, xii (1932), 84-6.

McNaught, William: [review], *The Musical Times*, lxxiii (1932), 68.

[review], *Boston Evening Transcript* (30 March 1933), 13.

Hughes, Spike: *Second Movement, continuing the autobiography of Spike Hughes*. London: Museum Press, 1951.

Foreman, Lewis: *From Parry to Britten: British Music in Letters 1900-1945*, 151, 152, 158, 189, 208, 280. Portland, OR: Amadeus Press, 1987.

Ward, Robert (b. Cleveland, OH, 13 September 1917).

Life: Ward attended the Eastman School (1935-9) where he studied composition with Bernard Rogers, Howard Hanson, and Edward Royce. He undertook graduate work at Juilliard (1939-42), studying composition with Frederick Jacobi, conducting with Arthur Stoessel and Edgar Schenkman, and orchestration with Bernard Wagenaar. During the summer of 1941, he was a composition student of Aaron Copland at Tanglewood. Following service as a bandleader in the Second World War, he turned to teaching. He taught composition at (1946-56) and Columbia University (1946-8). He also served as music director of the Third Street Music Settlement (1952-5) and was managing editor of Galaxy Music (1956-67). Ward then succeeded Louis Mennini to become the second Chancellor of the North Carolina School of the Arts (1967-75). He remained at NCSA as a composition instructor until 1979 when he was appointed Mary Duke Biddle professor of Music at Duke University, where he remains an emeritus faculty member since his retirement in 1987. Ward's music is fairly conservative with an excellent affinity for text and the stage. His works are tonal and rhythmically strong at times incorporating folk song and dance music in quotation and as models.[91]

Awards: MacDowell Colony Fellowship (1938), Alice M. Ditson Fellowship (1944), grant from the American Academy of Arts and Letters (1946), Pulitzer Prize and New York Critics' Circle Award (both in 1962 for *The Crucible*), elected to the National Institute of Arts and Letters (1967).

Principal Works: *opera - He who gets Slapped* (1955), *The Crucible* (1961), *The Lady from Colorado* (1964), *Abelard and Heloise* (1981), *Minutes till Midnight* (1978-82); *orchestral -* 5 symphonies: no. 1 (1941), no. 2 (1947), no. 3 (1950), no. 4 (1958), no. 5, "Canticles of America" (1976), *Jubilation* (1948), *Euphony* (1954), Piano Concerto (1968), *Sonic Structure* (1981), Saxophone Concerto (1984, revised 1987), *Festival Triptych* (1986), *Dialogue on the Tides of Time* (1987); *vocal - Epithalamion* (1937), *Fatal Interview* (1937), *Sacred Songs for Pantheists* (1951), *Let the Words go Forth* (1965).

Selected Composer Bibliography

Stambler, Bernard: "Robert Ward," *American Composers' Alliance Bulletin,* iv/4 (1955), 3.
"Ward, Robert (Eugene)," *Current Biography Yearbook,* xxiv (July 1963); New York: H. W. Wilson Company.
Fleming, Shirley: "Robert Ward," *HiFi/Musical America,* xxxii/5 (1982), 2.
Kreitner, Kenneth: *Robert Ward: A Bio-Bibliography.* Westport, CT: Greenwood Press, 1988.

Earth Shall Be Fair (1960)

Duration: ca. 26 minutes

Text: "Turn back O Man," by Clifford Bax and Psalms selected by John Dexter.

Performing Forces: *voices*: SATB choir, SATB youth choir, children's choir or soprano soloist; *orchestra*: 2 flutes (flute II

---

[91] Kenneth Kreitner: *Robert Ward: A Bio-Bibliography.* New York: Greenwood Press, 1988.

doubling piccolo), 2 oboes, 2 clarinets, 2 bassoons, 4 horns, 2 trumpets, 2 trombones, timpani, percussion (1 player - snare drum, cymbals, suspended cymbal, tam-tam, chimes), and strings.

First Performance: *with organ*: 20 November 1960; KRNT Theater, Des Moines, IA; Des Moines Council of Churches Choirs; Robert Speed, organ; conducted by Robert Ward.

with orchestra: 28 July 1963; Brevard Music Center, Brevard, NC; Transylvania Chamber Orchestra, Transylvania Chorus and Choral Ensemble; conducted by David Buttolph.

Edition: *Earth Shall Be Fair* is published by Highgate Press and distributed by Galaxy Music/E. C. Schirmer. The organ-vocal score is for sale; orchestral materials are available for rental.

Autograph: Sketches are housed in the Robert Ward Archive at Duke University, Durham, NC. The autograph score is in the possession of the composer.

Notes: This was commissioned by and dedicated to the Des Moines Council of Churches. The work is organized into 5 sections, the last of which uses a hymn tune by Louis Bourgeois (c. 1510-c. 1561). The sections are:

1. Lord, thou hast been our dwelling place
2. Then the kings of the earth
3. Thou changest man back to dust
4. Earth might be fair
5. Search me, O God, and know my heart!

Performance Issues: This score offers an unusual configuration of singers for a work of this length. It is well written for the abilities of the three age groups represented by the choirs. Much of the choral material is common to both the adult and youth choirs. Although a soprano soloist may be substituted for the children's choir it seems inappropriate for a piece written to celebrate a multi-generational ensemble. This is a tonal and mostly diatonic composition in which the choral pitches are carefully prepared by the accompaniment. The choral writing is mostly homophonic with scalar motion dominating each part. The harmonies of the choir are consistently supported in the orchestra. The opening of the second movement features the youth choir in a section which is full of changing meters emphasizing a variety of beat groupings. In the fifth movement, there are a number of *a cappella* passages for the adult choir which are based upon Bourgeois's hymn. Ward's harmonization is somewhat challenging and the unaccompanied opening of the movement in F minor immediately following a movement in E major may present some difficulties. This last movement and the opening of the second movement will require the greatest amount of rehearsal time. The organization of the score allows for most of the preparation of each choir to take place independently. The orchestral writing is conservative and arranged to balance well with the voices. In the third movement the horns have some exposed and sustained playing and first violins have some fairly high passagework, both of which will need to be considered when assigning parts. The orchestral portion of this piece is quite accessible to an average community orchestra and the choral parts are well within the grasp of a community choir or large church music program. The text is familiar and the music tuneful and skillfully arranged. It is a work which would be very effective as the focus of a church music festival for a church with choirs of different ages. *Choir*: medium easy; *Orchestra*: medium easy.

Discography: As of January 1993, no commercial recording has been made available.

Selected Bibliography

Boulware, Jane: "Premiere Performance of Cantata Here," *Des Moines Tribune* (19 November 1960).
Dwight, Ogden: "3,000 Hear Premiere of Cantata," *Des Moines Register* (21 November 1960).

Sweet Freedom's Song: a New England Chronicle (1965)

Duration: ca. 40 minutes

Text: Compiled by Robert and Mary (the composer's wife) Ward from William Bradford's *Of Plimouth Plantation*; traditional Thanksgiving hymns of Henry Alford, Anna Barbauld, and Leonard Bacon; William Tyler Page's "Epitaph of an Unknown Soldier of the Revolution"; James Russell Lowell's "Ode on the Hundredth

Anniversary of the Fight at Concord Bridge"; and Samuel Francis Smith's *America*, verse III.

Performing Forces: *voices*: narrator, soprano and baritone soloists; SATB choir; *orchestra*: 2 flutes, 2 oboes, 2 clarinets, 2 bassoons, 2 horns, 2 trumpets, 2 trombones, timpani, percussion (1 player - snare drum, cymbals, suspended cymbal, glockenspiel, celeste; the timpanist also plays bass drum and cymbals), and strings.

First Performance: 4 December 1965; Cary Hall, Lexington, MA; Lexington Choral Society; conducted by Allan Lannom.

Edition: It is published by Highgate Press and distributed by Galaxy Music/E. C. Schirmer. The piano-vocal score is for sale; orchestral materials are available for rental.

Autograph: Sketches are housed in the Robert Ward Archive at Duke University, Durham, NC. The autograph score is in the Library of Congress (M1533. 3. W37 S92)

Notes: *Sweet Freedom's Song* was commissioned by and dedicated to the Lexington Choral Society to commemorate their twenty-fifth anniversary. The work is divided into 8 movements as follows:

Prelude		orchestra
1.	It was a great design (William Bradford)	choir
2.	O, Lord God of My Salvation (Psalm 88)	soprano
3.	Come, Ye Thankful People, Come (Henry Alford, Anna Barbauld, Leonard Bacon, and William Bradford)	choir
4.	Ballad of Boston Bay (Robert and Mary Ward)	choir
5.	Damnation to the Stamp Act (a collage of quotations from colonial broadside and speeches; British views are given to one choir, colonial to the other)	double choir
6.	Epitaphs (William Tyler Page, James Russell Lowell)	baritone, choir
7.	Let Music Swell the Breeze (Samuel Francis Smith's *America*, verse III)	choir

There are two versions of the narration, and the composer notes that it may be performed without narration if the narrative material is included in the program notes.

Performance Issues: A distracting feature of the full score is that all stems which hang do so on the right side of the noteheads. There is also much inconsistency in the beaming of the vocal parts. The choral writing is diatonic, scalar, and generally doubled in the accompaniment. Many of the choral passages are homophonic including frequent choral unisons, although there are some well executed imitative sections including a delightful fugue in the third movement. There are a number of *a cappella* passages including the entire fourth movement and some which feature only the men. Much of the melodic material is tuneful and often folk-like. The narration is placed between movements so that integration between the speaker and the music is not a concern. The orchestra parts present few balance problems, and there are no significant rhythmic challenges. However, the strings and woodwinds are both given some occasional intricate and rapid passage work throughout the score. These parts require experienced players. *Soloists*: soprano, range: d'-b^{b}", tessitura: g'-e^{b}", a control of long phrases is required, the orchestration allows for a small voice to be used; baritone, range: B-g', tessitura: e-d', written in the treble clef, it is declamatory and light. This is a patriotic work particularly suitable for the Thanksgiving season. The choral part is appropriate for an amateur or college group of moderate experience. Considering the parts listed above, the accompaniment is within the range of an average community orchestra. *Choir*: easy to medium easy; *Orchestra*: medium easy.

Discography: As of January 1993, no commercial recording has been made available.

Selected Bibliography

Shertzer, Jim: "Ward's Music Finds Place in Bicentennial," *Winston-Salem [NC] Journal* (14 March 1976).
Carr, Genie: "Both Objectivity and Subjectivity," *Winston-Salem [NC] Sentinel* (1 April 1976).

Willan, Healey (b. Balham, England, 12 October 1880; d. Toronto, 16 February 1968).

Life: Willan attended St. Saviour's Choir School in Eastbourne, England (1888-95) singing under the direction of Walter Hay Sangster. He served as organist in a number of London-area churches studying organ privately with William Stevenson Hoyte and piano with Evelyn Howard-Jones, and became a Fellow of the Royal College of Organists in 1899. In 1913, he emigrated to Canada to head the theory department of the Toronto Conservatory of Music, and in 1914 became a lecturer and examiner for the University of Toronto where he also acted as music director of the Hart House Theatre (1919-25). He became precentor of the Church of St. Mary Magdalene in 1921, remaining there until his death. Willan was vice-principal of the Toronto Conservatory (1920-36), and professor (1936-50) and University Organist (1932-64) at the University of Toronto. He was one of the most influential church musicians in North America, encouraging the expansion of the role of plainsong in Anglican worship and promoting the reintroduction of Renaissance music to church use. Willan's music is historically retrospective combining ninteenth-century harmonic practice with sixteenth- and eighteenth-century counterpoint. He was a prominent authority in English plainchant and Latin church music. This he used to great effect in his hundreds of works for church use. His later orchestral music is in the mold of Wagner and Bruckner.[92]

Awards: honorary membership in the Canadian League of Composers (1955), Lambeth Doctorate from the Archbishop of Canterbury (1956), Canadian Council Medal (1961), FRSCM (1963), FRHCM (1965), Companion of the Order of Canada (1967, first musician so honored), and in his centenary year became the first Canadian musician to be depicted on a Canadian postage stamp.

Principal Works: *opera*: *The Order of Good Cheer* (1928), *Transit through Fire* (1942), *Dierdre* (1945); *orchestral*: Symphony no. 1 (1936), Symphony no. 2 (1941), Piano Concerto (1944), *Royce Hall Suite* (1949), Incidental Music for 16 plays; *choral*: *An Apostrophe to the Heavenly Hosts* (1921), *The Mystery of Bethlehem* (1923), Six Motets (1924), *Gloria Deo per immensa saecula* (1950), *The Story of Bethlehem* (1955); *works for church use: Red Carol Book* (1930),

---

[92] Frederick Robert Charles Clarke: *Healey Willan*. Toronto: University of Toronto Press, 1983.

13 Introits for the Church Year (1950), *Carols for the Seasons* (1959), *Canadian Psalter* (1963), *Introits, Graduals, and Responses* [Lutheran] (1967), 14 settings of the Missa Brevis (1928-63), 10 settings of the Communion Service, 35 fauxbourdon settings of Canticles, 15 full settings of Canticles, many hymns, anthems, and plainsong arrangements; numerous songs and pieces for organ.

Selected Composer Bibliography

Ridout, Godfrey: "Healey Willan," *Canadian Music Journal*, iii (1959), 4.

Marwick, William: *The Sacred Choral Music of Healey Willan*. Michigan State University: Dissertation, 1970.

Telschow, Frederick H.: *The Sacred Music of Healey Willan*. Eastman School of Music of the University of Rochester: Dissertation, 1970.

Bryant, Giles: *Healey Willan Catalogue*. Ottawa: National Library of Canada, 1972.

_____: "Healey Willan," in *The New Grove Dictionary of Music and Musicians*, edited by Stanley Sadie, xx: 428-30. 20 volumes. London: Macmillan, 1980.

Musical Canada [entire issue devoted to Willan], xlii (Spring 1980).

Clarke, Frederick Robert Charles: *Healey Willan*. Toronto: University of Toronto Press, 1983.

Coronation Suite, op. 57 (1952-53)

Duration: ca. 27 minutes

Text: John Milton, James Edward Ward, Liturgical (Veni sponsa Christi, Psalm 45, II John).

Performing Forces: *voices*: SSATB choir; *orchestra*: 2 flutes, 2 oboes, 2 clarinets, 2 bassoons, 4 horns, 3 trumpets, 3 trombones, tuba, timpani, percussion (3 players - snare drum, bass drum, cymbals and chimes), harp, and strings.

First Performance: 2 June 1953; CBC broadcast for the coronation of Elizabeth II, Toronto;

Edition: *Coronation Suite* is published and distributed by Berandol Music. The piano-vocal score is for sale; orchestral materials are available for rental. A separate octavo score of "Come Ready Lyre" is published by Clark and Cruickshank, and of "Ring Out, Ye Crystall Spheres" is published separately by BMI Canada. Both are distributed by Berandol.

Autograph: The full score distributed by the publisher is a facsimile of the manuscript.

Notes: *Coronation Suite* is in written in five sections as follows:

1.	Prelude	orchestra
2.	Ring Out Ye Crystall Spheres (Milton)	unaccompanied choir SSATB
3.	Intermezzo	orchestra
4.	Come Ready Lyre (Ward)	unaccompanied choir SATB
5.	Come, Thou Beloved of Christ (liturgy)	orchestra and choir, SSATB

Compare the setting of Milton's "Ring Out Ye Crystall Spheres" to that in Ralph Vaughan Williams's *Hodie*.

Performance Issues: A significant problem for the preparation of this piece is that the score is very difficult to read. It is also unfortunate that the two *a cappella* movements do not occur in the full score. The choral writing is diatonic and scalar. There is a good balance between polyphonic and homophonic writing. Willan uses a melodic language which is tonal, while borrowing occasional chromaticisms which lean toward modality. Each section of the choir must sustain passages of unison singing in a sectional solo. The final 24 measures of the work demand a large choir to balance with the orchestra. All sections of the choir have divisi and speech-like rhythms. There are some remarkable choral harmonies which are executed through practical linear movement. The vocal writing is eloquent and very approachable by choirs of moderate experience, and the orchestra part is playable by a college-level orchestra. The orchestration reflects the composer's experience as an organist: dynamic contrast is guaranteed by consistent expansions or reductions of players in response to the level of volume desired. Sections of the orchestra are engaged as if a stop were being pulled, or a section of the orchestra will enter diagonally in the score much like the effect of an organ's crescendo pedal. The result can be completely effective, but explaining this feature of the score could be helpful in establishing a good dynamic balance. The string writing is fairly thick and represents the majority of the orchestra material. The individual instrumental parts are fairly conservative with the greatest demands falling upon the strings, about whom the composer appears to have had the best knowledge. The winds generally double melodic lines from the strings. Occasionally there are glissando-like passages which create polyrhythms including 7 against 3, and 10 against 9. Most of the rhythmic material is straightforward and the harmonic language is triadic and functionally conceived. One notable characteristic of the orchestral writing is that although the texture changes regularly, there are virtually no silences. This is a grandiose and triumphant work which calls for a large and vibrant ensemble. It is an ideal piece for celebratory programs. *Choir*: medium easy; *Orchestra*: medium.

Discography: As of January 1993, no commercial recording has been made available.

Appendix I

Text Sources, Authors, and Translators

African-American Spirituals [found in: Delius - Appalachia, Dett - The Ordering of Moses, Tippett - A Child of Our Time]

Hugo Chayim Adler (1898-1955), a cantor and composer, he was born in Antwerp. He served as cantor at Mannheim (1921-39). Escaping the Nazis, he emigrated to Worcester, Massachusetts, where he became a cantor and reformed the music of the services. In Europe, he studied composition with Ernst Toch. There he developed an ethically-based cantata form modeled upon those of Brect and Hindemith. He is the father of the composer, Samuel Adler. His cantatas include: *Licht und Volk* (1931), *Balak und Bileam* (1934), *Akedah* (1938), *Parable of Persecution* (1946), *Behold the Jew* (1943), and *Jona* (1943). [found in: Adler - The Binding]

Aggadah (see Midrash) [found in: Adler - The Binding]

Ainsworth Psalter Translation prepared by English separatist, Henry Ainsworth (1571-1623?). He was a clergyman and scholar of rabbinical and Oriental studies. He joined the Brownists in Amsterdam (1593). His work was focused upon the Old Testament. This was the Psalter brought to Plymouth by the Pilgrims. [found in: Finney - Pilgrim Psalms]

Mark Akenside (1721-70), an English poet and physician, he was physician to the queen (1761). He studied theology at the

University of Edinburgh, but abandoned this for medicine. His works include: *Pleasures of the Imagination* (1744) and *Hymn to the Naiads* (1746). [found in: Finney - Still Are New Worlds]

Henry Alford (1810-71), an English clergyman and poet, he was born in London and became a Fellow of Trinity College, Cambridge. In 1857, he was made dean of Canterbury. He was the first editor of the Contemporary Review (1866-70). Among his many hymn texts is "Come ye thankful people, come." [found in: Ward - Sweet Freedom's Song]

The American Mercury Literary magazine founded in 1924, under the sponsorship of Alfred A. Knopf. It was an offshoot of *Smart Set* (1900-30). The American Mercury had as its initial editor, George Jean Nathan and H. L. Mencken. Its contributors included William Faulkner, Sinclair Lewis, Vachel Lindsay, Edgar Lee Masters, Margaret Mead, Louis Mumford, and Carl Sandburg. A regular section, "Americana," was a collection of outrageous aspects of popular culture arranged geographically. In later years it became a placard of right-wing propaganda. [found in: Thompson - Americana]

The Apocryphal Acts of St. John, about St. John the Evangelist who is also known as John the Divine. One of the twelve original apostles of Christ, he is the author of the Fourth Gospel. He is said to have taken the Virgin Mary to Ephesus after the crucifixion. At Domitian he escaped unharmed from a cauldron of boiling oil. He was banished to the Isle of Atmos where he authored the *Book of Revelation.* [found in: Holst - Hymn of Jesus]

Matthew Arnold (1822-88), English poet and critic. Son of Thomas Arnold, he was born in Laleham and educated at Winchester, Rugby, and then Balliol College, Oxford. From 1851 to 1886, he served as lay inspector of schools. He was appointed professor of poetry at Oxford in 1857. He gained fame not only for his many volumes of poetry and criticism, but also for his application of modern literary criticisms toward scripture. [found in: Sowerby - Canticle of the Sun (translator of St. Francis of Assisi), Vaughan Williams - Oxford Elegy]

W(ystan) H(ugh) Auden (1907-73), born in York, 21 February, he was schooled at St. Edmund's School, Grayshott; Gresham's

School, Holt; and Christ Church College (exhibitioner), Oxford (1925-8). He traveled through Europe, Iceland, and China in the 1930's. He emigrated to the U.S. in 1939 with Peter Pears and Benjamin Britten, becoming a citizen in 1946. He held many teaching posts in the U.S. and England. He received numerous awards including the Pulitzer (1948), Bollingen Prize (1954), and membership in the Academy of the American Academy and Institute of Arts and Letters (1954). A prolific writer, his works include: *Look, Stranger!* (1936), *The Double Man* (1941), *The Age of Anxiety: A Baroque Eclogue* (1948), *About the House* (1965), and *Collected Poems*, ed. Edward Mendelson (1976). [found in: Britten - Spring Symphony]

St. Augustine (354-430), the most influential of the Latin Church founders, converted with his son to Christianity by St. Ambrose, writings are concerned with his own spiritual struggle which is most significantly explored in *Confessions* (400) and *The City of God* (22 volumes: 412-27). [found in: Tippett - Vision of St. Augustine]

Leonard Bacon (1802-81), an American Congregational minister, he was a founder and editor of *The Independent*. He was a leader in the antislavery movement and author of *Slavery Discussed in Occasional Essays* (1846), and *The Genesis of New England Churches* (1874). [found in: Ward - Sweet Freedom's Song]

James Baldwin (1924-87), a black author and activist, he was born and raised in Harlem. As a teen he became a Pentecostal minister and preached in many Harlem churches. With the help of his teachers he began to explore the written word. He became a voice of the civil rights movement and seminal figure in African-American literature. Central topics in his writings are the social injustice toward blacks and coming to grips with his homosexuality. His works include: *Go Tell It On the Mountain* (1953), *Notes of a Native Son* (1955), *Giovanni's Room* (1956), *Nobody Knows My Name* (1961), *Another Country* (1962), *The Fire Next Time* (1963), and *Just Above My Head* (1979). [found in: Amram - A Year in Our Land]

William Ballet (16th cent.), a minor poet about whom little is known, he is remembered almost exclusively for his lullaby. [found in: Vaughan Williams - Hodie]

Anna Barbauld (1743-1825), a British poet who married a dissenting minister in 1774. She published *Miscellaneous Poems in Prose* in 1773 with her brother, John Aiken. Her other writings include: *Poems* (1773), *Early Lessons for Children, Hymns in Prose for Children,* and *Evenings at Home* (a series begun in 1792). [found in: Ward - Sweet Freedom's Song]

Richard Barnefield (1574-1627), an English poet [found in: Britten - Spring Symphony]

Clifford Bax (1886-1962), an English poet and playwright, he was the brother of the composer Arnold Bax. His works include: *The Poetasters of Ispahan* (1912), *Midsummer Madness* (1924), *Pretty Witty Nell* (1932), *The Rose Without a Thorn* (1932), *The House of Borgia* (1935), and *Ideas and People* (1936). [found in: Ward - Earth Shall Be Fair]

Benedicite, a hymn often called "Psalm Benedicite," or "Song of the Three Children." It is part of a Greek addition to the third chapter of the Book of Daniel which was based upon Psalm 148. [found in: Foulds - World Requiem]

Francis Beaumont (1584-1616), an Elizabethan English dramatist, he was educated at Broadgates Hall (now Pembroke College), Oxford. He became associated with a group of writers who met regularly at the Mermaid Tavern including Ben Jonson and John Fletcher. With the latter he coauthored virtually all of his theatrical works, these were compiled in two folios (1647 and 1679) containing 87 works. Among them are: The Woman Hater (1607), *The Knight of the Burning Pestle* (1609). He is buried in Westminster Abbey. [found in: Britten - Spring Symphony, Holst - First Choral Symphony]

Stephen Vincent Benét (1886-1950), American poet, playwright, novelist, and editor; he is best known for *The Devil and Daniel Webster* (1937) and *John Brown's Body* (1928) for which he received the 1929 Pulitzer prize. [found in: Dello Joio - Song of Affirmation]

Beowulf An Old English epic poem, it is the oldest in English or any of the Teutonic languages. Its authorship is unknown, but it surely predates the arrival of the Saxons to England. It has been modified since the arrival of Christianity to the British Isles. The present form is thought to date from the eighth century. The story takes place in Denmark or Sweden, and is concerned with Beowulf who kills the Grendel, a creature which is half-human and half-monster. Grendel's mother attempts to avenge her son's death and is also slain by Beowulf. Eventually, the hero becomes king, but is killed 50 years later by another dragon. [found in: Hanson - Lament for Beowulf]

Bible from *biblia*, the latinization of the Greek meaning books, it refers to the collection of principle sacred writings of the Jews (Old Testament) and Christians (New Testament). The Old Testament was authored in Hebrew and Aramaic, and the New Testament in Greek. There have been numerous translations including: Vulgate (translated into Latin by St. Jerome, c. 384-404, It is the edition sanctioned by the Roman Catholic Church.), Wyclif's Bible (earliest complete English translation (from Vulgate), c. 1384), Tyndale's Bible (influential English translation to incorporate original Greek manuscripts, 1525-35), Coverdale's Bible (first complete printed edition in English, 1535), Geneva Bible (versified English Bible, 1560), Douai Bible (English translation for Roman Catholics, 1582-1609), and Authorized of King James's Bible (still in current use in England, 1697-11). Later efforts of modern scholarship include: Revised Version (1881-95), Revised Standard Version (1946-52), New English Bible (1970), Jerusalem Bible (1966), New International Version (1978), and Revised English Bible (1989). [found in: Adler - The Binding, Behold Your God, Brubeck - Light in the Wilderness, Creston - Isaiah's Prophecy, Dett - The Ordering of Moses, Elgar - The apostles, The Kingdom, Foulds - World Requiem, Hovhaness - Praise the Lord With Psaltery, Howells - Hymnus Paradisi, Mennin - Cantata de Virtute, Christmas Story, Rogers - The Prophet Isaiah, Starer - Ariel, Stevens - Testament of Life, Thompson - The Passion According to St. Luke, Tippett - The Vision of St. Augustine, Vaughan William - Dona Nobis Pacem, Hodie, Sancta Civitas, Walton - Belshazzar's Feast]

(Robert) Lawrence Binyon (1869-1943), English poet and art critic whose style is reminiscent of Wordsworth and Arnold, worked in the British Museum from his graduation from Oxford until 1933, after which he was the Norton professor of poetry at Harvard University. Portions of "For the Fallen" appear on war memorials throughout Great Britain. [found in: Elgar - The Spirit of England]

William Blake (1757-1827), an English poet, engraver, and painter, he was born in London. In 1771, he apprenticed as an engraver and studied art at the Royal Academy School. He began his career making illustrations for magazines. He believed that he was regularly visited by members of the spirit world. He illustrated and engraved editions of many works including: Edward Young's *Night Thoughts* (1797), Robert Blair's *The Grave* (1808), and the *Book of Job* (1826) as well as his own writings. Among his poetical works are: *Poetical Sketches* (1783), *Songs of Innocence* (1789), *Songs of Experience* (1794); and the mystical writings: *Book of Thel* (1789), *The Marriage of Heaven and Hell* (1791), *The French Revolution* (1791), and *The Song of Los* (1795). [found in: Britten - Spring Symphony]

Edmund Charles Blunden (1896-1974), an English poet and critic, he was born in London and educated at Christ's Hospital and Queen's College, Oxford. He has taught in Tokyo (1924-7), University of Hong Kong (1953-66), and Oxford (1966-8). He has edited the works of many significant English poets and has authored books on Leigh Hunt, Lamb, and John Keats. His own poetry is inspired by the English country side and includes: *Pastorals* (1916), *The Waggoner and Other Poems* (1920), and the prose works: *The Bonadventure* (1922), and *Undertones of War* (1928). [found in: Finzi - For St. Cecilia]

Book of Common Prayer The book of official liturgy for the Church of England, it was first issued in 1549 with a series of revisions including the 1662 reissue following the restoration. An *Alternative Services Book* (1980) provided updated liturgies and services in contemporary English. In the United States, the Episcopal Church adopted revisions in 1928 (including Coverdale's translation of the *Psalter*) and 1979. [found in: Howells - Hymnus Paradisi, Vaughan Williams - Hodie]

John Bowring (1792-1872), a British diplomat and linguist. Following his schooling, he worked in a merchant's office where he gained a knowledge of 200 languages. In 1824, he became editor of *Westminster Review*. He travelled widely and prepared numerous international trade agreements. He served in parliament (1835-49) where he campaigned for free trade. He was made British consul in Hong Kong (1849) and in 1854 he was knighted and made Hong Kong's governor. He published numerous volumes of his translations of eastern European poetry. [found in: Cowell - The Creator (translator of Derzhavin)]

William Bradford (1590-1657), a founder of the Pilgrim Colony in Plymouth, Massachusetts. Born in Austerfield, England, he joined the Brownists (a separatist movement) in 1606 and moved to Amsterdam and then Leiden seeking religious freedom. He sailed with the Pilgrims in 1620 and signed the Mayflower Compact that same year. He was elected Governor of the Plymouth Colony 30 times between 1621-56. He is the author of *History of Plimoth Plantation* (1651). [found in: Ward - Sweet Freedom's Song]

John Bright (1811-89), a radical British statesman and orator, he denounced the Crimean War (1854). Bright was considered to be one of the most eloquent speakers of his era. [found in: Vaughan Williams - Dona Nobis Pacem]

Robert Browning (1812-89), an English poet, he was born in Camberwell and briefly attended University College in London, and then travelled abroad. He married Elizabeth Barrett in 1846 and the two settled in Italy. Following her death in 1861, he moved back to London. He established new methods of writing narratives which outmoded the epic and pastoral. His principal works include: *Paracelsus* (1835), *Men and Women* (1855), *Dramatis Personae* (1864), *The Ring and the Book* (1868-69), *Fifine at the Fair* (1872), *The Inn Album* (1875), *Pacchiarotto* (1876), and *Aslondo* (1889). [found in: Mennin - Cantata de Virtute]

Albert Camus (1913-60), a French author, he was born in Algeria where he studied philosophy between bouts of ill-health. After moving to Paris, he was active in the resistance during World War II. His work is existential and explores some of the inequities of human existence. In 1957, Camus was awarded the Nobel prize for literature. His works include: *L'Étranger* (1942), *Le Mythe de Sisyphe* (1942, trans. 1955), *La Peste* (1947), *Actuelles I* (1950), *L'Homme révolté* (1951, trans. 1953), *Actuelles II* (1953), and *La Chute* (1956). [found in: Finney - Still Are New Worlds]

Lewis Carroll, born Charles Dodgson (1832-98), English author and mathematician, he attended Rugby and Christ Church Colleges, Oxford. He joined the mathematics faculty of Christ Church in 1855. He was also an important early amateur photographer. He authored *Euclid and His Modern Rivals* (1879). His fictional works emphasize fantasy and word games, and many feature a character modeled on Alice Liddell, the daughter of Christ Church's Dean. They include: *Alice's Adventure in Wonderland* (1865), *Phantasmagoria and other poems* (1869), *Through the Looking Glass and What Alice Found There* (1871), *The Hunting of the Snark* (1876), *Rhyme? and Reason?* (1883), and *Sylvie and Bruno* (1889 and 1893). [found in: Adler - A Whole Bunch of Fun, Del Tredici - Pop-Pourri]

Guy Wetmore Carryl (1873-1904), American poet, novelist, children's writer, and humorist; he was the son of stockbroker/children's author, Charles Edward Carryl. Guy Wetmore is best known for his parodies of traditional children's tales which include: *Fables for the Frivolous* (1898), *Mother Goose for Grown-Ups* (1900), and *Grimm Tales Made Gay* (1902). [found in: Siegmeister - This is Our Land]

John Clare (1793-1864), English poet. He was born to and lived in poverty. He was primarily self-taught, and attracted attention with a number of self-published collections including: *Proposal for Publishing a Collection of Trifles in Verse* (1817), *Poems Descriptive of Rural Life* (1820), *Village Minstrel* (1821), *The Shepherd's Calendar* (1827), and *Rural Muse* (1835). In 1837, he was committed to an insane asylum where he remained until his death. [found in: Britten - Spring Symphony]

Jean Cocteau (1889-1963), a French poet, playwright, artist, and film maker; had a spectacular and multifaceted career. His associations included *Les Six*, Stravinsky, Diaghilev, de Chirico, and Picasso. His works are dramatic and reflect his affiliations with the Surrealist and Dadaist movements. His principal works include: novels - *La Lampe d'Alladin* (1909), *Le Grand Ecart* (1923), *Les Enfant terribles* (1929); plays - *Les Mariés de la Tour Eiffel* (1921), *Orphée* (1926), *L'Aigle à deux têtes* (1946); films - *Le sang du poète* (1932), *La Belle et la bête* (1945), *Orphée* (1949), and *Le Testament d'Orphée* (1960). [found in: Rorem - Poet's Requiem]

Miles Coverdale (1488-1568), English biblical scholar and Protestant activist, he was educated at Cambridge, after which he was ordained a Roman Catholic priest in 1514, but later converted to Protestantism. As a religious refugee in Zürich, he published an English translation of the Bible which was dedicated to Henry VIII.

The Psalter of that Bible was used in the Book of Common Prayer. [found in: Vaughan Williams - Hodie]

Abraham Cowley (1618-67), an English poet, he was schooled at Westminster School, Trinity College at Cambridge, and Oxford. During the British Civil War, he served as correspondent for the Queen. His best known work is *Davideis*. [found in: U. Kay - Phoebus Arise]

Eric Crozier (1914-), an English author and producer of opera and television, he frequently collaborated with Britten. He served as librettist for that composer's *Albert Herring* (1947), *Let's Make an Opera* (1949), *Billy Budd* (with E. M. Forster, 1951). He wrote the libretto to Lennox Berkeley's *Ruth* (1956), and co-translated Smetana's *The Bartered Bride* (with Joan Cross, 1943). Crozier produced the first performances of Britten's *Peter Grimes* (1945), and *The Rape of Lucretia* (1946). He is also the author of the narration for Britten's *The Young Person's Guide to the Orchestra* (1946). [found in: Britten - St. Nicolas]

Gavril Romanovich Derzhavin (1743-1816), Russian poet and aristocrat, his works are almost exclusively lyrical and charged with imagination. He is regarded as one of Russia's greatest poets. He was made Secretary of State in 1791, Imperial Treasurer in 1800, and Minister of Justice in 1802. [found in: Cowell - The Creator]

John Dexter, an American author of hymns [found in: Ward - Earth Shall be Fair]

John Donne (c. 1572-1631), Anglican priest and poet, he was born Roman Catholic, a denomination he would later attack in his writings. He attended Hart Hall, Oxford, and later graduated from Cambridge. His works are diverse reflecting his varied career as a court poet and then priest. He authored some of the most eloquent love poems in the English language, numerous tracts examining moral and religious issues, an a number of extant sermons. His works include: *Songs and Sonnets*, six *Satires*, *Of the Progress of the Soul* (begun 1601, published 1633), *Divine Poems* (1607), *Pseudo-Martyr* (1610), *An Anatomy of the World* (1611), *Anniversarie* (1611), *La Corona*, and *A Cycle of Holy Sonnets* (1618). [found in: Finney - Still Are New Worlds]

John Dos Passos (1896-1970), an American novelist, poet, and playwright; he was born in Chicago and educated at Harvard. His incorporation of montage techniques and the social and political content of his writing made him a prominent influence among American writers. His works include: *Manhattan Transfer* (1925), *The Garbage Man* (1926), *Facing the Chair: Story of the Americanization of Two Foreignborn Workmen* (1927), *U. S. A. Trilogy: 42nd Parallel* (1930), *Nineteen Nineteen* (1931), and *Big Money* (1936), *Adventures of a Young Man* (1939), and *Number One* (1943). [found in: Amram - A Year in Our Land]

William Drummond (1585-1649), a Scottish poet, he was educated in Edinburgh, Bourges, and Paris. He was closely associated with Ben Jonson and deeply opposed to the National Covenant. His works include: *Tears on the Death of Moeliades* (1613), *Forth Feasting* (1617), *Flowers of Sion* (1623), *A Cypress Grove* (1630), and *History of the Five Jameses*. [found in: U. Kay - Phoebus Arise, Vaughan Williams - Hodie]

Philip D. Eastman, an American author of children's literature, including *Sam and the Firefly* (1958). [found in: Adler - A Whole Bunch of Fun]

Eleanor Farjeon (1881-1965), an English author, she specialized in children's literature. There is an annual children's book award given in her honor. Her works include: *Nursery Rhymes of London Town* (1916), *Martin Pippin in the Apple Orchard* (1921), and *The Little Bookroom* (1955). [found in: Adler - A Whole Bunch of Fun]

Janet Flanner (1892-1978), an American writer, she served as the Paris correspondent to The New Yorker. These correspondences were compiled into two volumes under the title of Paris Journal (1965 and 1971). She is one of a very few women to be awarded the French Legion of Honor. Her other writings include: *The Cubical City* (1926), *American in Paris* (1940), *Men and Monuments* (1957), and a translation of Colette's *Claudine à l'école* (1930). [found in: Rorem - Paris Letters]

John Fletcher (1579-1625), an English Elizabethan dramatist. He attended Benet (now Corpus) College, Cambridge. He became associated with a group of writers who met regularly at the Mermaid Tavern including Ben Jonson and Francis Beaumont.

With the latter he coauthored many of his theatrical works of his theatrical works, these were compiled in two folios (1647 and 1679) containing 87 works. Among them are: The Woman Hater (1607), *The Knight of the Burning Pestle* (1609). His other collaborators included Massinger, Rowley and Shakespeare. Notable among his own plays are: *The Faithful Shepherdess, The Humorous Lieutenant* (1619), and *Rule a Wife and Have a Wife* (1624). He died of the plague. [found in: Bliss - Pastoral, Britten - Spring Symphony, Holst - First Choral Symphony]

Bernard la Bouvier de Fontenelle (1657-1757), a French author, he supported the movement away from classical models in French literature. He served as secretary and later president of the Académie des Sciences. His writings include: *Histoire des oracles* (1867) and *Entretiens sur la pluralité des mondes* (1868). [found in: Finney - Still Are New Worlds]

St. Francis of Assisi (1181-1226), an Italian religious figure, he was born Giovanni Bernadone. Following his conversion in 1205 he founded the Franciscan monastic order and the Poor Clares, the Franciscan order for women. Based upon early monastic sects, they were founded upon the principles of chastity, obedience, and, most importantly, poverty. His writings include: sermons, hymns, treatises, and *Canticle of the Sun.* [found in: Sowerby - Canticle of the Sun]

Sigmund Freud (1856-1939), an Austrian neurologist, he is the founder of psychoanalysis. He studied medicine in Vienna and served as a neurology specialist at the Vienna General Hospital. There, with Joseph Breuer, he began to treat hysteria with hypnosis. He later developed a number of theories regarding the subconscious, its manifestation in dreams, and its connections with sexuality. His principal writings are: *The Interpretation of Dreams* (1900), *The Psychopathology of Everyday Life* (1904), *Three Essays on the Theory of Sexuality* (1905), *Totem and Tabu* (1913), *Beyond the Pleasure Principle* (1919-20), *Ego and Id* (1923), *The Future of an Illusion* (on religion, 1927), and *Why War?* (with Albert Einstein, 1933). [found in: Rorem - Poet's Requiem]

André Gide (1869-1951), a French diarist and novelist, he became France's most prominent man of letters. His writings have included essays, biographies, criticism, memoirs, and translations. He received the 1947 Nobel prize for literature and was a founder of the magazine, *La Nouvelle Française*. His principal writings are: *L'Immoraliste* (1902), *Les Caves du Vatican* (1914), *La Symphonie Pastorale* (1919), *Les Faux Monnayeurs* (1925), *Journals* (1889-1949), and *Si le Grain ne meurt* (an autobiography, 1926). [found in: Rorem - Poet's Requiem]

Paul Goodman (1911-72), an American author, he first gained an audience through New Directions. He wrote in many fields sometimes reflective of his experience as a psychoanalyst. His works include: *non-fiction - Communitas* (1947), *Gestalt Therapy* (1951); *novels - The Grand Piano* (1949), *The Dead of Spring* (1950), *The Empire City* (1959), *Making Do* (1963); *plays - Faustina* (1949), *The Young Disciple* (1955), and *The Cave at Machpelah*. [found in: Rorem - Poet's Requiem]

Thomas Hardy (1840-1928), an English writer, he was the son of a stonemason, and initially pursued a career as an architect. A prolific novelist, he turned to poetry and drama in reaction to criticisms of the bleak outlook of his novels. His works include: *novels - Under the Greenwood Tree* (1873), *Far from the Maddening Crowd* (1874), *The Return of the Native* (1878), *Tess of the D'Urbervilles* (1891), *Jude the Obscure* (1895); *poetry - Wessex Poems* (1898), *Winter Words* (1928); *drama - The Dynasts* (1904-08). [found in: Vaughan Williams - Hodie]

Catherine R. Harris [found in: Riegger - In Certainty of Song]

Gabriel Harvey (1545-1630), an English poet noted as one of the first to utilize hexameter. The son of a rope maker, he was educated at Christ Church, Cambridge and was a fellow at Pembroke Hall. A curmudgeon, much of his efforts were spent attacking his contemporaries; however, he remained on friendly terms with Edmund Spencer. [found in: Finney - Still Are New Worlds]

Hebrew Liturgy [found in: Bernstein - Kaddish Symphony]

George Herbert (1593-1632), an Anglican priest and religious poet. He was the brother of Lord Herbert of Cherbury and is closely associated with John Donne. He was educated at Westminster and Trinity College, Cambridge; being made a fellow of the latter in 1614. His early adulthood was spent involved with parliament and the court of James VI. He took holy orders in 1630 and led a short, but agressive career as a parish priest. His sacred poetry is contained in *The Temple, Sacred Poems and Private Ejaculations*, which was published immediately after his death. [found in: Vaughan Williams - Hodie]

Lord Herbert of Cherbury (1583-1648), Born Edward Herbert, he was an English soldier, diplomat, and philosopher; he was the brother of George Herbert. Educated at Oxford, he served in the army of the Prince of Orange (1614), and he was ambassador to France (1619-24). At the outbreak of the English Civil War, Herbert was a royalist, but soon sided with parliament. His writing uses a Platonic basis to argue for the existence of God. He has come to be called the "Father of English Deism." His works include: *De Veritate* (1624), *De Religione Gentilium* (1645), and *Life of Henry VIII* (pub. 1649). [found in: U. Kay - Phoebus Arise]

Robert Herrick (1591-1674), an English poet and clergyman, he was the son of a goldsmith, and educated at Trinity Hall, Cambridge. He was deprived of his parish during the English Civil War from 1647 to 1662 for his royalist views. During this time he published his poetical works as *Hesperides: or the Works both Humane and Divine of Robert Herrick Esq.* (1648), the wealth of which represented pagan rather than clerical life. [found in: Britten - Spring Symphony]

Thomas Hood (1799-1845), and English humorist and poet with his brother-in-law, J.H. Reynolds, he wrote *Odes and Addresses to Great People* (1825). His annuals and magazines included: *Comic Annual* (1830-42), *Gem* (1829-), and *Hood's Magazine* (1844-). His other works include: *Eugene Aram's Dream* (1829), *Tylney Hall* (1834), *Song of the Shirt* (1843), *The Bridge of Sighs* (1844). [found in: U. Kay - Phoebus Arise]

Gerard Manley Hopkins (1844-89), an English poet, he studied at Bailliol College, Oxford where he formed a lifelong friendship with Robert Bridges and was led into the Roman Catholic church in 1866. He became a Jesuit novice in 1868 and was ordained a priest in 1877. He taught at Stoneyhurst School and then was the chair of Greek at University College, Dublin. None of his poems was published during his lifetime, but they were brought out in complete edition by Bridges in 1918. [found in: Rubbra - Inscape]

Jacopone da Todi (c. 1230-1306), an Italian religious poet and Franciscan monk, he is believed to be the author of the *Stabat*

Mater, Laude, and numerous Latin hymns. He was imprisoned (1298-1303) for his satirization of Pope Boniface VIII. [found in: Persichetti - Stabat Mater]

Ben Jonson (1572-1637), an English playwright, he was educated at Westminster School. He was associated with Dryden and Shakespeare, the latter of whom appeared in some of Jonson's early plays. His best known works are: *Cynthia's Revels* (1603), *Volpone* (1606), *The Silent Woman* (1609), *The Alchemist* (1610), and *Bartholomew Fair* (1614). [found in: Bliss - Pastoral]

Kabir (c. 1450-1518), a Hindu philosopher and poet, he believed in the admission of all castes and denounced the worship of idols. His writings in Hindi have been widely read by Hindus and Muslims. There is a Sikh religion called Kabirpanthi which is based upon his teachings. [found in: Foulds - World Requiem]

Franz Kafka (1883-1924), a Jewish Austrian novelist, he was born and educated in Prague. His works portray man as a helpless figure in an irrationally bureaucratic world. During his life, he published the short stories: "Der Heizer" ("The Boilerman,"1913), "Betrachtungen" ("Meditations," 1913), and "Die Verwandlung" ("Metamorphosis," 1916). His three unfinished novels were published posthumously by Max Brod; they are: *Prozess (The Trial)*, *Das Scloss (The Castle)*, and *Amerika*. [found in: Rorem - Poet's Requiem]

John Keats (1795-1821), an English romantic poet, he was associated with Leigh Hunt, Percy Byshe Shelley, and Lord Byron. His works include: *Endymion* (1818) and *Lamia and Other Poems* (1820). [found in: Holst - First Choral Symphony]

Johann Kepler (1571-1630), a German astronomer and mathematician, he was born in Württemberg. He is the founder of modern astronomy, his efforts being the foundation of Isaac Newton's work. His findings and theories were published in *Mysterium cosmographicum* (1596), *Astronomia nova* (1609), and *Harmonice mundi* (1619). [found in: Finney - Still Are New Worlds]

Jack Kerouac (1922-69), an American novelist, he has become a cult-hero and coined the term the "Beat Generation." He was closely associated with Allen Ginsburg and Gary Snyder. His second novel,

On the Road (1957), which tells of a cross-country trip of self-exploration, has became the touchstone of the American counter-culture of the 1960's. His other novels include: *The Town and the City* (1950), *The Dharma Bums* (1958), *Doctor Sax* (1959), and *Big Sur* (1962). [found in: Amram - A Year in Our Land]

Martin Luther King, Jr. (1929-68), American clergyman and civil rights leader, he achieved national recognition for his leadership of the Alabama bus boycott and the establishment of the Southern Christian Leadership Conference (1957). He led a major march on Washington (1963) which was crowned by his "I have a dream. . ." speech. In 1964, he was awarded the Kennedy peace prize and the Nobel peace prize. He was assassinated by James Earl Ray in Memphis, TN. [found in: Flagello - Passion of Martin Luther King, Siegmeister - I Have a Dream]

Latin Liturgy [found in: Bernstein - Mass, Britten - War Requiem, Creston - Missa Solemnis, Flagello - Passion of Martin Luther King, Foulds - World Requiem, J. Harrison - Mass in C and Requiem, Hovhaness - Magnificat, Howells - Hymnus Paradisi, Mennin - Cantata de Virtute, Rubbra - Mass, Willan - Coronation Suite, Coronation Te Deum]

Li Tai Po (c. 700-762), one of China's greatest poets, he was a member of the group "the Eight Immortals of the Wine Cup." He is believed to have drowned while intoxicatedly attempting to embrace the moon's reflection. [found in: Bliss - Morning Heroes]

Henry Wadsworth Longfellow (1807-82), an American poet, he was educated at Bowdoin College where he later served as chair of foreign languages. He later served as chair of modern languages and literature at Harvard. He was a classmate of Nathaniel Hawthorne and was acquainted with Thomas Carlyle. His works include: *Voices of the Night* (1839), *Ballads* (1840), *Poems on Slavery* (1842), *Evangeline* (1847), *Hiawatha* (1855), *The Courtship of Miles Standish* (1858), and *Tales of a Wayside Inn* (1863). [found in: Diamond - To Music]

James Russell Lowell (1819-91), an American poet and essayist, he was born in Cambridge, Massachusetts, and educated at Harvard. In addition to writing he did editorial work for the *The Pioneer, The Atlantic Monthly*, and *North American Review*. He was an ardent abolitionist addressing the issue of slavery in much of his writing.

He served as the US minister to Spain (1877-80) and to Great Britain (1880-85). His works include: *Conversations on Old Poets* (1845), *Biglow Paper* (1848 and 1867), *A Fable for Critics* (1848), *Among my Books* (1870), and *My Study Windows* (1871). [found in: Ward - Sweet Freedom's Song]

Martin Luther (1483-1546), German founder of the Protestant Reformation, he was ordained a Roman Catholic priest in 1508. He became a lecturer at the University of Wittenberg. He preached that salvation came from faith rather than works. His 95 theses on indulgences, which he nailed to the church door in Wittenberg (31 October 1517), denied the Pope of the power to forgive sins. He worked diligently to reform the church throughout his life. He authored a German translation of the Bible and wrote numerous hymns, and religious tracts. [found in: Vaughan Williams - Hodie]

Edward Mabley (b. 1906), an American author, and friend of Elie Siegmeister for whom he organized a number of texts. [found in: Siegmeister - I Have a Dream (arranger of King)]

Maud MacCarthy, an English violinist, mystic, and author, she was John Foulds's mistress. She was involved in the preparation of a number of his scores and served as the orchestra leader in numerous performances of Foulds's works. [found in: Foulds - World Requiem]

Stéphane Mallarmé (1842-98), a French poet, he was the leader of the Symbolist movement. He wrote primarily in free verse using unusual word construction and allegorical elements. His best known works are *L'Apres-midi d'un faune* (1876), *Les Dieux antiques* (1880), *Vers et Prose* (1893), and *Proésies* (1899). [found in: Rorem - Poet's Requiem]

Christopher Marlowe (1564-93), an English playwright, he was born in Canterbury where he attended the King's School. He then matriculated at Cambridge. He established a standard of excellence for English drama in the 16th century. His works served as a model for those of Shakespeare. Among his plays are *Tamburlaine the Great, The Tragical History of Dr. Faustus, The Jew of Malta,* and *Edward II.* [found in: Finney - Still Are New Worlds]

John Masefield (1878-1967), an English poet and novelist, he apprenticed as a seaman, but was forced to abandon this career due to poor health. He then turned to writing, becoming Poet Laureate (1930-67). His works include: *Salt Water Ballads* (1902), *Dauber* (1913), *Gallipoli* (1916), *Reynard the Fox* (1919), and *The Trial of Jesus* (1925). [found in: Diamond - To Music]

Thomas Middleton (c. 1570-1627), an English playwright, his work is found primarily in collaboration with other authors who include Beaumont and Fletcher, William Rowley, and Thomas Dekker. He annually wrote the Lord Mayor's (of London) pageant and was made city historian. His works include: *The Phoenix, Anything for a Quiet Life, The Honest Whore, The City Heiress, The Spanish Gypsy,* and *The Changeling.* [found in: U. Kay - Phoebus Arise]

Midrash (Hebrew: "to teach" or "to investigate") It refers to rabbinical commentary on Old Testament writings, or an oral interpretation of the Torah. Aggadah refers to interpretations of texts which are not Halakhal (rules or instructions). [found in: Adler - The Binding]

John Milton (1608-74), an English poet, he was the son of a Protestant poet and composer. He was educated at Christ's College, Cambridge. He became blind in 1652, and thereafter continued his work by amanuensis. He wrote numerous tracts on law and religion as well as epic poetry. Among his writings are *L'Allegro* (1632), *Areopagitica* (1644), *Paradise Lost* (1663, enlarged 1674), *Paradise Regained* (1671), and *Samson Agonistes* (1671). [found in: Britten - Spring Symphony, Vaughan Williams - Hodie, Willan - Coronation Suite. "Ring out ye crystal spheres" is used in the Vaughan Williams and Willan.]

Marianne Moore (1887-1972), an American poet, she was born in Kirkwood, Missouri, and educated at the Metzger Institute, Bryn Mawr College, and Carlisle Commercial College, teaching at the last. She served as editor of *The Dial* (1926-29). She was associated with T.S. Eliot, Ezra Pound, Wallace Stevens, and William Carlos Williams. Among her writings are *Predilections* (1955), *Complete Poems* (1968), and an English translation *The Fables of La Fontaine* (1952). [found in: Adler - A Whole Bunch of Fun]

Henry More (1614-87), and English philosopher, he was in Grantham and educated at Eton and Christ's College, Cambridge. The leader of the "Cambridge Platonists," he attempted to use philosophy to combine reason with faith. His writing include

Philosophical Poems (1647), *An Antidote against Atheism* (1653), *The Immortality of the Soul* (1659), and *Divine Dialogues* (1668). [found in: Finney - Still Are New Worlds]

William Morris (1834-96), an English artist, poet, and philospher, he was educated at Exeter College, Oxford. He became involved in the pre-Rapaelite movement. His design firm revolutionized English interior decorating. He also founded the Society for the Protection of Ancient Buildings. Much of the last two decades of his life were spent forwarding his Utopian beliefs in socialism. He was a prolific author and translator and founder of the Kelmscott Press at Hammersmith. He wrote English translations of Homer's *Odyssey* (1887) and Virgil's *Aeneid* (1875). His original writings include: *The Defense of Guinevere, and other poems* (1858), *The Earthly Paradise* (1868-70), *The Story of Sigurd the Volsung and the Fall of the Nibelungs* (1876), *News from Nowhere* (1891). [found in: Hanson - Lament for Beowulf (translator with Wyatt)]

Ogden Nash (1902-71), an American author of humorous poems, he was born in Rye, New York, and educated at Harvard. His poems which often border upon the absurd frequently used puns and alliteration. He established a wide audience through the regular appearance of his work in The New Yorker. His collections of verse include *Parents Keep Out: Elderly Poems for Youngerly Readers* (1951), *The Private Dining Room and Other New Verses* (1953), and *Boy is a Boy* (1960). [found in: Adler - A Whole Bunch of Fun]

Thomas Nashe (1567-1601), an English playwright, he was born in Lowestoft, and educated at St. John's College, Cambridge. His writing is filled with satire and social criticism. Nashe was once imprisoned for the content of his work. His works include: *Anatomie of Absurditie* (1589), *Pierce Penilesse, his Supplication to the Divell* (1592), *Summer's Last Will and Testament* (1592), and *The Unfortunate Traveller* (1594). [found in: Britten - Spring Symphony, Lambert - Summer's Last Will and Testament]

Pablo Neruda (1904-1973), a Chilean poet and diplomat, he was elected to Chile's Senate as a Communist in 1945. The party was outlawed in 1948 and he left to tour Russia and China returning to Chile in 1952. He received the Stalin prize in 1953 and the Nobel prize for literature in 1971. His best known works are: *Alturas de Macchu Picchu* (1945), *Residencia en la Terra* (I, II, and III, 1933,

1935, and 1947), and *Veinte poemas de amor y una canción desperada* (1924); the last of which is the source for "The Lovers." [found in: Barber - The Lovers]

Cardinal John Henry Newman (1801-90), an English Theologian, he was born in London, and educated at Trinity College, Oxford. The son of protestants, he was ordained a Anglican priest in 1824, but converted to Roman Catholicism in 1845. He was a champion of church reform and was made cardinal in 1879. He authored numerous sermons, tracts, and religious poems. Among his writings are *Anglican Difficulties* (1850), *Catholicism in England* (1851), *The Idea of a University* (1852), "The Dream of Gerontius" (1865), *Grammar of Assent* (1870). [found in: Elgar - The Dream of Gerontius].

Robert Nichols (1893-1944), an English poet and playwright, he was the son of the poet, John Nichols. His works include: *Invocation* (1915), *Ardours and Endurances* (1917), *Aurelia* (1920), *Guilty Souls* (1922), and *Fantastica* (1923). [found in: Bliss - Morning Heroes and Pastoral]

Marjorie Hope Nicholson (b. 1894), an American scholar and author, she was born in Yonkers, New York, and educated at the University of Michigan (AB and AM) and Yale (Phd). She served as Dean of Smith College and Professor of English Literature at Columbia University. She was the first woman to serve as national president of Phi Beta Kappa. She authored a number of volumes of literary criticism, as well as original writings. Her shorter works appeared widely in literary magazines. [found in: Finney - Still Are New Worlds]

Friedrich Wilhelm Nietzsche (1844-1900), a German philosopher, writer, and musician, he was born in Röcken, Saxony, and educated at Schulpforta and the Universotoes of Bonn and Leipzig. Nietzsche was associated with Wagner and was himself a gifted composer, particularly of piano music. Between 1872 and 1888, he wrote a vast quantity of "Romantic" and often poetic philosophical material. This includes: *Die Geburt der Tragödie* (*The Birth of Tragedy*, 1872), *Unzeitgemässe Betrachtungen* (*Untimely Meditations*, 1873-76), *Die fröhliche Wissenschaft* (*The Joyful Science*, 1882), *Also sprach Zarathustra* (*So Spoke Zarathustra*, 1883-92), *Jenseits von Gut und Böse* (*Beyond Good and Evil*, 1886), *Zur Genealogie der Moral* (*On the*

Genealogy of Morals, 1887), and an autobiography, *Ecce Homo* (1888, pub. 1908). [found in: Delius - Requiem]

Arthur O'Shaughnessy (1844-1881), an English poet, he was employed as a copyist in the library of the British Museum, later serving as a herpetologist in the museum's Zoological Department. Associated with the pre-Raphaelites, his writings include *An Epic of Women* (1870), *Lays of France* (1872), *Music and Moolight* (1874), and *Songs of a Worker* (1881). [found in: Elgar - The Music Makers]

Wilfred Owen (1893-1918), English poet killed in the First World War one week before the Armistice; his collected works were first published in 1920. [found in: Bliss - Morning Heroes, Britten - War Requiem]

William Tyler Page (1868-1942), an American author of hymn texts. [found in: Ward - Sweet Freedom's Song]

George Herbert Palmer (1824-1933), an English author, translator, and literary critic. [found in: Howells - Hymnus Paradisi (translator of Salisbury Diurnal)]

George Peele (c. 1558-98), an English playwright, he was educated at Oxford. He maintained a fairly pagan lifestyle and a high profile as an important London author, supporting himself by writing and acting. His works include: *The Arraignment of Paris* (1584), *Polyhymnia* (1590), *Honour of the Garter* (1593), *Edward I* (1593), *The Old Wive's Tale* (1595). [found in: Britten - Spring Symphony]

Pindar (c.522-c.440 BC), a Greek lyric poet, he was born near Thebes. His work exists in fragments with the exception of his Triumphal Odes. [found in: Finney - Still Are New Worlds]

Poliziano (1454-1494), an Italian poet, he is also know as Politian and Angelo Ambrogini. A close friend of Lorenzo de' Medici, he was one of the most prominent classical scholars of the Italian Renaissance. He made many Italian translations of Latin and Greek classics. Among his original writings is the first secular drama in Italian, *Orfeo* (1480). [found in: Bliss - Pastoral]

Kathleen Raine (b. 1908), an English poet, she was born in London, and studied natural science at Cambridge. Her works include: *Stone and Flower* (1943), *The Hollow Hill* (1965), *The Lost Country* (1971), and a number of commentaries on William Blake. [found in: Bliss - Golden Cantata]

Requiem Mass [found in: Britten - War Requiem, Foulds - World Requiem, Howells - Hymnus Paradisi]

The Revelation of St. John [found in: Holst - Hymn of Jesus]

Rainer Maria Rilke (1875-1926), an Austrian poet, he was born in Prague. He studied art history and became secretary to Rodin after marrying his pupil, Klara Westhoff, during which time he wrote masterful French poems. His early work bordered upon mystical imagery, but later he turned to a more classical approach imbuing the poetry with a muse-like quality. His works include *Die Sonette an Orpheus* and *Duisener Elegien*. [found in: Rorem - Poet's Requiem]

Charles Rodda [found in: Rogers - The Passion]

Theodore Roethke (1908-63), an American poet, he was born in Saginaw, Michigan, and educated at the University of Michigan and Harvard. He suffered from a lifetime of mental illness. His works include *The Waking* (1953 Pulitzer Prize for Poetry), and *Words for the Wind* (1958). [found in: Adler - A Whole Bunch of Fun]

William Rowley (c. 1585-c. 1642), an English playwright, he collaborated with Thomas Dekker and Thomas Middleton. His known works are *A New Wonder, a Woman Never Vext* (1632), *All's Lost by Lust* (1633), *A Match at Midnight* (1633), and *A Shoomaker a Gentleman* (1639). [found in: U. Kay - Phoebus Arise]

Salisbury Diurnal [found in: Howells - Hymnus Paradisi]

Carl Sandburg (1878-1967), an American poet, born in Galesburg, Illinois, he was educated at Lombard College. His poetry is realistic and representative of his America. He was an avid collector of folksongs which he published in *An American Songbag* (1927). He wrote a four-volume biography of Lincoln (1926-39) and his

Collected Poems was awarded the 1950 Pulitzer Prize for poetry. [found in: Foss - The Prairie, Lockwood - The Prairie]

Stephen Schwartz (b. 1948), an American poet, composer, and playwright, he gained early and instant success. Between 1971 and 1975 he co-authored the lyrics for Bernstein's *Mass* and created the musicals *Godspell* and *Pippin*. He has since written a few moderately successful plays and some children's books. [found in: Bernstein - Mass]

Heinrich Simon, translator of Nietzsche's Requiem text into English [found in: Delius - Requiem]

Sir Osbert Sitwell (1892-1969), an English poet and brother of Sacheverell Sitwell, he was associated with Ezra Pound, Wyndham Lewis, and T. S. Eliot. His sister Edith collaborated with Walton in *Facade*. His works include *Argonaut and Juggernaut* (1919), *Out of the Flame* (1923), *Triple Fugue* (1924), *Dumb Animal* (1930), and a series of autobiographical books. [found in: Walton - Belshazzar's Feast]

Sacheverell Sitwell (1897-1988), an English author and art critic, he was the younger brother of Dame Edith and Sir Osbert Sitwell. He wrote books on many topics including travel and music. He is greatly responsible for the the resurgence of interest in Baroque art. His books include: *The People's Palace* (1918), *Southern Baroque Art* (1924), *German Baroque Art* (1927), *The Gothic North* (1929), and *The Dance of the Quick and the Dead* (1986). [found in: Lambert - Rio Grande]

John Skelton (1460-1529), an English poet, he was educated at Oxford and Cambridge and made poet laureate of both. He served as a tutor to the young Henry VIII and was an ordained Roman Catholic priest who was defrocked for reasons of conjugal activity. His poetry is vivid, energetic and filled with satiric criticisms of the church. [found in: Vaughan Williams - Five Tudor Portraits]

Samuel Francis Smith (1750-1819), an American poet and Baptist minister, he was born in Boston. He served as editorial secretary of the American Baptist Missionary Union. He is author of "My country 'tis of Thee." [found in: Ward - Sweet Freedom's Song]

Edmund Spenser (1552-99), an English poet, he was born in London and educated at Merchant Taylor's School and Pembroke Hall, Cambridge. As a secretary to Lord Grey de Wilton during an attack upon an Irish rebellion, he was rewarded with the bequeath of Kilcolman Castle in Cork, which became his home. His friendships included Sir Phillip Sydney and Sir Walter Raleigh. Among his works are *The Faerie Queen, Mother Hubberd's Tale, The Early Tears of the Muses, Prothalamion,* and *Epithalamion.* [found in: Britten - Spring Symphony, Vaughan Williams - Hodie]

John Steinbeck (1902-68), an American novelist, he was born in California and for a short while studied marine biology at Stanford University. Many of his works served as a plea for social reform through their moving portrayal of the trials of the downtrodden. His works include: *Tortilla Flat* (1935), *Of Mice and Men* (1937, New York Critics' Circle Award for Best Drama), *The Grapes of Wrath* (1939, winner of the 1940 Pulitzer Prize for literature), *The Red Pony* (1945), *East of Eden* (1952), and *Winter of Our Discontent* (1961). He was awarded the Nobel prize for literature in 1962. [found in: Amram - A Year in Our Land]

Sumer is icumen in (medieval song) [found in: Britten - Spring Symphony, Tippett - Shires Suite].

Genevieve Taggard (1894-1948), an American poet, she was born in Waitsburg, Washington, and raised in Hawaii. She was founder and editor of The Measure, a Journal of Verse (1920-26) and a member of the faculties of Sarah Lawrence and Mount Holyoke Colleges. Her writings include: *For Eager Lovers* (1922), *Hawaiian Hilltop* (1923), *Traveling Standing Still* (1928), *Calling Western Union* (1936), *Long View* (1942), and a biography of Emily Dickinson (1930). [found in: Schuman - This is Our Time]

Taverner's Bible (1539), a translation prepared by Richard Taverner, it is notable for its use of idiomatic English. [found in: Vaughan William - Sancta Civitas]

Edward Taylor (1642-1729), an American Puritan minister, he was born in England and is supposed to have studied at Cambridge. In 1668 he immigrated to Boston. He graduated from Harvard and moved to Westfield, Massachusetts where he founded the town's first church in 1679, remaining its minister until his death. His literary works were deposited as manuscripts in the Yale University

Library by his grandson, Ezra Stiles. They were found in 1937 and published in 1939 under the editorship of Thomas Johnson as *The Poetical Works of Edward Taylor.* [found in: Cowell - . . . If he please]

Theocritus (c. 310-c. 250 BC), a Greek poet, he was born in Syracuse. His pastoral works elevated the form and served as models for generations to follow. Approximately 30 of his poems survive. [found in: Bliss - Pastoral]

Alvar Núñez Cabeza de Vaca (c. 1490-1557), a Spanish colonial official, soldier, and explorer, he served as the treasurer of the expedition of Narváez, which was shipwrecked off the coast of Texas. He was captured by Native Americans and eventually reached Mexico City seven year's later. His reports of his experience vitalized interest in exploration and settlement of the region. He led subsequent expeditions and was made colonial governor of Paraguay (1542-44), but was deposed (1544) and returned to Spain where he was imprisoned (1551-56). [found in: Schuller - The Power Within Us]

Henry Vaughan (1622-95), a Welsh poet and physician, he was born in Newton-by-Usk, Llansantfraed, Powys, and educated at Jesus College, Oxford. His twin brother was the chemist, Thomas Vaughan. His works include: *Poems, with the tenth Satyre of Juvenal Englished* (1646), *Silex Scintillans* (1650), *The Mount of Olives* (1652), *Thalia Rediviva: The Pastimes and Diversions of a Country Muse* (1678). [found in: Britten - Spring Symphony]

Ursula Vaughan Williams [nee: Wood] (b. 1911), she was the second wife of composer Ralph Vaughan Williams. Her texts appear in nine of his works. [found in: Vaughan Williams - Hodie, The Sons of Light]

Vespers for Christmas Day [found in: Vaughan Williams - Hodie]

James Edward Ward (1843-1925), an English psychologist and philosopher, he began his education by pursuing divinity studies at Spring Hill College, Birmingham, but abandoned this to study moral science at Trinity College, Cambridge. He helped to establish the validity of psychology as a science in England. [found in: Willan - Coronation Suite]

George Frisbie Whicher (1889-1954), an American author. [found in: Adler - A Whole Bunch of Fun]

Walt Whitman (1819-92) American poet, his style of free verse gave a distinctive voice to American poetry. His work is realistic and holds the elements of everyday in reverence. His experience as a volunteer nurse in the American Civil War was doubtlessly of great influence upon the many poems reacting to the horrors of man's self-destruction. *Leaves of Grass* is his collection of his poetical work which in its first edition (1855) was 95 pages and in its final form nearly 440. [found in: Amram - A Year in Our Land, Bliss - Morning Heroes, Delius - Sea Drift, Dello Joio - Songs of Walt Whitman, Hanson - Three Songs from "Drum Taps," Hindemith - When Lilacs Last in the Dooryard Bloom'd, U. Kay - Inscriptions from Whitman, Lees - Visions of Poets, Martino - Portraits, Rogers - Letter from Pete, Schuman - A Free Song, Sessions - When Lilacs Last in the Dooryard Bloom'd, Vaughan Williams - A Sea Symphony, Dona Nobis Pacem]

Thomas Wolfe (1900-38), an American novelist, the son of a stone cutter, he was born in Asheville, North Carolina, and was educated at the University of North Carolina at Chapel Hill, and Harvard. His works include: *Look Homeward Angel* (1929), *Of Time and the River* (1935), *The Web and the Rock* (pub. 1939), and *You Can't Go Home Again* (pub. 1940). [found in: Amram - A Year in Our Land]

William Wordsworth (1770-1850), an English poet, he was born in Cockermouth and orphaned at an early age. He was educated at Hawkshead and Cambridge. His mature poetry is concerned with the philosophical exploration of the world of the common people. In this effort he was closely associated with Samuel Taylor Coleridge. His works include: Lyrical Ballads (1798), The Prelude (1805), and Intimations of Immortality (1807). [found in: Finzi - Intimations of Immortality]

Alfred John Wyatt (1858-?), an English author, he was affiliated with the pre-Raphaelites and aided William Morris in the preparation of the 1894 edition of *Beowulf* in modern English translation for the latter's Kelmscott Press. [found in: Hanson - Lament for Beowulf (translator with Morris)]

Appendix II

A List of Publishers and Distributors

Associated Music Publishers, 866 Third Avenue, New York, NY 10022 distributed by G. Schirmer

Belwin-Mills Publishing Corp., 25 Deshon Drive, Melville, NY 11747 distributed by Theodore Presser Company

Berandol Music Ltd., 11 St. Joseph Street, Toronto, ONT M4Y 1J8
phone: 416-480-2561

Boosey and Hawkes, 200 Smith Street CSB6, Farmingdale, NY 11735
phone: 212-979-1090, ext. 26

Broude Bros. Ltd., 141 White Oaks Road, Williamstown, MA 01267
phone: 413-458-8131

Canadian Music Centre, 1263 Bay Street, Toronto, ONT M5R 2CI
phone: 416-961-6601

Franco Colombo Publications, a division of Belwin-Mills distributed by Theodore Presser Company

Dantalian, Inc., Eleven Pembroke Street, Newton, MA 02158

Educational Music Service, 13 Elkay Drive, Chester, NY 10918
phone: 914-469-5790

Elkan-Vogel Inc., Presser Place, Bryn Mawr, PA 19010
distributed by Theodore Presser Company

European American Music Corp., 2480 Industrial Boulevard,
Paoli, PA 19301
phone: 215-648-0506

Faber Music Ltd./Curwen, 3 Queen Street, London WC1N 3AW,
England
distributed by Educational Music Service

Carl Fischer, Inc., 56-62 Cooper Square, New York, NY 10003
phone: 800-762-2328

Mark Foster Music Co., 28 East Springfield Avenue, P.O. Box
4012, Champaign, IL 61820-1312
phone: 217-398-2760

St. Francis Music Co., a division of Shawnee Press

Galaxy Music Corp., 131 West 86th Street, New York, NY 10024
distributed by E. C. Schirmer

H. W. Gray Co., Inc., a division of Belwin-Mills
distributed by Theodore Presser Company

Lawson-Gould Music Publishers, Inc., 866 Third Avenue,
New York, NY 10022
distributed by G. Schirmer

Alfred Lengnick and Co., Ltd., Purley Oaks Studios, 421a
Brighton Road, South Croydon CR2 6YR, Surrey, England
distributed by Theodore Presser Company

MCA, 445 Park Avenue, New York, NY 10022, a division of
Belwin-Mills
distributed by Theodore Presser Company

E. B. Marks, 1619 Broadway, New York, NY 10019
distributed by Theodore Presser Company

Novello and Co., Fairfield Road, Borough Green, Sevenoaks, Kent
TN15 8DT England
distributed by Theodore Presser Company

Oxford University Press, 37 Dover Street, London, W1X 4AH
England
phone: New York office 800-334-4249 ext. 7168

Peer International Corp., 1740 Broadway, New York, NY 10019
phone: 212-265-3910

C. F. Peters Corp., 373 Park Avenue South, New York, NY
10016
phone: 212-686-4147

Theodore Presser Co., Presser Place, Bryn Mawr, PA 19010
phone: 215-525-3636

E. C. Schirmer Music Co., 112 South Street, Boston, MA
02111
phone: 617-236-1935

G. Schirmer, Inc., 866 Third Avenue, New York, NY 10022
phone: 914-469-2271

Schott and Co., Ltd., 48 Great Marlborough Street, London W1V
2BN England
distributed by European American Music Corp.

B. Schotts Söhne, Weihergarten 5, Postfach 3640, D-6500 Mainz,
Germany
distributed by European American Music Corp.

Shawnee Press, Inc., Delaware Water Gap, PA 18327
phone: 717-476-0550

Southern Music Publishing, a division of Peer International

Stainer and Bell, Ltd., 82 High Road, East Finchley, London N2
9PW England

General Bibliography

General Reference and Biography

Anderson, E. Ruth: *Contemporary American Composers: A Biographical Dictionary.* Boston: G. K. Hall, 1976.

Apel, Willi, editor: *The Harvard Dictionary of Music,* second edition. Cambridge, MA: Belknap Press of Harvard University Press, 1972.

Ardoin, John: *The Stages of Menotti.* Garden City, NY: Doubleday, 1985.

Austin, William W.: *Music in the Twentieth Century from Debussy through Stravinsky.* New York: W.W. Norton, 1966.

Bowen, Meirion: *Michael Tippett.* London: Robson, 1982.

Carnovale, Norbert: *Gunther Schuller: A Bio-Bibliography.* New York: Greenwood Press, 1987.

Chase, Gilbert: *America's Music,* second edition. New York: McGraw-Hill, 1966.

Clarke, Frederick Robert Charles: *Healey Willan.* Toronto: University of Toronto Press, 1983.

Cohn, Arthur, and Philip Miller: "The Music of Nicolas Flagello," *American Record Guide,* xxxi (1965), 1054.

Cooper, Martin, ed.: *New Oxford History of Music, volume X. The Modern Age, 1890-1960.* London: Oxford University Press, 1974.

Cowell, Henry, ed.: *American Composers on American Music: A Symposium.* New York: Frederick Ungar Publishing, 1933. Revised 1962.

Craggs, Stewart R.: *Arthur Bliss: A Bio-Bibliography*. New York: Greenwood Press, 1988.

_____: *William Walton: A Thematic Catalogue of his Musical Works*. London: Oxford University Press, 1977.

Day, James: *Vaughan Williams*. London: J. M. Dent, 1961.

Durant, Will and Ariel: *The Story of Civilization*. 11 volumes. New York: Simon and Schuster, 1975.

Eagon, Angelo, ed.: *Catalog of Published Concert Music by American Composers*, second edition. Metuchen, NJ: Scarecrow Press, 1969. Supplement, 1971; Second Supplement, 1974.

Evans, Ivor H., ed.: *Brewer's Dictionary of Phrase and Fable*, Centenary Edition, revised. New York: Harper and Row, 1981.

Gleason, Harold, and Walter Becker: *20th-Century American Composers*. Music Literature Outlines, series iv. Bloomington, IN: Indiana University Press, revised 1981.

Hines, Robert Stephan, ed.: *The Composer's Point of View: Essays on Twentieth-Century Choral Music by Those Who Wrote It*. Norman, OK: University of Oklahoma Press, 1963.

Hitchcock, H. Wiley: *Music in the United States: A Historical Introduction*, revised edition. Englewood Cliffs, NJ: Prentice-Hall, 1974.

Holst, Imogen: *The Music of Gustav Holst*, third edition; and *Holst's Music Reconsidered*. 1 volume. Oxford: Oxford University Press, 1986.

_____: *A Thematic Catalogue of Gustav Holst's Music*. London: Faber and Faber, 1974.

Huscher, Phillip: notes for recording of Samuel Barber's *The Lovers*. Performed by Dale Duesing, Sarah Reese; Chicago Symphony Orchestra and Chorus; conducted by Andrew Schenck. Koch International Classics: 3-7125-2HI, 1992.

Jerrold, Northrop Moore: *Spirit of England: Edward Elgar in His World.* London: Oxford University Press, 1984.

Kallmann, Helmut, Gilles Potvin, and Kenneth Winters: *Encyclopedia of Music in Canada.* Toronto University of Toronto Press, 1981.

Kennedy, Michael, editor: *The Concise Oxford Dictionary of Music,* third edition. London: Oxford University Press, 1980.

_____: *Portrait of Elgar,* revised. London: Oxford University Press, 1983.

_____: *A Catalogue of the Works of Ralph Vaughan Williams.* London: Oxford University Press, 1985.

Kreitner, Kenneth: *Robert Ward: A Bio-Bibliography.* New York: Greenwood Press, 1988.

Lambert, Bruce: "William Schuman Is Dead at 81; Noted Composer Headed Juilliard," *New York Times* (16 February 1992), 48-L.

MacDonald, Malcolm: *John Foulds and His Music: An Introduction.* White Plains, NY: Pro/Am Music Resources, 1989.

Machlis, Joseph: *Introduction to Contemporary Music.* New York: W.W. Norton, 1961.

MacMillan, Keith and John Beckwith, editors: *Contemporary Canadian Composers.* Toronto: Oxford University Press, 1975.

Magnusson, Magnus, editor: *Cambridge Biographical Dictionary.* Cambridge: Cambridge University Press, 1990.

Mead, Rita: *Henry Cowell's New Music 1925-36: The Society, the Music Editions, and the Recordings.* Ann Arbor, MI: UMI Research Press, 1981.

Mellers, Wilfrid: *Music in a New Found Land: Themes and Developments in the History of American Music,* second ed. New York: Hillstone, 1975.

Mize, Lou Stem: *A Study of Selected Choral Settings of Walt Whitman Poems.* Florida State University: Dissertation, 1967.

Morgan, Robert P.: *Twentieth-Century Music*. New York: W.W. Norton, 1991.

Morton, Brian and Pamela Collins, editors: *Contemporary Composers*. Chicago: St. James Press, 1992.

Palmer, Christopher: notes for recording of Herbert Howells's *Hymnus Paradisi*. Performed by Heather Harper, Robert Tear; The Bach Choir, Choir of King's College and New Philharmonia Orchestra; conducted by Sir David Willcocks. EMI CDM 7 63372 2, 1990.

Perkins, George, Barbara Perkins, and Phillip Leininger, eds.: *Benét's Reader's Encyclopedia of American Literature*. New York: Harper Collins, 1991.

Peyser, Joan: *Bernstein: A Biography*. New York: Beechtree Books, 1987.

Procter, Francis: *A History of the Book of Common Prayer*. London: Macmillan, 1898.

Redwood, Christopher: *A Delius Companion*, 2nd edition. London: Scolar Press, 1980.

Roach, Hildred: *Black American Music: Past and Present*. Boston: Crescendo Publishing, 1973.

Sabin, Robert: "It Takes a Great Strength to Remain Tender and Simple," *Musical America* (1 December 1950), 9.

Sadie, Stanley, editor: *The New Grove Dictionary of Music and Musicians*. 20 volumes. London: Macmillan, 1980.

Salzman, Eric: *Twentieth-Century Music: An Introduction*, second edition. Englewood Cliffs, NJ: Prentice-Hall, 1974.

Slonimsky, Nicholas: *Music Since 1900*, fourth edition. New York: Charles Scribner's Sons, 1971.

_____: *Baker's Biographical Dictionary of Musicians*, eighth edition. New York: Schirmer Books, 1991.

Smith, Carolyn J.: *William Walton: A Bio-Bibliography*. Westport, CT: Greenwood Press, 1988.

Southern, Eileen: *The Music of Black Americans: A History*. New York: W.W. Norton, 1971.

_____: *Biographical Dictionary of Afro-American and African Musicians*. Westport, CT: Greenwood Press, 1982.

Theil, Gordon: *Michael Tippett: A Bio-Bibliography*. New York: Greenwood Press, 1989.

Thomson, Virgil: *American Music Since 1910*. New York: Holt, Rinehart, and Winston, 1971.

Tirro, Frank: *Jazz: A History*. New York: W.W. Norton, 1977.

Vaughan Williams, Ursula: *R.V.W.: A Biography*, revised. London: Oxford University Press, 1985.

Vinson, James: *Contemporary Poets*, third edition. New York: St. Martin's Press, 1980.

Wannamaker, John Samuel: *The Musical Settings of the Poetry of Walt Whitman: A Study of Theme, Structure, and Prosody*. University of Minnesota: Dissertation, 1972.

Webster's Biographical Dictionary. Springfield, MA: G. and C. Merriam, 1964.

Whitall, Arnold: *Music Since the First World War*. London: J. M. Dent, 1977.

Repertoire

Aronowsky, Solomon: *Performing Times of Orchestral Works*. London: Ernest Benn Limited, 1959.

Burnworth, Charles C.: *Choral Music for Women's Voices*. Metuchen, NJ: Scarecrow Press, 1968.

Daniels, David: *Orchestral Music: A Source Book*, second edition. Metuchen, NJ: Scarecrow Press, 1982.

Daugherty, F. Mark, and Susan H. Simons, eds.: *Secular Choral Music in Print*, second edition, 2 volumes. Philadelphia: Musidata, 1987.

Dox, Thurston: *American Oratorios and Cantatas: A Catalog of Works Written in the United States from Colonial Times to 1985*. 2 volumes. Metuchen, NJ: Scarecrow Press, 1986.

Eslinger, Gary S., and F. Mark Daugherty, eds.: *Sacred Choral Music in Print*, second edition, 2 volumes. Philadelphia: Musidata, 1985.

Farish, Margaret K.: *Orchestra Music in Print*. Philadelphia: Musidata, 1979.

Kagen, Sergius: *Music for the Voice*, revised. Bloomington, IN: Indiana University Press, 1968.

Knapp, J. Merrill, editor: *Selected List of Music for Men's Voices*. Princeton, NJ: Princeton University Press, 1952.

Robertson, Alec: *Requiem: Music of Mourning and Consolation*. London: Praeger Press, 1985.

Ulrich, Homer: *A Survey of Choral Music*. New York: Harcourt, Brace, and Jovanovich, 1973.

Young, Percy M.: *The Choral Tradition*. New York: W.W. Norton, 1971.

Interviews

Adler, Samuel: August 1992, by telephone

Diamond, David: August 1992, by telephone

Fine, Vivian: numerous meetings, 1987-88

Hilbish, Thomas: July and September 1992, by telephone

McCarty, Frank: lecture given at the University of North Carolina at Greensboro, February 1990.

Discographies

Clough, Francis F., and G. J. Cuming: *The World's Encyclopedia of Recorded Music*. London: Sidgwick and Jackson, 1950. First supplement, 1951. Second supplement, 1953. Third supplement, 1957.

Gramophone Shop Inc., New York: *The Gramophone Shop Encyclopedia of Recorded Music*. New York: The Gramophone Shop, Inc., 1936. Second edition, 1942. Third edition, 1948.

Greenfield, Edward, Robert Layton, and Ivan March: *The Complete Penguin Stereo Record and Cassette Guide*. London: Long Playing Record Company, 1984.

Kolodin, Irving: *The New Guide to Recorded Music*, International edition. Garden City, NY: Doubleday and Company, 1950.

Oja, Carol J.: *American Music Recordings: A Discography of Twentieth-Century U.S. Composers*. Brooklyn, NY: Institute for Studies in American Music, 1982.

Schwann Catalogues (including: *Schwann Long Playing Record Catalog, Schwann Compact Disc Catalog*, and *Opus*). Boston: W. Schwann, 1949-1992.

U.S. Library of Congress: *Library of Congress National Union Catalogue, Music and Phonorecords*. Washington, DC: Library of Congress,1953- .

ABOUT THE AUTHOR

JONATHAN D. GREEN (BMus, Fredonia School of Music at SUNY Fredonia; MMus, University of Massachusetts; DMA, University of North Carolina Greensboro) is Director of Choral Music at Elon College in North Carolina. He has held conducting posts at Williams College, Amherst College, and Hampden-Sydney College; and he served as Music Librarian at Bennington College. Dr. Green is also Music Director of the Alamance Chorale. An active composer, he has written over 80 works to date, including 5 symphonies, 5 song cycles and many choral works. He is the recipient of numerous commissions, an Ornest Fellowship, and he was made an Excellence Fellow of the University of North Carolina Greensboro. Green is a member of the American Choral Directors' Association, American Music Center, American Symphony Orchestra League, Conductors' Guild, Composers Forum, Southeastern League of Composers, College Music Society, and Phi Mu Alpha Sinfonia. He currently resides in Greensboro, NC with his wife Lynn Buck.